COMPUTER PROGRAMMING

in

STANDARD MUMPS

Second Edition

Arthur F. Krieg
David H. Miller
Gregory L. Bressler

The Milton S. Hershey Medical Center at
The Pennsylvania State University
P.O. Box 850
Hershey, PA 17033

Editing and Production:
    Ruth E. Dayhoff
    Dianne C. Barker
    Donald E. Piccone
    Lori J. Doeg

Cover Design:
    Jack Ballestero

Published by:
    The MUMPS Users' Group
    4321 Hartwick Rd., Suite 510
    College Park, MD 20740
    (301) 779-6555

ISBN   0-918118-28-X

PREFACE AND ACKNOWLEDGEMENTS

In 1978, the senior author (AFK) had no training or experience in computer programming. At that time, he set out to learn MUMPS "on his own", using self-teaching materials available at that time. Although the "grammar" of the MUMPS language was quite simple, it required many months of "trial and error" before AFK could write useful programs. To shorten this learning process, AFK and a colleague (Lucille K. Shearer) developed a sequence of programmed learning experiences designed to help non- programmers learn MUMPS "on their own".

This material was published by the MUMPS Users'Group in 1981 under the title "Computer Programming in ANS MUMPS: A Self-Instruction Manual for Non-Programmers".

In late 1981, AFK was able to obtain assistance from a professional programmer, Mr. David H. Miller, who was then working in the Department of Pathology at the Pennsylvania State University School of Medicine. Mr. Miller generously shared his experience with various "techniques" commonly used by professional MUMPS programmers.

In 1982, DHM moved to a new position. But before leaving, he helped Mr. Gregory L. Bressler to "get started" as a MUMPS programmer. Since 1982, GLB and AFK have worked closely together to develop the series of exercises in this manual.

In 1983, a "first draft" of the present manuscript was circulated to various reviewers for comment and criticism. Many people provided helpful suggestions and constructive criticism. Some of the people who provided especially helpful suggestions and encouragement included:

Dr. Kevin O'Kane
University of Tennessee
Knoxville, TN

Dr. Richard Walters
University of California School of Medicine
Davis, CA

Mr. Phillip Ragon
InterSystems Corporation
Boston, MA

Mr. David Marcus
Micronetics Design Corporation
Rockville, MD

We gratefully acknowledge the contributions of these reviewers, who generously contributed their time and expertise.

Mrs. Karen Homisak repeatedly entered and re-entered this manuscript into our MUMPS Multiword ® word processing system during 1982, 1983 and 1984.

AFK   DHM   GLB

SUGGESTIONS FOR USING THIS MANUAL

It is easier to learn Standard MUMPS if you have access to a computer using this language. Standard MUMPS is available on:

(1)   A wide range of desk top computers including the IBM PC and XT, Apple IIe, Radio Shack TRS 80, and so on.

(2)   A wide range of minicomputers including the DEC PDP 11 and VAX, Data General Eclipse, and others.

(3)   Mainframe computers from IBM, Harris, Tandem and other vendors.

"Latest information" on Standard MUMPS for specific machines is available from the MUMPS Users' Group.

Each chapter in this book is organized into sections, with descriptive subtitles. Each section is organized into frames, with individual numbers. Some frames are followed by a solid line:

_____

which separates a question in the frame from an answer below the solid line. Try to answer the question, before reading below the solid line.

As you read through this book, some sections may be difficult to understand. When this occurs, we suggest:

(1)   Try to "figure it out" for half an hour or so.

(2)   If after half an hour you do not understand the material, either: set it aside for 2 to 24 hours, or seek help from a person with more experience. If you do not have access to such a person, the MUMPS Users' Group (MUG) has a list of people who can provide assistance to new users.

Some implementations of Standard MUMPS may have features not described in this manual. We recommend that you do NOT use this manual as a "replacement" for the documentation provided by your system vendor. Instead, we suggest that you use this manual as a series of "learning exercises" which progress from very simple examples to programs of "moderate" difficulty.

Editor's note: To accomodate typesetting restrictions, it has been necessary to continue long lines of MUMPS code onto the next line. We have used the convention of "....." in the line label column to signify the continuation of a line of code.

WHY MUMPS?

History

MUMPS is an acronym for **M**assachusetts General Hospital **U**tility **M**ulti-**P**rogramming **S**ystem. In 1967, The Laboratory of Computer Science at Massachusetts General Hospital began development of a computer language to store and retrieve free text within a random access data base. This new language became widely accepted in the medical community: by 1972, 14 different versions were in existence (1).

In 1972, the National Bureau of Standards and the National Center for Health Sciences Research sponsored an effort to define a single version of this language, i.e. Standard MUMPS. By 1976, the MUMPS Development Committee (MDC) had defined Standard MUMPS - and submitted this to the American National Standards Institute (ANSI). In 1977, ANSI approved the MDC definition for Standard MUMPS. At this time, there are only four computer languages for which ANSI standards are established: FORTRAN, COBOL, PL/1, and MUMPS.

The MUMPS Development Committee

Since 1977, MDC has continued to meet regularly. Proposed changes in Standard MUMPS are published by MDC as Type B releases.

After the MUMPS community has commented on proposed changes, these are republished by MDC as Type A releases. Type A releases eventually become part of the approved language standard.

MUMPS as a Computer Language

Unlike most computer languages, MUMPS is designed to store and retrieve free text information - such as names, addresses, and descriptive comments - rather than perform complex calculations.

Unlike most computer languages, MUMPS does not require the programmer to pre-define storage space, data types, or formats for information. Thus variables (such as a persons name, address, or occupation) do not need to be "declared in advance".

Most programming languages require the user to learn "sorting routines", such as the bubble sort, heap sort and so on. With MUMPS, such sorts are performed "automatically".

In comparison to other computer languages such as BASIC, Pascal, FORTRAN and COBOL:

    (1)   MUMPS is easier for beginners to learn.

    (2)   Programs for file management are easier to develop and revise.

A typical experience reported by one MUMPS user (2) was that in comparison to COBOL, MUMPS required:

8% as many lines of code

8-12% as much programmer time for system development.

Our own experience with MUMPS has been highly favorable. Not only is this computer language easy to learn, but it also:

(1)   provides "built in" capability for data base management.

(2)   can be used by experienced programmers to develop large and complex systems.

Additional information on Standard MUMPS is available from:

MUMPS Users' Group
4321 Hartwick Road - Suite #510
College Park, MD 20740
(301) 779-6555

We would welcome your suggestions and constructive criticism on this manual. Please address your comments to:

Arthur F. Krieg
The Milton S. Hershey Medical Center of
   The Pennsylvania State University Box 850
Hershey, PA 17033

REFERENCES

1.   Walters RF, Bowie J, Wilcox JC: MUMPS Primer. MUMPS Users' Group, 1982

2.   Munnecke T: A Linguistic Comparison of MUMPS and COBOL. Paper presented at the National Computer Conference, 1980.

TABLE OF CONTENTS

CHAPTER ONE

BASIC CONCEPTS

This chapter will present an introduction to basic computer concepts and terminology. If you are already experienced in use of computers - or already "computer literate" - you may choose to skip most of this material and read only the sections on Standard MUMPS (frames 19-25).

COMPUTER HARDWARE AND SOFTWARE

1. "Software" refers to instructions which tell the computer "what to do". "Hardware" is the machine that runs the instructions.

2. A computer system requires both hardware and software: either component is incomplete by itself.

3. Computer hardware commonly includes:

- The "computer": internal components include a "central processing unit" (accepts data and performs operations on this data under the direction of a program), and "primary storage" (stores instructions and data during program execution).

- Input/output units which: allow you to enter programs and data; display results of running programs.

- Secondary storage, also known as "external memory": this provides "extra storage" of programs and data.

These components are shown schematically in Figure 1-1.

4. Figure 1-1 depicts combined input/output devices. However, input and output may be performed either by: (1) a single input/output unit such as a video terminal; (2) separate units for input and output.

1

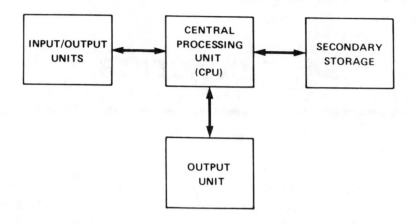

FIGURE 1-1. RELATIONSHIP OF COMPUTER HARDWARE COMPONENTS

5. Input and output units include:

- "Input units" which only accept input: for example, card readers and document readers.

- "Output units" which only produce output: for example, printers with no keyboards for data entry.

- "Input/output units" or "I/O units" which both receive input and produce output: for example, video display terminals (VDT) which allow you to enter data, as well as display output.

Input and output units are sometimes called "terminals". Input terminals allow entry of data and/or programs into the computer, output terminals display results from running a program, and input/output terminals allow two way communication with the computer.

Terminals which produce printed records on paper often are called "hard copy devices", since they produce "hard copy output". Video display terminals (VDT) which produce transient displays are considered as "soft copy devices".

6. Most "standard" video display terminals display 80 columns with 22 to 25 lines. A second type of "standard" terminal displays 132 columns with 22-25 lines. A third type of "standard" terminal displays 80 columns with 66 lines: this is equivalent to one sheet of 8-1/2" X 11" paper.

7.   For hard copy I/O terminals, the "industry standard" print widths are 80 and 132 columns. Smaller "non-standard" widths are available - but are less convenient for entering and displaying programs.

8.   Secondary storage or "external storage" is commonly provided by either:

  • magnetic tape drives

  • disk drives.

9.   Magnetic tape drives are sometimes referred to as "sequential access" since data stored on magnetic tape must be read sequentially.

One type of magnetic tape is the "industry standard" tape reel used with large computer systems. This is also referred to as "nine track half inch tape". Information is stored as magnetic spots along nine tracks as shown in Figure 1-2. One position (a total of nine magnetized spots across the tape) stores one character (such as a letter or a number). Common densities of character storage include 800 bits per inch (bpi), 1600 bpi and 2400 bpi. Since there are nine tracks, one "bit per inch" is equivalent to one "character per inch".

Magnetic tapes provide an inexpensive way to store large amounts of data: a tape with 1600 bpi accommodates about 23 million characters.

Data storage on magnetic tape commonly is expressed as "bytes". One "byte" of storage is equivalent to one character (such as a letter or number). One Kilobyte (Kb) is equal to approximately 1000 characters (actually 1024), and one Megabyte (Mb), to approximately 1,000,000 characters (actually 1,024,000).

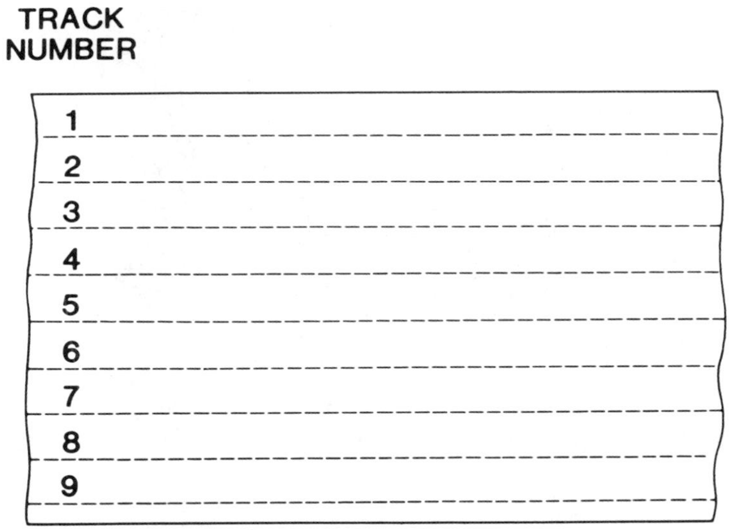

**TRACK
NUMBER**

FIGURE 1-2. A SECTION OF NINE TRACK HALF INCH TAPE

10. A wide variety of tape cartridges and cassettes are available. Some of these include:

    (a)   1/4" tape cartridges, sometimes known as "3M cartridges", with
           typical storage capacities in the 10 Mb range.

    (b)   audio tape cartridges (5/32" tape), sometimes used with home com-
           puters, having storage capacities in the 0.25 Mb range.

11.   Magnetic disk storage is sometimes referred to as "random access storage", in contrast to the "sequential access" of magnetic tape. While a magnetic tape must be read "in
sequence", the read/write head on a disk drive can move directly to a specific "address". Data
retrieval from magnetic disk usually is more rapid than sequential access from magnetic tape.

Figure 1-3 depicts a commonly used layout for magnetic disk storage. Data is stored as
magnetized spots, located along concentric "tracks". A typical eight inch disk as depicted in
Figure 1-3 would have about 77 tracks.

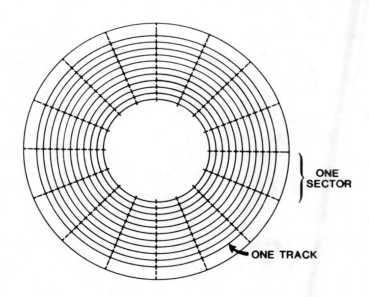

ONE
SECTOR

ONE TRACK

FIGURE 1-3. TRACK AND SECTOR LAYOUT OF A DISK

A commonly used "bit density" is 6800 bits per inch (bpi). Usually, this bit density applies to the innermost track, with decreasing bit densities along the outer tracks. The capacity of the single sided 8 inch 77 track disk depicted in Figure 1-3 would be about 0.82 Mb. Recording on both sides would provide a capacity of about 1.6 Mb.

What about the "dotted lines" in Figure 1-3? For disk storage, each track is divided into multiple "sectors": 16 sectors is common practice, but other numbers also are used.

Disk storage is sometimes specified in terms of "data blocks". A common data block size is 1024 bytes. Thus, the disk depicted in Figure 1-3 would require two sectors for one data block. Most of the time, we need not concern ourselves with considerations such as tracks per inch, bits per inch, or number of sectors per data block.

12.   A floppy disk is a piece of flexible plastic, enclosed either in a cardboard jacket, or plastic "hard shell". The plastic disk is coated with a thin film of metallic oxide. Each data item on a floppy disk has a specific "address", based on track and sector number.

Floppy disks are available in a variety of sizes including 8 inches, 5-1/4 inches ("minifloppy") and 3-1/2 inches ("microfloppy"). The only "industry standard" floppy disk is the eight inch, single density "IBM 3740 standard" unit. Just as magnetic tape cassettes are often incompatible between different manufacturers, "minifloppy" and "microfloppy" disks often are incompatible between different vendors.

Floppy disks also may be classified as: (1) hard sector; (2) soft sector.

A hard sectored disk might have 16 holes at the inner radius to establish the start point for each sector, plus a 17th hole to establish the start position for each track.

A soft sectored disk has only one punched hole that defines the start position: the number of sectors per track is defined by the disk control unit.

Transfer of programs and data between floppy disk units from different computers frequently presents problems - unless both systems are specified as eight inch, single density "IBM 3740 standard", analogous to half inch "industry compatible" magnetic tape.

Typical storage for one side of a floppy disk ranges from about 90 Kb to over 1 Mb. The number of tracks per inch of radius is known as the "density" of the disk. "Double density" refers to 48 t.p.i. (tracks per inch), while "grad density" refers to 96 t.p.i. Even higher track densities are available.

13. A hard disk has random access capability, quite similar to floppy disks. However, as compared with floppy disks, hard disks have:

- greater data storage for a given disk diameter

- faster access times.

The greater data storage is achieved by:

(1)   Greater track density - allowing more tracks within a given disk diameter.

(2)   Greater bit densities - typically in the range of 6000 to 15,000 bits per inch (innermost track) as compared with about 6000 to 8,000 bits per inch (innermost track) for floppy disks.

Descriptions of hard disks often specify "fci" (flux changes per inch), as a synonym for "bpi" (bits per inch).

Faster access times are achieved by greater rotational speed - typically in the range of about 3000 to 4000 rpm as compared with about 300 rpm for floppy disks.

The read-write head for a hard disk "flies" above the surface, at a "flying height" in the range of 15-100 microinches for different disk drives. In contrast, the read-write head or a floppy disk physically rests on the disk surface.

14.   Hard disks may be classified as:

(1)   Winchester drives

(2)   non-Winchester drives.

The "Winchester disk" typically is a sealed unit, with very light read/write head (about 10 grams vs over 300 grams), and very low head flying height (about 20 microinches vs over 50 microinches). These characteristics allow higher storage capacity for a given disk size and price, as compared with conventional disks.

Disk drives also may be classified as:

(1)   removable disk units

(2)   non-removable disk units.

Until recently, the term "Winchester drive" implied a non-removable disk. Recently, removable Winchester disks have become available - although costs are somewhat higher than traditional non-removable Winchester units.

15.   "Software" refers to computer programs which "tell the hardware what to do".

Computer programs often exist in the form of floppy disks or magnetic tapes, which can be kept "on the shelf", and loaded into the computer as desired.

Of course, computer programs can also be stored as printed text: such as the examples in this manual. Before use, programs stored as printed text must be translated into machine-readable form: either by typing the program into a terminal, or by entering it onto a machine-readable medium such as disk or magnetic tape.

16.   Two types of computer software are: applications programs and operating systems. Application programs are written to perform specific functions for end users. This manual will illustrate over 100 different application programs, each of which provides one or more functions for an end user.

An operating system is the "master program" which provides: (1) a "programming environment" for the person writing an applications program; (2) an "operating environment" for people using an applications program.

Some typical functions provided by an operating system include:

- control the "log on" process

- compile or interpret programs written in a high level language

- allow programmers to make changes via a "program editor"

- allow programmers to list programs and data stored on disk

- allow users to store, retrieve and run programs as needed.

Some implementations of Standard MUMPS run under a "separate" operating system such as CPM or MS DOS. Other implementations of Standard MUMPS combine both an operating system and a MUMPS interpreter. For additional information, consult the user manual supplied by your system vendor.

17.   Application programs are usually written in a high level language, such as BASIC, MUMPS, or FORTRAN.

Different high level languages are designed to perform different functions. Some high level languages - such as Standard MUMPS - are designed for easy and efficient management of files.

Other high level languages - such as FORTRAN - are designed for rapid performance of complex calculations. Still other high level languages - such as BASIC - represent a "compromise" between file management and calculation.

The term "high level language" implies that:

- one "high level instruction" is translated into several "machine level instructions"

- the "high level instructions" are relatively easy for humans to understand, as compared with "machine level instructions".

18.   High level languages can be implemented as:

- compiled languages

- interpreted languages.

A compiler translates "source code", written in a high level language, into "object code". This object code may be machine language, directly executed by the computer, or an intermediate language that requires a second translation step into machine language.

After a program is written, it is run through the compiler, which translates the code into machine language. This process is called "compiling the program". If the compiler identifies any errors, it will stop compiling. The programmer must then correct these errors, and recompile the program. Usually several "recompiles" are needed to produce a satisfactory program. When the compiler does not identify any errors while compiling, it can then execute the machine language version of the program.

An interpreter does not produce machine language object code for an entire program. Instead, source code is interpreted one line at a time, when the program is executed.

Interpreted code often executes more slowly than compiled source code. However, interpreters offer an important advantage: programs can be stopped, modified, and execution resumed far more easily than with most compilers. With an interpreted language, you can write a few lines of code, run the program, modify it as needed, write a few more lines, check whether the program operates properly, and so on.

Some languages are available both as compiled and interpreted versions. The interpreted versions are more convenient for program development, while the compiled versions usually execute more rapidly.

STANDARD MUMPS AS A COMPUTER LANGUAGE

19.   Standard MUMPS is also known as:

- American National Standard MUMPS

- ANS MUMPS

- American National Standard Institute MUMPS

- ANSI MUMPS.

MUMPS is an acronym for Massachusetts General Hospital Utility Multi-Programming System; it was at Massachusetts General Hospital that this language was first developed, during the late 1960's. MUMPS originally was developed as an interpreted language, with one objective being easy and rapid program development. Standard MUMPS implementations now include:

    (1)   a compiled language, running under a separate operating system

    (2)   an interpreted language, running under a separate operating system such as CPM (Control Program for Microcomputers)

    (3)   an operating system combined with an interpreted language.

Thus, it is possible to develop programs with interpreted MUMPS - then compile these programs to achieve faster execution speeds. However, a unique feature of MUMPS - called indirection - requires that an interpreter be available "as needed" to handle new constructs created by indirection when programs are executed.

20.   In many cases, after a computer language is developed, several different versions are introduced. This occurred with BASIC, COBOL, FORTRAN - and also with MUMPS, during the late 1960's and early 1970's.

The MUMPS Users' Group (MUG), and MUMPS Development Committee (MDC) of MUG identified some important advantages if this new language could be "standardized". Advantages of "standardization" include:

    (1)   A "standard language" can be used with minimal changes on hardware from several different manufacturers.

    (2)   The "standard" provides detailed specifications which contribute to development of new implementations.

    (3)   A well defined "standard" increases the value of "public domain" software, available to all users at minimal cost.

(4)   A standard which is subject to continued review and revision can coordinate the evolution of a computer language. This coordinated evolution can prevent compatibility problems between the "old language" and "new revisions" proposed by vendors.

In 1975, MUMPS was accepted as a Standard Language by the American National Standards Institute (ANSI). Other computer languages accepted as "standard" by ANSI include COBOL, FORTRAN, and PL/I.

21.   Standard MUMPS has been implemented on a wide range of computer hardware. Information on these implementations is available from the MUMPS Users' Group.
(4321 Hartwick Road, Suite 510, College Park, MD 20740)

Standard MUMPS implementations from different vendors may differ in six principal areas:

- "log on" and "log off" procedures used to gain access to computer resources, and terminate this access

- procedures used to name, save and retrieve programs

- conventions, such as error messages

- utility programs, such as programs used to list the names of application programs stored on disk

- the program editor, used to modify programs after they are written

- vendor-specific commands, functions and variables, which are identified by the prefix "Z".

In addition, some implementations provide features approved by the MUMPS Development Committee, but not yet accepted by ANSI as part of the approved standard.

22.   Standard MUMPS may be implemented either as:

- a single user system ("single user environment")

- a multi-user system ("multi-user multi-programming environment").

Within multi-user MUMPS systems, primary storage usually is divided into multiple "partitions", so that each user has his own "space".

23.   Typical allocation of primary storage is represented schematically in Figure 1-4. Different implementations may vary slightly from the layout depicted.

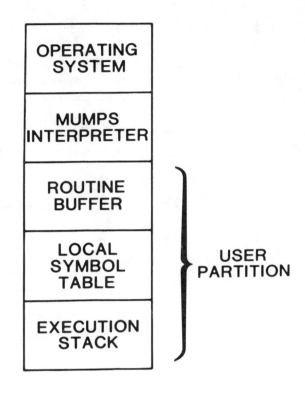

FIGURE 1-4. TYPICAL ALLOCATION OF PRIMARY STORAGE IN A MUMPS SYSTEM

At the "upper level", we have the operating system and the MUMPS interpreter.

Also within primary storage are one or more user partitions. A multi-user system will have many such partitions (typically from 4 to 20 or more). Space within each user partition is dynamically allocated among several areas. These typically include the:

- routine buffer

- symbol table

- execution stack.

A "routine" can be considered as a program which is stored on disk. Before a routine can be executed, it must be moved from disk into the routine buffer of a user partition. The routine buffer can be considered the "workplace" for a routine within a given partition.

The symbol table contains names of all "local variables" within a partition. For example, we might have the local variable ADDRESS with a value of "500 University Drive". These local variables can be stored on disk as "global variables", also known as "globals". This process, actually quite simple, will be demonstrated in later chapters.

The execution stack stores the names of routines and subroutines as these are performed during the execution of a larger program which contains several routines. We can consider the execution stack as "keeping track" of the routine (or subroutine) to be executed next.

The space available to a user partition may be fixed or variable in size. Some implementations of Standard MUMPS regard all partitions as fixed size, while other implementations allow variable partition size.

24.   When you "log on" to a MUMPS system, you are assigned your own user partition.

After you "log on", you may load programs from disk into your partition, and access data from disk. Programs and data loaded into your partition from disk will remain on disk, and are not "lost" after you "log off".

However, programs and data entered into your partition and NOT saved on disk will be LOST when you "log off" the system.

25.   Are you running Standard MUMPS on a single user personal computer? In this case, you probably have only one user partition.

Are you running Standard MUMPS on a multi-user system? In this case, contact the system manager for a user class identification (UCI) code, and a "password" which will allow you to write programs.

Typically, two types of "password" are available:

- passwords that provide "User Access" - this allows you to use existing programs but not write new programs.

- passwords that provide "Programmer Access" - this allows you to write new programs as well as to run existing programs.

With Programmer Access, you can enter and execute MUMPS statements in either:

(1)   the Direct Mode

(2)   the Indirect Mode.

With User Access, you can execute MUMPS statements only in the Indirect Mode.

In the next chapter, we will demonstrate how to enter and execute MUMPS statements in the Direct Mode.

12

SUMMARY OF NEW CONCEPTS - CHAPTER 1

Log on - a procedure used to gain access to computer resources (implementation specific).

Log off - a procedure used to terminate access to computer resources (implementation specific).

Partition - the "space" allocated to user within primary storage: typically includes a routine buffer, symbol table and execution stack (see Figure 1-4). Programs and data entered into your partition are "lost" when you log off the system - unless they have been "stored" on disk (or an equivalent device used for secondary storage).

Routine - a program which is stored on disk and moved into the routine buffer of user partition prior to execution.

Symbol table - a space within user partition which contains the names of all "local variables".

Execution stack - a space within user partition which stores the names of routines and subroutines as they are performed.

User Access - access to the computer which allows you to use existing programs, but not write new programs.

Programmer Access - access to the computer that allows you to write new programs as well as use existing programs.

CHAPTER TWO

ENTERING AND EXECUTING MUMPS STATEMENTS IN THE DIRECT MODE

In this chapter, we will demonstrate the Direct Mode for entering and executing MUMPS code. Topics in this chapter include:

- your computer terminal

- the log on procedure

- the Direct Mode

- an introduction to MUMPS syntax

- correcting mistakes

- wrap around

- the log off procedure.

When you complete this chapter, you will be able to:

- log on to your MUMPS system

- enter and execute MUMPS statements in the Direct Mode

- log off your MUMPS system.

YOUR COMPUTER TERMINAL

1.   MUMPS systems commonly use two types of terminals: hardcopy terminals, and video display terminals (VDT). Hardcopy terminals mark your current typing position by position of the print head. Video display terminals mark your current typing position by a cursor (a flashing underscore or a flashing box).

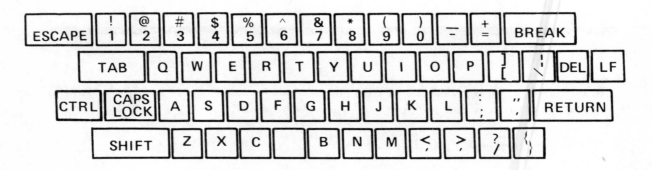

FIGURE 2-1. LAYOUT OF A TERMINAL KEYBOARD

2.   Your terminal keyboard will resemble the keyboard for an electric typewriter. One possible layout is illustrated in Figure 2-1.

Notice that there are some "additional keys" which include:

    ESCAPE (or "ESC")
    BREAK
    DEL (or "DELETE")
    CTRL (or "CONTROL")
    CAPS LOCK
    LF (or "LINE FEED")

Also, there are some "special character" keys which include:

    ^ (on the top row as a shift character)
    ] and [(on the second row)
    { and } (on the fourth row)
    < and > (on the lower row as shift characters)
    / and \ (on the fourth and second rows respectively)

Actual layout of your keyboard may differ from Figure 2-1. The "RETURN" key may be labelled "ENTER". There may be more (or fewer) "additional keys" and "special character" keys. Computer terminal keyboards are not "standardized" to the same extent as typewriters! Review the positions of all keys on your terminal.

3.   For a typewriter keyboard, we are concerned with physical appearance of printed characters. For a typewriter, the following characters are interchangeable:

(1)   numeric "1" (one) and lower case alpha character "l" (lower case "L")

(2)   numeric "0" (zero) and upper case alpha character "O" (upper case "O").

For a computer terminal, each character transmits a unique electric signal. The numeric "1" and the lower case alpha "l" transmit different electrical signals and are NOT interchangeable. Likewise, the numeric "0" and the upper case alpha "O" transmit different electrical signals and are NOT interchangeable.

THE LOG ON PROCEDURE

4.   Three important keys are (1) TAB, (2) RETURN (or ENTER) and (3) CONTROL (sometimes labelled CTRL). Locate the positions of these keys on your terminal.

Are you running MUMPS on a personal microcomputer? Then check the instruction manual for information on "log on".

Are you sharing a computer with other users? Then ask your system manager how to "log on". Practice this a few times, and write down the procedure, so you needn't worry about remembering!

Here is a sample log on sequence. The user responses are underlined.

BREAK (user strikes the BREAK key)

MUMPS LINE #64

UCI: CPD:TOM

>

For this example, log on requires two access codes:

(1)   "UCI". In this example, CPD is the user class identification code. This UCI also identifies the programs written and saved by a given "user" of the system.

(2)   A programmer access code, sometimes referred to as a "PAC". In this example, TOM is the programmer access code.

5. Ask your system manager for passwords (such as a UCI and PAC) which will allow you to write new programs.

Different MUMPS systems may have slightly different log on procedures. Enter the log on procedure for your own system in the space below.

6. What about the ">" symbol displayed by the computer in frame 4? This symbol, commonly used to designate a "greater than" relationship, is also called a "right caret". In our system, the right caret represents a "system prompt" - to notify the user that a response is expected. Some MUMPS systems use a "?" to signal that a response is expected.

THE DIRECT MODE

7. The Direct Mode implies that:

- MUMPS statements or commands are entered "directly" after a right caret (or equivalent symbols displayed by other MUMPS systems)

- MUMPS statements or commands are executed "directly" after you strike the RE-TURN key (or the ENTER key, used on some terminals).

8. Enter the following at any right caret (or the system prompt for your implementation):

>WRITE "THIS IS AN EXAMPLE"

Start typing "WRITE" directly after the right caret (no space). Use exactly one space after "WRITE". Press RETURN after completing your entry.

What happens?

MUMPS displays on your terminal:

THIS IS AN EXAMPLE

9. Now enter at any right caret:

```
>WRITE "10+5=",10+5 L
```

Again, start typing "WRITE" directly after the right caret (no space). Use exactly one space after "WRITE", before entering the first quote. Do NOT use a space between the second quote and the comma. Do NOT use a space after the comma. Press RETURN after completing your entry. What happens?

MUMPS displays on your terminal:

10+5=15

10. Try a few more entries, using frames 8 and 9 as models use one space after WRITE, but NO spaces before or after the comma.

What happens if you make a mistake?

MUMPS displays an error message such as "<SYNTX>".

INTRODUCTION TO MUMPS SYNTAX

11. Frames 8 and 9 illustrate MUMPS statements with a command which specifies an action to be performed. This command may be followed by one or more arguments.

The WRITE command for our MUMPS statements in frames 8 and 9 can be translated as: "display these arguments following the WRITE command".

12. Commands represent the "verbs" for MUMPS statements. Arguments are the "objects" of a MUMPS command. A command may have either:

● no arguments (argumentless command)

● one argument

● several arguments.

In frame 8 the WRITE command has one argument. In frame 9 the WRITE command has two arguments. One space is used between a command and it's first argument. Multiple arguments to a command are NOT separated by spaces - but by commas, as shown in frame 9. A series of arguments following a command is called an argument list.

19

13. MUMPS arguments are composed of expressions used in MUMPS are:

- string literals

- numeric literals

- variables.

14. String literals consist of letters, numbers, or symbolic characters, enclosed within quotation marks. What two string literals are used in frame 8 and 9?

```
"THIS IS AN EXAMPLE"
"10+5="
```

15. MUMPS will accept lower case letters for both commands and string literals. However, in this manual, we will use lower case letters only for string literals.

16. Numeric literals consist of numbers not enclosed within quotation marks. What numeric literal is used in frame 9?

```
10+5
```

17. Notice from frame 9 that the string literal "10+5=" is output as:

10+5=

The numeric literal 10+5 is output as 15.

18. Arithmetic operations can be performed with numeric literals using the arithmetic operators:

    +   (addition)

    -       (subtraction)

    *   (multiply)

    /   (divide)

19. Enter the following examples at your terminal:

```
>WRITE "3+2=",3+2

>WRITE "3-2=",3-2

>WRITE "3x2=",3*2

>WRITE "1/3=",1/3
```

What are the outputs?

_____

3+2=5

3-2=1

3x2=6

1/3=.33333

20. The number of decimal places output for 1/3 will vary for different MUMPS implementations.

21. Variables are symbolic names for data stored in computer memory. MUMPS provides three types of variables:

- local variables

- global variables

- special variables.

In this chapter, we are only concerned with local variables. A local variable is "local" to your user partition. Your local variable names and values will "disappear" when you log off the system. MUMPS keeps the names and current values for your local variables in the symbol table of your user partition.

22.   The SET command allows us to create a variable name and assign a value to this name. Here is an example:

```
>SET VALUE="$100"
>
```

Enter this MUMPS statement into your terminal. Now at the next right caret, enter the WRITE command with no argument. What happens?

In our implementation, MUMPS displays the value $100. The effect of MUMPS commands entered in the direct mode is implementation specific. For our implementation of MUMPS, the WRITE command with no argument entered at a system prompt displays the names and values for all local variables in our partition. Your implementation may be different: study the user manual for your system and identify the method used to display the local variables in your partition.

23.   Our implementation also allows us to display the value of a specific variable via the WRITE command. For example:

```
>SET VALUE2="$50"

>WRITE VALUE2
$50
>
```

Here is a second example:

```
>SET SUM2="4 DOGS"+"1 CAT"

>WRITE SUM2
5
>
```

If MUMPS finds valid numeric characters at the beginning of a string literal (literal string), it uses these characters as the numeric values for the string. A third example:

```
>SET SUM3="ONE DOG #13"+"1 CAT"

>WRITE SUM3
1
>
```

Strings which do not begin with one or more numeric characters are assigned a numeric value of zero. And a fourth example:

```
>SET SUM4=6+"10"

>WRITE SUM4
16
>
```

A numeric literal within quotation marks is assigned its true numeric value. As demonstrated above, numeric literals are evaluated correctly even when NOT enclosed within quotation marks.

24. In MUMPS, we can freely assign values to any variable. We do not need to plan in advance whether a particular variable will be expressed as alpha characters, numbers, or a mixture of number and alpha characters.

CORRECTING MISTAKES

25. When you make a typing error, MUMPS displays an error message such as: <SYNTX>. After receiving such an error message, you can simply retype the line.

26. You can also correct a line before you execute it, by using either:

- the DELETE key

- CONTROL U (entered by holding down the CONTROL or CTRL key, while typing U).

27. Each stroke of the DELETE key erases the right-most character on the line. On some hardcopy terminals, DELETE may write a backslash, to designate that the right most character has been deleted. On other hard copy terminals, both a backslash and the character deleted are displayed. On video display terminals, DELETE erases the last character, and backspaces over it.

28. CONTROL U erases an entire line. Each time you enter CONTROL U, MUMPS deletes the line you are typing, and places the print head or curser back at the beginning of this line.

WRAP-AROUND

29. It is possible to enter more than one statement on a single line. When you enter multiple statements on the same line, separate each new command from the preceding statement by at least one space. Here is an example:

```
>SET RESULT1=1+4 SET RESULT2=6+7 SET RESULT3=RESULT2/RESULT1 WRITE RESULT3
```

30.   You can enter any number of statements on one line so long as the total number of characters does not exceed 255. What happens if we enter more than 80 characters on a video display terminal which is only 80 columns wide? Try entering the following as one line of code:

```
>SET RESULT1=(1+4)*3 SET RESULT2=RESULT1*RESULT1 SET RESULT3=7/3 SET RESULT4=RES
ULT2/RESULT3 SET RESULT5=RESULT4/6.32 WRITE RESULT5
```

This line of code contains more than 80 characters - but less than 255. What happens?

_____

Our code "wraps around" onto the next line, as illustrated above.

31.   If you enter more than 80 characters as one line of code, this single line of code will "wrap around" - into the next line of your video screen, starting with the 81st character. Although wrap around will not affect how your code executes, it makes your code more difficult to read. We recommend that you avoid wrap around.

THE LOG OFF PROCEDURE

32.   One way to log off is to enter HALT - or its abbreviation H - at a right caret. Different MUMPS systems have slightly different log off procedures. Enter the log off procedure for your system in the space below.

SUMMARY OF NEW CONCEPTS - CHAPTER 2

UCI - user class identifier: an identification code used for log on, which also identifies the programs written and saved by a specific user.

System Prompt - a signal to the user that a response is expected (e.g. right caret, asterisk or question mark displayed at the left margin).

Direct Mode - entry of MUMPS code "directly" after a system prompt. The code entered is executed "directly" after you strike the RETURN or ENTER key.

Command - an instruction which specifies an action to be performed. Typical MUMPS commands include WRITE, PRINT, SET and so on. Operation of certain commands - such as WRITE and PRINT - is implementation specific when used in the direct mode.

Statement - one or more MUMPS commands accompanied by one or more arguments.

Argument - the "object" of a MUMPS command.

String literal - a string of characters enclosed within quotation marks.

Numeric literal - numbers used without quotation marks as part of a MUMPS statement.

Arithmetic operators - symbols which denote an arithmetic operation to be performed: the symbols + , -, * and / denote addition, subtraction, multiplication and division.

Variable - a symbolic name for data stored within the computer. Each variable has two components: a name and a value. For example: SET VAR = "$100" creates the variable VAR, with a value of "$100".

Correcting Mistakes - DELETE key deletes one or more characters on a given line before you strike RETURN.
- CTRL/U deletes an entire line before you strike RETURN.

CHAPTER THREE

ENTERING AND EXECUTING MUMPS STATEMENTS IN THE INDIRECT MODE

In Chapter Two, we used the Direct Mode to display results of simple arithmetic operations. This chapter will demonstrate how to write and execute simple programs, or "routines". Topics in this chapter include:

- The Indirect Mode

- Correcting mistakes and making changes

- Saving programs on disk

- Formatting output

- Simple arithmetic

- Error messages.

When you complete this chapter, you will be able to:

- write simple programs, using the READ, WRITE and SET commands

- enter a program into your computer

- DO (or execute) a program

- remove unwanted errors in your program

- display programs currently in computer memory

- perform arithmetic operations

- save programs on disk

- recall programs from disk.

INDIRECT MODE

1. A MUMPS routine is one or more lines of code that are executed and stored as a unit. A MUMPS program is one or more routines, that perform specific functions, and provide outputs.

2. At this point, there are two ways you can "clear" your partition after creating a series of variables in the direct mode:

- Log off your terminal, then log on again

- Enter the KILL command at any right caret.

For our implementation, the KILL command, entered in the direct mode, erases or "kills" all local variables in your partition. However, operation of MUMPS commands in the direct mode is implementation specific - if necessary, study the user manual for your system.

3. Create a few local variables by using the SET command in the direct mode. Display these variables with the WRITE command entered at any right caret (also referred to as "direct execution" - since the WRITE command is executed "directly", without delay). Now enter the KILL command in the Direct Mode. Again, enter the WRITE command at any right caret. What happens?

Your local variables have disappeared!

4. Let's use direct execution (the direct mode) to perform some simple addition:

```
>SET  A=1
>SET  B=4
>SET  SUM=A+B
>SET  AVERAGE= (A+B) /2
>WRITE  "Sum=", SUM
>WRITE  "Average=", AVERAGE
```

What if we wanted to perform a series of additions using different numbers each time? With the direct mode, we would have to re-enter these six MUMPS statements for each addition. However, we can use the indirect mode to create a small program, or routine, which need not be re-entered for each addition.

5.　Here is a simple program which:

- Displays a message "Enter first number: "

- Accepts whatever entry is made as the value of A

- Displays a message "Enter second number: "

- Accepts whatever entry is made as the value of B

- Calculates the sum and average

- Displays the sum and average.

```
CH3EX1 ; EXAMPLE 1 - ADDING MACHINE PROGRAM WITH READ, SET AND WRITE
        WRITE !,"Enter first number: "
        READ A
        WRITE !,"Enter second number:  "
        READ B
        SET SUM=A+B
        SET AVERAGE=SUM/2
        WRITE !,"Sum = ",SUM
        WRITE !,"Average = ",AVERAGE
```

6.　Let's consider the format and functions line by line:

(1)　The first line does not resemble anything we've seen in direct mode. This first line begins with the line label CH3EX1. A line label is a name which identifies a program line. For our implementation of Standard MUMPS, line labels must begin with an uppercase letter or %. A line label may be as short as one character, or as long as eight characters. After the first character, additional characters must be uppercase letters or digits. The first line of any MUMPS code to be executed in the indirect mode should begin with a line label. This line label indicates where the starting point of the program is.
In Frame 5, the line label appears to be followed by a space. Actually, it is followed by a tab, then a semicolon. The semicolon means: "everything which follows on this line will represent comments rather than executable MUMPS code". It is common practice for MUMPS programmers to follow the first line label of each program with comments that describe what the program does, and why it was written.

(2)　The second line begins with a tab, preceding the WRITE command. In indirect mode, each line of code must begin with a "line start character". For our implementation, this line start character is a tab (enter by pressing the tab key on your terminal). For some other implementations, this line start character is a single space.

Is there a tab (or equivalent) in the first line? Yes! However, it is "obscured" by the line label. The tab (or other line start character) signifies: "this is a program line, to be executed in indirect mode". Two arguments follow our first WRITE command: an exclamation mark, separated by a comma from the literal string "Enter first number :   ". The exclamation mark means: "execute one line feed and return the print head (or cursor) to column zero".
This code outputs one line feed and carriage return, then outputs the literal string "Enter first number: ".

(3)   Our third line also begins with a line start character (in this case, the tab), followed by a new command: READ. The READ command "reads" whatever entry was made as the current value for the variable A. This line accepts whatever entry is made as the current value for A. You signal the computer that your entry is done by striking the RETURN key.

(4)   The fourth line is similar in format and function to the second.

(5)   The fifth line is similar in format and function to the third.

(6)   The sixth line SETs the value of SUM equal to A plus B.

(7)   The seventh line SETs the value of AVERAGE equal to SUM divided by two.

(8)   The eighth line outputs one line feed/carriage return, displays the message "Sum = " and the value of SUM.

(9)   The ninth line outputs one line feed carriage return, displays the message "Average = ", and the value of AVERAGE.

7.   Log onto your terminal, and enter the program from frame 5 into your terminal. But first, remove any program lines that may exist in your partition of internal memory. Different vendors handle this differently. Commands beginning with the letter Z are vendor specific; that is, they are not part of standard MUMPS. For our implementation, to remove programs from internal memory, we enter at any right caret the letters ZR, then press the key marked RETURN. The letters "ZR" stand for "ZREMOVE". Enter ZREMOVE or ZR (or your system's equivalent) at any right caret.

At the next right caret, enter "CH3EX1". MUMPS recognizes this as a "line label".

Next, enter the line start character for your system. In our implementation, the line start character is entered by striking the tab key. In other implementations, this may be done by striking the space bar once.

Check how to enter the line start character for YOUR system. Don't worry about making mistakes! You can always enter "ZR" (or the equivalent) to remove all program lines in your partition of memory.

After you enter a line label, be sure to follow this by the line start character for your system.

The semicolon indicates that this first line of code represents comments, rather than instructions to be executed. Enter this first line, then strike RETURN.

8.   After you strike RETURN, a second system prompt - such as a right caret - will appear. Enter the line start character (a tab or space, depending on your implementation of MUMPS), the second line of code, and RETURN.

9.   Now enter the remaining lines of code, starting each time with a line start character after the right caret. If you make a mistake, use the DELETE key, CTRL/U, or ZR to make the correction.

Notice that this program has only one line label. Some computer languages (such as some versions of BASIC) require a separate numeric label for every line of code. If you are familiar with a language that requires numeric labels for each line, it may take a while to feel "comfortable" with using line labels only where necessary!

10.   To "do" a routine, enter the DO command at a right caret (direct execution) followed by one space, and the line label at which execution should start. Commands within the routine are then executed "indirectly" - in the "indirect mode". At the next right caret enter:

```
>DO  CH3EX1
```

The computer should ask for a series of two numbers and then print the sum and the average. Here is a sample - the user entries are underlined. A carriage return is indicated by the symbol <CR>.

```
>DO  CH3EX1<CR>


Enter first number: 5<CR>
Enter second number:  15<CR>
Sum = 20
Average = 10
```

After typing in each number, enter RETURN, to signal the computer that you have completed your entry.

The program should execute from top to bottom sequentially. Execution stops when the program runs out of code.

11.   If your program does not work properly, type ZR at a right caret, re-enter your program exactly as shown in frame 5, and try again. The program CH3EX1 can be read as:

(1)   Regard the first line of code as a line label, a line start character, and a "comment line". The semicolon signals the computer that whatever follows on the same line will be "explanatory comments", rather than code to be executed.

(2)   WRITE, or "output", a line feed (signaled by one exclamation mark) and display the message "Enter first number: ".

(3)   READ the entry made as the value of A.

(4)   WRITE, or "output", one line feed (signaled by one exclamation mark) and display the message "Enter second number: ".

(5)   READ the entry made as the value of B.

(6)   SET the value of SUM equal to the value of A plus B.

(7)   SET the value of AVERAGE equal to SUM divided by 2.

(8)   WRITE or "output" one line feed, display the message "Sum = ", and the value of SUM.

(9)   WRITE or "output" one line feed, display the message "Average = ", and the value of AVERAGE.

12.   In this program, the WRITE, READ, and SET commands specify actions to be performed. The subject of a command is called an "argument". In line CH3EX1 + 1 (the first line after the one labelled CH3EX1), the WRITE command is followed by two arguments: ! and "Enter first number: ".

Here are two simple rules to follow:

(1)   Use one space between a command and its first argument.

(2)   Separate multiple arguments after the same command by commas (no spaces).

If you use two spaces between a command and its first argument, MUMPS will display an error message when you DO the program.

If you use a space (with or without a comma) between two arguments of the same command, MUMPS will display an error message when you DO the program.

13.   Notice the line label - CH3EX1. Line labels may be up to 8 characters long. The first character of a line label must be either alphabetic or "%". No decimals, hyphens, spaces, or punctuation are permitted.

14.   Your program is not altered or erased from primary storage when you DO it. Every time you type DO CH3EX1 and press RETURN, the computer will run your program.

15.   The right caret is a prompt to indicate you may enter either a command (in direct mode), or a program line (preceded by a line start character). Other implementations may use some other symbol than a caret: eg. "?" or "*". The results of computer output - as depicted in frame 10 - have no carets.

16.   Literal strings are output exactly as they appear, that is, literally For example:

```
WRITE "Sum=", SUM
```

"Sum = " is a string,
and will be output
exactly as written

SUM is not a string: the value
assigned to the variable SUM will
be displayed

A literal string may include:

(a)   numerals (0,1,2...)

(b)   letters (A,B,C,a,b,c...)

(c)   special characters (+,-,*,/,\,#,^,(,),{,}, comma, period, semicolon, quotation marks, and so on).

Since quotation marks define the beginning and end of a literal string, they require special handling when used within a literal string. To signify one quotation mark within a string, use two quotation marks together. For example:

```
>WRITE !,"This program performs the function of an ""adding machine""."
```

33

17. In Chapter Two, we introduced the concept of a "variable". We can think of a variable as a "name" whose value can " vary" - while a program is being run. In CH3EX1, the value of SUM and AVERAGE can vary each time you execute this program.

CORRECTING MISTAKES AND MAKING CHANGES

18. Did you make any errors when you entered CH3EX1 into your terminal? Even experienced programmers make typing errors from time to time!

Also, you may want to change your programs at a later date. For example, you may want to revise CH3EX1 to accept three numbers, or to perform multiplication rather than addition.

To correct mistakes and make changes in your programs, you need to perform three functions:

- change a specified line

- delete a specified line

- add a new line at a specified location in your program.

CHANGING A SPECIFIED LINE

19. In Chapter Two, we described two ways to change a line BEFORE striking RETURN.

If you notice a mistake before entering RETURN, you can remove individual characters via the DELETE key. The DELETE key is sometimes marked RUBOUT. Some implementations use the BACKSPACE key or CONTROL/H to perform this function.

When you mis-type most of a line, you may wish to "start-over". You can do this by typing a CONTROL/U: hold the control key down and strike the U key. CONTROL/U deletes an entire line, while the DELETE key deletes individual characters. Be sure to check your instruction manual: some implementations may use different characters, in place of CONTROL/U.

Neither DELETE nor CONTROL/U can be used after you strike RETURN for that line.

20. How can you change one or more lines after you strike RETURN? Most implementations of Standard MUMPS include an editor program supplied by the vendor.

The editor programs ("editors") from different vendors operate differently. For a given editor, different techniques must be used with hard copy terminals as compared to video display terminals - since hard copy terminals do not allow the print head to "back up" and "reprint" a given line (unlike a VDT, the printer cannot erase its output).

In the next few frames, we'll illustrate how our editor can be used with a video display terminal. At this point, refer to your user manual, and note how your editor differs from these examples. We suggest that you note these differences as marginal comments.

21.   For most MUMPS implementations, you begin the editor by typing X ^% at a right caret. In these examples, all user responses will be underlined. Note the space after "X" in this entry:

>X ^%

The character "X" is shorthand for the "XECUTE" command. The characters "^%" represent the name of the editor program. The XECUTE command performs a function for our ^% program (the editor) quite comparable to the function performed by the DO command for our CH3EX1 program in Frame 10.

When we enter X ^% at a right caret, we are using direct execution of the XECUTE command, with ^% as the argument for this command.

Why didn't we DO ^%? There is a good reason which is covered later, in our discussion of the XECUTE command.

The editor responds with:

EDIT:

Your editor may respond with a different prompt, such as LINE>.

Let's edit CH3EX1 so that the last lines read:

```
WRITE !,"The sum is ",SUM
WRITE !,"The average is ",AVERAGE
```

To do this , we need to change lines CH3EX1 + 7 and CH3EX1 + 8. The " + 7" and the " + 8" are called "offsets" from the line label CH3EX1.

At the prompt EDIT:, enter CH3EX1 + 7, and strike RETURN:

EDIT: CH3EX1+7<CR>

The editor responds by displaying the line you selected, with a single space separating the line label (if any) from the rest of the routine line. The cursor is positioned over the first character and the line is ready for editing:

```
WRITE ! , "Sum = " , SUM
```

To edit this line, you must position the cursor over the first character to be edited. For our system, you can position the cursor by:

(1)   Pressing the space bar - this moves the cursor forward to the next space or comma.

(2)   Typing a period (".") - this moves the cursor forward one character position.

(3)   Pressing the backspace key - this moves the cursor backward one character position.

Once the cursor has been positioned for our system, you can perform one of five operations:

(1)   Press the DELETE (or RUBOUT) key to delete the single character under the cursor.

(2)   Type the character "D" (for "delete") to delete the character under the cursor plus all characters up to (but not including) the next space or comma.

(3)   Type the character "E" (for "enter") to enter new characters.

(4)   Press the RETURN key (after you have performed a delete and/or entry operation) to return the cursor to the beginning of the line.

(5)   Press the RETURN key while the cursor is at the beginning of the line to return to the EDIT: prompt.

After you change this line, press RETURN to return the cursor to the beginning of the line. Press RETURN again to redisplay the prompt:

```
EDIT:
```

Now make the changes in line CH3EX1 + 8.

When you have no further changes, enter a period and strike RETURN to exit the Editor.

22. For our system, you can list your revised program, by entering a PRINT command at any right caret:

```
>PRINT
CH3EX1 ; EXAMPLE 1 - ADDING MACHINE PROGRAM WITH READ, SET AND WRITE
      WRITE !,"Enter first number: "
      READ A
      WRITE !,"Enter second number: "
      READ B
      SET SUM=A+B
      SET AVERAGE=SUM/2
      WRITE !,"The sum is ",SUM
      WRITE !,"The average is ",AVERAGE
```

Use of PRINT with direct execution is implementation specific. Refer to your user manual to determine how this operation is performed on your system.

After making a change, it's a good idea to display your revised program for a "final review".

DELETING A SPECIFIED LINE OR LINES

23. To delete an entire line before striking RETURN, use CONTROL/U, as described in frame 19 of this chapter.

24. Several options are available for deleting one or more lines after you strike RETURN.

For our system, one option is direct execution of the ZREMOVE command, which may be abbreviated as ZR.

Suppose you want to remove a line from a program without replacing it with another line. To remove a single line, at any right caret type ZR and the label or label plus offset. Let's remove line CH3EX1+8, so that average is no longer displayed:

```
>ZR CH3EX1+8
>PRINT
CH3EX1 ; EXAMPLE 1 - ADDING MACHINE PROGRAM WITH READ, SET AND WRITE
      WRITE !,"Enter first number: "
      READ A
      WRITE !,"Enter second number: "
      READ B
      SET SUM=A+B
      SET AVERAGE=SUM/2
      WRITE !,"The sum is ",SUM
```

The ZREMOVE command may not exist as such in your MUMPS system, but there should be a very similar command available for you.

25.   For our system, you can "ZRemove" all lines after CH3EX1+2 by typing ZR CH3EX1 + 3:CH3EX1 + 7. Now all lines of your program will be removed, except for the first three lines.

26.   For our system, you can remove all programs in your partition by typing at any right caret ZR and RETURN. Try this with the corresponding command for your system, and then check your partition via direct execution of the PRINT command or its equivalent. What happens?

Your partition is empty!

27.   Re-enter CH3EX1, and practice using it until you are satisfied the program works properly.

28.   Your system may allow you to delete one or more specified lines from a program via the Editor. Here is an example using our system:

```
>X ^%
EDIT:  .REMOVE LINES
```

The .R signifies "remove a range of lines from the routine specified".

```
FROM LINE: BEG=> CH3EX1+8    TO LINE: END=> CH3EX1+8
EDIT:  .
```

ADDING A NEW LINE AT A SPECIFIED LOCATION

29.   We have already used direct execution of the PRINT command to display programs in our partition (this is implementation specific). With our system, we can also use the PRINT command to add a new line at any desired location in our program.

Assume CH3EX1 is currently in computer memory and we want to add a new line CH3EX1 + 9 to our program CH3EX1. This new line will be: WRITE !,"The end". First, PRINT the line preceding the new line:

```
>PRINT CH3EX1+8
WRITE !,"The average is ",AVERAGE
```

Now type in the new line (remember to include a tab):

><tab>WRITE !,"The end"

and press RETURN. This new line is incorporated into the existing program.

To verify this, at any right caret type PRINT, then press RETURN. The computer will display our program with the new line.

Since the PRINT command is implementation specific, your system may be somewhat different.

30.   To insert a new line after line CH3EX1, we can print line CH3EX1 and then enter the new line:


```
>PRINT CH3EX1
CH3EX1 ; EXAMPLE 1 - ADDING MACHINE PROGRAM WITH READ, SET AND WRITE

>&lt;tab&gt;WRITE !,"This program allows you to add two numbers"

>PRINT
CH3EX1 ; EXAMPLE 1 - ADDING MACHINE PROGRAM WITH READ, SET AND WRITE
       WRITE !,"This program allows you to add two numbers"
       WRITE !,"Enter first number: "
       READ A
       WRITE !,"Enter second number: "
       READ B
       SET SUM=A+B
       SET AVERAGE=SUM/2
       WRITE !,"The sum is ",SUM
       WRITE !,"The average is ",AVERAGE
       WRITE !,"The end"
```


31.   You can also use the Editor to insert new program lines. Here is how this is done with our implementation:


```
>X ^%
EDIT: .INSERT AFTER: CH3EX1
INSERT:  ; THIS IS AN ADDED COMMENT LINE
INSERT: <CR>
EDIT: .
>PRINT
```

```
CH3EX1 ; EXAMPLE 1 - ADDING MACHINE PROGRAM WITH READ, SET AND WRITE
       ; THIS IS AN ADDED COMMENT LINE
       WRITE !,"Enter first number: "
       READ A
       WRITE !,"Enter second number: "
       READ B
       SET SUM=A+B
       SET AVERAGE=SUM/2
       WRITE !,"The sum is ",SUM
       WRITE !,"The average is ",AVERAGE
       WRITE !,"The end"
```

32.   Different implementations of Standard MUMPS may vary in:

  • Function of the PRINT command in Direct Mode

  • Function of the Editor.

Your implementation of Standard MUMPS may provide other "ZCommands" such as:

  • ZCHANGE

  • ZINSERT

  • ZMOVE

  • ZPRINT

  • ZWRITE

Check your user manual to review:

  • How the PRINT and WRITE commands function in the direct mode with your implementation of Standard MUMPS.

  • How the ZREMOVE command functions with your implementation.

  • Whether "ZCommands" such as ZCHANGE, ZINSERT, ZMOVE, ZPRINT and ZWRITE exist - and if so, how they operate.

  • How the Editor functions for your implementation of Standard MUMPS.

SAVING PROGRAMS ON DISK

33.   What will happen to your program CH3EX1, when you log off your terminal? Your program will disappear - just as if you had entered ZREMOVE at right caret!

MUMPS allows you to save programs on disk. In our implementation, we save programs on disk by the ZSAVE command, and load programs from disk into our partition by the ZLOAD command. As noted before:

- all "ZCommands" are implementation specific

- operation of the PRINT command in Direct Mode is implementation specific

- operation of the Editor is implementation specific.

Check your user manual for a discussion of how the ZSAVE and ZLOAD commands - or their equivalents - are used to save programs on disk, and load programs from disk. Although the following discussion is specific to our implementation, most versions of Standard MUMPS use similar methods for saving programs on disk, and loading programs from disk to your partition.

34.   Use the PRINT command (or its equivalent) to display CH3EX1 in your partition of memory. Ask your system manager if you may use the program names "AAAA" and "BBBB". If these names are NOT permitted, select two other names, in place of AAAA and BBBB, for the following exercises.

Enter ZSAVE (or its equivalent) at any right caret, a space, AAAA and RETURN. You have just saved CH3EX1 onto disk under the program name AAAA.

Now enter ZSAVE and BBBB. You have saved CH3EX1 onto disk again - this time, under the program name BBBB. As long as you have a routine in your partition, you can use ZSAVE to copy this routine onto disk under many different names.

35.   Now enter ZR (or its equivalent) display all programs in your partition. What happens?

_____

The screen remains blank. CH3EX1 has been removed from your partition of memory.

36.   Now type at any right caret ZLOAD AAAA, and strike RETURN. What happens when you enter PRINT?

_____

Your program is back!

37.   Again enter ZR and use PRINT to confirm that your partition is empty. Now enter ZSAVE, space and BBBB. You have just "saved" an empty partition onto disk under the name BBBB.

Try to ZLOAD the program BBBB. What happens?

You get an error message such as <NOPGM>. You removed the program BBBB from disk when you saved an empty partition under the name BBBB. If someone else had a program called BBBB on disk, it would be gone! And if someone else had a program called AAAA on disk, your first ZSAVE operation would have replaced their program with your own! So be careful about assigning names to programs!

38.   Before you select a program name, empty your partition with ZREMOVE, and try a ZLOAD with the name you are considering. If you get a message such as <NOPGM>, it's safe to proceed. Otherwise, when you ZSAVE your program, you will zap some other program on disk!

39.   Some rules for program names:

    (1)   a program name may be 1 to 8 characters long

    (2)   the first character must be either alphabetic or %

    (3)   no punctuation marks or spaces are permitted.

We recommend that you do NOT begin program names with the "%" character: program names beginning with "%" usually are "reserved" for implementation specific "utility programs", provided by your system vendor.

It is common practice to use program names which are identical to the first line label of the program. However, as you can see from the preceding frames, any name can be used!

In this book, we will name most programs by a chapter number plus an example number. For instance:

CH3EX1
CH3EX2

and so on.

A common convention is to have related programs start with the same first two letters. For example, the programs which relate to a file of names might include: NABUILD to build the file, NAMOD to modify the file, NADEL to delete names from the file, and NADISPLAY to display data for a specific name. Alternatively, these programs could be called NA00001, NA00002, NA00003, and so on. Since all these programs begin with NA (an abbreviation for NAME), they will appear together in your "routine directory".

40.   What is a "routine directory"? A routine directory is a list of all programs saved on disk under a given UCI (user class identification code). Most implementations of Standard MUMPS provide a utility program which displays the routine directory for your UCI, with program names listed in alphabetic order.

Our implementation of Standard MUMPS provides a utility program called %RD. To display our routine directory we enter:

```
>DO ^%RD
```

Your user manual will have instructions on the equivalent utility program for your system.

At this point, your routine directory should contain two program names: AAAA and CH3EX1.

41.   Which of the following are not valid program names?

    a.   CH3EX2

    b.   CH3EX2.1

    c.   FILE10

    d.   MODULE

    e.   CH3EX#1

---

b and e (no punctuation or spaces allowed)

42.   To "erase" your partition of internal storage, use the ZREMOVE command (or its equivalent).

To load a named program from disk, use the ZLOAD command (or its equivalent).

To display a program in your portion of main memory, use the PRINT command (or its equivalent).

To remove a program from disk, clear your partition (ZREMOVE), then do a ZSAVE using the name of the program to be removed. When you save empty memory, any program stored on disk under the same name is "overwritten", and hence removed.

Commands beginning with the letter Z are vendor specific. The Z-commands used by other vendors may have different names, and may operate differently from our implementation of Standard MUMPS.

Utility programs also are vendor specific. In your system, the utility program to display routine names in alphabetic order may be called %R, %RD, or some other name.

43.   What happens if you enter ZSAVE without specifying a program name?

For our implementation, if the program in our partition has a name previously assigned via ZSAVE, this program is saved on to disk, overwriting the earlier version of the program with the same name. Otherwise an error message occurs.

44.   We recommend the following procedure for modifying a program on disk:

(1)   ZLOAD the program into your partition.

(2)   ZSAVE this program under a new name - in case the new version doesn't work!

(3)   Edit the program as desired, and make sure it works properly.

(4)   Save the edited program onto disk, using the original program name.

FORMATTING OUTPUT

HORIZONTAL FORMATTING

45.   We can provide horizontal formatting by including blank spaces within string literals. For example, in CH3EX1 we used blank spaces within the string literals:
```
"Sum = "   and
"Average = "
```

When we DO CH3EX1, our outputs would be:

```
Sum = 44
Average = 22
```

rather than:

```
Sum=44
Average=22
```

46.   We can also use tab stops, as on a typewriter. The horizontal tab character is a question mark ("?"). The horizontal tab character plus a number moves our print head (or curser) to the column number specified. For example, to print sum and average on the same line, we could use:

```
WRITE !,"Sum = ",?10,SUM,?20,"Average = ",?30,AVERAGE
```

This code means: "line feed and carriage return, write "Sum = ", "tab to column 10, write the value of SUM with the first character appearing in column 10, tab to column 20, write "Average = ", tab to column 30, write the value of AVERAGE with the first character appearing in column 30".

The first column on each line is considered as "column zero", rather than "column one".

47.   To keep track of the horizontal position of the print head or cursor, you can use the $X special variable.

The $X special variable contains a numeric value corresponding to the current column number at which the print head or cursor is positioned. You can reposition the print head or cursor by adding values to $X, and using this sum after the horizontal tab character. For example:

```
WRITE ?$X+6,5
```

means: "tab six spaces past current position of print head and type a 5 in this location".

This technique is useful if we want to output both SUM and AVERAGE on the same line, with six spaces after the last character of SUM. To do this, modify the last two lines of CH3EX1 to read:

```
WRITE !,"Sum = ",SUM,?$X+6,"Average = ",AVERAGE
```

With this code, we will output "Average = " starting six spaces after the last number printed for SUM.

48.   Which of these three techniques is best for spacing on output? For spaces following a message, it is easiest to include these in the string. For results printed in multiple columns, the tab stop is easiest. For a sequence of messages on the same line, interspersed with variables of unknown length, $X is the most convenient.

VERTICAL FORMATTING

49.   We have already used the linefeed formatting character, depicted by an exclamation mark ("!"). This is interpreted as: "move to the next line, and bring the print head or cursor to column zero". You may use the two formatting characters "?" and "!" in the same argument. For example:

```
WRITE !!!?10, "Sum = ", SUM
```

is interpreted as:

> " move down three lines, tab to column 10, output the string literal
> "Sum = ", and the value of SUM."

SIMPLE ARITHMETIC

50.   We have already seen that the plus symbol (+) indicates addition, the slash (/) indicates division, the minus symbol (-) indicates subtraction, and the asterisk (*) indicates multiplication.

Try running CH3EX1 with the following entries for A and B:

(1)   CAT and 9

(2)   A1 and 2A

(3)   1A and 2A

(4)   1A2 and 2;3

For the first two sets of entries, MUMPS treats each entry which begins with one or more alpha characters as having a numeric value of zero. An entry of ",2" also would be treated as having numeric value of zero.

For the last two sets of entries, numbers followed by alpha characters or punctuation marks are treated as having numeric values equal to those numbers which precede the first alpha character or punctuation mark. The remaining characters are "discarded" insofar as numeric values are concerned.

51. MUMPS does arithmetic in strict left to right order. Multiplication and division do NOT take priority over addition and subtraction.

Here are some expressions with multiple operations. For the first one, we have shown the value computed. You complete the rest.

Expression	Value Computed
2*3-4	2
2+3*4	—
2*3+4*5	—
2+3*4-5	—
2*3-4*5+6*7	—

      20

      50

      15

      112

52. What happens if we try to divide by zero? Enter a new program, CH3EX2:

```
CH3EX2 ; PROGRAM TO DIVIDE TWO NUMBERS
       WRITE !,"Enter first number   "
       READ A
       WRITE !,"Enter second number   "
       READ B
       WRITE !,"First number divided by the second number = ",A/B
```

Now DO this program, entering 0 as the second number. What happens?

Our system displays an error message <DIVER> for "divide error", resulting from the attempt to divide by zero. Your system may display a different error message. Error messages, such as <SYNTX> and <DIVER>, are implementation specific just like Z-commands, utility programs, direct execution of the PRINT command, and operation of the Editor.

53. Now try these:

Expression	Value Computed
2*3/4	—
8/4*5	—
8/4/2	—
2*3/2 + 3/2*5	—

1.5   Multiply 2 by 3, then divide result by 4.

10   Divide 8 by 4, then multiply result by 5.

1   Divide 8 by 4, then divide result by 2.

15   Multiply 2 by 3, divide result by 2, add 3 to result, divide by 2, and multiply result by 5.

54. If you want to change the order, use parentheses:

$2*3+4 = 10$

$2*(3+4) = 14$ Compute $3+4$, then multiply result by 2.

$2+3*4+5 = 25$

$(2+3)*(4+5) = 45$ Compute $2+3$, then compute $4+5$, then multiply.

55. Complete the following:

Expression	Value Computed
(7+3)/(4*5)	—
2+3*(4+5)	—
1/(5+5)	—

.5

45

.1

56.   Write a correct MUMPS expression for each of the following multiplication and division operations with the proper MUMPS symbol.

Problem   MUMPS Expression

2x3 + 6-5
16(33-212)
3.14x2x2
<u>88-52</u>
19 + 47

2*3 + 6-5

16*(33-212)

3.14*2*2

(88-52)/|(19 + 47)

ERROR MESSAGES

58.   MUMPS tells us when we make a typographical mistake at your terminal in Direct Mode:

```
>WRITE 2*)3+4)
```

Our implementation of Standard MUMPS returns the error message:

```
<SYNTX>
```

A "syntax error" means an error with respect to MUMPS grammar. Common examples include: omitting the space between a command and its first argument; adding a space between two arguments of the same command; and incorrect spelling of command names. The manual for your implementation of Standard MUMPS will list the error messages for your system, and what they mean.

59.   Now enter the following code in Indirect Mode, and then DO it:

```
CH3EX4 ; EXAMPLE OF ERROR MESSAGE
      WRITE 2*)3+4)
>DO CH3EX4
<SYNTX>CH3EX4+1 WRITE 2*)3+4)
```

This same error, with indirect execution, produces a three part error message which includes: (1) the type of error (syntax); (2) the line in which the error occurred (CH3EX4 + 1); (3) the code within this line where processing stopped.

60.   What about error messages for programs stored on disk? Let's add an extra space after the comma in CH3EX1 + 1:

```
>ZR  CH3EX1+1
>PRINT CH3EX1
CH3EX1 ; EXAMPLE 1 - ADDING MACHINE PROGRAM WITH READ, SET AND WRITE
>WRITE !, "Enter first number: "
>ZSAVE CH3EX1

>ZR
>DO ^CH3EX1
<SYNTX>CH3EX1+1^CH3EX1 , "Enter first number: "
```

When we do CH3EX1, our error message displays: (1) the type of error (syntax);   (2) the line in which the error occurred;   (3) the program name with a '^' which indicates that the program CH3EX1 exists on disk.

SUMMARY OF NEW CONCEPTS - CHAPTER 3

Routine - one or more lines of code that are executed and stored as a unit. A routine is assigned a name at the time it is stored on disk. The way in which a routine is named and stored is implementation specific: on our system, this is done via the ZSAVE command.

Line Label - a name 1 to 8 characters long; the first character must be either an alpha character or %.

Offset - a line reference consisting of a line label plus a positive number.

KILL Command - can be used to "erase" all local variables in your partition.

ZREMOVE - an implementation specific command which in our system can be used to:

- "erase" all programs in our partition (ZREMOVE with no argument)

- "erase" one line in a program (e.g. ZREMOVE CH1EX1 + 1)

- "erase" a range of lines in a program (e.g. ZREMOVE CH1EX1 + 1: CH1EX1 + 3).

SET Command - creates a variable with a name and an assigned value.

WRITE Command - with direct execution, WRITE with no argument displays all variables in your partition (implementation specific).
- with indirect execution, outputs format control characters (such as ! for line feed carriage return), literal strings, and values of variables.

Indirect Mode - execution of MUMPS code as part of a routine (each line is preceeded by a line space character, rather than entered "directly" at a system prompt). Also referred to a "indirect execution".

Format control characters - characters which control output format:

- ! for "single line feed" and !! for "double line feed"

- ? for "horizontal tab" to a specified column.

READ Command - accepts the value for a variable.

DO Command - entered at any system prompt, initiates execution of the routine specified: e.g. DO CH1EX1.

Line start character - an implementation specific character which allows code to be executed in Indirect Mode via the DO command. Our implementation uses the tab as a line start character.

Quotation marks within literal strings - to signify one quotation mark, use two quotation marks together.

System Editor - an implementation specific program which allows you to "edit" program lines in your partition. For our implementation, the editor is "called" by entering X ,% at any right caret.

PRINT Command - with direct execution (implementation specific), can be used to:

- display all lines of MUMPS code currently in your partition

- display any given line of MUMPS code currently in your partition

- display a range of lines via PRINT LINEX:LINEY

- add a new line via PRINT specified line, then enter tab and the new line.

ZSAVE - an implementation specific command which in our system is used to "save" programs onto disk.

ZLOAD - an implementation specific command which in our system is used to "load" programs from disk into a user partition.

Routine directory - a list of all programs saved on disk under a given UCI (user class identifier). Most implementations of Standard MUMPS provide a implementation-specific utility program to display the routine directory for your UCI.

$X special variable - contains numeric value corresponding to current position of print head or cursor.

MAKING DECISIONS AND CREATING LOOPS

In Chapter Three, you learned how to: write simple MUMPS programs; modify these programs; store programs on disk; and retrieve programs from disk. In this chapter you'll: review the concept of a "variable"; create simple "loops" using the IF and GOTO commands; use "operators" to evaluate expressions; and use "post conditional syntax" to express an "implied IF command".

Topics in Chapter Four include:

- Review of simple variables

- Using the IF and GOTO commands to make decisions and create loops

- Using operators to evaluate expressions

- Post conditional syntax.

When you have finished this chapter, you will be able to:

- use tables to depict the names and values of variables;

- use the IF and GOTO commands to create simple loops;

- use numeric relational operators, string relational operators, and logical operators to evaluate expressions;

- use post conditional syntax to express an "implied" IF.

REVIEW OF SIMPLE VARIABLES

1.   As originally written, your program CH3EX1 looks like:

```
CH3EX1 ; EXAMPLE 1 - ADDING MACHINE PROGRAM WITH READ, SET AND WRITE
        WRITE !,"Enter first number: "
        READ A
        WRITE !,"Enter second number: "
        READ B
        SET SUM=A+B
        SET AVERAGE=SUM/2
        WRITE !,"Sum = ",SUM
        WRITE !,"Average = ",AVERAGE
```

Log on to your terminal, and use ZLOAD (or its equivalent) to load CH3EX1 from disk to your partition.

2.   What function is performed in line CH3EX1 + 2?

_____

This code creates a simple variable called A.

After executing this line, the program waits for a carriage return. The variable A is assigned the value of whatever entry is made before the carriage return. If no entry is made before the carriage return ("<CR>"), then A is assigned the value of "null" (expressed as ""). If no carriage return is made, the program "just sits there", waiting for a carriage return.

3.   What values of A are created by:

    (a)   a carriage return with no other entry

    (b)   entries of 0, ? 1A, and A1

_____

    (a)   a null entry, depicted as " "

    (b)   0, ? 1A and A1

4.   In our implementation of Standard MUMPS:

- direct execution of the PRINT command displays all program lines in your partition

- direct execution of the WRITE command displays all variables in your partition.

Your implementation of Standard MUMPS may use different methods to:

- display all program lines in your partition

- display all variables in your partition.

Check your user manual on how to perform these functions.

5.   Run CH3EX1 several times. Each time , enter different values for A and B. And each time, write down the values you enter for A and B. Now, display all variables for your partition. What happens?

The last values of A, B, SUM, and AVERAGE are displayed.

For some implementations, a null entry of carriage return at line CH3EX1+2 will be displayed as 'A = ""'; for other implementations, a null entry will be displayed as 'A = '; for still other implementations, a null entry is not displayed.

6.   With some computer languages, you must "declare the variable name and type" before you can create a variable. With MUMPS, you can create variables "as you go". There is no need to "specify in advance" that a given variable must contain: numbers only, alpha characters only, or a mixture of numbers, alpha characters and punctuation marks.

Figure 4-1 illustrates what happens to the values of A, B, SUM and AVERAGE when we DO CH3EX1 twice: the first time entering 30 and 20 as values, and the second time entering 6 and 4. Each time we DO CH3EX1, the values of these four variables take on different values.

NAME OF VARIABLE	VALUE OF VARIABLE		
	CYCLE ONE	CYCLE TWO	CYCLE THREE
A	30	6	
B	20	4	
SUM	50	10	
AVERAGE	25	5	

FIGURE 4-1. SAMPLE VALUES OF VARIABLES FOR THE PROGRAM CH3EX1

7. We can create variable names, together with the values of these variables, via the READ and SET commands. We can display the values of all variables within our partition by entering WRITE at any right caret.

8. Enter at any right caret:

>SET A="ZZZ"

Now enter WRITE at the next right caret. What is the current value of A?

_____

ZZZ

9. Now enter at any right caret:

>SET A=ZZZ

What happens?

_____

You get an error message, such as <UNDEF>, meaning "undefined variable". The exact nature of this error message will be implementation specific.

In frame 8, we set A equal to the literal string ZZZ: notice that ZZZ was enclosed in quotes. In frame 9, ZZZ was considered a second variable - since ZZZ was not enclosed in quotes.

10. In frame 9, what would have happened if we had entered:

>SET ZZZ=""
>SET A=ZZZ

_____

Our first command would have created the variable ZZZ, having a "null value". Our second command would have created the variable A, having the same value as ZZZ.

We could also express these two lines of code as two arguments of a single SET command:

>SET ZZZ="", A=ZZZ

11.   From the preceding frames, we see that a variable can have the value of:

(1)   a number, eg. SET A = 1

(2)   a literal string, eg. SET A = "ZZZ"

(3)   one or more other variables, eg.

SET ZZZ=" " , A=ZZZ
SET SUM=A+B+C+D

When we set one variable equal to a second variable, this second variable MUST be created or "defined" in advance, either by a READ or a SET command.

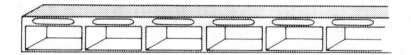

FIGURE 4-2. A REPRESENTATION OF VARIABLE 'NAMES' AND 'CONTENTS'

12.   To further illustrate the concept of a variable, imagine a collection of little boxes within the main memory of your computer. Such a collection of boxes could be visualized as Figure 4-2. Each box has space for a name, and room for contents.

With our program CH3EX1, as line CH3EX1 + 2 is executed, our READ command creates box "A", and assigns as contents whatever entry was made before striking RETURN. As the line CH3EX1 + 4 is executed, our READ command creates box "B", and assigns as contents whatever entry was made before striking RETURN. Each time you enter a new value for A or B, your new value replaces the old value within the box named A or B.

What would be the contents of box A and box B if you made the following entries:

(a)   carriage return and 0

(b)   1.0 and A74

(c)   ? and 16

a null entry (sometimes expressed as " ") and zero

1 and A74

? and 16

You can confirm this by DOing CH3EX1, and entering a WRITE command at the next right caret.

13.   In CH3EX1, the command SET SUM = A + B creates a box with the name SUM, and the contents equal to A + B. The command SET AVERAGE = SUM/2 creates a box with the name AVERAGE, and the contents equal to SUM/2.

14.   Use a pencil to "work through" different values for A, B, SUM and AVERAGE within the first four boxes of Figure 4-2.

Each time you re-run CH3EX1, the contents of A, B, SUM and AVERAGE change, depending upon your entries.

15.   Can we remove the label from a box in Figure 4-2, as well as removing it's contents?

Yes. This operation is done by the KILL command. At any right caret, enter KILL. At the next right caret, enter a WRITE command (or equivalent for your implementation). What happens?

We removed all variables from our partition by using the KILL command with no argument.

16.   Most implementations of Standard MUMPS allow up to 8 characters as a variable name, so long as the first character is alphabetic or %. As with line labels and program names, open spaces and punctuation marks are NOT accepted. Here are some examples of variables:

SMITHSAM
ZIP17033
RESULT

We recommend that you use meaningful variable names, such as SUM for sum, AVERAGE for average and ANS for answer. Alpha characters plus numbers may be useful, such as ANS1 for answer 1, ANS2 for answer 2, and so on.

USING THE IF AND THE GOTO COMMANDS TO CREATE LOOPS

17.   How can we revise CH3EX1 to allow entry of one hundred numbers? One way is to rewrite our program with over one hundred lines of code. Here is a better way, using the IF command and the GOTO command:

```
CH4EX1  ;ADDING MACHINE PROGRAM WITH 'GOTO' LOOP
        SET COUNTER=0
        SET SUM=0
        WRITE !,"Number of entries = "
        READ ENTRIES
LOOP    WRITE !,"Enter number "
        READ ENTRY
        SET COUNTER=COUNTER+1
        SET SUM=SUM+ENTRY
        IF COUNTER<ENTRIES GOTO LOOP
        WRITE !,"Sum = ",SUM
        WRITE !,"Average = ",SUM/COUNTER
```

18.   Let's examine each line of this program:

Line CH4EX1 + 1 creates a variable called COUNTER, and sets the value of this variable equal to zero.

Line CH4EX1 + 2 creates a variable called SUM, and sets the value of this variable equal to zero.

Line CH4EX1 + 3 outputs a line feed and displays the message "Number of entries = "

Line CH4EX1 + 4 creates a variable called ENTRIES. The value of this variable is equal to whatever entry was made in response to the prompt in line CH4EX1 + 3. This variable is created only after the user also enters a carriage return.

Line LOOP outputs a line feed and the message "Enter number ".

Line LOOP + 1 assigns the value entered to the simple variable ENTRY.

Line LOOP + 2 increments COUNTER by one.

Line LOOP + 3 increments SUM by the value of ENTRY.

Line LOOP + 4 checks the value of COUNTER: IF value of COUNTER is less than the value of ENTRIES, execution will GOTO line LOOP; else execution passes to line LOOP + 5.

Line LOOP + 6 outputs one line feed, a string literal, and the value of SUM divided by the value of COUNTER.

19.   This program allows us to add any series of numbers, so long as we know in advance how many entries we will have.

Let's examine what happens to our variables COUNTER and ENTRY each time the loop is executed. Assume that we respond with "6" to the prompt "Number of entries = ", and enter the number "4" at each prompt "Enter number ".

EXECUTION OF LOOP	VALUE OF COUNTER	ENTRY
1	1	4
2	2	4
3	3	4
4	4	4
5	5	4
6	6	4

The sixth time through our loop, COUNTER is no longer less than 6: therefore, our GOTO command is not executed, and control passes to line LOOP + 5.

20.   We can depict the logic for line LOOP + 4 by Figure 4-3.

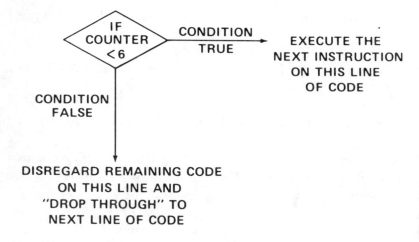

FIGURE 4-3. THE 'IF' COMMAND IN LINE LOOP + 4

The statement: IF COUNTER<ENTRIES GOTO LOOP

tells the computer:

- examine the value of COUNTER

- IF the numeric value of COUNTER is less than the numeric value of ENTRIES, GOTO line LOOP

- otherwise, disregard the remaining code on this line and "drop through" to the next line of code.

60

21.   When the argument to our IF command is true (numeric value of COUNTER less than the numeric value of ENTRIES), the rest of this line is executed, and we GOTO line LOOP. When the argument to our IF command is false (numeric value of COUNTER is equal to or greater than the numeric value of ENTRIES), the rest of this line is NOT executed, and control passes to the next line of code.

22.   What happens if we change our variable names in CH4EX1?

Enter 'ZR' at a right caret to erase any program lines in your partition. Now enter CH4EX1 into your terminal, and make sure it runs properly. Then use the ZSAVE command (or equivalent) to save CH4EX1 onto disk under the name CH4EX1. Now edit the program in your partition as follows:

-   change the variable name COUNTER in lines CH4EX1 + 1, LOOP + 2, LOOP + 4 and LOOP + 6 to ZZZ

-   change the variable name ENTRIES in line CH4EX1 + 4, and LOOP + 4 to XXX

-   change the variable name ENTRY in lines LOOP + 1 and LOOP + 3 to YYY

What do you expect will happen when you run this revised program?

        If you have made these changes correctly, your program will run just fine! The names you choose for your variables have no intrinsic meaning or significance so far as the computer is concerned! However, to make your programs more readable, we suggest that you choose variable names which are meaningful to humans.

23.   If after this revision your program does not run properly, use the WRITE command to display the values of each variable. This is one way to "check the logic" of your program. Another way is to "step through" each line of the program manually and write down the values of each variable after each command is executed.

USING OPERATORS TO EVALUATE EXPRESSIONS

24.   Standard MUMPS provides:

-   numeric relational operators
-   string relational operators
-   logical operators.

These three types of operators may be used with either:

(1)   the IF command

(2)   post conditional syntax (an "implied" IF command).

NUMERIC RELATIONAL OPERATORS

In CH4EX1, the symbol "<" is a numeric relational operator, which signifies that the expression on its left is less than the expression on its right. In line LOOP + 4 of CH4EX1, IF the numeric value of COUNTER is less than the numeric value of ENTRIES, the "truth value" of our argument is "true", and the rest of this line is executed. IF the numeric value of COUNTER is equal to or greater than the numeric value of ENTRIES, the "truth value" of our argument is false, and control "drops through" to the next line of code.

25.   Standard MUMPS provides two numeric relational operators:

Symbol	Operator
<	binary LESS THAN
>	binary GREATER THAN

26.   The unary NOT logical operator - expressed as an apostrophe - reverses the truth value of a binary relational operator. Thus:

'<	binary NOT LESS THAN
'>	binary NOT GREATER THAN

STRING RELATIONAL OPERATORS

27.   Standard MUMPS provides four string relational operators:

Symbol	Operator
=	Binary EQUAL TO
[	Binary CONTAINS
]	Binary FOLLOWS
?	Binary PATTERN MATCH

28.   Again, the unary NOT logical operator reverses the truth value of a binary string relational operator:

'=	Binary NOT EQUAL TO
'[	Binary NOT CONTAINS
']	Binary NOT FOLLOWS
'?	Binary NOT PATTERN MATCH

29.   Here is a modified version of CH4EX1, which displays the numbers entered, and allows the user to decide whether division should be performed:

```
CH4EX2 ; DIVIDE TWO NUMBERS, AND DISPLAY ENTRIES FOR USER
        WRITE !,"This program allows you to enter two numbers, "
        WRITE !,"The first number entered is divided by the second"
        WRITE !,"Enter first number "
        READ A
        WRITE !,"Enter second number "
        READ B
        IF B=0 WRITE !,"Division by zero not allowed" GOTO CH4EX2
        WRITE !,"First number was ",A
        WRITE !,"Second number was ",B
        WRITE !,"Are these entries correct?  Please answer 'YES' OR 'NO' "
        READ ANS
        IF ANS="NO" GOTO CH4EX2
        WRITE !,"First number divided by second number = ",A/B
```

30.   In line CH4EX2+7, the binary "equal to" string relational operator in effect acts as a numeric relational operator.

In line CH4EX2+12, the user might respond "N" instead of "NO". What would happen in this case? The response of "N" does not equal "NO", and control passes to the last line of code!

31.   In this case, we can improve our code by using the contains operator. The contains operator checks whether the string to the right of the operator is contained within the string on the left of the operator.

```
IF ANS["N" GOTO CH4EX2
```

means: IF ANS contains the character "N", GOTO to the line CH4EX2.

32.   What if the user strikes Y and then strikes N by mistake, before entering RETURN? Then, ANS will contain both Y and N: since ANS contains "N", control passes to line CH4EX2!

33.   The binary pattern match string relational operator provides a solution to this problem. The pattern match operator allows us to check the value of a string against a pattern.

For example, a social security number can be checked against the pattern of 3 digits, a dash, 2 digits, dash, 4 digits. In MUMPS, this particular pattern match is expressed as:

```
?3N1"-"2N1"-"4N
```

We can translate this code as:

> pattern match (the "?" character)
> 3 numbers
> 1 "-"
> 2 numbers
> 1 "-"
> 4 numbers

The "?" character tests whether a string literal or variable on its left matches a pattern (specified by pattern code characters) on its right.

34. Here is the code for pattern match on social security number:

```
LOOP    WRITE !,"Social security no:    "
        READ SS
        IF SS'?3N1"-"2N1"-"4N WRITE !,"Format error" GOTO LOOP
```

Here, we check for failure of match, then display an error message. We do do this with the unary NOT operator (').

35. The pattern code characters and their meanings are as follows:

Character	Meaning
N	numerics 0 to 9
U	upper case alphabetics A to Z
L	lower case alphabetics a to z
P	punctuation (including space,$,&,#,+,-,*, /,\,?, comma, period, and so on)
A	any alphabetics A to Z and a to z
C	control characters (dual characters such as CTL/C and CTL/U)
E	everything (any character)

36. We can also use literal strings for pattern verification. In frame 33, we used "-" as part of our pattern match.

37. In a different context, the question mark signifies "tab to column #", rather than a pattern match. MUMPS interprets the question mark as either a tab or a pattern match, depending on the statement preceding it.

38. In frame 33, each pattern match code as well as the literal string "-", is preceded by a number to indicate the required number of entries. In place of this number, we can use a period to indicate "zero or greater number of entries".

Here are some examples of pattern verification. The first two are completed; you answer the rest:

```
"873"?3N              TRUE
"873"?.N.U            TRUE
"873"?1N.E            _____
"873"?.A.N.P          _____
"873"?.A              _____
```

_____

TRUE
TRUE
FALSE (although there are zero alpha characters, there are three numbers)

39. MUMPS also allows you to specify an "either or" match checks for either one alphabetic or one numeric. Notice that the two codes are next to each other.

Some more examples:

```
"873"?3AN                          TRUE
"203-872-4722"?3NA1P3NA1"-"4N      TRUE
"203-872-4722"?3NA.A3NA1"-"4N      FALSE (the "-" represents
                                          punctuation)

"AB"?2NA                           _____
"+72"?1P2N                         _____
"+72"?3PN                          _____
```

_____

TRUE
TRUE
TRUE

40. Be careful with these:

```
"+72"?."+"2N               TRUE
"72"?."+"2N                _____
"AB"?.N                    _____
"5:15PM"?.N1":"2N.E        _____
"72"?1N.N                  _____
"SAM"?4AP                  _____
```

65

TRUE (. indicates "zero or greater number of entries")
FALSE (N indicates numerics and 2 alpha does not match zero numerics)
TRUE
TRUE
FALSE

41. Let's go back to our "YES/NO" problem. Here is one possible pattern match you might use:

    IF ANS? 1 "N" . A GOTO CH4EX2

Now, "NYET", "NO", "N", and "NOT" pass the pattern check, while YN is rejected.

The test you use (equals, contains, or pattern verification) is your decision.

But whatever method you chose, try to be consistent with the response you require from the user. For example, do NOT require "YES" in one part of your program, and "Y" in another part of your program. Make every effort to avoid confusion for the people who use your programs!

42. A null entry is a special case for pattern verification

A null entry is signaled by a carriage return,, and is identified in MUMPS code as "".

A null entry is consistent with a "zero or greater number" of numerics, alphabetics, punctuation, control character, etc.

Thus a null entry will pass the following pattern verification:

                .N
                .U
                .L
                .P
                .A
                .C
                .E

However, a null entry will fail:

1N. N

43. Modify CH4EX2 to allow a null entry (carriage return) in place of "Y" to accept the numbers entered. Also, provide pattern matches so that only numbers (no alpha characters) will be accepted. Call your new program CH4EX3.

Here's how we did it:

```
CH4EX3 ; DIVIDE TWO NUMBERS, AND DISPLAY ENTRIES
        WRITE !,"This program allows you to enter two numbers,"
        WRITE !,"The first number entered is divided by the second"
        WRITE !,"Enter first number "
        READ A
        IF A'?1N.N WRITE !," Numbers only, please" GOTO CH4EX3
        WRITE !,"Enter second number "
        READ B
        IF B'?1N.N WRITE !," Numbers only, please" GOTO CH4EX3
        IF B=0 WRITE !,"Division by zero not allowed" GOTO CH4EX3
        WRITE !,"First entry= ",A
        WRITE !,"Second entry= ",B
        WRITE !,"Enter carriage return if these entries are correct"
        WRITE !,"Otherwise enter 'N' "
        READ ANS
        IF ANS?1"N".E GOTO CH4EX3
        WRITE !,"First number divided by the second number = ",A/B
```

44. The pattern match operator also can be used to ensure that the length of an entry does not exceed a specified value. For example:

AGE?1.3N

accepts any numeric value from one to three digits in length.

LOGICAL OPERATORS

45. Standard MUMPS provides three logical operators:

Symbol	Operator
&	Binary AND
!	Binary OR
'	Unary NOT

67

We have already used the unary NOT to reverse the truth values for arithmetic and string relational operators. Likewise, we can use the unary NOT to reverse the truth values for binary AND as well as binary OR:

Symbol	Operator
'&	Binary NOT AND
'!	Binary NOT OR

46.   In CH4EX3 line CH4EX3+15, we can use the binary AND to allow entry of either carriage return or Y:

```
IF  (ANS'="") & (ANS'?1"Y".E)  GOTO CH4EX3
```

The GOTO command is executed if (ANS'="") and (ANS'?1"Y".E). In other words, if both expressions are true, then the entire argument of our IF command is true. If either expression is false, then the entire argument of our IF command is false.

47.   We can also express this logic as:

```
SET FLAG="NOT OK"
IF (ANS="") ! (ANS?1"Y".E)  SET FLAG="OK"
IF FLAG'="OK"  GOTO CH4EX4
```

With the binary OR, if one element of the expression is true, then the entire argument of our IF command is true. If both expressions are false, then the entire argument of our IF command is false.

48.   To avoid confusion, we recommend you place the NOT operator within parentheses when you perform logical AND or OR operations. The three expressions below are similar to the logical expression in frame 46:

```
IF  '(ANS="") &' (ANS?1"Y".E)
IF ANS'=""&ANS'?1"Y".E
IF (ANS="") '& (ANS?1"Y".E)
```

However, only one of the above expressions is the logical equivalent of the expression in frame 46. Which one is it?

Here is a program that can help us determine which expression is equivalent:

```
CH4EX4  ;  EVALUATE LOGICAL OPERATORS
        WRITE !,"Enter 'Y' or RETURN for yes, enter 'N' for no: "
        READ ANS
        IF (ANS'="")&(ANS'?1"Y".E) WRITE !,"Expression ONE is true"
        IF '(ANS="")&'(ANS?1"Y".E) WRITE !,"Expression TWO is true"
        IF ANS'=""&ANS'?1"Y".E WRITE !,"Expression THREE is true"
        IF (ANS="")'&(ANS?1"Y".E) WRITE !,"Expression FOUR is true"
        GOTO CH4EX4
```

Expression ONE is the logical expression in frame 46. With expression ONE, the message is NOT printed if you enter "Y" or RETURN - the message will appear when any other entry is made. If expressions TWO, THREE and FOUR are the equivalent of expression ONE, then they should respond to input in the same manner as expression ONE.

Enter this program into the computer and run it.

What do you obtain as output when you answer 'Y'? When you answer 'RETURN'? When you answer 'N'?

With an answer of 'Y' and RETURN our output is:

> Expression THREE is true
> Expression FOUR is true

With an answer of 'N' (or anything else) our output is:

> Expression ONE is true
> Expression TWO is true
> Expression THREE is true
> Expression FOUR is true

Expression TWO is the logical equivalent of expression ONE. Expressions THREE and FOUR do NOT have the same logical significance as expression ONE! We can see from our output that expressions THREE and FOUR are always true!

To avoid confusion, we recommend that you place the NOT operator within parentheses when you perform logical AND or OR operations.

POST-CONDITIONAL SYNTAX

49.   What about combining several IF commands on the same line? For example, we might change the line of code in frame 46 to read:

```
IF ANS="" GOTO CH4EX3 IF ANS'?1"Y".E GOTO CH4EX3
```

What will happen if:

    (1)   ANS passes the first pattern match?

    (2)   ANS fails the first pattern match?

---

    (1)   The first GOTO command is executed, and the second pattern check

             is not examined.

    (2)   Control passes to the next line of code, and the second pattern match

             is not examined.

In this case, regardless of whether the first IF statement is true or false, the second IF statement is never examined! Although we can place several IF commands on the same line, there is no point in doing so since only the first one will be examined!

50.   How can we solve this problem?

MUMPS allows us to append an "implied IF" to: (1) arguments of the GOTO command or the DO command; (2) to most MUMPS commands, including READ, WRITE, SET, GOTO, DO and QUIT. The DO and QUIT commands will be discussed in Chapter Five. This "implied IF" is called a post conditional. With a post conditional, program execution continues along the same line, regardless of whether the "implied IF" is true or false. The "implied IF" is depicted by a colon.

Here is an example:

```
CH4EX5 ; DIVIDE TWO NUMBERS AND DISPLAY ENTRIES
       WRITE !,"This program allows you to enter two numbers,"
       WRITE !,"The first number entered is divided by the second"
ENTRYA WRITE !,"Enter first number "
       READ A
       IF A'?1N.N WRITE !," Numbers only, please" GOTO ENTRYA
```

```
ENTRYB WRITE !,"Enter second number "
       READ B
       IF B=0 WRITE !,"Division by zero not allowed" GOTO ENTRYB
       IF B'?1N.N WRITE !," Numbers only, please" GOTO ENTRYB
       WRITE !,"Enter carriage return if both entries are correct,"
       WRITE !,"Enter '1' if you want to revise both entries,"
       WRITE !,"Enter '2' if you want to revise only the second entry "
       READ ANS
       GOTO ENTRYA:ANS?1"1".E GOTO ENTRYB:ANS?1"2".E
       WRITE !,"First number divided by the second number = ",A/B
```

The second to last line is read as:

> GOTO ENTRY A on the condition that ANS pattern matches 1 "1"
> followed by any number of everything; GOTO ENTRY B on the
> condition that ANS pattern matches 1 "2" followed by any number
> of everything.

51.   In the second to last line of CH4EX5, we could use post conditionals on the GOTO commands instead of the arguments:

```
GOTO:ANS?1"1".E ENTRYA GOTO:ANS?1"2".E ENTRYB
```

Logical interpretation of this code is identical to frame 50.

SUMMARY OF NEW CONCEPTS - CHAPTER 4

IF Command - used with a "comparative argument" (e.g. IF COUNTER <ENTRIES).
- code following on the same line is executed if the argument is true; otherwise, execution "drops through" to the next line of code.

GOTO Command - transfers control of execution to the line specified. Commonly used in combination with the IF command to create "conditional loops", as depicted in Figure 4-3.

Numeric relational operators -

<	binary LESS THAN
>	binary GREATER THAN

String relational operators -

=	binary EQUAL TO
[	binary CONTAINS
]	binary FOLLOWS
?	binary PATTERN MATCH

Logical operators -

&	binary AND
!	binary OR
'	unary NOT

The unary NOT can be used to "reverse the meaning" of any binary operator.

Pattern match codes -

N	numerics
U	upper case alphabetics
L	lower case alphabetics
P	punctuation
A	alphabetics (either case)
C	control characters
E	everything
" "	anything enclosed within quotes
.	a zero or greater number of the specified entry

Examples of pattern match syntax:

     IF ANS?3N.A - if ANS pattern matches 3 numbers, any number of upper or lower case alpha characters (including zero alpha characters).

     IF ANS?3NA - if ANS pattern matches 3 numbers and/or alpha characters (can have one number plus two alpha characters).

     IF ANS?1.3NA - if ANS pattern matches between 1 and 3 numbers and/or alpha characters.

Post conditional syntax - an implied IF command, expressed as a colon (:).
     - code following on same line is executed regardless of whether the implied IF is true or false.
     - may be used on arguments of GOTO and DO. For example: GOTO CH1EX1:ANS["N"
     - may be used on the READ, WRITE, SET, GOTO, DO and QUIT commands. For example: GOTO:ANS["N" CH1EX1

CHAPTER FIVE

PERFORMING ITERATIVE OPERATIONS WITH FOR LOOPS

In Chapter Four, we used the IF and GOTO commands to create a "loop" for our adding machine program. We also used IF and GOTO to create loops for checking data entries, with the pattern match operator.

In this chapter, we introduce the FOR loop. The FOR loop provides a convenient "shorthand" method to create loops. In most situations, you will find FOR loops much easier to use than loops created with IF and GOTO.

Topics discussed include:

- The FOR loop

- The QUIT command

- The BREAK key and BREAK command

- The DO command

- Abbreviations

- Practice Exercises.

By the end of this chapter you will be able to:

- create closed or open FOR loops to perform iterative operations

- use a single READ command to output literal strings as well as accept values for variables

- use the QUIT command to exit an open FOR loop

- use the DO and QUIT commands to perform subroutines

- use abbreviations for MUMPS code.

THE FOR LOOP

1.   The FOR loop allows us to perform iterative operations as originally written with IF and GOTO.

```
CH4EX1 ; ADDING MACHINE PROGRAM WITH 'GOTO' LOOP
        SET COUNTER=0
        SET SUM=0
        WRITE !,"Number of entries = "
        READ ENTRIES
LOOP    WRITE !!!,"Enter number "
        READ ENTRY
        SET COUNTER=COUNTER+1
        SET SUM=SUM+ENTRY
        IF COUNTER<ENTRIES GOTO LOOP
        WRITE !,"Sum = ",SUM
        WRITE !,"Average =",SUM/COUNTER
```

Here is CH4EX1 rewritten as CH5EX1 using a closed FOR loop:

```
CH5EX1 ; ADDING MACHINE PROGRAM WITH 'FOR' LOOP
        SET SUM=0
        WRITE !,"Number of entries = "
        READ ENTRIES
        FOR I=1:1:ENTRIES WRITE !,"Enter number: " READ NUM SET SUM=SUM+NUM
        WRITE !!,"Sum = ",SUM
        WRITE !,"Average = ",SUM/I
```

2.   In CH4EX1, a GOTO command instructs the computer to "go to" line LOOP, until the value of COUNTER is no longer less than the value of ENTRIES.

In CH5EX1, we use a FOR loop to accomplish the same thing. The FOR command in line CH5EX1 + 4 tells the computer:

(1)   Assign the variable I an initial value of 1.

(2)   Perform all MUMPS commands on the same line as the FOR command.

(3)   Increment the variable I by 1.

(4)   Perform steps 2 and 3 above until I equals the value of ENTRIES. If we enter "6" at the prompt in line CH5EX1 + 3, the FOR loop is executed six times.

(5)   Pass control to the next line of code when I passes this "limiting value" equal to the numeric value of ENTRIES.

76

3.   The FOR loop variable, initial value, increment, and limiting value are depicted in Figure 5-1. In Figure 5-1, the FOR command indicates that the variable I should be initially assigned the value 1, then incremented by 1 each time the FOR loop is executed, until I passes the limiting value of 6.

The "scope" of a FOR loop includes all MUMPS statements on the same line as the FOR command.

Following the final execution of the FOR loop, control passes to the next line. In CH5EX1, when the value of I reaches 7, control passes to line CH5EX1 + 5.

Enter CH5EX1 into your terminal, and practice using this program.

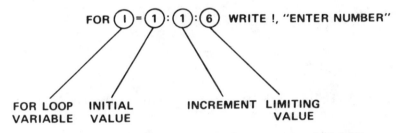

FIGURE 5-1. THE STRUCTURE OF A 'FOR' LOOP

4.   The name of the FOR loop variable is irrelevant. In CH5EX1, we could have used COUNTER, A, MOUSE, or any other variable name.

The initial value may be any integer; a decimal value; a variable; or an expression (such as the value of a variable incremented or decremented by an integer or another variable). Possible expressions include START-1, START + 1, START-ANS, and so on.

The increment and the limiting value also may be any integer, a decimal value, a variable, or an expression.

Any variables used as the initial value, increment or limiting value must be created and assigned numeric values by READ or SET commands earlier in the program. It is the numeric values of such variables which are used by the FOR loop: their names are irrelevant.

5.   Here is CH5EX1 rewritten with "COUNTER" as the name of our FOR loop variable, and NO as the limiting value.

```
CH5EX2 ; ADDING MACHINE PROGRAM WITH 'FOR' LOOP
       ; THIS PROGRAM ALLOWS THE USER TO SPECIFY NUMBER OF ENTRIES
       SET TOTAL=0
       WRITE !,"Number of entries = "
       READ NO
       FOR COUNTER=1:1:NO WRITE !,"Enter number " READ N SET TOTAL=TOTAL+N
       WRITE !,"Total = ",TOTAL
       WRITE !,"Average = ",TOTAL/COUNTER
```

This program will execute in the same manner as CH5EX1.

6.   What will happen if we revise this program and place our initial SET command on the same line as our FOR loop?

```
CH5EX3  ;  ADDING MACHINE PROGRAM WITH 'FOR' LOOP
        ;  THIS PROGRAM ALLOWS USER TO SPECIFY NUMBER OF ENTRIES
        WRITE !,"Number of entries " READ NO
        SET T=0 FOR I=1:1:NO WRITE !,"Enter number " READ N SET T=T+N
        WRITE !,"Total = ",T,!,"Average = ",T/I
```

This new program will work just fine!

The SET command preceding the FOR command is outside the scope of the FOR loop, and is executed only once.

The scope of a FOR loop starts with the FOR command and terminates at the end of the line. Commands within this scope are executed as many times as indicated in the FOR command.

7.   In CH5EX3, we can combine the WRITE command and READ command in line CH5EX3 + 2. The following two lines of code function in exactly the same manner:

```
WRITE !,"Number of entries:  " READ NO

READ !,"Number of entries:  ",NO
```

8.   The WRITE command can be used to:

-   output literal strings

-   output the values of variables.

The READ command can be used to:

-   output literal strings

-   input the values to variables.

From this point on, we will use the READ command to perform both functions, rather than separate WRITE and READ commands.

9.   What if we don't know in advance how many numbers we want to enter? MUMPS allows us to use an "open-ended" FOR loop with no limiting value:

```
FOR  I=1:1  READ  !, "ENTER  NUMBER  ",N  SET  T=T+N
```

What would you predict as output from this line of code?

_____

Since there is no limiting value, this code will repeatedly display the message "ENTER NUMBER", accept a value of N, and SET T = T + N. This FOR loop will run indefinitely, until you strike the BREAK key to interrupt output!

How can we exit an open-ended FOR loop without using the BREAK key? We can do this by the QUIT command, combined with IF or a post conditional.

THE QUIT COMMAND

10.   The QUIT command is used to:

(1)   terminate execution of a FOR loop

(2)   terminate execution of a subroutine

(3)   terminate execution of a routine.

We will consider the second and third uses of the QUIT command in the next section of this chapter (discussion of the DO command).

Commands with arguments are followed by one space to separate the command from its argument. If another command is on the same line, then at least one space must separate the arguments of the first command from the second command. If your implementation of MUMPS is based on the 1977 standard, then your system may allow only one space to separate the last argument of one command from the next command on the same line. Multiple spaces between commands are allowed by the revised Standard proposed in 1982.

The QUIT command is used with no argument - and therefore must be followed by at least two spaces.

Other argumentless commands (to be discussed later) also must be followed by at least two spaces.

11.   To terminate the execution of a FOR loop, we can use the QUIT command with an IF command or a post conditional. Even when the QUIT command has a post conditional, it still must be followed by two spaces. A post conditional is not considered as an "argument".

Here are two examples of QUIT, used to exit a FOR loop. Notice that in CH5EX5, the QUIT command is followed by two spaces.

```
CH5EX4 ;  ADDING MACHINE PROGRAM WITH UNSPECIFIED NUMBER OF ENTRIES
         ; EXIT FOR LOOP VIA IF AND QUIT COMMAND
         SET T=0 FOR I=1:1 READ !,"Enter number ",N SET T=T+N IF N="" QUIT
         WRITE !,"Total = ",T,!,"Average = ",T/(I-1)

CH5EX5 ;  ADDING MACHINE PROGRAM WITH UNSPECIFIED NUMBER OF ENTRIES
         ; EXIT FOR LOOP VIA QUIT AND POST CONDITIONAL
         SET T=0 FOR I=1:1 READ !,"Enter number ",N QUIT:N=""  SET T=T+N
         WRITE !,"Total = ",T,!,"Average = ",T/(I-1)
```

With both programs, we terminate the FOR loop on an entry of carriage return (a "null entry"), after the prompt "ENTER NUMBER".

12.   In the program CH5EX4, we SET T = T + N before the IF command which terminates our FOR loop on a null entry. However, in CH5EX5, we perform this SET command after our post conditional. What would happen with the code:

```
SET T=0 FOR I=1:1 READ !,"Enter number ",N IF N="" QUIT  SET T=T+N
```

_____

Here, if N does NOT equal a null entry, the argument of our IF command is "false", and we return to the FOR loop without executing our QUIT or SET commands. If N DOES equal a null entry, we execute the QUIT command, and drop out of our FOR loop: again, the command SET T = T + N is not executed!

13.   Compare the "last lines" of CH5EX4 and CH5EX5 to the "last line" of CH5EX3. What difference do you notice?

_____

In CH5EX3, we divide T by the value of NO. In CH5EX4 and CH5EX5, we divide by the value of I, decremented by one.

14. After we exit our open-ended FOR loop in CH5EX4 and CH5EX5, should we divide T by I to obtain an average, or should we use (I-1)?

Let's examine the values of each variable for each iteration of our FOR loop in CH5EX4. Let's assume that we enter the number 4 three times, and then enter a carriage return.

Iteration of FOR Loop	Values of Variables		
	I	N	T
1	1	4	4
2	2	4	8
3	3	4	12
4	4	" "	12

It is apparent that we must divide by I-1. Now let's construct a similar table for CH5EX5:

Iteration of FOR Loop	Values of Variables		
	I	N	T
1	1	4	4
2	2	4	8
3	3	4	12
4	4	" "	12

Again, it is apparent that we must divide by I-1.

When we exit our closed FOR loop at I = NO (NO is a number entered by the user), we divide our total by NO. However, when we exit our open FOR loop on a null entry, we must subtract one from the last value of I.

The BREAK Key and BREAK Command

15. In frame 8, we used the BREAK key to exit an indefinite FOR loop

Some implementations of MUMPS allow you to manually strike the BREAK key, examine your local variables with WRITE (or its equivalent) in the direct mode, and then resume program execution with the implementation specific ZGO command (or its equivalent). Check your user manual - or experiment to see what happens when you do this!

16.   Some implementations of MUMPS allow you to insert a BREAK command into your code, which will "freeze" execution of your program at any point. You can then examine all variables in your partition.

Here is an example (user responses are underlined):

```
CH5EX6 ; ADDING MACHINE PROGRAM WITH UNSPECIFIED NUMBER OF ENTRIES
       ; BREAK COMMAND PERMITS EVALUATION OF VARIABLES
       ; AFTER BREAK COMMAND USE ZGO COMMAND TO RESUME FOR LOOP
       SET T=0 FOR I=1:1 READ !,"Entry: ",N QUIT:N=""  SET T=T+N BREAK
       WRITE !,"Total = ",T,!,"Average = ",T/(I-1)

>DO CH5EX6
 Entry:  6
<BKERR>CH5EX6+3
>WRITE
 I=1
 N=6
 T=6
>
```

The message <BKERR> is implementation specific. In our system, this message includes the line label plus any code which may follow on the same line. Your implementation may display a different message.

After reviewing the values of our variables, we resume program execution by typing ZGO at any right caret. Since all "Z commands" are implementation specific, your system may be somewhat different.

After you use the BREAK command to examine your FOR loop variables, be sure to remove it - otherwise you will have to manually enter ZGO for every execution of the loop!

THE DO COMMAND

17.   What if we wanted to include some pattern matches and error messages within the FOR loop of CH5EX5 - similar to our programs in Chapter Four?

In Chapter Four, our IF-GOTO loops extended over several lines, allowing lots of space for pattern matches and error messages. But the "scope" of our FOR loop is limited to a single line.

18.   The DO command provides a solution to this problem.

We have already used the DO command at a right caret to DO a specified program. This ability to execute code immediately, and not as part of a program, is called "direct execution".

We can also use the DO command within programs. When used within a program, the DO command transfers control to the line indicated, where code is executed sequentially until a QUIT transfers control back to the command following the DO statement.

19. Enter the following code into your terminal as CH5EX7:

```
CH5EX7  ; SIMPLE EXAMPLE OF 'DO' COMMAND
        WRITE !,"THIS PROGRAM"
        DO MODULE
        WRITE !,"OF THE USE"
        WRITE !,"OF THE DO COMMAND"
        WRITE !,"ONCE AGAIN THIS"
        DO MODULE
        WRITE !,"THIS IS THE END"
        QUIT
MODULE  WRITE !,"WILL SERVE AS AN EXAMPLE"
        QUIT
```

A DO of this program yields:

```
        THIS PROGRAM
        WILL SERVE AS AN EXAMPLE
        OF THE USE
        OF THE DO COMMAND
        ONCE AGAIN THIS
        WILL SERVE AS AN EXAMPLE
        THIS IS THE END
```

20. Let's follow the processing:

DO CHEX7

THIS PROGRAM	Line CH5EX7 + 1 is processed.
DO MODULE	In line CH5EX7 + 2, the DO command indicates that processing should move to line MODULE.
WILL SERVE AS AN EXAMPLE	Line MODULE is processed.
QUIT	Line MODULE + 1 is processed - a QUIT is found. Since we got to MODULE by means of a DO command, processing returns to the command following this original DO command.
OF THE USE	Line CH5EX7 + 3 is processed.
OF THE DO COMMAND	Line CH5EX7 + 4 is processed.
ONCE AGAIN THIS	Line CH5EX7 + 5 is processed.
DO MODULE	In line CH5EX7 + 6, the DO command indicates that processing should again move to line MODULE.

WILL SERVE AS AN EXAMPLE	Line MODULE is processed.
QUIT	Line MODULE + 1 is processed - a QUIT is found. Since we got to MODULE by means of a DO command, processing returns to the command following this original DO command.
THIS IS THE END	Line CH5EX7 + 7 is processed.
QUIT	Line CH5EX7 + 8 is processed, and a QUIT is found. This QUIT stops the entire program, since we did not access this QUIT via a DO command. Without this QUIT, we would process line MODULE one more time, and then QUIT.

21.   On finding a DO command, processing moves to the line specified. Processing continues from that new point until a QUIT is found. Then, processing returns to the next command following the DO command - either on the same line as the DO command, or on the following line.

22.   Again, notice that QUIT on line CH5EX7 + 8. When we reach a QUIT that is not "arrived at" via a DO command, our program stops. This QUIT - which is NOT "paired" with a DO comand - halts execution of our program.

What would happen if we omitted this QUIT in line CH5EX7 + 8?

Execution would "run over", and the line MODULE would be processed one more time. In this example, one extra output of "WILL SERVE AS AN EXAMPLE" would not cause serious problems. But in more complex programs, this "run over" could present severe problems!

23.   In MUMPS, a routine is a collection of command lines, associated with a single name. This name is created when you save your routine on disk. It is common practice to begin each routine with a line label identical to the routine name, followed by one or more comment lines which briefly describe the purpose of the program.

Routines may contain subroutines, also referred to as modules, which are "called" by the DO command. The simple module subroutine in CH5EX7 is called twice, by two separate DO commands. It is common practice to "call" or "do" each subroutine by a line label.

An offset is a line label, followed by a " + " sign, followed by an integer number which specifies a line number in relation to the line label. For example, in CH5EX7, we could refer to our MODULE subroutine as CH5EX7+9. However, we recommend that you always "call" subroutines by line labels and NOT by offsets. If you use an offset in a DO, then later add or delete a program line, you may forget to change the offset in the DO. This is "trivial" in a simple routine such as CH5EX7, but can create serious problems with complex routines.

24. Do you feel "comfortable" with the DO and QUIT command? If so, feel free to skip this frame. If not, the following explanation may be helpful.

In CH5EX7, we can think of the initial DO command as placing a routine (or a subroutine) on top of a "stack". This "stack" is similar to a stack of trays in a cafeteria. Each time program execution encounters an explicit or implied QUIT, the "top" routine or subroutine is removed from this stack. Let's use this analogy to follow processing in CH5EX7. The operations described are depicted graphically in Figure 5-2.

>DO CH5EX7

DO command places CH5EX7 on the stack (Fig 5-2/1).

CH5EX7+1

DO command places MODULE on the stack: execution continues at the line label MODULE. (Fig. 5-2/2)

MODULE+1

QUIT command removes MODULE from the stack: execution continues at line CH5EX7+3 (Fig 5-2/3).

CH5EX7+5

DO command replaces MODULE on stack (back to Fig 5-2/2): execution continues at the line label MODULE.

MODULE+1

QUIT command removes MODULE from the stack, execution continues at line CH5EX7+7 (fig 5-2/3)

CH5EX7+8

QUIT command removes CH5EX7 from stack, and execution stops(fig. 5-2/4). If this QUIT command were deleted, execution would continue until an explicit or an implied QUIT removed CH5EX7 from the stack.

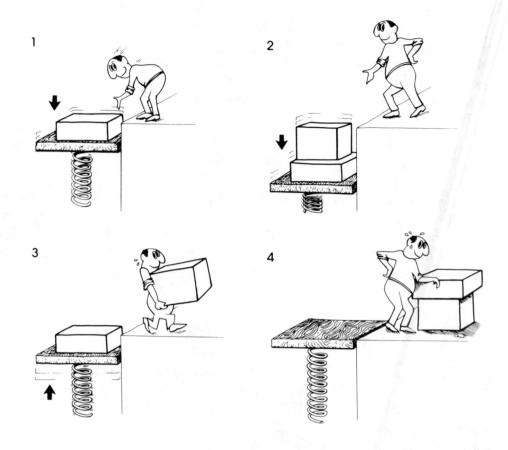

FIGURE 5-2. OPERATION OF THE 'DO' AND 'QUIT' COMMANDS IN CH5EX7 - ADDING AND REMOVING MODULES FROM 'THE STACK'

25.   Here is another example:

```
CH5EX7A   ;  EXAMPLE  OF  MODULES  WITH  DO  AND  QUIT  COMMANDS
          WRITE !,"MARY HAD A"
          DO MOD1
          WRITE !,"THE LAMB WAS"
          WRITE !,"SURE TO GO"
          QUIT
MOD1      WRITE !,"LITTLE LAMB"
          WRITE !,"ITS FLEECE WAS"
          DO MOD2
          WRITE !,"MARY WENT"
          QUIT
MOD2      WRITE !,"WHITE AS SNOW"
          WRITE !,"AND EVERYWHERE THAT"
          QUIT

>DO CH5EX7A
MARY HAD A
LITTLE LAMB
ITS FLEECE WAS
WHITE AS SNOW
AND EVERYWHERE THAT
MARY WENT
THE LAMB WAS
SURE TO GO
```

Can you follow the processing?

Before the DO of MOD1 is completed, we DO MOD2, return to MOD1 and finally return to CH5EX7A + 3. The DO of MOD2 is "nested" within the DO of MOD1. We can consider MOD1 as our first "subroutine", with MOD2 as a "sub-subroutine".

26.   We can now revise our adding machine program CH5EX5 to include:

(1)   an open-ended FOR loop, to accept any desired number of entries, until the user enters a carriage return

(2)   a DO command to access an entry module, which provides pattern checks and error messages as desired.

Here is one way to make this revision:

```
CH5EX8  ;  ADDING MACHINE PROGRAM WITH OPEN-ENDED FOR LOOP
        ;  THIS PROGRAM PROVIDES PATTERN CHECKS AND ERROR MESSAGES
        ;  AN ENTRY MODULE IS ACCESSED VIA DO COMMAND FROM FOR LOOP
        SET SUM=0
        FOR I=1:1 DO ENTRY QUIT:NUM=""   SET SUM=SUM+NUM
        WRITE !,"Sum = ",SUM
        WRITE !,"Average = ",SUM/(I-1)
        QUIT
ENTRY   WRITE !,"Enter number "
        READ NUM
        IF NUM="" QUIT
        IF NUM'?1N.N WRITE !,"Whole numbers only please" GOTO ENTRY
        QUIT
```

27.   Notice that we need two QUIT commands: one to exit our ENTRY module if NUM = "", and one to exit our FOR loop if NUM = "".

28.   Now revise CH5EX8 to:

(1)   display the "total so far" after each entry

(2)   allow entry of negative numbers and decimal fractions as well as positive whole numbers

(3)   display the number entered, ask the user "Is this entry ok?", and accept entry if user enters "Y", or carriage return.

Call your new program CH5EX9

Here's how we did it:

```
CH5EX9  ;  IMPROVED ADDING MACHINE PROGRAM WITH OPEN-ENDED FOR LOOP
        ;  THIS PROGRAM:
        ;     . DISPLAYS "TOTAL SO FAR" AFTER EACH ENTRY
        ;     . ACCEPTS NEGATIVE NUMBERS AND DECIMAL FRACTIONS
        ;     . DISPLAYS ENTRY ON NEW NUMBER FOR USER TO ACCEPT OR REJECT
        ;  WRITTEN BY AFK 1 SEP 82   REVISED BY GLB 6 NOV 82
        ;
        SET SUM=0
        FOR I=1:1 DO ENTRY QUIT:N="'
        WRITE !,"Sum = ",SUM
        WRITE !,"Average = ",SUM/(I-1)
        QUIT
```

```
ENTRY   READ !,"Enter number or carriage return to exit program ",N
        IF N="" QUIT
        IF (N'?1N.N)&(N'?1"-"1N.N)&(N'?1N.N1"."1N.N)&(N'?1"-"1N.N1"."1N.N) D
O ERROR GOTO ENTRY
        WRITE !,"The number you entered was ",N
        WRITE !,"Entry ok? "
        WRITE !,"Enter 'Y' or carriage return to accept"
        READ !,"Yes=> ",ANS
        IF (ANS'?1"Y".E)&(ANS'="") GOTO ENTRY
        SET SUM=SUM+N WRITE !,"Total so far = ",SUM
        QUIT
ERROR   WRITE !,"Please enter either a positive number (no plus sign)"
        WRITE !,"or a negative number preceded by a minus sign."
        WRITE !,"Fractions may be entered as decimals."
        QUIT
```

29.   The "wrap around" in line ENTRY + 2 makes our code more difficult to read. Later, we will present methods to avoid this problem. For the present, we will accept occasional "wrap arounds" on long pattern checks.

30.   In CH5EX9, notice how the pattern checks on entry are more complex - and consume more lines of code - than anything else in our program.

Also, notice the "comment lines" at the beginning of our program. It is common practice to begin each program with comments which clearly describe:

   (1)   purpose of the program

   (2)   how the program operates

   (3)   who wrote the program and when

   (4)   who revised the program and when.

31.   In CH5EX9, our routine is constructed from a FOR loop and two modules (or sub-routines):

   ● The FOR loop in CH5EX9 + 8 calls an ENTRY module

   ● The ENTRY module calls an ERROR module.

We use the DO and QUIT commands to move from module to module, and use GOTO only for moving within a module. We recommend that you follow this same practice. If you use GOTO to move from one module to another, your code will become very difficult to read when you write complex programs with many modules!

32.   Figure 5-3 is a diagram of CH5EX9. This type of diagram is sometimes called a "structure chart". Our routine CH5EX9 calls a module, ENTRY, via the DO command from a FOR loop. The DO command from a FOR loop is depicted by a curved line.

Our ENTRY module calls a module, ERROR, via a DO command from an IF statement. The DO command from an IF is depicted by a diamond.

Professional programmers frequently use structure charts to graphically depict how complex programs are organized. You may want to use structure charts to plan your own programs.

The structure chart implies that you use the DO and QUIT commands to move from module to module - rather than the GOTO command. We recommend that you use GOTO only to return to another line within the same module. If you use GOTO to move from one module to another, your code will become very difficult to read!

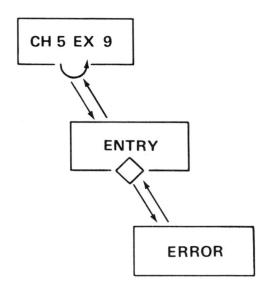

FIGURE 5-3. A STRUCTURE CHART OF CH5EX9

33.   Let's look at the logic for our pattern matches in CH5EX9. Here is line ENTRY + 2:

```
IF  (N'?1N.N)&(N'?1"-"1N.N)&(N'?1N.N1"."1N.N)&(N'?1"-"1N.N1"."N.N)
DO ERROR GOTO ENTRY
```

The interpretation of this code is:

IF (N does not pattern match one number followed by any number of numbers) AND (N does not pattern match one minus sign followed by one number followed by any number of numbers) AND (N does not pattern match one number followed by any number of numbers followed by one decimal point followed by one number followed by any number of numbers) AND (N does not pattern match one minus sign followed by one number followed by any number of numbers followed by one decimal point followed by one number followed by any number of numbers), DO the ERROR module, and then GOTO the line labelled ENTRY.

Can you express the same logic without using any NOT operators?

We can express the logic of four "failures to pattern match" connected by Boolean ANDs, as four "correct pattern matches", connected by Boolean ORs. Here's how we did it:

```
IF  (N?1N.N) ! (N?1"-"1N.N) ! (N?1N.N1"."1N.N) ! (N?1"-"1N.N1"."1N.N)  DO OK QUIT
    DO ERROR GOTO ENTRY
OK ;This module would contain code from ENTRY+3 thru ENTRY+8 and terminate
   ;with a QUIT
```

In most cases, it is easier to check for failure of pattern match, using Boolean ANDs and an ERROR module, rather than check for correct pattern matches.

34. Can you think of a way to make the required entry format in CH5EX9 easier for the "occasional user" who is not familiar with how this program operates?

We could add a "help" module to specify the formats accepted. The help module is similar to an error module except we allow the user to "ask" for help instead of displaying an error message when an error occurs. By convention, the user asks for help by entering a question mark. Of course, the help module can double as an error module. For example:

```
HELP  WRITE !,"Enter a number. Precede decimal numbers by a leading zero."
      WRITE !,"Examples of acceptable entries: "
      WRITE !,"        6.0        (a positive number)"
      WRITE !,"        6          (a positive number)"
      WRITE !,"       -6.0        (a negative number)"
      WRITE !,"       -6          (a negative number)"
      WRITE !,"        0.2        (a positive decimal)"
      WRITE !,"       -0.2        (a negative decimal)"
      WRITE !,"Enter RETURN if you have no further entries"
      QUIT
```

We recommend that you include "help prompts" with sample entries in programs that will be used by many different people. These people often will be unfamiliar with the "internal logic" of your programs!

35.   Our program CH5EX9 still has one defect.

What if our very first entry were a carriage return? Try this at your terminal. What happens?

Line CH5EX9 + 10 divides our SUM of zero by I-1, or zero. Zero as a numerator is no problem - but with our implementation of Standard MUMPS, any attempt to divide by zero gives an error message! In our system this error message is displayed as <DIVER> for "divide error". Your implementation may display a different message.

36.   How can we correct this problem?

We can add some code in our ENTRY module to check for the condition of N = " " and I = 1.

37.   Add this "additional code", plus our HELP module from frame 34, to create a new program CH5EX10:

Here's how we did it:

```
CH5EX10 ; ADDING MACHINE PROGRAM - REVISED VERSION OF CH5EX9
        ;
        SET SUM=0
        FOR I=1:1 DO ENTRY QUIT:N=""
        WRITE !,"Sum = ",SUM
        WRITE !,"Average = ",SUM/(I-1)
        QUIT
ENTRY   READ !,"Number = ",N
        IF (N="")&(I=1) WRITE !,"First entry must be a number" GOTO ENTRY
        IF N="" QUIT
        IF N="?" DO HELP GOTO ENTRY
        IF (N'?1N.N)&(N'?1"-"1N.N)&(N'?1N.N1".".1N.N)&(N'?1"-"1N.N1".".1N.N)
......  DO HELP GOTO ENTRY
        WRITE !,"The number you entered was ",N
        WRITE !,"Entry ok? "
        WRITE !,"Enter 'Y' or carriage return to accept"
        READ !,"Yes=> ",ANS
        IF (ANS'?1"Y".E)&(ANS'="") GOTO ENTRY
        SET SUM=SUM+N WRITE !,"Total so far = ",SUM
        QUIT
```

```
HELP    WRITE !,"Enter a number.  Precede decimal numbers by a leading zero. "
        WRITE !,"Examples of acceptable entries: "
        WRITE !,"          6.0        (a positive number)"
        WRITE !,"          6          (a positive number)"
        WRITE !,"         -6.0        (a negative number)"
        WRITE !,"         -6          (a negative number)"
        WRITE !,"          0.2        (a positive decimal)"
        WRITE !,"         -0.2        (a negative decimal)"
        WRITE !,"Enter RETURN if you have no further entries"
        WRITE !,"Please do not enter a RETURN as your first entry"
        QUIT
```

We could replace line ENTRY+2 with:

```
        IF  (N="")&(I=1)  DO ERR GOTO ENTRY
```

In this case, we would add an ERR module after our HELP module:

```
ERR     WRITE !,"First entry cannot be a carriage return. "
        WRITE !,"Please enter a number as your first entry. "
        QUIT
```

This provides a somewhat longer error message if the first entry is a carriage return.

ABBREVIATIONS

38.   MUMPS allows us to use just the first letter of a command. Implementation specific Z commands are abbreviated by the first two letters. Thus:

```
        S = SET
        R = READ
        W = WRITE
        G = GOTO
        D = DO
        P = PRINT
        Q = QUIT
        ZR = ZREMOVE
        ZS = ZSAVE
        ZL = ZLOAD
        I = IF
        F = FOR
        K = KILL
```

From here on, we will often use abbreviations rather than the full names of MUMPS commands.

PRACTICE EXERCISES

39.   Here is a simple adding machine program using an open FOR loop with QUIT and a post conditional:

```
CH5EX11 ; SIMPLE ADDING MACHINE PROGRAM WITH QUIT AND POST CONDITIONAL
        SET T=0 WRITE !,"Enter numbers, I will calculate sum and mean."
        FOR I=1:1 WRITE !,"Number: " READ N QUIT:N=""   SET T=T+N
        WRITE !!,"Sum = ",T,!,"Average = ",T/(I-1)
        WRITE !,"A total of ",(I-1)," numbers were entered."
```

Notice the expression (I-1). The last time through our FOR loop, I is incremented, but no number is entered. Therefore, I must be reduced by one in the calculation step.

Enter this program into your terminal. Be sure to include at least two spaces after the post conditionalized QUIT! A command with no argument requires at least two spaces before the next command. Attaching a post conditional to QUIT does not affect this requirement! A post conditional is NOT an argument!

Practice using this program until you are sure it operates properly. This process - "checking" a program to make sure it functions as intended - is called "debugging".

40.   Here is a new program, CH5EX12:

```
CH5EX12 ; EXIT FOR LOOP WITH QUIT AND IF COMMAND
        SET T=0 WRITE !,"Enter numbers, I will calculate sum and mean."
        FOR I=1:1 WRITE !,"Number: " READ N IF N="" QUIT  SET T=T+N
        WRITE !!,"Sum = ",T,!,"Average = ",T/(I-1)
        WRITE !,"A total of ",(I-1)," numbers were entered."
```

Here, we use IF, rather than a post conditional, to exit our FOR loop.

What problem would you expect when you DO this program?

_____

Each time through the FOR loop, if N is not equal to null, execution returns to the beginning of the FOR loop - and the SET command is not executed. If N is equal to null, we quit the FOR loop - and again, the SET command is not executed.

Here is a DO for CH5EX12

```
>DO CH5EX12
```

Enter numbers - I will calculate sum and mean
Number: 4
Number: 4
Number: 6
Number: 6

 Sum = 0
 Average = 0
 A total of 4 numbers were entered.

41.   We can rearrange our program so our SET command is executed before we come to the
IF:

```
CH5EX13 ; EXIT FOR LOOP WITH IF COMMAND AT END OF LINE
        SET T=0 WRITE !,"Enter numbers, I will calculate sum and mean."
        FOR I=1:1 WRITE !,"Number:  " READ N SET T=T+N IF N="" QUIT
        WRITE !!,"Sum = ",T,!,"Average = ",T/(I-1)
        WRITE !,"A total of ",(I-1)," numbers were entered."
```

What would you expect with this revised program?

    Our program works properly! We can exit an open ended FOR loop with IF, provided we do
not follow the IF command with code which must to be executed each time through the FOR
loop. Always try to keep IF commands at the END of your FOR loops!

42.   Now write a program to calculate grade point average using READ statements. The
program should: (1) prompt for entry of A's, B's, C's, D's, and F's; (2) write grade point average.
For those who have been out of school for many years: an A = 4.0 points, B = 3.0 points, C =
2.0 points, D = 1.0 points, and F = 0.0 points.

    Here is one solution:

```
CH5EX14 ;PROGRAM TO COMPUTE GRADE POINT AVERAGE
        READ !,"How many A's?",A
        READ !,"How many B's?",B
        READ !,"How many C's?",C
        READ !,"How many D"s?',D
        READ !,"How many F's?",F
        SET SUM=A+B+C+D+F
        SET GPA=((4*A)+(3*B)+(2*C)+(1*D))/SUM
        WRITE !!,"Your grade point average is ",GPA
```

Here is a DO of CH5EX14, with values of A,B,C,D and F supplied by the user:

>DO CH5EX14

How many A's? 4
How many B's? 6
How many C's? 6
How many D's? 0
How many F's? 0

Your grade point average is 2.875

43.   We can use one READ statement to assign values for several variables:

```
READ "Numbers of A's, B's, C's, D's and F's ",A,B,C,D,F
```

What would happen if we replace the first five lines of CH5EX14 with this code, and enter "2" as the number for each grade?

_____

The user responses are underlined:

>DO CH5EX14

Number of A's, B's, C's, D's and F's 22222

44.   Why do we see "22222" on the DO of this program?

After we enter the first 2, we enter RETURN to signal the computer we have completed our entry. BUT, unlike a typewriter, RETURN does NOT move the print head. We need an exclamation mark, or some other format characters, to move the print head! This is why our entries "ran together".

To avoid confusion when a series of entries are expected, we recommend that you provide:

  (1)   separate prompts for each entry

  (2)   spaces or line feeds between each entry.

45.   To shorten our program, we might combine multiple arguments to the READ command on a single line, following each argument with a line feed, or multiple spaces. For example:

```
READ !,"A'S ",A,!,"B'S ",B,!,"C'S ",C,!,"D'S ",D,!,"F'S ",F
```

Is this "shorter version" of code from CH5EX14 any "better"? Not necessarily! If you shorten a program - but make it more difficult to read and to use - you have made it worse, not "better"! The criteria for a "good program" include:

- Program is "easy to operate" for the end user

- Logic is easy to follow and code is easy to read

- Sufficient "comment lines" within the program to clearly explain program operation.

46.   The following program is quite similar to previous programs in this chapter.

```
CH5EX15 ; SIMPLE ADDING MACHINE PROGRAM
        S T=0
        F I=1:1 D ENTRY S T=T+N I N="" Q
        W !,"Total = ",T,!,"Average = ",T/(I-1)
        Q
ENTRY R !,"Enter number ",N
        S T=T+N
        Q
```

What will happen if you enter a carriage return at the first prompt?

_____

You will get an error message such as <DIVER> for "divide error" - since I-1 = 0. The nature of this error message may vary for different implementations.

47.   How might you correct this problem?

_____

One way would be insert a new line right after the FOR loop:

```
I I=1 W !,"No numbers entered.  Program terminated." Q
```

This new line, ending with QUIT, terminates our program before the division operation can be executed.

48.   Briefly discuss the three ways that QUIT may be used in a MUMPS program

---

(1)   To terminate an open FOR loop, using an IF or a post conditional. Here, QUIT is NOT paired with a DO command.

(2)   To stop execution of a module or subroutine. In this case, QUIT is paired with the DO command used to "call" execution of the module.

(3)   To stop execution of a routine, as in frame 47. Here, QUIT is NOT paired with a DO command.

49.   We can use the READ command to:

• output string literals

• output format characters (such as #, !, ?5, and ?$X + 4)

• input values to variables.

50.   We can use the WRITE command to:

• output strings

• output format characters

• output the values of variables.

51.   What do you expect would happen in the following program:

```
CH5EX15 ; SIMPLE ADDING MACHINE PROGRAM
        S FOR=0
        F F=1:1 D ENTRY S FOR=FOR+N I N="" Q
        I F=1 W !,"No numbers entered. Program terminated." Q
        W !,"Total = ",FOR,!,"Average = ",FOR/(F-1)
        Q
ENTRY   R !,"Enter number ",N
        Q
```

This program would run fine! We can use "FOR" as a variable name - and we can use "F" as our FOR loop variable! MUMPS does NOT get "confused" if we use variable names that are identical to command names.

However, we recommend that you use variable names that are distinctly different from command names. Henceforth, we will use J1, J2,... Jn as FOR loop variables - rather than I, which can be confused with the abbreviation for an IF command.

Even a simple routine such as CH5EX15 can become difficult to read when: F may be either the FOR loop command or a variable name; S may be either the SET command or a variable name; D may be either the DO command or a variable name.

Even a beginner can write MUMPS code which is cryptic and hard to read. A "good program" has logic that is easy to follow, and code that is easy to read.

SUMMARY OF NEW CONCEPTS - CHAPTER 5

FOR loop (F I = A:B:C) - closed FOR loop with repeated execution of code
following on the same line
- does not go beyond final value specified.

FOR loop (F I = A:B) - open ended FOR loop may be exited via:

- QUIT with post conditional

- IF command (do NOT follow the IF command with
code which needs to be executed each time through
the FOR loop).

READ - outputs literal strings and/or format characters; inputs values of variables.

WRITE - outputs literal strings and/or format characters; outputs values of variables.

DO - moves execution to line indicated; code is executed sequentially until QUIT
encountered; execution then returns to code following the DO statement.

QUIT - terminates an open ended FOR loop (NOT paired with DO command)
- stops execution of a module (paired with DO command)
- stops execution of routine (NOT paired with a DO command).

BREAK key - terminates execution of program and outputs implementation-specific error
message
- some implementations allow you to resume program via
direct execution of ZGO command after using the BREAK
key.

BREAK command - may be used in manner similar to BREAK key (implementation-
specific - see your user manual).

Abbreviations - Standard MUMPS commands may be abbreviated to one letter (you may
NOT use "shortened versions" such as WR for WRITE)
- Z commands may be abbreviated to first two
letters.

CHAPTER SIX

USING FOR LOOPS TO BUILD AND SEARCH FILES

In Chapter Five, we used FOR loops to perform iterative operations. Some of these iterative operations were performed within modules, accessed by DO commands from the FOR loop. In this chapter, you will learn how to: (1) build and search local arrays; (2) build and search files on disk.

Topics discussed include:

- Subscripted variables and local arrays

- Using the FOR loop to build local arrays

- Displaying local variables

- Deleting local variables - the KILL command

- Using the FOR loop to build global arrays

- Displaying global arrays.

By the end of this chapter you will be able to:

- use FOR loops to build and display local arrays

- display local variables

- delete local variables using the KILL command

- use FOR loops to build and display global arrays.

SUBSCRIPTED VARIABLES AND LOCAL ARRAYS

1.   Here is our adding machine program CH5EX8:

```
CH5EX8  ; ADDING MACHINE PROGRAM WITH OPEN-ENDED FOR LOOP
        ; THIS PROGRAM PROVIDES PATTERN CHECKS AND ERROR MESSAGES
        ; AN ENTRY MODULE IS ACCESSED VIA DO COMMAND FROM FOR LOOP
        SET SUM=0
        FOR I=1:1 DO ENTRY QUIT:NUM=""  SET SUM=SUM+NUM
        WRITE !,"Sum = ",SUM
        WRITE !,"Average = ",SUM/(I-1)
        QUIT
ENTRY   WRITE !,"Enter number "
        READ NUM
        IF NUM="" QUIT
        IF NUM'?1N.N WRITE !,"Whole numbers only please" GOTO ENTRY
        QUIT
```

2.   In CH5EX8, the values of our simple variables I, NUM and SUM change each time the FOR loop is executed.

We can visualize simple variables as "labelled boxes", or "labelled envelopes" within the computer. Each box (or envelope) has:

- a label

- contents.

Both the label and contents can be created by either:

- a READ command, or

- a SET command.

For example:

```
READ "Enter number ",N
SET SUM=SUM+N
```

3. MUMPS also allows us to create subscripted variables. Subscripted variables in MUMPS consist of a simple variable name followed by a subscript: e.g. N(1),N(2),N(3),N(4) and so on.

Say it like this: "N sub 1", "N sub 2", and so on.

4.   The name part of a subscripted variable uses the same rules we introduced in Chapter Four:

- the first character must be alphabetic or %

- subsequent characters must be alphabetic or numeric

- the first eight characters must be unique

- may be 1 to 63 characters long (only the first eight have meaning to the system).

5.   The subscript part of a subscripted variable has slightly different rules:

- must be enclosed within parentheses

- multiple subscripts must be separated by commas

- the maximum length of a subscript is implementation specific

- the maximum length of multiple subscripts is also implementation specific.

Subscripts may be either:

(1)   a number

(2)   a literal string enclosed in quotation marks

(3)   a simple variable

(4)   a mathematic expression (such as I*2)

(5)   a second subscripted variable.

Some implementations based on the 1977 version of Standard MUMPS may not allow negative numbers, non-integer numbers, or literal strings as subscripts. The revised 1981 MUMPS Standard allows all these types of subscripts.

In this chapter, we will consider only subscripted variables with numeric subscripts.

6.   Which of these is a subscripted variable:

NAME   NAME1   NAME (1)

NAME(1); NAME and NAME1 are simple variables.

If these three variables appear in the same program, the computer will recognize them as distinct, separate variables.

7. A simple variable has a name and a value. The value may be either a number or a literal string. For example:

```
S  N=10
S  NAME="RODGER  YOUNG"
```

Likewise, a subscripted variable has a name and a value. For example:

```
S  NAME(1)="JOHN  SMITH"
S  NAME(2)="MARY  JONES"
```

8. A subscripted variable is often called an array element. An array is a group of subscripted variables which have the same simple variable. The following example represents the "N array".

```
array elements                          values
     N(1)                                  2
     N(2)                                  4
     N(3)                                  6
     N(4)                                  8
```

	array elements			
	N(1)	N(2)	N(3)	N(4)
VALUES	2	4	6	8

FIGURE 6-1. THE 'N' ARRAY

9. Such an array may be depicted as a table (Figure 6-1). Each array element has a name and a value. We can create new array elements via the SET or READ commands. For example:
```
SET  N(5)="10";READ !,"Enter result ",N(6)
```

We can change the value of an existing array element via the SET or READ command. How could we change the value of N(1) to "null"?

_____

Enter at any right caret SET N(1)=""

USING THE FOR LOOP TO BUILD LOCAL ARRAYS

BUILDING AN ARRAY WITH NUMERIC DATA

10.   This "adding machine" program uses a FOR loop incremented by one to create a "NUMBER array" with numeric subscripts; each array element has a numeric value:

```
CH6EX1  ;  ADDING MACHINE PROGRAM WHICH CREATES SUBSCRIPTED ARRAY
        ;  NAME OF ARRAY = 'NUMBER'
        ;  NUMERIC SUBSCRIPTS CREATED BY FOR LOOP INCREMENTED BY ONE
        ;
        S  T=0
        F  INDEX=1:1 R !,"Number: ",N Q:N=""  S T=T+N S NUMBER(INDEX)=N
        W  !,"Sum = ",T,!,"Average = ",T/(INDEX-1)
        W  !,"Number of entries = ",INDEX-1
        Q
```

In this program, we used "INDEX" as the FOR loop variable.

We suggest that you avoid use of single letter variables which could be confused with commands (such as I for INDEX, S for SUM, or D for DATA).

Henceforth, we will use the letter J, with or without a number, as our FOR loop variable.

11.   Let's modify CH5EX8 to create a subscripted array. We will call this revised program CH6EX2:

```
CH6EX2  ;  ADDING MACHINE PROGRAM WHICH CREATES SUBSCRIPTED ARRAY
           SET SUM=0
           FOR J=1:1 DO ENTRY QUIT:N=""
           WRITE !,"Sum = ",SUM,!,"Average = ",SUM/(J-1)
           QUIT
           ;
ENTRY      READ !,"Enter number ",N QUIT:N=""
           IF N'?1N.N WRITE !,"Whole numbers only please" GOTO ENTRY
           SET NUMBER(J)=N
           SET SUM=SUM+N
           QUIT
```

12.   In CH6EX1, the SET command which creates our subscripted array is part of the FOR loop. In CH6EX2, this SET command is part of our ENTRY module.

With both programs, each execution of the FOR loop creates a new element, in the NUMBER array.

With both programs, the value of N changes on each execution of the FOR loop. However, each entry is saved as a separate array element, identified by a numeric subscript.

13.   Do either of these programs. Enter 4,11,3, and a carriage return. Now enter at any right caret WRITE (or the equivalent command for your system) to display your local variables. What is the result?

CH6EX1   CH6EX2

J="4"   J="4"
N=" "   N=" "
NUMBER   NUMBER
NUMBER(1)="4"   NUMBER(1)="4"
NUMBER(2)="11"   NUMBER(2)="11"
NUMBER(3)="3"   NUMBER(3)="3"
T="18"   SUM=18

Both programs create exactly the same array. The only difference is that CH6EX2 uses the simple variable SUM, while CH6EX1 uses T, to accumulate totals.

14.   Notice that MUMPS created the simple variable NUMBER as the "array name" - no READ or SET command was needed to do this!

We can depict our NUMBER array as an outline:

NUMBER
        NUMBER(1)="4"
        NUMBER(2)="11"
        NUMBER(3)="3"

as an inverted "tree":

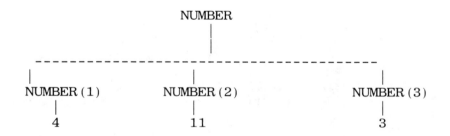

or as an inverted tree rotated 90 degrees:

                    <NUMBER(1)="4"
         NUMBER-<NUMBER(2)="11"
                    <NUMBER(3)="3"

15.   Why bother creating a "number array" with our adding machine program? One reason would be to display an "audit trail" of all entries during a single terminal session. In frame 13, we displayed these entries via direct execution of the WRITE command.

We can modify CH6EX2 to print out this "audit trail" via a FOR loop, rather than using the WRITE command in direct mode:

```
CH6EX3 ; ADDING MACHINE PROGRAM WITH DISPLAY OF ALL ENTRIES
        SET SUM=0
        FOR J1=1:1 DO ENTRY QUIT:N=""
        DO DISPLAY
        WRITE !,"Sum = ",SUM,!,"Average = ",SUM/(J1-1)
        WRITE !,"Number of entries = ",J1-1
        QUIT
ENTRY   READ !,"Enter number ",N QUIT:N=""
        IF N'?1N.N WRITE !,"Whole numbers only please" GOTO ENTRY
        SET NUMBER(J1)=N
        SET SUM=SUM+N
        QUIT
DISPLAY SET END=J1-1
        WRITE !!,"Numbers entered"
        FOR J2=1:1:END WRITE !,?5,NUMBER(J2)
        QUIT
```

16.   In CH6EX3, we set the simple variable END equal to J1-1, and use a second FOR loop to display our entire number array.

In CH6EX3, the FOR loop which built our NUMBER array used a FOR loop variable J1. The FOR loop which displayed our NUMBER array used a FOR loop variable of J2. THE NAMES OF OUR FOR LOOP VARIABLES ARE IRRELEVANT!

What would happen if we change our DISPLAY module as follows:

```
DISPLAY W !!,"Numbers entered"
        F XXX=1:1:J1-1 W !,?5,NUMBER(XXX)
        Q
```

Nothing! This revised module will run without difficulty! However, it is "common practice" to assign the FOR loop variable a "conventional name". Such "conventional names" include:

(1)   A single letter such as I, J, K, L and so on. This practice of using I (and subsequent letters) to name the FOR loop variable represent a "carry over" from other computer languages such as FORTRAN.

(2)   A "meaningful" name such as INDEX, or COUNTER.

(3)   A single letter plus a number: this provides a simple way to "keep track" of different FOR loop variables within a single program.

17.   Here are some subscripted variables with values:

    N(1) = 4
    N(2) = 3
    N(3) = 5
    N(4) = 6

If I = 2, what is the value of N(I)? If I = 4, what is the value of N(I)? If J = 2, what is the value of N(J)? If J = 4, what is the value of N(J)?

    3
    6
    3
    6

When we use a FOR loop to "search" our array, our array elements are selected by the value of our FOR loop variable - not by the name of our FOR loop variable!

18.   Let's revise CH6EX3 so we can modify one or more entries before the total and average are printed.

```
CH6EX4  ;  ADDING MACHINE PROGRAM WITH:
        ;  DISPLAY OF ALL ENTRIES
        ;  OPTION FOR USER TO CHANGE ANY ENTRY BEFORE RESULTS CALCULATED
        ;
        S  SUM=0
        F  J1=1:1 D ENTRY Q:N=""
        D  DISPLAY
        F  J2=1:1:END S SUM=SUM+NUMBER(J2)
        W  !,"Sum = ",SUM,!,"Average = ",SUM/(J1-1)
        W  !,"Number of entries = ",J1-1
        Q
        ;
        ;  THE ENTRY MODULE BUILDS N(J1) ARRAY
        ;  ONLY NUMERIC ENTRIES ARE ACCEPTED
        ;
ENTRY   R  !,"Enter number ",N Q:N=""
        I  N'?1N.N W !,"Whole numbers only please " G ENTRY
        S  NUMBER(J1)=N
        Q
        ;
        ;  THE DISPLAY MODULE DISPLAYS ENTRIES SO THAT USER CAN CHANGE
        ;  VALUES BEFORE RESULTS ARE CALCULATED
        ;
DISPLAY S  END=J1-1
        W  !!,"ENTRY NUMBER",?20,"ENTRY"
        F  J2=1:1:END W !?5,J2,?20,NUMBER(J2)
        ;
```

```
          ;  THE DISPLAY1 MODULE PROVIDES OPTION TO CHANGE ONE OR MORE ENTRIES
          ;
DISPLAY1  R  !,"Do you want to change one or more entries? ",ANS
          I  ANS?1"Y".E D REVISE Q
          I  ANS?1"N".E Q
          W  !,"ANSWER WITH 'Y' OR 'N'" G DISPLAY1
          ;
          ;  THE REVISE MODULE PROMPTS FOR AN ENTRY NUMBER
          ;  THIS "ENTRY NUMBER" IDENTIFIES ENTRY TO BE REVISED
          ;
REVISE    F  J3=0:0 R !,"Entry number to be revised? ",NUM Q:NUM=""  D REVISE1
          Q
          ;
          ;  THE REVISE1 MODULE PROMPTS FOR CORRECT RESULT ON A GIVEN ENTRY
......    ;  NUMBER
          ;
REVISE1   I  NUM'?1N.N W !,"ENTER A NUMBER FROM 1-",END Q
          W  !,"Please give correct result for entry number ",NUM,": "
          R  ANS
          S  NUMBER(NUM)=ANS
          Q
```

19.   Notice how NUMBER(J1), NUMBER(J2), and NUMBER(NUM) all are used to reference our "adding machine array". When we have an array with numeric subscripts, and reference this array with variables as subscripts, it is the numeric value of the variable which determines "what we get".

What would happen if we created a NUMBER array with CH6EX3, and then ran our program CH6EX4?

The elements of our NUMBER array created via CH6EX3 would be replaced by the elements of our NUMBER array created via CH6EX4. The converse would happen if we ran CH6EX4, followed by CH6EX3.

BUILDING AN ARRAY WITH FREE TEXT DATA

20.   Can we adapt our "adding machine program" to perform a more useful function - such as keeping track of names and telephone numbers? Yes! Here is a program to accomplish this function:

```
CH6EX5  ;  CREATE 'NAME' ARRAY WITH NUMERIC SUBSCRIPTS
        F  J1=1:1 D ENTRY Q:NAM=""
        W  !!,"Finished" Q
ENTRY   R  !,"Enter name and phone: ",NAM
        I  NAM="" Q
        I  NAM'?1A.E W !,"Please enter alpha characters for name" G ENTRY
        S  NAME(J1)=NAM
        Q
```

Each time through the FOR loop, we increment J1 to create the NAME array.

21. Use CH6EX5 to enter the following data (or data of your own) into your terminal:

```
JOHN SMITH, 111-111-1111
MARY DOE, 222-222-2222
<CR>
```

The last entry of "<CR>" signifies a carriage return. This carriage return creates "null value" for NAM via the READ command in our ENTRY module. What will happen if we DO CH6EX5 again and enter:

```
DONALD DUCK, DISNEY WORLD, 333-333-3333
```

_____

Our FOR loop will begin at 1, and new data will overwrite our previous entry at NAME(1)! DO CH6EX5 again, make one or two entries, then display your local variables.

22. How can we solve this problem? We could:

(1)   save the last value of J1 as the simple variable START, and

(2)   begin our FOR loop at START, rather than at 1.

Revise CH6EX5 to read:

```
CH6EX5A ; CREATE 'NAME' ARRAY WITH NUMERIC SUBSCRIPTS
        ; SAVE LAST VALUE OF J1 AS THE SIMPLE VARIABLE 'START'
        F J1=START:1 D ENTRY Q:NAM=""
        W !!,"Finished" S START=J1 Q
ENTRY   R !,"Enter name and phone: ",NAM
        I NAM="" Q
        I NAM'?1A.E W !,"Please enter alpha characters for name" G ENTRY
        S NAME(J1)=NAM
        Q
```

This program saves the last value of J1 as the simple variable START.

What happens when we DO this program?

_____

We get an error message, <UNDEF>: this occurs because START is an undefined variable. Before we can use a variable, we must "define" or "initialize" this variable via a SET or READ command.

110

23.   We can define our simple variable START via direct execution of a SET command.

Enter at any right caret:

>S START=3

Now run CH6EX5A. Enter a few names, addresses and phone numbers. Exit via an entry of carriage return. Then DO the program a second time. Display your local variables to verify that the new entries did NOT overwrite your previous data.

24.   We do not have to "initialize" START by direct execution of a SET command before we run CH6EX5A. MUMPS allows us to check whether START is undefined, and if so, SET START equal to one.

The $DATA function returns a zero if a variable does not exist. Here is an example:

IF $DATA (START) =0 SET START=1

This code says: "if the $DATA function for START returns zero, set START equal to one".

25.   Another way to say the same thing:

IF ' $DATA (START) SET START=1

Here, IF is used with an "implied comparison". The code:

IF $DATA (START) SET START=1

has the same meaning as:

IF $DATA (START) =0 SET START=1

The NOT operator, used with $DATA and a variable, provides a "shorthand method" to determine whether the $DATA function for this variable returns zero.

26.   Modify CH6EX5A so the variable START is initialized "automatically" Call you new program CH6EX5B.

_____

Here's how we did it:

```
CH6EX5B  ;  CREATE 'NAME' ARRAY
        ;  THIS PROGRAM:
        ;      (1) USES A FOR LOOP TO STORE DATA IN A LOCAL ARRAY
        ;      (2) STORES THE LAST VALUE OF FOR LOOP VARIABLE AS 'START'
        ;      (3) INITIALIZES 'START' THE FIRST TIME PROGRAM IS RUN
        ;
        I '$DATA(START) S START=1
        F J1=START:1 D ENTRY Q:NAM=""
        W !!,"Finished" S START=J1 Q
ENTRY   R !,"Enter name and phone:  ",NAM
        I NAM="" Q
        I NAM'?1A.E W !,"Please enter alpha characters for name" G ENTRY
        S NAME(J1)=NAM
        Q
```

DISPLAYING LOCAL VARIABLES

27.   Now display all the local variables in your partition. In our implementation, you can do this via direct execution of WRITE at any right caret; your implementation may be somewhat different.

The display will look something like this:

```
>WRITE
START="6"
J1="6"
NAM=""
NAME
NAME(1)="DONALD DUCK,  333-333-3333"
NAME(2)="MARY DOE,  222-222-2222"
```

You will see everything in your NAME array, plus other variables from recently run programs.

The simple variable NAME was automatically created by our READ command, as a "by product" of creating NAME(1).

28.   We can depict our NAME array as an outline:

```
NAME
        NAME(1)="DONALD DUCK,  DISNEY WORLD,  333-333-3333"
        NAME(2)="MARY DOE,  222-222-2222"
```

as an inverted "tree":

112

```
                    NAME
                     |
    -----------------------------------------
    |                   |                    |
NAME (1)            NAME (2)             NAME (3)
```

or as a tree "turned on its side":

```
         <NAME (1)="DONALD  DUCK,  DISNEY  WORLD,  333-333-3333"
         <   .
NAME-<   .
         <   .
         <NAME (n)
```

29. For our implementation:

- You can display all program lines in local memory via direct execution of the **PRINT** command (check user manual for your implementation).

- You can display all variables in local memory via direct execution of the **WRITE** command (check user manual for your implementation).

30. Save your programs from this chapter on disk using direct execution of the **ZSAVE** command (or its equivalent for your implementation). Now "clear" your partition using direct execution of the **ZREMOVE** command (or its equivalent for your implementation).

Now display all programs in your partition using direct execution of the **PRINT** command (or its equivalent) - to confirm that your programs have disappeared.

Now display all variables in your partition using direct execution of the **WRITE** command (or its equivalent). Your NAME array, plus other variables from recently run programs are still there! MUMPS considers "programs" and "variables" as separate entries!

DELETING LOCAL VARIABLES - THE KILL COMMAND

31. Enter at any right caret the command KILL NAME(2). Now display all variables in your partition. What happens?

The local variable NAME(2) has disappeared!

32.   You can delete a specified local variable via the KILL command - either via direct execution or as part of a program.

33.   Now enter at any right caret the command KILL, with no qualifications. Again, display all variables in your partition. What happens?

All variables in your partition have disappeared!

34.   You can "clear" programs from your partition via:

- The ZREMOVE command (or its equivalent)

- Logging off your terminal.

You can "clear" variables from your partition via:

- The KILL command

- Logging off your terminal.

You can "save" programs to disk via the ZSAVE command (or its equivalent).

Starting in frame 35, you will learn how to save variables to disk, so they do not disappear when you log off your terminal.

USING THE FOR LOOP TO BUILD GLOBAL ARRAYS

35.   We can save programs from local memory to disk via ZSAVE. We can also save variables and arrays on disk - so they aren't lost when we sign off our terminal.

All of the variables we've used so far are local variables: they exist only within local memory, and are NOT saved on disk. When you sign off the system, your local variables disappear, just as programs disappear, unless saved on disk.

36.   Saving a local variable to disk is done by converting a "local" variable to a "global" variable. In MUMPS, the terms "global variable" and "global array" refer to a variable or array which is saved on disk. The term "global" may refer to either a global array on disk, or a global variable on disk.

37.   We can create local variables by:

```
(1)   the READ command:   READ "NAME=",NAM
(2)   the SET command:    SET NAME(I)=NAM
```

We cannot create global variables by the READ command. But we CAN create global variables by the SET command. Simply precede the name of the variable with an up arrow or circumflex:

SET ^NAME (J1) =NAM

This SET command:

(1)   creates the global variable ^NAME(J1)

(2)   SETs the contents of this global variable equal to NAM.

38.   Here is the program CH6EX5B used to build our NAM array:

```
CH6EX5B ; CREATE 'NAME' ARRAY
        ; THIS PROGRAM:
        ;     (1) USES A FOR LOOP TO STORE DATA IN A LOCAL ARRAY
        ;     (2) STORES THE LAST VALUE OF FOR LOOP VARIABLE AS 'START'
        ;     (3) INITIALIZES 'START' THE FIRST TIME PROGRAM IS RUN
        ;
        I '$DATA(START) S START=1
        F J1=START:1 D ENTRY Q:NAM=""
        W !!,"Finished" S START=J1 Q
ENTRY   R !,"Enter name and phone: ",NAM
        I NAM="" Q
        I NAM'?1A.E W !,"Please enter alpha characters for name" G ENTRY
        S NAME (J1) =NAM
        Q
```

Develop a new program CH6EX6 so that each time through the FOR loop, we create an array element in the global array ^NAME. Also, we suggest that you save START as a global variable - so it does not disappear when you log off your terminal!

_____

Here's the way we did it:

```
CH6EX6 ; CREATE 'NAME' ARRAY ON DISK
       ;
       I '$DATA(^START) S ^START=1
       F J1=^START:1 D ENTRY Q:NAM=""
       W !!,"Finished" S ^START=J1 Q
ENTRY  R !,"Enter name, address and phone: ",NAM
       I NAM="" Q
       I NAM'?1A.E W !,"Please enter alpha characters for name" G ENTRY
       S ^NAME (J1) =NAM
       Q
```

In this program we've made only two minor changes:

(1)   we SET ⊰NAME(J1) = NAM to create a global array, rather than a local array

(2)   we SET ⊰START = J1, to create a global variable rather than a local variable.

39.   We can save the last value of J1 as the value of:

(1)   the global variable ⊰START via SET ⊰START = J1

(2)   the global variable ⊰NAME(0) via SET ⊰NAME(0) = J1

(3)   the global variable ⊰NAME via SET ⊰NAME = J1.

Either the second or third alternative has several advantages over saving the last value of J1 as ⊰START:

(1)   If all the data needed by your program is stored in the ⊰NAME array, there is no need to 'look up' data in a second global, hence your program will run faster.

(2)   When you list the contents of your ⊰NAME array, you obtain the last value of J1, with no need to find this from a second array.

Which is better - to save the last value of J1 at ⊰NAME(0), or at ⊰NAME? This is a matter of personal preference. Your program will operate equally well, either way.

40.   Change our program CH6EX6 to store the last value of J1 at ⊰NAME rather than at START. Call the new program CH6EX7.

```
CH6EX7 ; CREATE 'NAME' ARRAY ON DISK
       ; LAST VALUE OF J1 SAVED AS VALUE OF ^NAME
       ;
       I '$DATA(^NAME) S ^NAME=1
       F J1=^NAME:1 D ENTRY Q:NAM=""
       W !!,"Finished" S ^NAME=J1 Q
ENTRY R !,"Enter name, address and phone: ",NAM
       I NAM="" Q
       I NAM'?1A.E W !,"Please enter alpha characters for name " G ENTRY
       S ^NAME(J1)=NAM
       Q
```

This program is identical to CH6EX6, except we use ^NAME in place of ^START. Save CH6EX7 on disk.

41.   Now use CH6EX7 to re-enter data into your global array, ^NAME. Make up your own names - or use the following:

CHURCHILL WINSTON	000-000-0000
CARTER JIMMY	111-111-1111
DOE JANE	222-222-2222
SMITH JOHN	333-333-3333
DUCK DONALD	444-444-4444
EINSTEIN ALBERT	555-555-5555

We suggest that you use "fake" telephone numbers to keep track of the entry order.

42.   At the next right caret, enter WRITE to display your local variables What's there?

```
J1="6",  NAM="",  START=1
```

The WRITE command displays only our local variables - everything else has been stored in the ^NAME global array.

DISPLAYING GLOBAL ARRAYS

UTILITY PROGRAMS: Global Display and Global Directory

43.   How can we display our global array?

Most implementations of Standard MUMPS provide a utility program which displays the contents for specified globals. The utility program may be called "global display", "global lister", or some similar name. Check whether your system provides this. If you system does NOT have such a utility, we suggest you move directly to frame 52.

44.   In our implementation, we call the global display utility by entering at any right caret DO ^%G. Your implementation may be different.

The global display utility for our implementation asks three questions:

(1)   DEVICE:

Enter return (or a zero) for output at your terminal. For output at some other device, such as a printer, enter the device number. MUMPS assigns a specific number for each terminal; this number is available from your system manager.

(2)   Right margin 80 = >

Enter return for an 80 character line. Enter 132 for a 132 character line.

(3)   GLOBAL

Enter the name of your global array (in this case, NAME).

In our system, this utility displays the NAME array in numeric order:

```
>D ^%G
DEVICE: 0                    RIGHT MARGIN 80=>
GLOBAL ^NAME=7
^NAME("1")=CHURCHILL WINSTON, 000-000-0000
^NAME("2")=CARTER JIMMY, 111-111-1111
^NAME("3")=DOE JANE, 222-222-2222
^NAME("4")=SMITH JOHN, 333-333-3333
^NAME("5")=DUCK DONALD, 444-444-4444
^NAME("6")=EINSTEIN ALBERT, 555-555-5555
```

45.   How do you know what globals exist on disk? Most implementations of Standard MUMPS provide a utility program which allows you to list the names for all globals on disk.

You can think of the global names in your system as residing in a global directory. The utility program which lists global names on your system may be called "global directory", or some similar name. Check whether your system provides this.

46.   In our implementation, we call the global directory utility by entering at any right caret DO .%GD.

All globals on disk are listed in alphabetic order: at present, you probably have only one global on disk, ,NAME.

In your system, the global directory may contain either:

● only those globals which you have created

● both your own globals, plus globals created by other users.

If you are sharing your global directory with other users, before you create a global, you should check whether this global name is already being used by someone else!

Just as it's a good idea to have names of related programs start with the same first two letters, it's also a good idea to have names of related globals start with the same first two letters.

47.   What would happen if we used the following program to enter a few names:

```
CH6EX8 ;  CREATE NAME ARRAY ON DISK
       ;
       I '$D(^NAME) S ^NAME=1
       F INDEX=^NAME:1 R !,"Enter name:  ",NAM Q:NAM=""  S ^NAME(INDEX)=NAM
       W !!,"Finished" S ^NAME=INDEX Q
```

The new entries would be "added on" to your ﹢NAME array created with CH6EX7! You can confirm this by making a few entries via CH6EX8, and then using your global display utility.

48.   What would happen if CH6EX8 used a "starting point" of 1 rather than ﹢NAME?

Then, the new entries made with CH6EX8 would overwrite previous entries made via CH6EX7!

When you select names for globals, first check if your proposed name is already being used for some other global on disk!

UTILITY PROGRAMS: Routine Directory

49.   Most implementations of Standard MUMPS provide a utility program which allows you to list the names for programs stored on disk. You can think of the program names in your system as residing in a routine directory.

In your system, the routine directory may contain either:

- only those routines which you have created

- both your own routines, plus routines created by other users.

If you are sharing your routine directory with other users, then before you save a routine to disk, you should check whether this routine name is already being used by someone else! There are two ways to do this:

(1)   Try to load the proposed routine name into your partition from disk. If you get an error message such as <NOPGM>, it's safe to proceed.

(2)   Check whether the proposed name already exists in your directory.

50.   For our implementation, we call Routine Directory by:

>DO ˆ%RD

The system responds with a prompt:

REFRESH ROUTINE DIRECTORY? NO=>

Enter 'N' or carriage return if you do NOT want to "refresh" the routine directory.

If you have recently saved a routine to disk, or deleted a routine from disk, the "current list" in routine directory may be "out of date". When you "refresh" the routine directory, you "update" this list of routines to reflect any additions or deletions since the last "refresh" procedure.

51.   Here are a few review questions:

(1)   To display variables and arrays from local memory:

(2)   To display programs from local memory:

(3)   To display variables and arrays from disk:

(4)   To display program names from disk:

(5)   To display programs from disk:

---

(1)   In our implementation, enter WRITE at any right caret (may differ for your implementation)

(2)   In our implementation, enter PRINT at any right caret (may differ for your implementation)

(3)   Use Global Directory (or equivalent utility program for your implementation)

(4)   Use Routine Directory (or equivalent utility program for your implementation)

(5)   Use Routine Directory (or equivalent) load the desired program into your partition, then enter PRINT at any right caret

USING THE FOR LOOP TO DISPLAY A GLOBAL ARRAY

52.   Can we display our global ^NAME array without all the extraneous data obtained with our utility program?

Yes! We can use FOR loops to display global arrays in the same way we used FOR loops to display local arrays.

53.   Here is a program to display our ^NAME array:

```
CH6EX9  ;DISPLAY GLOBAL ARRAY ^NAME
        S END=^NAME-1
        W !!,"This is a display of the global array ^NAME",!!
        F INDEX=1:1:END W !,^NAME(INDEX)
        W !!,"Finished" Q
```

Why did we SET the limiting value of our FOR loop at ^NAME-1, rather than ^NAME?

Our previous programs SET ^NAME equal to the next available numeric subscript, rather than the last subscript at which data is stored. If we use ^NAME as the limiting value of our FOR loop, we will get an error message such as <UNDEF> when we try to WRITE an undefined variable.

54.   Rather than use the local variable END, we could rewrite CH6EX9 + 3 as:

```
        F INDEX=1:1:^NAME-1 W !,^NAME(INDEX)
```

However, each time through this FOR loop we make two "global references". A "global reference" occurs when you "refer to a global name" in your program.

It is considered "good practice" to minimize the number of global references when you perform a repetitive operation. You can decrease the number of global references by converting global variables such as ^NAME-1 to local variables such as END.

121

SUMMARY OF NEW CONCEPTS - CHAPTER 6

Local Array - a group of subscripted variables which share the same simple variable. Local arrays - like local variables - are not stored on disk, and disappear from your partition when you log off. Local arrays with numeric subscripts commonly are created via a FOR loop incremented by one.

$DATA Function - returns zero if the specified variable does not exist. For example:

IF $DATA (START) =0 SET START=1

KILL command - deletes the variable specified. For example:

KILL NAME (2)

- KILL with no argument deletes all local variables from your partition.

Global Array - a group of subscripted variables which share the same simple variable, and are stored on disk. Global arrays with numeric subscripts commonly are created via a FOR loop incremented by one. Global array elements must be created via the SET command, in contrast to local array elements, which may be created via the READ or SET commands.

Utility Programs - implementation specific. Refer to the User Manual provided by your system vendor for information on utility programs which:

- list routine names (e.g. routine directory)

- list global names (e.g. global directory)

- display contents for specified globals (e.g. global display).

CHAPTER SEVEN

BUILDING FILES WITH THE CONCATENATE OPERATOR RETRIEVING DATA WITH THE $PIECE FUNCTION

In this chapter, you will learn how to: (1) store multiple "pieces" within global nodes via the concatenate operator; (2) retrieve specific "pieces" from global nodes via the $PIECE function.

Topics include:

- Deleting global nodes and arrays with the KILL command

- Storing multiple "pieces" within global nodes - the concatenate operator

- Retrieving "pieces" from global nodes - the $PIECE function

- Checking length of entries: the one argument form of $LENGTH; the # syntax of READ; the "range syntax" of pattern match

- Checking the number of "pieces" in a string: the two argument form of $LENGTH

- Building files with multi-level subscripts.

By the end of this chapter, you will be able to:

- use the concatenate operator to store multiple entries as separate "pieces" within a single global node

- retrieve specific "pieces" of a global node via the $PIECE function

- check data entries with the $LENGTH function

- build nodes with variable numbers of "subpieces"

- retrieve data from nodes which contain variable numbers of "subpieces"

- use multi-level subscripts to store more than 255 characters of data for each record in a global file.

DELETING GLOBAL NODES AND ARRAYS WITH THE KILL COMMAND

1. Local variables "disappear" when you:

   - log off your terminal

   - enter KILL via direct execution at any right caret

   - execute KILL with no argument in the programming mode (you must follow this argumentless command with at least two spaces!)

2. Global variables do NOT disappear when you log off your terminal. The only way to get rid of a global variable is via the KILL command. At this time, you probably have entered onto disk:

   - the global variable ^START

   - the global array ^NAME.

You can delete these via:

   (1)   Direct execution of the KILL command:

                >KILL ^START, ^NAME

   (2)   Indirect execution of this same code, as part of a routine.

To delete ^START and ^NAME, we had to specify the names for these global variables. An argumentless KILL affects only our local variables - not globals. When we KILL ^NAME, our entire ^NAME array disappears - not just the "top node" designated as ^NAME.

3. In the next section, we will create a new ^NAME array. Therefore, we suggest that you either:

   - delete your present ^NAME array via the KILL command

   - give your new array a different name, such as ^NAME1.

STORING MULTIPLE "PIECES" WITHIN GLOBAL NODES - THE CONCATENATE OPERATOR

4. Remember those entries of name and phone number in our ^NAME file from Chapter Six? Wouldn't it be nice if we could:

124

- use separate READ statements for different items such as name, phone number, address, and so on

- combine these different variables into a single string

- store this string as the data for one global node

- retrieve any portion of this string on demand?

MUMPS allows you to: (1) use separate READ statements to create several variables; (2) join these variables into a single "data string" via the concatenate operator. You can then store this "data string" as the value of a global node within a global array. You can retrieve specific portions of this global node with the $PIECE function.

5. The concatenate operator joins several strings into one string. Standard MUMPS uses an underline as the symbol for concatenation.

Here is an example:

```
R !,"Name: ",NAM,!,'"Street address: ",ST,!,"Town: ",TWN,!,"State: ",STATE
R !,"Zip code: ",ZIP,!,"Phone: ",PHONE
S DATA=NAM_"^"_ST_"^"_TWN_"^"_STATE_"^"_ZIP_"^"_PHONE
```

The first two lines of code ask for entries of name, street address, town, state, zip code, and phone.

The third line of code creates a local variable DATA, whose value equals the value of NAM, concatenated with an up arrow (^), concatenated with the value of ST, concatenated with another up arrow (^), and so on. When we create a variable such as DATA by concatenation, it is common practice to separate the "components" with "delimiters". Commonly used delimiters include the up arrow, the reverse slash("\"), the asterisk and the pounds sign ("#").

We can also perform concatenation without using delimiters. For example:

```
SET DATA=NAM_ST_TWN_STATE_ZIP_PHONE
```

However, the value of using delimiters will soon become apparent!

6. You can use any character you like as a delimiter. However, we recommend that you choose delimiters which do not appear as "valid characters" within the strings entered.

The characters ^, \, *, >, <, !, and] are good delimiters, since they are unlikely to appear as "valid characters" for most strings entered. Throughout this text, we will use the ^ as our "first choice" for a delimiter.

We can use either literal strings or variables as delimiters. For example:

```
S ^NAME=NAM_"ZZZ"_ST_"YYY"_TWN_"XXX"_STATE_"WWW"_ZIP_"VVV"_PHONE
S DEL1="^",DEL2=">|<",DEL3="XXX"
S DATA=NAM_DEL1_ST_DEL2_TWN_DEL3_STATE_"YYY"_ZIP_"ZZZ"_PHONE
```

7.   Here is a program which creates our ^NAME array with concatenated data at each node:

```
CH7EX1  ; CREATE NAME ARRAY WITH CONCATENATED DATA ITEMS
        ;
        I '$D(^NAME) S ^NAME=1
        F J1=^NAME:1 D ENTRY Q:NAM=""
        W !!,"Finished" S ^NAME=J1 Q
        ;
ENTRY   R !!,"Enter name: ",NAM Q:NAM=""
        I NAM'?A.E W !,"Enter alpha characters for name" G ENTRY
        R !,"Enter address: ",ADR
ENTRY1  R !,"Telephone:  ",TEL
        I TEL'?3N1"-"3N1"-"4N D ERR G ENTRY1
        S ^NAME(J1)=NAM_"^"_ADR_"^"_TEL
        Q
        ;
ERR     W !!,"Enter phone number in the format nnn-nnn-nnnn" Q
```

8.   In this new program, we store name, address and phone as three separate "pieces". The three "pieces" are separated by a delimiter: the literal string "^".

Study this program until you understand how it operates, and what functions are performed by each line of code. We will use CH7EX1 as the "model" for a slightly more complex program to be developed in the next few frames.

9.   Now plan a program to:

- READ a name entry

- allow user to enter street address, town, state, zip code, and phone for each name

- store each data item, concatenated with a delimiter, as the contents of ^NAME(n)

First, outline the structure of your global.

_____

The first thing to consider is our file structure. Here is one approach:

$$<\text{^NAME}(1) = \text{DATA}$$
$$\text{^NAME} - <$$
$$<\text{^NAME}(n)$$

$$\text{DATA} = \underset{\#1}{\text{NAM}}\_"\text{^}"\_\underset{\#2}{\text{ST}}\_"\text{^}"\_\underset{\#3}{\text{TWN}}\_"\text{^}"\_\underset{\#4}{\text{STATE}}\_"\text{^}"\_\underset{\#5}{\text{ZIP}}\_"\text{^}"\_\underset{\#6}{\text{PHONE}}$$

Six pieces of data are concatenated to form the contents of each node. Numeric subscripts are used, as in previous examples.

10. Next, write the code to build this global:

_____

Here's how we did it:

```
CH7EX2  ;  BUILD GLOBAL ARRAY - CONCATENATED OPERATOR AND NUMERIC SUBSCRIPTS
        ;
        I  '$D(^NAME) S ^NAME=1
        S  START=^NAME
        F  INDEX=START:1 R !,"Name: ",NAM Q:NAM=""  D ENTRY
        W  !!,"Finished" S ^NAME=INDEX Q
        ;
ENTRY   R !,"Enter street address: ",ST
        R !,"Town: ",TWN
ENTRY1  R !,"Enter state (two initials): ",STATE I STATE'?2A D ERR1 G ENTRY1
ENTRY2  R !,"Enter zip code: ",ZIP I ZIP'?5N D ERR2 G ENTRY2
ENTRY3  R !,"Enter phone: ",PHONE I PHONE'?3N1"-"3N1"-"4N D ERR3 G ENTRY3
        S ^NAME(INDEX)=NAM_"^"_ST_"^"_TWN_"^"_STATE_"^"_ZIP_"^"_PHONE Q
        ;
ERR1    W !,"Please enter two initials for name of state" Q
ERR2    W !,"Please enter five number for zip code" Q
ERR3    W !,"Please enter phone number in the format nnn-nnn-nnnn" Q
```

11. Briefly describe how this program operates.

_____

We use a FOR loop incremented by one to: (1) provide a series of unique identification numbers; (2) READ each entry into the simple variable NAM; (3) QUIT if NAM is a null entry; (4) DO the ENTRY module.

The ENTRY module includes ENTRY1, ENTRY2, and ENTRY3 - and is similar to the ENTRY modules used in Chapter Six.

Line ENTRY3 + 1 SETs the value of our global node equal to six simple variables concatenated with "^" as a delimiter.

Those error messages which cannot "fit" on the same line with a pattern match are grouped in a series of "error message modules" at the end of our program.

12.   We selected "^" as a delimiter because this character is unlikely to appear in an entry of name, address or phone. What other characters might be used as delimiters?

>,<,*,\,!,], and "compound delimiters" such as >< or XXX

Some programmers choose delimiters so the contents of a global node will be easily readable when displayed by the "global lister" utility program. The delimiters ><, ^^ and ** are good for this purpose, and can be combined with spaces, if desired.

RETRIEVING "PIECES" FROM GLOBAL NODES - THE $PIECE FUNCTION

AN INTRODUCTION TO $ PIECE

Delimiters do more than simply allow us to separate multiple entries stored within a single global node. Delimiters also allow us to retrieve specific "pieces" of global nodes via the $PIECE function.

13.   The $PIECE function returns a specified piece of a specified string, according to it's position as demarcated by a specific delimiter. You can use two, three or four arguments with $PIECE.

Syntax for the two argument form of $PIECE is:

        $PIECE(string,delimiter)

This form returns the first piece of the string specified, for example:

        WRITE !, $PIECE (^NAME(1), "^")

would return the first piece of our global node ^NAME(1).

Syntax for the three argument form of $PIECE is:

        $PIECE(string,delimiter,position of the desired piece)

For example:

        WRITE !, $PIECE (^NAME(1), "^", 6)

would return the sixth piece of our global node ˄NAME(1).

If the third argument specifies a number greater than the number of pieces present, then $PIECE returns a null.

Syntax for the four argument form of $PIECE is:

$PIECE(string,delimiter,position of first piece,position of last piece)

For example:

```
WRITE !,$PIECE(^NAME(1),"^",1,4)
```

would return the first, second, third and fourth pieces of our global node ˄NAME(1). All characters, including delimiters, would be returned.

$PIECE(string,delimiter,position of first piece,position of last piece)

For example:

```
WRITE !,$PIECE(^NAME(1),"^",1,4)
```

would return the first, second, third and fourth pieces of our global node ˄NAME(1). All characters, including delimiters, would be returned.

If the fourth argument specifies a number greater than the number of pieces present, then $PIECE returns all characters from the third argument thru the end of the string.

14.   Here is the code to display names from our ˄NAME array created in CH7EX2:

```
CH7EX3 ; PRINT NAME FROM GLOBAL ARRAY WITH CONCATENATED DATA
       ;
       S END=^NAME-1
       F INDEX=1:1:END W !,$PIECE(^NAME(INDEX),"^")
       W !!,"Finished" Q
```

15.   Here is the code to display name and phone from this array:

```
CH7EX4 ; DISPLAY NAME AND PHONE FROM GLOBAL ARRAY WITH CONCATENATED DATA
       ;
       S END=^NAME-1
       F INDEX=1:1:END D PRINT
       W !!,"Finished" Q
       ;
```

```
PRINT  S  DATA=^NAME (INDEX)
       S  NAM=$PIECE (DATA, "^")
       S  PHONE=$PIECE (DATA, "^", 6)
       W  ! , NAM, ? 30, PHONE
       Q
```

Why did we SET DATA equal to ^NAME(INDEX) and then perform our $PIECE operations on DATA? It might seem easier to perform our $PIECE operations on ^NAME(INDEX):

```
PRINT  S  NAM=$PIECE (^NAME (INDEX) , "^")
       S  PHONE=$PIECE (^NAME (INDEX, "^", 6)
       W  ! , NAM, ? 30, PHONE
       Q
```

If we perform our $PIECE operations on DATA(INDEX), then each execution of our PRINT module involves only one "global reference". If we perform our two $PIECE operations on ^NAME(INDEX), then each execution of our PRINT module requires two global references.

Each "global reference" involves at least one disk access - which takes much longer than "access" to a local variable in your partition. Typical "access times" to disk range from 20 milliseconds to 300 milliseconds, while "access times" for internal storage range from 1 microsecond to 3 microseconds: several thousand times faster!

Some implementations of MUMPS load the entire contents of your ^NAME array into local memory when you perform the disk access:

```
       S  NAM=$PIECE (^NAME (INDEX) , "^")
```

In this case, there may be little difference in speed between our two PRINT modules. However, as a general rule, we suggest that you plan your code to minimize the number of global references. This is especially important if you have a file of 100,000 names on disk, and perform repeated searches of this entire file!

16.   The following code would return name, street, town, state, zip code, and phone:

```
       S  END=^NAME-1
       F  INDEX=1: 1: END W  ! , $PIECE (^NAME (INDEX) , "^", 1, 6)
```

With the four argument form of $PIECE, our delimiter "^" would be included in this output. To avoid getting the "^", you could use the three argument form:

```
       S  END=^NAME-1
       F  INDEX=1: 1: END D  PRINT
       Q
```

```
PRINT S DATA=^NAME (INDEX)
      W !, $PIECE (DATA, "^", 1)
      W !, $PIECE (DATA, "^", 2)
      W !, $PIECE (DATA, "^", 3)
      W !, $PIECE (DATA, "^", 4)
      W !, $PIECE (DATA, "^", 5)
      W !, $PIECE (DATA, "^", 6)
```

17.   Rather than six WRITE commands, we can use a FOR loop with the three argument form of $PIECE:

```
      S END=^NAME-1
      F J1=1:1:END D PRINT
      Q
PRINT S DATA=^NAME (INDEX)
      F J2=1:1:6 W !, $PIECE (DATA, "^", J2)
```

18.   Revise CH7EX4 to return all six "pieces", with separate headings.

Here's how we did it:

```
CH7EX5 ; PRINT ALL SIX 'PIECES' FROM NAME FILE
       W !!, "NAME", ?20, "STREET ADDRESS", ?40, "TOWN", ?53, "STATE"
       W ?59, "ZIP CODE", ?68, "PHONE", !!
       S END=^NAME-1
       F J1=1:1:END W ! D PRINT
       W !!, "Finished" Q
       ;
PRINT  S DATA=^NAME (INDEX)
       F J2=1:1:6 D PRINT1
       Q
       ;
PRINT1 W:J2=2 ?20 W:J2=3 ?40 W:J2=4 ?53 W:J2=5 ?59 W:J2=6 ?68
       W $P (DATA, "^", J2) Q
```

19.   What if we wanted to print pieces #1, #3, #4 and #6? We could use separate WRITE commands, as in Frame 16. Or we could use a "special" form of FOR loop. Up to now, we have used two forms of FOR loop:

```
      F I=X:Y:Z              (closed FOR loop)

      F I=X:Y                (open FOR loop)
```

A third form of the FOR loop is:

```
      FOR I=X,Y,Z
```

Here is a simple example:

```
F INDEX=1,2,5 W INDEX,?$X+3
W !,"Finished" Q
```

Execution of this FOR loop will output:

```
1   2   5
Finished
```

The FOR loop is executed once for each of the three values listed. On each execution, the FOR loop variable is assigned one of these values. Execution ceases when we run out of values for the FOR loop variable.

20.   Revise CH7EX5 to output only pieces #1, #3, #4 and #6, using this third form of FOR loop. Name your program CH7EX5A:

_____

Here's how we did it:

```
CH7EX5A ; PRINT PIECES 1, 3, 4 AND 6 FROM NAME FILE
        ;
        W !!,"NAME",?25,"TOWN",?40,"STATE",?55,"PHONE"
        S END=^NAME-1
        F J1=1:1:END W ! D PRINT
        W !!,"Finished" Q
        ;
PRINT   S DATA=^NAME(J1)
        F J2=1,3,4,6 D PRINT1
        Q
        ;
PRINT1  W:J2=3 ?25 W:J2=4 ?40 W:J2=6 ?55
        W $P(DATA,"^",J2)
        Q
```

21.   Now write the code to print out only the names and phone numbers from our primary file. Remember - name is piece #1, and phone number is piece #6!

_____

```
CH7EX6 ; PRINT NAME AND PHONE NUMBER FROM PRIMARY FILE
       ;
       W !!,"NAME",?40,"PHONE"
       S END=^NAME-1
       F INDEX=1:1:END D PRINT
       W !!,"Finished" Q
       ;
```

```
PRINT  S  DATA="NAME (INDEX)
       S  NAM=$P (DATA, "^")
       S  PHONE=$P (DATA, "^", 6)
       W  !, NAM, ?40, PHONE
       Q
```

This program is essentially identical to CH7EX4. We simply SET the simple variable NAM equal to piece #1, and the simple variable PHONE equal to piece #6. We then print these two simple variables, using a tab at column 40.

Notice that our PRINT modules in CH7EX5A and CH7EX6 use only one "global reference" to ∧NAME. It is good practice to minimize the number of global references in your code.

Enter some names, with street address, town, state, zip code and phone, using CH7EX2. Enter name in the format: last name (comma) first name (space) middle initial. Now use CH7EX3, and CH7EX4 to display your data.

COMPOUND $PIECE OPERATIONS

22.   Within the "first piece" of each node of our ∧NAME array, we can identify three "subpieces":

> last name (delimited by comma from first name and middle initial)
> first name (delimited by comma from last name and by space from
> middle initial)
> middle initial (delimited by space from first name).

23.   Write a program to print name, address, town, state and zip code in the following format:

> First name (space) middle initial (period) (space) last name
> Street address
> Town (comma) (double space) State (double space) zip code

Here's one way:

```
CH7EX7  ;  PRINT MAILING ADDRESS LABELS
        ;
        S  END=^NAME-1
        F  INDEX=1:1:END D PRINT
        W  !!,"Finished" Q
        ;
```

```
PRINT   S  DATA=^NAME (INDEX)
        S  NAM=$P (DATA, "^", 1) ,LASTNAM=$P (NAM, ", ", 1) ,RESTNAM=$P (NAM, ", ", 2)
        S  FIRSTNAM=$P (RESTNAM, "  ", 1) ,MI=$P (RESTNAM, "  ", 2)
        S  STADDR=$P (DATA, "^", 2)
        S  TWNADDR=$P (DATA, "^", 3) _",    "_$P (DATA, "^", 4) _"   "_$P (DATA, "^",5 )
        W  !! ,FIRSTNAM_"  "_MI_". "_LASTNAM
        W  ! , STADDR
        W  ! , TWNADDR
        Q
```

24.   We can also use $PIECE within itself to accomplish the same thing, with fewer SET commands. Here is a revision of lines PRINT + 1 and PRINT + 2:

```
        S  NAM=$P (DATA, "^", 1) ,LASTNAM=$P (NAM, ", ", 1)
        S  FIRSTNAM=$P ($P (NAM, ", ", 2) , "  ", 1)
        S  MI=$P ($P (NAM, ", ", 2) , "  ", 2)
```

In the second line of code, our "innermost" $PIECE operation obtains first name plus middle initial; then our "outer" $PIECE operation obtains first name.

In the third line of code, our "innermost" $PIECE operation obtains first name plus middle initial; then our "outer" $PIECE operation obtains middle initial.

This code with "compound" $PIECE operations requires fewer SET commands, as compared with CH7EX7. In some implementations of Standard MUMPS, the reduced number of SET commands might execute a little faster than CH7EX7.

Should you use compound $PIECE operations to "speed up" your programs? Yes - if this does not make your code difficult to understand!

Four "suggestions for programmers" which we recommend to beginners:

The first time you write it, make it easy to understand.

A program that is slow but easy to understand can always be speeded up.

A program that is hard to understand may eventually become a problem rather than a solution.

Keep your logic and program flow simple. Resist the temptation to "show off" by writing tricky code which is difficult to understand.

CHECKING LENGTH OF ENTRIES

THE ONE ARGUMENT FORM OF $LENGTH

25.   What would happen if the length of concatenated data in our primary file exceeded 255 characters?

We would get an error message - only 255 characters can be stored as the contents of a node.

26.   Use CH7EX2 to enter:

   (1)   Any string of 80 characters for name

   (2)   Any string of 80 characters for street address

   (3)   Any string of 80 characters for town

   (4)   Any two characters for state

   (5)   Any five numbers for ZIP

   (6)   000-000-0000 for phone

What happens?

You will get an error message such as <MXSTRNG>. The exact nature of this message is implementation specific.

27.   One way to avoid this problem is via the $LENGTH function

The one argument form of $LENGTH returns the number of characters in a specified variable. You may use either local or global variables with $LENGTH. The syntax is:

   $LENGTH(variable, expression, or string literal)

28.   Write the code to check $LENGTH of our concatenation in line ENTRY3+2 of CH7EX2.

Insert the following line before line ENTRY3 + 2:

```
I  $LENGTH (NAM) +$L (ST) +$L (TWN) +$L (STATE) +$L (ZIP) +$L (PHONE) +5>250  D  ERR4
```

And add to the end of your program:

```
ERR4
    W !,"USE ABBREVIATIONS AS NEEDED TO SHORTEN YOUR ENTRIES. THE MAXIMUM"
    W !,"NUMBER OF CHARACTERS ALLOWED AS THE TOTAL FOR ALL ENTRIES IS 250."
    Q
```

This code ensures that our SET command will not be executed unless total length of the concatenation is 255 or less (the five delimiters are considered as part of our string).

29. We can use $LENGTH with expressions. The code in frame 28 could be written:

```
I  $L (NAM_ST_TWN_STATE_ZIP_PHONE)>250  D  ERR4  Q
```

And we can use $LENGTH function with string literals. For example:

```
I  $LENGTH("JONES, ROBERT")>20  D  MODULE
```

$LENGTH with expressions is frequently useful. However, it is seldom necessary to check the length of a string literal.

30.   We could of course, use $LENGTH to limit our NAM entry to 30 characters, our ST entry to 20 characters, and so on.

THE # SYNTAX OF THE READ COMMAND

31.   A second way to check the length of each entry is provided by a new syntax for the READ command, recently approved by MUMPS Development Committee. The following code specifies maximum length of 30, 40, 20, 2 and 5 characters respectively for NAM, ST, TOWN, STATE, and ZIP.

```
        READ !!,"Enter name: ",NAM#30
        READ !,"Street address: ",ST#40
        READ !,"Town: ",TWN#20
        READ !,"State: ",STATE#2
        READ !,"Zip code: ",ZIP#5
```

If you enter this maximum number of characters, the last character provides an automatic "RETURN". If you enter fewer than the specified maximum number of characters, you may terminate this entry by manually striking RETURN.

Consult the User Manual for your system to determine whether your implementation provides the #syntax of READ.

THE "RANGE SYNTAX" OF PATTERN MATCH

32.   A third way to check the length of each entry is provided by a new syntax for pattern match, recently approved by the MUMPS Development Committee. The following code specifies from three to 30 characters for NAM:

```
ENTRY1 R !!,"Enter name: ",NAM I NAM'?3.30A W !,"ENTER 3-30 CHARACTERS"
...G ENTRY1
```

This code specifies from zero to three numbers for AGE:
```
ENTRY2 I AGE'?.3N W !"ENTER 0-3 CHARACTERS" G ENTRY2
```

And this code specifies at least three characters for TWN:

```
ENTRY3 I TWN '?3.A W !"ENTER 3 OR MORE CHARACTERS" G ENTRY3
```

Your user manual will have information on whether your implementation provides the range syntax for pattern match.

33.   In most cases, length is best checked at the time of data entry, using the new syntax for pattern match. If this is NOT available on your implementation of Standard MUMPS, you can use $LENGTH plus some other form of pattern match.

34.   Even if your implementation of MUMPS provides the new syntax for pattern match, the $LENGTH function is uniquely useful for checking concatenations, before you use the SET command to store concatenated data as the contents of a global node.

CHECKING THE "NUMBER OF PIECES" IN A STRING WITH THE TWO ARGUMENT FORM OF $LENGTH

35.   The two argument form of the $LENGTH function returns the number of pieces which are separated by a specified delimiter.

We can depict this syntax in the general form:

```
$LENGTH(variable,"delimiter")
```

For example:

```
$LENGTH(^NAME(6),"^")
```

returns the number of pieces within ^NAME(6) which are separated by the "^" delimiter.

The two argument syntax of $LENGTH was recently approved by the MUMPS Development Committee.

Your users manual will have information on whether your implementation provides the two argument form of $LENGTH.

36.   In Frame 23, our program CH7EX7 used multiple $PIECE operations to obtain first name, last name and middle initial from our .NAME(n) global. We can use the two argument form of $LENGTH to check whether RESTNAM contains a middle initial:

```
PRINT S DATA=^NAME(INDEX)
        S NAM=$P(DATA,"^",1),LASTNAM=$P(NAM,",",1),RESTNAM=$P(NAM,",",2)
        S FIRSTNAM=$P(RESTNAM," ",1) K MI
        I $LENGTH(RESTNAM," ")>1 D INITIAL
        ;
        I '$D(MI) W !!,FIRSTNAM_" "_LASTNAM Q
        W !!,FIRSTNAM_" "_MI_". "_LASTNAM Q
        ;
INITIAL S MI=$P(RESTNAM," ",2) Q
```

In line PRINT+2, we KILL MI before DOing our INITIAL module. The KILL command is needed to delete any "left over" values for MI from a previous execution of our PRINT module.

In our original program, if there were no middle initial, S MI = $P(RESTNAM,"",2) would return a null value so in this case, the two argument form of $LENGTH is not really needed.

37.   What if we wanted to allow either one, or more, entries of phone number?

One approach would be to allow multiple entries of phone number, concatenated together by a "sub-delimiter", within the sixth piece of each node. We could then use the two argument form of $LENGTH to obtain the number of "sub pieces" within this sixth piece.

Modify CH7EX2 to allow multiple entries of "phone number", stored together within the sixth piece of each node, using "]" as a sub-delimiter.

Here's how we did it:

```
CH7EX8 ; BUILD GLOBAL ARRAY - CONCATENATE OPERATOR & NUMERIC SUBSCRIPTS
        ; PIECE #1 = NAME
        ; PIECE #2 = STREET ADDRESS
        ; PIECE #3 = TOWN
        ; PIECE #4 = STATE
        ; PIECE #5 = ZIP CODE
        ; PIECE #6 = PHONE NUMBERS
        ; DELIMITER = "^"
        ;
```

```
            ;
            ;  MULTIPLE PHONE NUMBERS ALLOWED WITHIN PIECE #6
            ;  SUB-DELIMITER = "]"
            ;
            K  I '$D(^NAME) S ^NAME=1
            S  START=^NAME
            F  INDEX=START:1 R !,"Enter name: ",NAM Q:NAM=""  D ENTRY
            W  !!,"Finished" S ^NAME=INDEX Q
            ;
ENTRY       R  !,"Enter street address: ",ST
            I  $LENGTH(ST)>30 W !,"THIRTY CHARACTERS OR LESS, PLEASE" G ENTRY
            ;
ENTRY2      R  !,"Enter town: ",TWN
            I  TWN'?1A.A!($L(TWN)>30)  W !,"THIRTY CHARACTERS OR LESS, PLEASE"
......      G  ENTRY2
            ;
ENTRY3      R  !,"Enter state (two initials): ",STATE
            I  STATE'?2A W !,"TWO ALPHA CHARACTERS, PLEASE" G ENTRY3
            ;
ENTRY4      R  !,"Enter zip code: ",ZIP
            I  ZIP'?5N W !,"PLEASE ENTER FIVE NUMBERS" G ENTRY4
            ;
ENTRY5      R  !,"How many phone numbers do you wish to enter? ",P
            F  J=1:1:P W !,"Phone number(",J,"): " R PH(J) D CHECK
            S  PHONE=PH(1) F K=2:1:P S PHONE=PHONE_"]"_PH(K)
            S  ^NAME(INDEX)=NAM_"^"_ST_"^"_TWN_"^"_STATE_"^"_ZIP_"^"_PHONE
            Q
            ;
CHECK       I  PH(J)?3N1"-"3N1"-"4N Q
            S  J=J-1
            W  !,"PLEASE ENTER PHONE NUMBER IN THE FORMAT 'nnn-nnn-nnnn'"
            Q
```

38.   Study the code in the ENTRY5 module of CH7EX8 closed FOR loop to build a local array, checking each entry via our CHECK module.

Line ENTRY5 + 2 uses another closed FOR loop to concatenate the entries in this array into a local variable, using our sub-delimiter.

Line ENTRY5 + 3 creates our global array element, by concatenating a series of local variables with our primary delimiter.

If you find ENTRY5 + 3 a little hard to follow, the following explanation may help. Imagine that we have a PH array with three elements:

```
PH(1)="A"
PH(2)="B"
PH(3)="C"
```

Our first SET command creates PHONE = "A". The first iteration of our FOR loop creates

PHONE = "A" concatenated with "B". The second iteration of our FOR loop creates PHONE = "A" concatenated with "B" concatenated with "C".

You can modify this code for other global files, where the number of "pieces" within a given node will vary for different array elements.

39.   Use CH7EX8 to enter a few names with multiple phone numbers into your .NAME global. After you have done this, for any given node, you do not know in advance how many phone numbers are in piece #6.

Now write a program to output name and phone numbers for the .NAME global. Use $LENGTH to determine how many phone numbers exist in piece #6 of each node.

```
CH7EX9  ; DISPLAY NAME AND PHONE NUMBERS FOR ALL ENTRIES IN ^NAME FILE
        ;
        W !!,"PHONE LIST" S END=^NAME-1
        F INDEX=1:1:END W !,$P(^NAME(INDEX),"^",1) D PHONE
        W !!,"Finished" Q
        ;
PHONE   S PH=$P(^NAME(INDEX),"^",6)
        S LAST=$L(PH,"]")
        F J=1:1:LAST W !?5,$P(PH,"]",J)
        Q
```

40.   Study the code in our routine CH7EX9

First, we use a closed FOR loop with $PIECE to obtain the first piece of each array element and to DO our PHONE module.

Second, we use the two argument syntax for $LENGTH to find the number of subpieces within our sixth piece.

Third, we use another closed FOR loop to WRITE the desired subpieces.

With a large file, we would create a local array via our first FOR loop, and then perform our two $PIECE operations on this local array, rather than use two global accesses for each global array element.

BUILDING FILES WITH MULTI-LEVEL SUBSCRIPTS

41.   What if the data for a given array element exceeds 255 characters? For example, for one "name", we might want to enter date of birth, education, work history, and so on. In this

case, we can use a second level of numeric subscripting. We can represent two levels of subscripting as an outline:

```
NAME
  NAME (1) =NAME_"ˆ"_DOB_"ˆ"_ST_"ˆ"_TOWN_"ˆ"_STATE_"ˆ"_ZIP CODE_"ˆ"_PHONE
      NAME (1, 1) =PROJECT #1_"ˆ"_TARGET DATE_"ˆ"_PROJECT #2...
      NAME (1, 2) =PREVIOUS ADDRESS #1_"ˆ"_PREVIOUS ADDRESS #2...
      NAME (1, 3) =EDUCATION #1_"ˆ"_EDUCATION #2...
      NAME (2) =
        .
        .
        .
      NAME (n) =
```

As an "inverted tree":

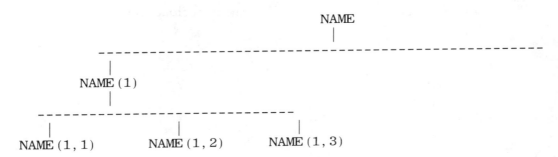

Or as an inverted tree which has been "turned on its side":

```
                        <NAME (1, 1)
            <NAME (1) --<NAME (1, 2)
            <    .       <NAME (1, 3)
            <    .
  NAME--<         .
            <    .
            <NAME (n)
```

42. We can consider our global array ₙNAME as a "hierarchical file". Each "record" is represented by an array element with one level of subscripting. Each record has a unique identifier - its numeric subscript plus one or more "ancesters". At the first level, within each record, we can have:

43.   For most implementations of Standard MUMPS, the maximum length for the "contents" of one global node is 255 characters. However, some implementations of Standard MUMPS allow 1000 or more characters as the "contents" for a global node. Check your user manual to determine what limitations apply to your system.

If your implementation of Standard MUMPS is limited to 255 characters as the maximum "content" for any one global node, then you will need a second level of subscripting for those records which contain more than the 255 character limit.

44.   Plan and write a program to create a ^NAME array with the following features:

(1)   Eight pieces at the first level of subscripting to include:

name
address
town
state
zip code
home phone
office phone
department

(2)   A second level of subscripting to provide one node for each "project". Each node at the second level should include six pieces:

project name
target date
description
classification
priority
cost

This new "global file" will allow an unlimited number of projects on each name.

Here is a possible file structure:

```
CH7EX10 ; CREATE NAME/PROJECT FILE WITH UNLIMITED NUMBER OF PROJECTS
        ; FILE STRUCTURE
        ;   ^NAME = NEXT AVAILABLE SUBSCRIPT AT THE FIRST LEVEL
        ;     FIRST LEVEL
        ;           PIECE #1 - NAME<31 CHARACTERS
        ;           PIECE #2 - ADDRESS<51 CHARACTERS
        ;           PIECE #3 - TOWN<21 CHARACTERS
        ;           PIECE #4 - STATE=2 LETTERS
        ;           PIECE #5 - ZIP CODE=5 NUMBERS
        ;           PIECE #6 - HOME PHONE=12 CHARACTERS IN FORMAT nnn-nnn-nnnn
        ;           PIECE #7 - OFFICE PHONE=12 CHARACTERS IN FORMAT nnn-nnn-nnnn
        ;           PIECE #8 - DEPARTMENT<16 CHARACTERS
        ;           PIECE #9 - NEXT AVAILABLE SUBSCRIPT AT THE SECOND LEVEL
        ;     SECOND LEVEL
        ;           PIECE #1 - PROJECT NAME<31 CHARACTERS
        ;           PIECE #2 - TARGET DATE=6 NUMBERS IN FORMAT YYMMDD
        ;           PIECE #3 - DESCRIPTION<101 CHARACTERS
        ;           PIECE #4 - CLASSIFICATION<21 CHARACTERS
        ;           PIECE #5 - PRIORITY=NUMBER BETWEEN 1 AND 10
```

142

```
    ;              PIECE #6 - COST<1000000  (NO CENTS)
    ;
    ; NAMES OF FOR LOOP VARIABLES WILL BE J, J1, J2, ETC.
    ;
```

_____

Here's how we did it:


```
CH7EX10 ; CREATE NAME/PROJECT FILE WITH UNLIMITED NUMBER OF PROJECTS
        ;
        K  I '$D(^NAME) S ^NAME=1
        S START=^NAME
        F J=START:1 R !,"Enter name:  ",NAM Q:NAM=""  D ENTRY
        W !!,"Finished" S ^NAME=J K   Q
        ;
        ; ENTRY MODULE
        ;
ENTRY   I $L(NAM)>30 W !,"Thirty characters or less, please" S J=J-1 Q
        ;
ENTRY2  R !,"Street address:  ",ST
        I $L(ST)>50 W !,"Fifty characters or less, please" G ENTRY2
        ;
ENTRY3  R !,"Town:  ",TWN
        I $L(TWN)>20 W !,"Twenty characters or less please" G ENTRY3
        ;
ENTRY4  R !,"Enter two letters for state:  ",STATE
        I STATE'?2A W !,"Two alpha characters, please" G ENTRY4
        ;
ENTRY5  R !,"Zip code:  ",ZIP
        I ZIP'?5N W !,"Five numbers, please" G ENTRY5
        ;
ENTRY6  R !,"Home phone:  ",HPHONE
        I HPHONE'?3N1"-"3N1"-"4N W !,"Please use format nnn-nnn-nnnn"
......  G ENTRY6
        ;
ENTRY7  R !,"Office phone:  ",OPHONE
        I OPHONE'?3N1"-"3N1"-"4N W !,"Please use format nnn-nnn-nnnn"
......  G ENTRY7
        ;
ENTRY8  R !,"Department:  ",DEPT
        I $L(DEPT)>15 W !,"Fifteen characters or less, please" G ENTRY8

        F J1=1:1 R !!,"Project name:  ",PROJ Q:PROJ="" D PROJECT
        ;
        S ^NAME(J)=NAM_"^"_ST_"^"_TWN_"^"_STATE_"^"_ZIP_"^"_HPHONE_"^"
......  _OPHONE_"^"_DEPT_"^"_J1
        Q
        ;
        ; PROJECT ENTRY
        ;
```

143

```
PROJECT  I $L(PROJ)>30 W !,"Thirty characters or less, please" S J1=J1-1 Q
         ;
PROJ2    R !,"Target date in format YYMMDD: ",TDATE
         I TDATE'?6N W ,"Please enter date as 6 numbers in format YYMMDD"
......   G PROJ2
         ;
PROJ3    R !,"Project description: ",DESCR
         I $L(DESCR)>100 W !,"One hundred characters or less, please" G PROJ3
         ;
PROJ4    R !,"Project classification: ",CLASS
         I $L(CLASS)>20 W !,"Twenty characters or less, please" G PROJ4
         ;
PROJ5    R !,"Priority: ",PR
         I PR>10!(PR'?.N) W !,"Please enter a number between 1 and 10" G PROJ5
         ;
PROJ6    R !,"Estimated cost as dollars (no decimals): ",COST
         I COST'?.N!(COST>999999) W !,"Enter a number between 1 & 999999"
......   G PROJ6
         S ^NAME(J,J1)=PRO_"^"_TDATE_"^"_"^"_DESCR_"^"_CLASS_"^"_PR_"^"_COST
         Q
```

45.   This program uses two FOR loops: one in line CH7EX10+4 and one in line ENTRY8+3.

The first FOR loop creates numeric subscripts at our first level of subscripting, while the second FOR loop creates the numeric subscripts at our second level of subscripting. We can have any number of projects for a given name.

SUMMARY OF NEW CONCEPTS - CHAPTER 7

Deletion of global variables and global arrays - use KILL command (specify name of global array or global node).

Concatenate operator - used with SET command to create global array element via joining multiple local variables into a single "data string" with delimiters.

$PIECE function - two argument form:

example: $P(^NAME(n),"^") returns first piece in relation to delimiter.

- three argument form:

$PIECE(string,delimiter,position of piece)

example: $P(^NAME(n),"^",3) returns third piece in relation to delimiter.

- four argument form:

$PIECE(string,delimiter,1st position,2nd position)

example: $P(^NAME(n),"^",3,6) returns the third through sixth pieces including delimiters.

FOR loop - closed form:

FOR INDEX=1:1:END

- open form:

FOR INDEX=1:1

- discrete form:
FOR INDEX=1,4,6

can be used to retrieve specific "pieces" of an array element, in combination with $PIECE function.

Compound $PIECE operations - may be used with sub-delimiters:

example: if the name "DOE, JOHN" is represented by $PIECE(NAM,"",1), then

$P ($P (NAM, "^", 1) , ", ", 1)

will return "DOE"

$LENGTH function - one argument form:

$LENGTH(string)

example: $LENGTH(NAM) returns the number of characters in simple variable NAM.

- two argument form:

$LENGTH(string,delimiter)

example: $LENGTH(DATA,"^") returns the number of pieces in DATA separated by the delimiter "^".

syntax for READ command:

READ NAM#30 limits number of characters in NAM to 30 or less.

Range syntax for pattern match:

```
IF NAM'?3.30A WRITE !,"Enter between 3 and 30 alpha characters"
IF AGE'?.3N WRITE !,"Enter zero to three numbers"
IF TWN'?3.A WRITE !,"Enter at least three alpha characters"
```

Multi-level subscripts - can represent global array as a multi-level hierarchical file
- most implementations of Standard MUMPS allow up to 255 characters as the "value" for a local or global variable (some implementations allow more - check your user manual)
- global array may be represented as an inverted tree which has been "turned on its side":

```
                                      <^NAME (1, 1)
                    <^NAME (1) --<       .
    ^NAME--<            .         <^NAME (1, n)
             <^NAME (n)
```

146

CHAPTER EIGHT

BUILDING FILES WITH STRING SUBSCRIPTS

In this chapter you will learn how to: (1) build files with string subscripts; (2) display these files in alpha order.

Topics include:

- String subscripts

- The $ORDER function

- The $NEXT function

- Negative Subscripts

- Potential problems with string subscripts.

By the end of this chapter you will be able to:

- build files with string subscripts

- display these files in alphabetic order

- identify potential problems caused by identical string subscripts.

If you are using a computer to work out examples, you should remove all previous programs and variables from local memory. To do this, either: (1) log off and then log on, or; (2) enter KILL and then ZREMOVE at any right caret. But first, be sure to ZSAVE any programs you plan to use later! We recommend that you ZSAVE all programs used in the previous chapters.

STRING SUBSCRIPTS

1.   In Chapter Seven we used FOR loops to:

    (1)   READ data into a simple variable such as NAM

    (2)   Create global arrays with one level of numeric subscripting

    (3)   Create global arrays with two levels of numeric subscripting

    (4)   Retrieve data from global arrays.

In Chapter Seven, our subscripts were numeric. Each record in our file was identified by a unique numeric subscript. However, when we retrieve data from such a file, we must do so in numeric order.

How can we display our name file in alphabetic order, rather than numeric order? We can do this by creating a new type of array, using alphabetic strings as subscripts.

2.   This simple program builds a name file with string subscripts:

```
CH8EX1 ; NAME FILE WITH STRING SUBSCRIPTS
       ;
       F INDEX=0:0 D ENTRY Q:NAM=""
       W !!,"Finished" Q
       ;
ENTRY  R !,"Enter name: ",NAM
       I NAM="" Q
       I NAM'?1A.E W !,"NAME MUST BEGIN WITH AN ALPHA CHARACTER" G ENTRY
       R !,"Address and phone: ",DATA
       S ^NAME(NAM)=DATA
       Q
```

3.   In this program:

    (1)   Our FOR loop is incremented by zero rather than by one

    (2)   There is no need to check $D for a variable which represents the starting value of our FOR loop variable

    (3)   There is no need to save the ending value of our FOR loop variable

    (4)   Part of our data - the name - is saved as the string subscript itself, while other parts of our data are saved as the value of our array element.

Each time through the FOR loop:

    (1)   the simple variable NAM changes to a new value

    (2)   a new element is created in our ^NAME global.

Nearly all implementations of Standard MUMPS allow you to use alpha strings (such as "DOE, JOHN") as subscripts. Before proceeding to the next frame, check your user manual to make sure that your implementation provides this feature. In most implementations, string subscripts may be 1 to 31 characters in length.

    4.   Enter CH8EX1 into your computer. Now enter three or four names followed by a null entry.

Use the global display utility program provided by your implementation to display these new entries in the ^NAME global. For our implementation of MUMPS, this is done by entering at any right caret DO ^%G. What happens?

For our implementation, the numeric subscripts appear first, followed by string subscripts sorted in alpha order!

    5.   We can depict our ^NAME array with mixed numeric and string subscripts as an outline:

```
^NAME
        ^NAME (1)
            .
            .
            .
        ^NAME (n)
        ^NAME (A)
            .
            .
            .
        ^NAME (ZZZ)
```

As an inverted tree:

```
                        ^NAME
                          .
                          .
                          .
                          .
    . . . . . . . . . . . . . . . . . . . . . . . .
       .                  .                  .
       .                  .                  .
    ^NAME (1)          ^NAME (N)          ^NAME (A)
```

Or as an inverted tree which has been "turned on its side":

```
        <^NAME (1)
            <     .
            <^NAME (n)
  ^NAME  -  <^NAME (A)
            <     .
            <     .
            <^NAME (ZZZ)
```

6. In MUMPS, each array element is called a node. Local nodes:

    (1)   are created by the READ or SET command

    (2)   have a name (created by the READ or SET command)

    (3)   have contents (entered by the READ or SET command).

Global nodes:

    (1)   must be created by the SET command

    (2)   have a name (created by the SET command)

    (3)   have contents (created by the SET command).

Contents of a local or global node may be:

    (1)   A "null entry" - created by carriage return or a SET command such as

            SET ^NAME (NAM) =" "

    (2)   Any alpha numeric character string, up to 255 characters in length.

An array element with a "null value" is considered as having data.

7. The term "global" refers to a simple variable or an array which is stored on disk.

We can think of each array element as a "pigeon hole", with a label (or name) and contents, as shown in Figure 8-1.

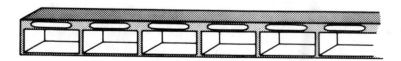

FIGURE 8-1. ARRAY ELEMENTS AS 'PIGEON HOLES'

8.   Standard MUMPS specifies: a variable name can be up to 8 characters long; subscripts may be up to 31 characters in length. Check the user manual for your system regarding:

(1)   The maximum number of characters allowed for a variable name
        (typically 8 characters)

(2)   The maximum number of characters allowed for a single subscript
        (typically 31 characters)

(3)   The maximum number of characters allowed for a variable name
        plus multiple subscripts (63 characters in our implementation).

9.   Nodes may be created "automatically" by MUMPS in order to "fill in" the tree structure of an array. For example, ^NAME is created automatically when we SET ^NAME(NAM)=""; ^NAME(1) is created automatically when we SET ^NAME(1,2)= "SMITH, ROBERT".

Nodes created "automatically" in this manner are considered to have no data.

THE $ORDER FUNCTION

AN INTRODUCTION TO $ORDER

10.   Remember how in Chapter Six, we displayed global arrays with numeric subscripts, by using a FOR loop incremented by one? What will happen if we run CH6EX9 on our ^NAME array, now that we have added a few string subscripts?

This program will not print the nodes with string subscripts!

A FOR loop incremented by one will NOT display our global array with string subscripts!

11.   You can display global arrays with string subscripts via:

(1)   The global display utility program for your implementation

(2)   The $ORDER function.

12.   We can depict our ^NAME array, which now contains both numeric subscripts and string subscripts, as an inverted tree which has been "turned on its side":

```
                <^ NAME (1) =
                <^ NAME (2) =
                <^ NAME (3) =
                <^ NAME (4) =
^NAME  -  <^ NAME ("BEETHOVEN,  LUDWIG") =
                <^ NAME ("BUNYAN,  JOHN") =
                <^ NAME ("CEASAR,) JULIUS") =
                <^ NAME ("CHURCHILL,  WINSTON") =
                <^ NAME ("ZIGGY PIG") =
```

This array, like most of the arrays we have created so far, has only one level of subscripting.

13.   The $ORDER function examines subscripts at a specified level of a specified array, and returns the next subscripts at this level.

Performing $ORDER on a null subscript at a specified level returns the first subscript at that level.

Performing $ORDER on the last subscript at a specified level returns null.

Using the array in frame 12:

$ORDER (^ NAME (""))	returns 1
$ORDER (^ NAME (1))	returns 2
$ORDER (^ NAME (2))	returns 3
$ORDER (^ NAME (3))	returns 4
$ORDER (^ NAME (4))	returns BEETHOVEN, LUDWIG
$ORDER (^ NAME ("BEETHOVEN, LUDWIG"))	returns BUNYAN, JOHN
$ORDER (^ NAME ("BUNYAN, JOHN"))	returns CAESAR, JULIUS
$ORDER (^ NAME ("CAESAR, JULIUS"))	returns CHURCHILL, WINSTON
$ORDER (^ NAME ("CHURCHILL, WINSTON"))	returns ZIGGY PIG
$ORDER (^ NAME ("ZIGGY PIG"))	returns ""

Note that $ORDER returns the next subscript - rather than the contents of the node.

14.   How can we express the concept depicted in Frame 13 as MUMPS code? Here is one approach:

```
CH8EX2 ; DISPLAY NAME ARRAY WITH MIXED NUMERIC AND STRING SUBSCRIPTS
       ; INITIAL INTRODUCTION TO $ORDER FUNCTION
       ;
       W !!,"SUBSCRIPT",?30,"CONTENTS OF  GLOBAL NODE",!!
       S A1=""
LOOP   S A2=$ORDER(^NAME(A1))
       I A2'="" W !,A2,?30,^NAME(A2) S A1=A2 G LOOP
       W !!,"Finished" Q
```

How would you "translate" lines CH8EX2+4 thru LOOP+1?

line CH8EX2+4	sets the simple variable A1 equal to null
line LOOP	sets the simple variable equal to the next subscript after the current value of A1. The first time this line is executed, it will return the first subscript for NAME.
line LOOP+1	examines the subscript returned by $ORDER. If this subscript is NOT equal to null, we WRITE the value of A2, tab to column 30, WRITE the value of ^NAME(A2), SET the value of A1 equal to A2, and GOTO LOOP

The first time through our LOOP module, A2 will be equal to 1. After we SET A1 = A2, then the second iteration of our LOOP module will return the second subscript.

15.   Here is a slightly different version of the same program:

```
CH8EX3 ;  SECOND EXAMPLE OF $ORDER FUNCTION
       ;
       W !!,"SUBSCRIPT",?30,"CONTENTS OF GLOBAL NODE",!!
       S A=""
LOOP   S A=$ORDER(^NAME(A))
       I A'="" W !,A,?30,^NAME(A)  G LOOP
       W !!,"Finished" Q
```

Remember in our adding machine program how we would SET SUM = SUM + N? With our SET command, we can use the same variable on both sides of our equals sign! The "old" value of our variable is on the right of our equals sign; the "new" value is created to the left of our equals sign.

Therefore, we really do not need the two separate variables A1 and A2. Our program CH8EX3 is identical in function to CH8EX2.

Of course, our variable name is irrelevant. As a "convention", we like to use A as the $ORDER variable at our first level of subscripting, B as the $ORDER variable at our second level, and so on.

16.   Remember how we've used FOR loops in place of GOTO loops? We can simplify CH8EX3 as follows:

```
CH8EX3 ; DISPLAY NAME ARRAY WITH MIXED NUMERIC AND STRING SUBSCRIPTS
       ; THIS PROGRAM USES FOR LOOP TO REPLACE GOTO LOOP
       ;
       W !!,"SUBSCRIPT",?30,"CONTENTS OF GLOBAL NODE",!!
       S A=""
       F INDEX=0:0 S A=$ORDER(^NAME(A)) Q:A=""  W !,A,?30,^NAME(A)
       Q
```

This FOR loop is considerably shorter than the code used in CH8EX2!

17.   How would you "translate" lines CH8EX3+4 and CH8EX3+5?

---

line CH8EX3+4:   SET the simple variable A equal to a null value

line CH8EX3+5:   SET the simple variable A equal to the value returned by $ORDER for ^NAME(A). If the value of A is null, drop out of the FOR loop. Otherwise, WRITE the values for A and ^NAME(A), and resume the FOR loop

SUBSCRIPT SEQUENCE FOR $ORDER

18.   Frames 12 and 13 both depict a "mixed array", containing numeric as well as string subscripts. Notice the sequence: numeric subscripts appear first, in numeric order, followed by string subscripts, in alphabetic order. Standard MUMPS "automatically" sorts your local or global array, in a specific subscript sequence. This subscript sequence is then used by $ORDER. The sequence used in your global display utility program may be similar - but is implementation specific.

19.   Let's consider the subscript sequence used by $ORDER more closely. The concept of "numeric subscripts in numeric order, followed by string subscripts in alpha order" seems simple.

But in some cases, we may have several different numeric subscripts - all with the same numeric value. For example:

```
  11
 +11
 011
 11.00
```

could be different subscripts - with the same numeric value.

Likewise:

```
    . 1
  0. 1
  0. 10
  +. 1
```

could be different subscripts - with the same numeric value.

20.   Standard MUMPS recognizes three types of numbers:

   (a)   Positive vs negative - for example 4 vs -4

   (b)   Integer vs non-integer - for example 4 vs 4.2

   (c)   Canonic vs non-canonic - for example:

```
   . 4  vs  0. 4
   . 4  vs  . 40
     1  vs  001
    10  vs  10. 0
  -. 4  vs  -0. 40
  +. 4  vs  +0. 40
   1. 2 vs  1. 20
```

A "canonic number" has no non-significant leading zeros or trailing zeros after a decimal point. Thus, the left hand numbers above are "canonic" - while the right hand numbers are "non-canonic".

21.   A canonic number may be:

   ●   positive or negative

   ●   an integer (whole number) or a non-integer (decimal fraction).

22.   Check your user manual to determine whether your system allows:

   ●   negative subscripts

   ●   non-integer subscripts (decimal subscripts).

Our implementation allows both negative subscripts and non-integer subscripts. We will use both in the examples which follow. If your implementation does NOT allow these, you should omit or modify these examples.

23.   The "collating sequence" in Standard MUMPS is:

   (1)   canonic numbers

   (2)   followed by all other subscripts in string order.

24.   We can think of "string order" as identical to "alphabetic order" for the ASCII character set. The ASCII character set is depicted in Table I. Each ASCII character has a code.

TABLE I

CODE	CHARACTER	CODE	CHARACTER	CODE	CHARACTER	CODE	CHARACTER
0	NUL	32	SP	64	@	96	`
1	SOH	33	!	65	A	97	a
2	STX	34	"	66	B	98	b
3	ETX	35	#	67	C	99	c
4	EOT	36	$	68	D	100	d
5	ENQ	37	%	69	E	101	e
6	ACK	38	&	70	F	102	f
7	BEL	39	'	71	G	103	g
8	BS	40	(	72	H	104	h
9	HT	41	)	73	I	105	i
10	LF	42	*	74	J	106	j
11	VT	43	+	75	K	107	k
12	FF	44	,	76	L	108	l
13	CR	45	−	77	M	109	m
14	SO	46	.	78	N	110	n
15	SI	47	/	79	O	111	o
16	DLE	48	0	80	P	112	p
17	DC1	49	1	81	Q	113	q
18	DC2	50	2	82	R	114	r
19	DC3	51	3	83	S	115	s
20	DC4	52	4	84	T	116	t
21	NAK	53	5	85	U	117	u
22	SYN	54	6	86	V	118	v
23	ETB	55	7	87	W	119	w
24	CAN	56	8	88	X	120	x
25	EM	57	9	89	Y	121	y
26	SUB	58	:	90	Z	122	z
27	ESC	59	;	91	[	123	{
28	FS	60	<	92	\	124		
29	GS	61	=	93	]	125	}
30	RS	62	>	94	^	126	~
31	US	63	?	95	_	127	DEL

The first 31 characters are "non-printable". Character 32 is a "space"; characters 33-126 are "standard" printable characters; character 127 represents "delete".

25. Here is a subscript sequence, as listed by our implementation of Standard MUMPS:

-20.6	.1	02
-20	1	022
-15	1.2	1.0
-4	2	30.0
-.5	2.5	6.0

In the first group, the five subscripts are negative canonic numbers, and appear in true numeric order. For our implementation of Standard MUMPS, negative subscripts collate in "true numeric order" prior to positive subscripts. Notice that non-integers are allowed as negative numbers. Your implementation may handle negative subscripts differently. We recommend that you avoid negative subscripts, unless there is a definite reason to use them.

The second five subscripts are positive canonic numbers and appear in true numeric order. Notice that decimal numbers collate in "true numeric order" regardless of whether the value is positive or negative.

The third group of five subscripts are non-canonic numbers, returned in "string sequence". Compare this order with the ASCII collating sequence in Table I. Notice that string order is comparable to "alphabetic order" - where our "alphabetic sequence" is represented by the ASCII collating sequence.

For some implementations of Standard MUMPS:

(1)   negative subscripts may collate in "string order" rather than "true numeric order"

(2)   non-integer subscripts (decimal numbers) may collate in "string order" rather than "true numeric order".

26.   Remember those last five non-canonic numbers from frame 25? Here is a sequence of subscripts in "string order":

                    0.9
                    0.90
                00748
                032
                06
                06.0
                    1.0
                    1.00
                    1.000
                100.0
            1000.0
                    2.0
                    2.00

```
200.0
  3.0
 30.0
  A
  AA
  AAA
  AAB
  B
  B1
  B2
  BA
  Z
  Z1
  Z9
  ZA
  a
  aA
  aa
  b
  b1
  bAZ
  bZ
  ba
  baA
  c
```

Carefully study this sequence. Compare this order with the ASCII collating sequence in Table I. What conclusion can you draw?

String order, or "ASCII string sequence", is comparable to an "alphabetic order" - in which our "alphabetic sequence" is represented by the ASCII collating sequence.

27. The Standard MUMPS subscript sequence is canonic numbers, followed by string subscripts in string order. "String order" implies non-canonic numbers followed by alpha characters in the ASCII collating sequence.

When you use non-canonic numbers (such as ZIP codes with leading zeros) as subscripts, they will appear in string order, rather than true numeric order. And when you use "mixed" upper and lower case characters as alpha subscripts, an upper case "Z" will collate before a lower case "a".

THE $NEXT FUNCTION

28.   The $NEXT function works exactly like $ORDER, except that $NEXT:

- starts with -1 (rather than "") as an initial value to return the first subscript at a specific level

- returns -1 (rather than "") after the last subscript found at a specific level.

29.   Here is an example of $NEXT used to display our ^NAME array:

```
CH8EX4 ; DISPLAY ^NAME ARRAY WITH $NEXT
       ;
       W !!,"SUBSCRIPT",?30,"CONTENTS OF GLOBAL NODE",!!
       S A=-1
LOOP   S A=$NEXT(^NAME(A))
       I A'<0 W !,A,?30,^NAME(A)  G LOOP
       W !!,"Finished " Q
```

30.   Rather than "A", we could use any name for the $NEXT variable in this program. We personally prefer "A" to indicate the first level of a global array, "B" to indicate the second level, "C" to indicate the third level, and so on.

31.   Is line CH8EX4+3 really needed? Yes! When using $NEXT to search an array, we begin by setting the $NEXT variable equal to -1, to ensure that the value retrieved by $NEXT will be the very first subscript.

32.   What if we wanted to display only these names beginning with "B"? Write the code to do this with $NEXT:

_____

Here's how we did it:

```
CH8EX5 ; DISPLAY PORTION OF NAME ARRAY WITH $NEXT
       ;
       W !!,"SUBSCRIPT",?30,"CONTENTS OF GLOBAL NODE",!!
       S A="AZZZ"
LOOP   S A=$NEXT(^NAME(A))
       I A?1"B".E D DISPLAY G LOOP
       W !!,"Finished" Q
       ;
DISPLAY W !,A,?30,^NAME(A)  Q
```

33.   Revise CH8EX5 to search the ^NAME array using $ORDER, and a FOR loop. Display only those names beginning with "V".

```
CH8EX6 ;  SEARCH ^NAME ARRAY WITH $ORDER
       ;  DISPLAY ONLY THOSE NAMES BEGINNING WITH "V"
       ;
       S  A="UZZZZ"
       F  INDEX=0:0  S  A=$ORDER(^NAME(A))  Q:A'?1"V".E   W  !,A,?30,^NAME(A)
       W  !!,"Finished"  Q
```

34.   We can build an array with string subscripts using an open-ended FOR loop incremented by zero.

We can search this same array with an open-ended FOR loop incremented by zero. Each time through the loop, $ORDER or $NEXT returns the next subscript for the previous value of A.

35.   What would happen if we use the following program to display our array:

```
CH8EX7 ;  DISPLAY ^NAME ARRAY WITH $ORDER
       ;
       S  PUSSYCAT=""
       F  J=0:0  S  PUSSYCAT=$ORDER(^NAME(PUSSYCAT))  Q:PUSSYCAT=""   D  PRINT
       W  !!,"Finished"  Q
       ;
PRINT  W  !,PUSSYCAT,?30,^NAME(PUSSYCAT)  Q
```

This program would run just fine! Try it and see!

36.   When we search an array using $ORDER or $NEXT, we can use any name we want for our subscript variable, so long as we specify the correct name for our global - in this case ^NAME. MUMPS finds the correct place to start with $ORDER or $NEXT by the global name, ^NAME, plus the position of PUSSYCAT as a first level subscript. The "temporary name" used for our first level subscript is irrelevant. The code in CH8EX7 + 3 uses the current VALUE of "PUSSYCAT" - NOT the "name" of this variable.

NEGATIVE SUBSCRIPTS

37.   Here is an array with numeric subscripts starting at -10:

```
                        <^NAME  (-10)
                        <^NAME  (-9)
                        <^NAME  (-1)
            NAME  -     <^NAME  (0)
                        <^NAME  (1)
                        <^NAME  (6)
                        <^NAME  (20)
```

What would happen if we tried to search this array with the following FOR loop:

```
    F INDEX=-10:1:20 W !,^NAME(INDEX)
```

Our FOR loop would stop, and we would see an error message, since ^NAME(-8) is un-defined.

38.   If we have an array with one or several array elements missing, we should search this array using $NEXT or $ORDER, rather than a FOR loop incremented by one.

39.   In the above array, what subscripts would be returned by the following line of code:

```
    S A=-1
    F J=0:0 S A=$NEXT(^NAME(A)) Q:A=-1   W !,A
    W !,"Finished" Q
```

---

            0 thru 20

We would miss all the negative subscripts - since we started with A = -1!

40.   What would happen if we started with SET A = -100?

We would QUIT the FOR loop after $NEXT returned the first two subscripts: -10 and -9.

41.   We cannot search this particular array with $NEXT. But we can search and print this array with $ORDER, starting with: SET A = " ".

42.   If you have an array with only numeric subscripts, and you are certain there is no gap in the sequence, you can search this with a FOR loop incremented by one.

If you have an array with mixed string and numeric subscripts, and you are certain there are no numeric subscripts with negative numbers, you can search this with $NEXT.

If you have an array with mixed string and numeric subscripts where some numeric subscripts may have negative values, use $ORDER. We suggest that you always use $ORDER to avoid potential problems!

43.   Different implementations of MUMPS may handle negative numeric subscripts somewhat differently.

Some implementations do not allow negative numeric subscripts.

Some implementations allow negative numeric subscripts, but return them in "string order", rather than in true numeric order.

The following negative subscripts appear in "string order":

$$-1$$
$$-120$$
$$-20$$
$$-300$$

The following negative subscripts appear in true numeric order:

$$-300$$
$$-120$$
$$-20$$
$$-1$$

44.   Here is some code that you can use to check whether your implementation returns negative subscripts in true numeric order.

```
CH8EX8  S  ^Z(-300)="",^Z(-20)="",^Z(-1)="",^Z(0)="",^Z(-120)=""
        S  A=""
        F  INDEX=0:0 S A=$ORDER(^Z(A)) Q:A=""  W !,A
        W !!,"Finished" Q
```

If your implementation accepts negative subscripts and returns these in true numeric order, CH8EX8 will return:

$$-300$$
$$-120$$
$$-20$$
$$-1$$
$$0$$

As a general rule, we recommend that you avoid using negative subscripts unless:

(1)   Your implementation allows negative subscripts and returns them in true numeric order, and

(2)   You really need to use negative subscripts for a specific application.

POTENTIAL PROBLEMS WITH STRING SUBSCRIPTS

45.   Here is our original routine to build a name file with string subscripts:

```
CH8EX1 ; NAME FILE WITH STRING SUBSCRIPTS
         ;
         F INDEX=0:0 D ENTRY Q:NAM=""
         W !!,"Finished" Q
         ;
ENTRY    R !,"Enter name: ",NAM
         I NAM="" Q
         I NAM'?1A.E W !,"NAME MUST BEGIN WITH ALPHA CHARACTER" G ENTRY
         R !,"Enter address and phone: ",DATA
         S ^NAME(NAM)=DATA
         Q
```

46.   Use your global display utility program or CH8EX3 to display your ^NAME file. If there is a node with the string subscript SMITH, JOHN in your ^NAME array, KILL this node. Or, if you prefer, you may KILL your entire ^NAME array.

47.   Use CH8EX1 to make the following entries in your ^NAME global:

        SMITH, JOHN, 123 PERCY PLACE, 111-111-1111

        SMITH, JOHN, 204 WALNUT STREET, 222-222-2222

        SMITH, JOHN, 999 MAPLE STREET, 333-333-3333

48.   Now use either your global display utility program or CH8EX3 to display your ^NAME global. What happens?

There is only one "SMITH, JOHN" in our file! Each time through the FOR loop, our final SET command in CH8EX1 considered ^NAME("SMITH, JOHN") as a single subscripted variable - rather than three separate entries!

To avoid problems with string subscripts, every node in your array must be identified by a unique set of alpha characters!

49.   String subscripts allow us to display arrays in alphabetic order via $ORDER.

However, if we enter two different items with the same string subscript, new data will overwrite old!

Some solutions to this problem will be described in the next chapter.

SUMMARY OF NEW CONCEPTS - CHAPTER 8

String Subscripts - alpha string subscripts (as well as decimal subscripts) provided by most implementations of Standard MUMPS

- arrays typically created via FOR loop incremented by zero.

$ORDER function - used to display global arrays with string or numeric subscripts using null string as the starting and default values.

Example:

```
S  A=""
F  INDEX=0:0  S A=$ORDER(^NAME(A))  Q:A=""   W !,A,?30,^NAME(A)
```

- "canonic numbers" have no non-significant leading zeros or trailing zeros after a decimal point. For example:

.4 vs 0.4
.4 vs .40

- collating sequence for $ORDER is canonic numbers in true numeric sequence followed by non-canonic numbers and alpha characters in string order.

- "string order" is analogous to "alphabetic order" using the ASCII character set.

- some implementations treat negative numbers, numbers preceded by " + " and non-integers (decimals) as non-canonic numbers (see your user manual for information).

$NEXT function - operates in same manner as $ORDER, using "-1" in place of null string.

- use $ORDER rather than $NEXT with negative subscripts

- may begin $NEXT (or $ORDER) at any starting point within array, and either QUIT or DO display module on pattern match.

Potential problems with string subscripts - if two different entries use the same string subscript, new data will overwrite old.

CHAPTER NINE

CROSS REFERENCE FILES

In the previous chapter, we created and displayed global arrays with string subscripts. We used $ORDER to display our array elements with canonic number subscripts in true numeric order, followed by non-canonic number and string subscripts in "string order".

For a global array with string subscripts, if we use the same string subscript for two different entries, new data will overwrite old. This has the same effect as saving two different programs under the same name on disk.

In this chapter, we will demonstrate two different methods for avoiding problems with identical string subscripts.

Topics include:

- using second-level subscripts as unique identifiers

- building cross reference files from a primary file

- building combined global files (primary and cross reference files combined in the same global)

- checking new entries against existing data.

By the end of this chapter you will be able to:

- use "second level subscripts" as unique identifiers

- display data from a file which uses second level subscripts as unique identifiers

- build cross reference files from a primary file with numeric subscripts

- build cross reference files at the same time as you build a primary file

- build combined global files, which provide numeric subscripts for your primary file, and string subscripts for your cross reference files

- use cross reference files to display data from your primary file

- use a cross reference file to automatically display data on previous entries with the same "name" as a new entry in your primary file.

Before continuing with this chapter, we recommend you KILL the ^NAME global created in Chapter Eight. As an alternative, you may create a global array such as ^NAME1 or ^NAMECH9.

SECOND LEVEL SUBSCRIPTS AS UNIQUE IDENTIFIERS

1.   One way to solve our problem with identical string subscripts is to use second level subscripts as unique identifiers. In this example, the second level numeric subscripts provide unique identifiers:

```
                                    <^NAME("A",1)=DATA
                    <^NAME("A")  - <
^NAME  - <          .           <^NAME("A",n)=DATA
          <         .
          <         .
          <         .
          <^NAME("ZZZ")
```

Our data is stored at the second level of subscripting. With three people named SMITH, JOHN, we will see:

```
          <^NAME("A")
          <                           <^NAME("SMITH, JOHN",1)=DATA 1
^NAME  - <^NAME("SMITH, JOHN") -<^NAME("SMITH, JOHN",2)=DATA 2
          <                           <^NAME("SMITH, JOHN",3)=DATA 3
          <^NAME("ZZZ")
```

---

2.   The string subscripts at the first level ensure that our file will be sorted in alpha order. Numeric subscripts at the second level provide unique identifiers for each entry within a given string subscript.

The data for each record is stored at the second level of subscripting. There is no data stored at the first level.

3.   Where might we store the next available numeric subscript for a fourth person with the name "SMITH, JOHN"?

One option is the contents of ˷NAME("SMITH, JOHN")

A second option is the contents of ˷NAME("SMITH, JOHN",0)

We prefer the first option. We have already used this to build files with sequential numeric subscripts.

4.   What steps are needed to build this file?

_____

(1)   Use an open-ended FOR loop incremented by zero to read a name into a simple variable such as NAM:

• QUIT if NAM equals a null entry

• then DO an entry module.

(2)   Within the entry module:

• IF $DATA of NAME(NAM) returns zero, set NAME(NAM) equal to one

• SET SUB (the number for our next second level subscript) equal to NAME(NAM)

• READ address and phone into a simple variable such as DATA

• SET NAME(NAM,SUB) equal to DATA

• SET NAME(NAM) equal to SUB+1 and then QUIT.

5.   Now, write the code to perform these functions.

_____

Here's how we did it:

```
CH9EX1  ;  BUILD NAME FILE WITH TWO LEVELS OF SUBSCRIPTING
        ;
        F J1=0:0 R !,"Name: ",NAM Q:NAM=""  D MOD1
        W !!,"Finished" K  Q
        ;
MOD1    I '$D(^NAME(NAM))  S ^NAME(NAM)=1
        S SUB=^NAME(NAM)
        R !,"Address & phone: ",DATA
        S ^NAME(NAM,SUB)=DATA
        S ^NAME(NAM)=SUB+1
        Q
```

6. What functions are performed by each line of code in CH9EX1?

Line CH9EX1 + 2:

>   reads name into the simple variable NAM, quits if NAM is a null entry, and does MOD1.

Line CH9EX1 + 3:

>   writes 'Finished', KILLS all local variables and quits. It is common practice to KILL all local variables at the end of a program - however, this is not really necessary.

Line MOD1:

>   sets ˄NAME(NAM) equal to 1, if this node does not already exist.

Line MOD1 + 1:

>   sets SUB equal to ˄NAME(NAM).

Line MOD1 + 2:

>   reads address and phone into the simple variable DATA.

Line MOD1 + 3:

>   sets NAME(NAM,SUB) equal to DATA.

Line MOD1 + 4:

>   sets ˄NAME(NAM) equal to SUB + 1.

Line MOD1 + 5:

>   quits MOD1.

170

Enter this program into your terminal, and practice using it until you feel "comfortable" with this code, and how the program operates.

7.   Now that we've written a program to build our file at two levels, how can we print names in alphabetic order from this two level array?

Look at the diagram in Frame 1. What operations must be performed?

___

(1)   Use a FOR loop incremented by zero with $ORDER to go through

subscripts at the first level.

(2)   DO a second FOR loop incremented by one, from one to the value of

ˆNAME (NAM) -1.

(3)   WRITE the value of the first level subscript, and the contents of

ˏNAME(NAM,J) (assume J is your second FOR loop variable).

8.   Now write the code for this program as CH9EX2

___

```
CH9EX2 ; DISPLAY NAME FILE WITH TWO LEVELS OF SUBSCRIPTING
       ; THIS PROGRAM CAN BE USED WITH THE FILE CREATED BY CH9EX1
       ;
       K   S A=""
       F INDEX=0:0 S A=$O(ˆNAME(A))  Q:A=""   D LEVEL2
       W !!,"Finished" K   Q
       ;
LEVEL2 S END=ˆNAME(A)-1
       F J=1:1:END W !,A,?40,ˆNAME(A,J)
       Q
```

BUILDING CROSS REFERENCE FILES FROM A PRIMARY FILE

9.   Remember our original global array with numeric subscripts from Chapters 6 and 7? We can compare this type of global array with numeric subscripts to a file of "reference cards" where each new reference card "automatically" receives a numeric accession number - corresponding to a numeric subscript. We can depict the layout of such a card as Figure 9-1. At the "name and subscript level", we have a global name and unique numeric subscript. At the "data level", we have multiple "pieces".

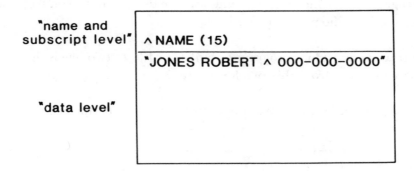

FIGURE 9-1. A GLOBAL NODE WITH NUMERIC SUBSCRIPT

10.   Remember our global array with string subscripts from Chapter Eight? We can compare this type of global array with string subscripts to a file of "reference cards" with the layout illustrated in Figure 9-2.

In Figure 9-2, if we create a second card with the subscript at the "name and subscript level", new data will overwrite our old data at the "data level".

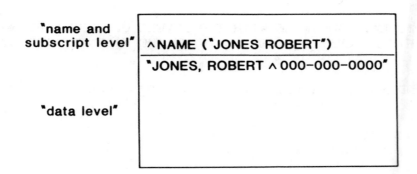

FIGURE 9-2. A GLOBAL NODE WITH STRING SUBSCRIPT

11.   Our program CH9EX1 solved this problem with a "second level of subscripting". This is depicted in Figure 9-3.

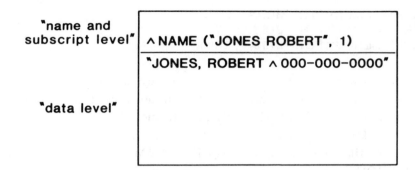

FIGURE 9-3. A GLOBAL NODE WITH TWO LEVELS OF SUBSCRIPTING: STRING AND NUMERIC SUBSCRIPTS

12. A different approach would be to maintain two files:

● a "primary file" by accession number, as shown in Figure 9-1

● a "cross reference file", where our "second level of subscripting" is the unique accession number in our primary file.

A node within such a cross reference file is depicted in Figure 9-4.

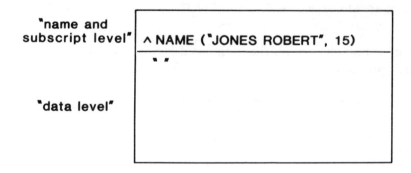

FIGURE 9-4. A GLOBAL NODE IN A CROSS REFERENCE FILE

Within the cross reference file, our second subscript serves as a "pointer" to the primary file, which is ordered by accession number. For a NAME file with three entries "SMITH, JOHN", our cross reference file might have:

```
^XREFNAME ("SMITH,   JOHN", 26)
^XREFNAME ("SMITH,   JOHN", 37)
^XREFNAME ("SMITH,   JOHN", 109)
```

The second level subscripts in our cross reference file are identical to the first level numeric subscripts in our primary file (e.g. Figure 9-1). Within our cross reference file, we use these second level numeric subscripts to identify specific nodes within our primary file. For ^XREFNAME ("SMITH, JOHN",26), the second level subscript refers us to numeric subscript #26 in our primary file. Within our primary file, ^NAME(26) contains information on a specific "SMITH, JOHN". In Figure 9-4, notice that nothing is stored at the "data level".

13.   Here is a diagram corresponding to the file structure implied by Figure 9-4:

```
         <NAME (1)=data                    <XNAME ("AAA", n) =""
         <    .                            <    .
^NAME-<       .                   ^XNAME-<      .
         <    .                            <    .
         <NAME (n)=data                    <XNAME ("ZZZ", nnn) =""
```

We have a primary file with one level of numeric subscripts, plus a cross reference file with two levels of subscripting.

To search the first level of our cross reference file, we will need $ORDER for use with string subscripts.

To search the second level of our cross reference file, we again need $ORDER, since the numeric subscript(s) at our second level will NOT be in sequential order.

14.   Assume we have a primary file, organized in order of accession number. Here is the structure of this primary file:

```
         <NAME (1)=concatenated data
         <    .
         <    .
^NAME-<       .
         <    .
         <    .
         <NAME (n)
```

Assume that:

(1)   the next available numeric subscript is stored at the first level of subscripting as contents of ^NAME.

(2)   Contents at first level are concatenated data with "ᐱ" as delimiter:

piece #1 = name
piece #2 = street address
piece #3 = town
piece #4 = state (two initials)
piece #5 = zip code
piece #6 = phone (format 000-000-0000)

15.   At this point, we suggest that you KILL the ᐱNAME global built from CH9EX1. Alternatively, you may want to think of a new global name for the next series of exercises in this chapter.

Use CH7EX2 to build the primary file depicted in Frame 14. About 6 to 12 entries should be sufficient. Enter names in the format: "SMITH, JOHN H". Now, see if you can write a program which will go through our primary file, and create a cross reference file with the following structure:

```
                              <XNAME ("AAA", nnn)
              <XNAME ("AAA") -<         .
              <          .        <          .
<XNAME -<         .
              <          .
              <XNAME ("ZZZ")
```

Assume that:

(1)   First level string subscripts will be named in format SMITH, JOHN H.

(2)   Second level numeric subscripts correspond to first level subscripts in primary file.

(3)   No data (null) is stored as values for the nodes in this cross reference file.

Here's how we did it:

```
CH9EX3 ; BUILD CROSS REFERENCE FILE ORGANIZED BY NAME FROM PRIMARY FILE
       ;
       S END=^NAME-1 W !,"STARTING TO CREATE CROSS REFERENCE FILE ^XNAME"
       F J=1:1:END S DATA=^NAME(J) S NAM=$P(DATA,"^",1) S ^XNAME(NAM,J)=""
       W !!,"CREATION OF CROSS REFERENCE FILE ^XNAME COMPLETED" Q
```

16.   Describe in words what is accomplished by each line of code in Frame 16.

Line CH9EX3 + 2 obtains the last numeric subscript in our primary file, and displays a message to let the user know the program is running.

Line CH9EX3 + 3 obtains content for each subscripted node within our primary file, obtains the first piece from each node within our primary file, and creates our cross reference file. The following nodes of our cross reference file are created "automatically": ^XNAME, and ^XNAME(NAM).

Line CH9EX3 + 4 displays a message to let the user know the cross reference file has been created.

17.   What would happen if we tried to run this program, after deleting a single node within our primary file? This might happen if we used the KILL command to delete an entry.

_____

Our FOR loop would stop with an error message when we encountered the "missing numeric subscript" causing a "gap in the sequence" within our primary file.

18.   How could we solve this problem, created by a "missing node" in our primary file?

_____

We could use $ORDER to build our cross reference file.

19.   Now write a revised program to build our cross reference file.

_____

Here's how we did it:

```
CH9EX4  ; BUILD CROSS REFERENCE FILE ORGANIZED BY NAME FROM PRIMARY FILE
        ;
        K  W !!,"STARTING TO CREATE CROSS REFERENCE FILE" S A=""
        F J=0:0 S A=$O(^NAME(A)) Q:A=""  D MOD
        W !!,"CREATION OF CROSS REFERENCE FILE COMPLETED" Q
        ;
MOD     S DATA=^NAME(A)
        S NAM=$P(DATA,"^",1)
        S ^XNAME(NAM,A)=""
        Q
```

20.   Run this program. Use your global display utility to confirm that you really have built the array XNAME.

21.   Now write the code to print name and phone number in alphabetic order from our primary file. Before running this program, be sure to run either CH9EX3 or CH9EX4 so you will have built your cross reference file!

Here's how we did it:

```
CH9EX5  ;  PRINT NAME AND PHONE NUMBER FROM PRIMARY FILE ^NAME
        ;  THIS PROGRAM REQUIRES USE OF CH9EX3 OR CH9EX4 TO BUILD
        ;  THE ^XNAME CROSS REFERENCE FILE
        ;
        K  W !!,"NAME",?40,"PHONE NUMBER",!!
        S  A=""
        F  J1=0:0 S A=$O(^XNAME(A)) Q:A=""  D MOD
        W  !!,"Finished" Q
        ;
MOD     S  B=""
        F  J2=0:0 S B=$O(^XNAME(A,B)) Q:B=""  D PRINT
        Q
        ;
PRINT   S  DATA=^NAME(B)
        W  !,$P(DATA,"^",1),?40,$P(DATA,"^",6)
        Q
```

22.   Now that we have printed name and phone number in alpha order by name - what should we do with our cross reference file ˄XNAME? Options include:

(1)   KILL ˄XNAME - and rebuild this cross reference file if we need it again at future date.

(2)   Modify the program which builds our primary file, so this automatically "updates" our cross reference file when we add a new entry.

If we plan to frequently print our primary file in alphabetic order by name, it is better NOT to KILL our ˄XNAME global. Instead, we should modify the program which builds our primary file, so this automatically "updates" our cross reference file when we add a new entry in our primary file.

If our ˄NAME file has thousands of records, it might take an hour or longer to rebuild our ˄XNAME global. In this case, if you anticipate even an infrequent future need to display the primary file in alpha order by name, it is better NOT to KILL the ˄XNAME global. The cost of keeping your cross reference file on disk may be relatively low, compared to the cost of "delay" while the data is not available in alphabetic order.

BUILDING COMBINED GLOBAL FILES (PRIMARY AND CROSS REFERENCE FILES IN THE SAME GLOBAL)

23.   Modify CH7EX2 to "automatically" update the ^XNAME global with every new entry to your primary file.

Here's how we did it:

```
CH9EX6  ;  CREATE PRIMARY FILE WITH NUMERIC SUBSCRIPTS AS UNIQUE IDENTIFIERS
        ;  AND CROSS REFERENCE FILE WITH STRING SUBSCRIPTS
        ;
        I '$D(^NAME) S ^NAME=1
        S START=^NAME
        F INDEX=START:1 R !,"Name: ",NAM Q:NAM=""  D ENTRY
        W !!,"Finished" S ^NAME=INDEX Q
        ;
ENTRY   R !,"Enter street address: ",ST
        R !,"Enter town: ",TWN
ENTRY1  R !,"Enter state (two initials): ",STATE I STATE'?2A D ERR1 G ENTRY1
ENTRY2  R !,"Enter zip code: ",ZIP I ZIP'?5N D ERR2 G ENTRY2
ENTRY3  R !,"Enter phone: ",PHONE I PHONE'?3N1"-"3N1"-"4N D ERR3 G ENTRY3
        S ^NAME(INDEX)=NAM_"^"_ST_"^"_TWN_"^"_STATE_"^"_ZIP_"^"_PHONE
        S ^XNAME(NAM,INDEX)=""
        Q
        ;
ERR1    W !,"Please enter two initials for name of state" Q
ERR2    W !,"Please enter five number for zip code" Q
ERR3    W !,"Please enter phone number in the format nnn-nnn-nnnn" Q
```

24.   This program is identical to CH7EX2, except we have added a single line of code (ENTRY3 + 2) to create our cross reference file.

This line of code - S ^XNAME(NAM,INDEX) = " " - is all we need to create our cross reference file.

25.   Now write a program to print name and phone number from the primary file in alphabetic order by name.

Here's how we did it:

```
CH9EX7  ;  DISPLAY PRIMARY FILE IN ALPHA ORDER VIA
        ;  CROSS REFERENCE FILE WITH STRING SUBSCRIPTS
        ;
```

```
              W  !!,"NAME",?30,"PHONE",!!
              S  A=""
              F  J1=0:0  S  A=$O(^XNAME(A))  Q:A=""    D  MOD
              W  !!,"Finished"Q
              ;
MOD           S  B=""
              F  J2=0:0  S  B=$O(^XNAME(A,B))  Q:B=""   D  PRINT
              Q
              ;
PRINT         S  DATA=^NAME(B)
              W  !,$P(DATA,"^",1),?30,$P(DATA,"^",6)
              Q
```

First, we use two FOR loops with $ORDER to obtain a second level subscript from our cross reference file. Then, we DO a PRINT module to display the first and sixth "pieces" from our primary file.

BUILDING COMBINED GLOBAL FILES

26.   Remember the examples in Chapter Eight, where we had nodes with numeric subscripts, as well as string subscripts, within the same global? With $ORDER, the canonic number subscripts appeared first, in true numeric order, followed by non-canonic number and string subscripts, in string order.

We can combine our cross reference file and primary file within the same global, by using literal strings as "demarcation subscripts" at the first level. Here is a combined file structure based on previous examples in this chapter:

```
                    <^NAME(1)=concatenated data
                    <    .
                    <    .
        ^NAME-<^NAME(n)
                    <^NAME("A",name,n)=""
                    <    .
                    <^NAME("A",name,nnn)=""
```

This "combined global file" combines a primary file with a cross reference file in the same global. Within this file, we have three types of subscripts at the first level:

- Numeric subscripts assigned by a FOR loop incremented by one, which serve as unique identifiers. Some gaps in the sequence may occur, if we delete one or more nodes via the KILL command.

- The string literal "A" which serves as "demarcation" between the primary file and the cross reference file.

- String subscripts, which provide "automatic sorting" for our cross reference file.

27.   Now, modify the code in CH9EX6 to create the file described in Frame 27.

_____

Here's how we did it:

```
CH9EX8  ;  BUILD COMBINED GLOBAL FILE WITH THREE CROSS REFERENCE FILES
        ;
        I '$D(^NAME) S ^NAME=1
        S START=^NAME
        F INDEX=START:1 R !,"Name: ",NAM Q:NAM=""  D ENTRY
        W !!,"Finished" S ^NAME=INDEX Q
        ;
ENTRY   R !,"Enter street address: ",ST
        R !,"Enter town: ",TWN
ENTRY1  R !,"Enter state (two initials): ",STATE I STATE'?2A D ERR1 G ENTRY1
ENTRY2  R !,"Enter zip code: ",ZIP I ZIP'?5N D ERR2 G ENTRY2
ENTRY3  R !,"Enter phone: ",PHONE I PHONE'?3N1"-"3N1"-"4N D ERR3 G ENTRY3
        S ^NAME(INDEX)=NAM_"^"_ST_"^"_TWN_"^"_STATE_"^"_ZIP_"^"_PHONE
        S ^NAME("A",NAM,INDEX)=""
        Q
        ;
ERR1    W !,"Please enter two initials for name of state" Q
ERR2    W !,"Please enter five number for zip code" Q
ERR3    W !,"Please enter phone number in the format nnn-nnn-nnnn" Q
```

28.   This program is identical to CH9EX6 - except for line ENTRY3 + 2, which creates the cross reference file within our combined global file.

29.   How would you write a program to print name and telephone number from this file, in alphabetic order by name?

It is apparent that we must limit our $ORDER operation to that portion of our "tree" which shares the first level subscript "A" as a "common root". To do this, we could:

(1)   Begin our $ORDER search at the second level of subscripting

(2)   Perform a second $ORDER search at the third level of subscripting

(3)   Use the third level subscript to display data from our primary file.

Try to write this code yourself, before proceeding further.

_____

Here's how we did it:

```
CH9EX9 ; PRINT NAME AND PHONE NUMBER IN ALPHA ORDER BY NAME WITHIN TOWN
```

```
    ; THIS PROGRAM USES THE 'A' CROSS REFERENCE FILE FROM CH9EX8
    ; NAME IS STORED AT THE SECOND LEVEL OF CROSS REFERENCE FILE
    ; PHONE IS PIECE #6 OF PRIMARY FILE
    ;
    S B=""
    F J2=0:0 S B=$O(^NAME("A",B)) Q:B=""  D LEVEL3
    W !!,"Finished" Q
    ;
LEVEL3 S C=""
    F J3=0:0 S C=$O(^NAME("A",B,C)) Q:C=""  W !,B,?40,$P(^NAME(C),"^",6)
    Q
```

Notice that:

(1)   We used "B" as the $ORDER variable at our second level of sub-scripting, and "C" as the $ORDER variable at our third level of subscripting.

(2)   We use the line label "LEVEL3" to denote the level of subscripting operated on by this module.

(3)   We use the FOR loop variables J2 and J3 to denote the level of subscripting operated on by each FOR loop.

Such "conventions" can make your code easier to read - if you use them consistently.

CHECKING NEW ENTRIES AGAINST EXISTING DATA

30.   Imagine that we have 50 or 100 names in our primary file. Each time we start to make a new entry into our file, it would be convenient to:

- display any previous data entered under this name

- allow user to decide whether the proposed entry is really "new" - or go on to another name entry.

What steps would be needed to build a combined global file, and produce this display for each new entry?

Assume that our combined global file has the structure:

```
            <NAME(1)=concatenated data
            <     .
            <     .
    ^NAME-  <NAME(n)
            <NAME("A",name,n)=""
            <     .
            <NAME("A",name,nnn)=""
```

Allow a name entry, and use $D to check whether ⁁NAME("A",NAM) already exists.

If ⁁NAME("A",NAM) already exists, use $ORDER to search the third level of subscripting; then WRITE the contents of ⁁NAME(nnn) from our primary file.

Display a message which allows the user to either: (1) enter new data for a new person with the same name; or (2) go on to another name entry.

31. Try to write your own program before proceeding further.

Here's how we did it:

```
CH9EX10  ;  BUILD COMBINED GLOBAL FILE WITH CROSS REFERENCE BY NAME
         ;  PROGRAM DISPLAYS INFORMATION ON DUPLICATE NAMES AT TIME OF ENTRY
         ;  USER HAS OPTION TO CONSIDER NEW ENTRY UNIQUE OR GO ON TO NEXT
         ;  NAME ENTRY
         ;
         I  '$D(^NAME)  S  ^NAME=1
         S  START=^NAME
         F  INDEX=START:1 S FLAG="OK" R !,"Name: ",NAM Q:NAM=""   D ENTRY
         W  !!,"Finished" S ^NAME=INDEX Q
         ;
ENTRY    I  $D(^NAME("A",NAM)) D DISPLAY
         I  FLAG'="OK" Q
         R  !,"Enter street address: ",ST
         R  !,"Enter town: ",TWN
ENTRY1   R  !,"Enter state (two initials): ",STATE I STATE'?2A D ERR1 G ENTRY1
ENTRY2   R  !,"Enter zip code: ",ZIP I ZIP'?5N D ERR2 G ENTRY2
ENTRY3   R  !,"Enter phone: ",PHONE I PHONE'?3N1"-"3N1"-4N D ERR3 G ENTRY3
         S  ^NAME(INDEX)=NAM_"^"_ST_"^"_TWN_"^"_STATE_"^"_ZIP_"^"_PHONE
         S  ^NAME("A",NAM,INDEX)=""
         Q
         ;
ERR1     W  !,"Please enter two initials for name of state" Q
ERR2     W  !,"Please enter five number for zip code" Q
ERR3     W  !,"Please enter phone number in the format nnn-nnn-nnnn" Q
         ;
DISPLAY  S  C=""
         F  J1=0:0 S C=$O(^NAME("A",NAM,C)) Q:C=""   W !,NAM,?$X+5,^NAME(C)
         R  !,"Do you want to continue with this entry? ",ANS
         I  ANS?1"N".E S FLAG="NOT OK"
         Q
```

32.   What functions are performed by each line of this program?

_____

Line CH9EX10 + 5 initializes ∧NAME the first time this program is run.

Line CH9EX10 + 6 sets the local variable START equal to ∧NAME

Line CH9EX10 + 7 sets the simple variable FLAG equal to "OK", reads NAM, quits if NAM is a null entry, and does ENTRY module.

Line ENTRY does the DISPLAY module, if we already have NAM as a second level subscript in our cross reference file.

Line ENTRY + 1 quits the ENTRY module if FLAG was changed by our DISPLAY module.

Lines ENTRY + 2-ENTRY3 read in data and DO error modules if data is invalid.

Lines ENTRY3 + 1 and ENTRY3 + 2 create new nodes for our primary file and cross reference file.

Lines ERR1-ERR3 display error messages for improper data entries.

Lines DISPLAY and DISPLAY + 1 display the data for all primary file entries having the same second level subscript as NAM.

Line DISPLAY and DISPLAY + 2-3 ask the user whether to continue with this entry. A response of "N" or "NO" sets FLAG to 'NOT OK'. We then return to ENTRY.

33.   If we DO our DISPLAY module from line ENTRY and answer "NO", we lose one numeric subscript in our primary file. We can still continue to build the primary file with our FOR loop incremented by one. But to search numeric subscripts within our primary file, we now must use $ORDER. What would happen if we tried to search our primary file, with a few numeric subscripts missing, via a FOR loop incremented by one?

_____

Our program would stop, with an error message such as "<UNDEF>". Of course, we could decrement our FOR loop variable INDEX within the DISPLAY module on a "NO" answer. However, if you want to search a file with numeric subscripts, where a few numbers may be missing, it's best to use $ORDER!

34.   What changes would be needed in CH9EX10 to display all entries for user approval or disapproval before "filing" as contents of new nodes in our ∧NAME global?

What changes would be needed in CH9EX10 to display "previous data under the same name" without delimiters?

To display all entries for user approval or disapproval, we could modify our first FOR loop:

```
F INDEX=START: 1 S FLAG="OK" R !, "Name": ", NAM Q: NAM=""   D ENTRY, FILE
```

Our FILE module would display all entries, ask whether entries were correct, and then perform the two SET commands from ENTRY3 + 1 and ENTRY3 + 2.

To display "previous data under the same name" without delimiters, we could modify the FOR loop in our DISPLAY module:

```
F J1=0: 0 S C=$O (^NAME ("A", NAM, C))  Q: C=""   D DISPLAY1
```

Our DISPLAY1 module would then use a FOR loop to display each piece of the data stored as "contents" of a node in our primary file.

Thus, the only changes needed in CH9EX10 would be:

CH9EX10 + 7: DO ENTRY,FILE

ENTRY3 + 1 and ENTRY3 + 2: this code would become part of our FILE module

FILE module: to be added

DISPLAY module: to DO DISPLAY1 module with a FOR loop to output the six pieces from our primary file.

35.   Now write CH9EX11 to include these new features.

Here's how we did it:

```
CH9EX11 ; BUILD COMBINED GLOBAL FILE - MODIFICATION OF CH9EX10
        ; CHANGES INCLUDE:
        ;   DISPLAY ALL ENTRIES FOR USER TO APPROVE OR DISAPPROVE BEFORE FILING
        ;   DISPLAY "EXISTING DATA" WITHOUT DELIMITERS
        ;
        I '$D (^NAME) S ^NAME=1
        S START=^NAME
```

```
        F INDEX=START:1 S FLAG="OK" R !,"Name: ",NAM Q:NAM=""
.......D ENTRY,FILE:FLAG= "OK" ; *
        W !!,"Finished" S ^NAME=INDEX Q
        ;
ENTRY   I $D(^NAME("A",NAM)) D DISPLAY
        I FLAG'="OK" Q
        R !,"Enter street address: ",ST
        R !,"Enter town: ",TWN
ENTRY1  R !,"Enter state (two initials): ",STATE I STATE'?2A D ERR1 G ENTRY1
ENTRY2  R !,"Enter zip code: ",ZIP I ZIP'?5N D ERR2 G ENTRY2
ENTRY3  R !,"Enter phone: ",PHONE I PHONE'?3N1"-"3N1"-"4N D ERR3 G ENTRY3
        Q
        ;
ERR1    W !,"Please enter two initials for name of state" Q
ERR2    W !,"Please enter five number for zip code" Q
ERR3    W !,"Please enter phone number in the format nnn-nnn-nnnn" Q
        ;
FILE    W !!,"Name entry = ",?20,NAM              ; *
        W !,"Address entry = ",?20,ST             ; *
        W !,"Town entry = ",?20,TWN               ; *
        W !,"State entry = ",?20,STATE            ; *
        W !,"Zip code entry = ",?20,ZIP           ; *
        W !,"Phone entry = ",?20,PHONE            ; *
        ;
FILE1   R !!,"Are all entries correct? ",ANS                              ; *
        I ANS?1"N".E W !!,"NOT FILED" K NAM,ST,TWN,STATE,ZIP,PHONE Q  ; *
        I ANS'?1"Y".E W !!,"PLEASE ENTER 'Y' OR 'N'" G FILE1             ; *
        ;
        S ^NAME(INDEX)=NAM_"^"_ST_"^"_TWN_"^"_STATE_"^"_ZIP_"^"_PHONE
        S ^NAME("A",NAM,INDEX)=""
        Q
        ;
DISPLAY S C=""
        F J1=0:0 S C=$O(^NAME("A",NAM,C)) Q:C=""  D DISPLAY1            ; *
        R !,"Do you want to continue with this entry? ",ANS
        I ANS?1"N".E S FLAG="NOT OK"
        Q
        ;
DISPLAY1 S DATA=^NAME(C)  W !,$P(DATA,"^",1)                            ; *
        F J2=2:1:6 W ?$X+2,$P(DATA,"^",J2)                             ; *
        Q                                                               ; *
```

36. The only changes from CH9EX10 are:

> Line CH9EX11 + 7
> The FILE module
> The DISPLAY module
> Our SET commands are moved from the ENTRY module to the new
> FILE module

Otherwise, these two programs are identical.

Each line that's been changed - or added - ends with a semicolon (to indicate an appended comment) and an asterisk. This makes it easy to identify the "differences" between our new program and CH9EX10.

SUMMARY OF NEW CONCEPTS - CHAPTER 9

One approach to "sorting" global arrays is to provide string subscripts at the first level, with numeric subscripts as unique identifiers at the second level. For example:

```
                              <^NAME(A,1)=DATA
              <^NAME(A)-<            .
^NAME-<            .          <^NAME(A,n)=DATA
              <^NAME(ZZZ)
```

A second approach to "sorting" global arrays is to provide cross reference files as part of a "combined global file". For example:

```
              <^NAME(1)=DATA
              <            .
              <^NAME(n)=DATA
^NAME-<^NAME("A",name,n)=""
              <    .
              <    .
              <^NAME("A",name,nnn=""
```

Cross reference files may be created:

(1)   From primary file, at the time when display in alpha order is needed.

(2)   "Automatically " as entries are made in primary file.

To use $ORDER with a cross reference file within a "combined global file" we begin $ORDER at second level of subscripting. For example:

```
          S  B=""
          F  J2=0:0  S  B=$O(^NAME("A",B))  Q:B=""    D  LEVEL3
          Q
LEVEL3    F  J3=0:0  S  C=$O(^NAME("A",B,C))  Q:C=""    W !,^NAME(C)
          Q
```

This code goes through second level string subscripts in cross reference file, identifies third level subscripts in cross reference file, and displays nodes from primary file in the desired order.

When "building" a primary file, it is easy to simultaneously "build" those cross reference files you expect will be needed in the future.

When "building" a primary file, your program can display previous entries under the same "name" - and allow the user to decide whether the proposed entry is really "new". To do this, you can:

(1)   check whether a node with the same string subscript already exists

(2)   display data for this node (if it exists)

(3)   allow user to either exit or continue with the entry.

For example:

```
          F  J=START:1  S  FLAG="OK"  D  ENTRY  I  NAM=""  Q
          Q
          ;
ENTRY     R  !,"Name:  ",NAM  I  NAM=""  Q
          I  $D(^NAME("A",NAM))  D  DISPLAY
          I  FLAG'="OK"  Q
          .
          .
          .
DISPLAY   S  C=""
          F  J3=0:0  S  C=$O(^NAME("A",NAM,C))  Q:C=""   W  !,^NAME(C)
          R  !,"Are you making a new entry?  ",ANS
          I  ANS?1"N".E  S  FLAG="NOT OK"
          Q
```

In the above code, our DISPLAY module: uses $ORDER to obtain third level subscripts from our cross reference file; displays existing data from our primary file; and allows the user to decide whether the proposed entry is really "new".

CHAPTER TEN

USING PRIMARY AND CROSS REFERENCE FILES

In Chapter Nine, we did not introduce any new commands, functions or operators: we merely demonstrated the use of commands, functions and operators presented in previous chapters.

This chapter will continue the presentation started in Chapter Nine. One new function - $EXTRACT - will be introduced. We will demonstrate how to:

- Make changes in a primary file

- Make changes in cross reference files

- Use the $EXTRACT function to: select file entries for change; prevent problems with "long entries" used as subscripts

- Check new entries against a dictionary file

- Perform sorts with mixed numeric subscripts (canonic plus non-canonic numbers).

By the end of this chapter you will be able to:

- change entries in primary files

- change entries in cross reference files

- display all items which match a "partial entry" (such as "SM" for "SMITH")

- prevent problems which may arise when a very long entry must be used as the subscript in a cross reference file (for example, a name which is 60 or 70 characters in length)

- create and use a "dictionary file" to check new entries in your primary and cross reference files.

- sort arrays with mixed numeric subscripts (canonic plus non- canonic numbers).

MAKING CHANGES IN A PRIMARY FILE

1. Assume we have a combined global file with the structure:

$$< \hat{}\ NAME\ (1) = DATA$$
$$< \qquad .$$
$$< \qquad .$$
$$\hat{}\ NAME - <\hat{}\ NAME\ (n) = DATA$$
$$< \hat{}\ NAME\ ("A", NAM, n) = ""$$
$$< \qquad .$$
$$< \hat{}\ NAME\ ("A", NAM, nn) = ""$$

DATA = Name_Street Address_Town_State_Zip_Phone

To change an entry in our primary file, we need to perform the following operations. First, allow the user to enter a name. Then, use $ORDER to look for a "match" in our "A" cross reference file. If a match is found, display each piece from the node in our primary file, and allow the user to enter a new value.

To display each piece from the node in our primary file, use a FOR loop with $PIECE to build a local array which contains the six pieces from our primary file. Then display each element of our local array, and allow the user to enter either RETURN or a new value. If the user enters RETURN, accept the original value. Then reset contents of the global node in our primary file.

Here's how to do it:

```
CH10EX1 ;  CHANGING AN ENTRY IN PRIMARY FILE
        ;  THIS PROGRAM OPERATES ON PRIMARY FILE PORTION OF ^NAME GLOBAL
        ;    THIS PRIMARY FILE HAS SIX PIECES OF DATA WITH '^' AS THE
        ;    DELIMITER
        ;
        ;     PIECE #1 = NAME
        ;     PIECE #2 = STREET ADDRESS
        ;     PIECE #3 = TOWN
        ;     PIECE #4 = STATE
        ;     PIECE #5 = ZIP CODE
        ;     PIECE #6 = PHONE
        ;
        ;
        F J1=0:0 S FLAG=0 R !!,"Enter name: ",NAM Q:NAM=""  D DISPLAY,
......  CHANGE:FLAG
        W !!,"Finished" Q
        ;
DISPLAY I '$D(^NAME("A",NAM))  W !!,"NOT FOUND" Q
        S C=""
        F J3=0:0 S C=$O(^NAME("A",NAM,C))  Q:C=""  D DISPLAY1
        D DISPLAY2
        Q
        ;
```

190

```
DISPLAY1 W !!,"Accession number = ",C,?25,"Name = ",NAM
         W !?12,"Data = ",^NAME(C)
         Q
         ;
DISPLAY2 R !!,"Enter accession number to change: ",NUM I NUM="" Q
         I '$D(^NAME("A",NAM,NUM)) W !!,"INCORRECT ACCESSION NUMBER!"
......   G DISPLAY2
         S FLAG=1
         Q
         ;
CHANGE   ; THIS MODULE ALLOWS USER TO CHANGE DATA IN PRIMARY FILE
         ;
         S NODE=^NAME(NUM)
         F J=1:1:6 S DATA(J)=$P(NODE,"^",J)
         W !,"Name: ",DATA(1),"// "
         R NAM I NAM="" S NAM=DATA(1)
         W !,"Street address: ",DATA(2),"// "
         R ST I ST="" S ST=DATA(2)
         W !,"Town: ",DATA(3),"// "
         R TWN I TWN="" S TWN=DATA(3)
         W !,"State: ",DATA(4),"// "
         R STATE I STATE="" S STATE=DATA(4)
         W !,"Zip code: ",DATA(5),"// "
         R ZIP I ZIP="" S ZIP=DATA(5)
         W !,"Phone: ",DATA(6),"// "
         R TEL I TEL="" S TEL=DATA(6)
         ;
         S ^NAME(NUM)=NAM_"^"_ST_"^"_TWN_"^"_STATE_"^"_ZIP_"^"_TEL
         Q
```

2. What functions are performed by each module in this program?

CH10EX1

Does FOR loop that initializes the variable FLAG, and allows the user to enter a name. We exit the FOR loop and the program on a null entry for name.

On any entry except a null entry, we DO DISPLAY. If DISPLAY resets our simple variable FLAG, we DO CHANGE - otherwise, we allow the user to enter another name via the FOR loop.

Notice our use of a non-comparative post conditional argument:

DO CHANGE:FLAG

If FLAG is any value other than zero, we DO the CHANGE module.

If FLAG is zero, we continue our FOR loop.

DISPLAY	Using $DATA, we check whether our entry is in the "A" cross reference file. If a "match" is found, we DO DISPLAY1 for each entry in the cross reference file. We then DO DISPLAY2, and quit.
DISPLAY1	Displays the accession number, name entry, and data for each node in our primary file found by DISPLAY.
DISPLAY2	We ask the user to enter an accession number to be changed. If null is entered, we quit the module. If an accession number is entered that does not exist at the third level of our cross reference file for the name entered, we print an error message and re-prompt for accession number. If the accession number is valid, we set FLAG to '1' and quit.
CHANGE	We create a local variable equal to value of the global node in our primary file.
	We use a FOR loop to create a local array, containing all six pieces from the node in our primary file. We then display the value of each "piece" - and allow the user to enter either return or a new value. A null entry (created by entering RETURN) sets our local variable equal to the original value for our local array element. Finally, we create a new global node by concatenation.

3.   This program does NOT update our cross reference file.

MAKING CHANGES IN CROSS REFERENCE FILES

4.   To change a node in our primary file, we simply use the same numeric subscript - and overwrite old data with new entries.

To change our cross reference file is more complex. With string subscripts, we cannot simply overwrite old data with a new entry. Instead, we must:

(1)   Determine if the "new" data is different from our "old" data.

(2)   If the "new" data is different from our "old" data, we:

(a) KILL the old node

(b) create a new node with new string subscript.

192

Assume that we have the following structure for our cross reference file:

$$^NAME ("A", NAM, n) = ""$$

We need to modify CH10EX1 so that when we update our primary file, we also:

(1)   Compare the "new" value of NAM with "existing" value of the first "piece" in our primary file.

(2)   If the "new" value differs from "existing" value, KILL the old node in our cross reference file, and create a new node with appropriate string subscript at the second level.

A single line of code, added to our CHANGE module, can perform both these functions:

```
I  DATA(1)'=NAM K ^NAME("A",DATA(1),NUM)  S ^NAME("A",NAM,NUM)=""
```

5.   Here is our revised CHANGE module with the new line of code:

```
CH10EX2 ; FIRST REVISION OF CHANGE MODULE FROM CH10EX1
CHANGE  ; THIS MODULE ALLOWS USER TO CHANGE DATA IN PRIMARY FILE
        ; AND ALSO UPDATE DATA IN CROSS REFERENCE FILE
        ;
        S NODE=^NAME(NUM)
        F J=1:1:6 S DATA(J)=$P(NODE,"^",J)
        W !,"Name: ",DATA(1),"// "
        R NAM I NAM="" S NAM=DATA(1)
        W !,"Street address: ",DATA(2),"// "
        R ST I ST="" S ST=DATA(2)
        W !,"Town: ",DATA(3),"// "
        R TWN I TWN="" S TWN=DATA(3)
        W !,"State: ",DATA(4),"// "
        R STATE I STATE="" S STATE=DATA(4)
        W !,"Zip code: ",DATA(5),"// "
        R ZIP I ZIP="" S ZIP=DATA(5)
        W !,"Phone: ",DATA(6),"// "
        R TEL I TEL="" S TEL=DATA(6)
        ;
        I DATA(1)'=NAM K ^NAME("A",DATA(1),NUM)  S ^NAME("A",NAM,NUM)=""
        ;
        S ^NAME(NUM)=NAM_"^"_ST_"^"_TWN_"^"_STATE_"^"_ZIP_"^"_TEL
        Q
```

We suggest you save this module as CH10EX2. You can then DO CH10EX2 from the first FOR loop in CH10EX1.

6.   What if we had several cross reference files? For example, we might add a "B" cross reference file within our combined global file:

```
              <^NAME(1)=DATA
              <        .
              <^NAME(n)=DATA
              <^NAME("A",NAM,n)=""
    ^NAME--<       .
              <^NAME("A",NAM,nnn)=""
              <^NAME("B",TWN,NAM,n)=""
              <        .
              <^NAME("B",TWN,NAM,nnn)=""
```

This "B" cross reference file provides names (in alphabetic order) within town in alphabetic order).

In this case, we need a second line of code to update our second cross reference file:

```
I  (DATA(3)'=TWN)!(DATA(1)'=NAM)  K ^NAME("B",DATA(3),DATA(1),NUM)
S  ^NAME("B",TWN,NAM,NUM)=""
```

Although this code is a little longer than our code from frame 5, the logic is identical. Here, we check string subscripts at the second and third levels, rather than check one string subscript at the second level.

7.   How would you revise our CHANGE module from frame 5 so the user can delete a node in our primary file, and the associated node in our cross reference file, by entering "@" as response to our "NAME" prompt in line CHANGE+5? Assume that we have a "B" cross reference file, as described in frame 6.

Here is the new line to insert after line CHANGE+5

```
I NAM="@" K ^NAME(NUM),^NAME("A",DATA(1),NUM),^NAME("B",DATA(3),
DATA(1),NUM)
```

USING THE $EXTRACT FUNCTION

SELECTING FILE ENTRIES FOR CHANGE

8.   In CH10EX1, our DISPLAY module requires an "exact match" in order to display "existing data" from our primary file. Thus, if you enter "SMITH, JOHN", you will NOT see the data for:

```
                "SMITH,  JOHN  P"
                        or
                "SMITH,  JOHN  PAUL"
```

We can solve this problem by using the $EXTRACT function.

9.   The one argument form of $EXTRACT returns the first character of a specified string. Syntax is:

> $EXTRACT(variable, expression or literal string)

For example:

```
    SET NAM="Smith, John P"
    WRITE $EXTRACT(NAM)
```

would return "S".

The two argument form of $EXTRACT returns a character from any position within the specified string. The two arguments consist of:

- the string from which you wish to extract a character

- an integer which specifies the position of this character within the string.

Syntax is:

> $EXTRACT(variable,position)

For example:

```
    SET NAM="Smith, John P"
    WRITE $EXTRACT(NAM,3)
```

would return "i".

If the value specified for the second argument exceeds the length of the specified string, $EXTRACT returns a null.

The three argument form of $EXTRACT returns a sequence of characters of specified length, starting at a specified position within a specified string. The three arguments consist of:

- the string from which you wish to extract a sequence of characters of specified length

- an integer which specifies the position of the first character in this sequence

- an integer which specifies the position of the last character in this sequence.

Syntax is:

```
$EXTRACT(variable,first position,last position)
```

For example:

```
SET NAM="Smith, John P"
WRITE $EXTRACT(NAM,1,5)
```

would return "Smith"

10.   We can use the three argument form of $EXTRACT to solve the problem noted in Frame 8. This will require extensive changes in our DISPLAY module from CH10EX1. The basic idea is relatively simple:

- use $DATA to check the cross reference file for an exact match to the user response and display these exact matches

- set length of user response to the prompt "Enter name:" equal to a local variable, LENGTH, via the $LENGTH function

- use $ORDER to display entries from our cross reference file that are partial matches, using NAM as the "starting point" for our $ORDER operation

- exit our $ORDER operation if:

    (1) $ORDER returns null from the second level of our cross reference file - the end of the cross reference file

    (2) our NAM entry is no longer equal to $EXTRACT(second level subscript,1,LENGTH).

In this way, all entries which "partially match" our user entry will be displayed via the $ORDER function.

Do we really need both $DATA and $ORDER here? Yes!

If the user enters an exact match, and we use this exact match as the starting point for our $ORDER operation, the first subscript returned will be the "next one past" our exact match!

11.   Now write a revised DISPLAY module to perform the four functions outlined in Frame 10. At this stage, rather than develop revised DISPLAY1 and DISPLAY2 modules, assume we can DO a single DISPLAY1 module which performs all required output functions.

Here's how we did it:

```
DISPLAY S B=NAM, LENGTH=$L (NAM)
        I $D(^NAME("A",NAM)) D DISPLAY1
        F J2=0:0 S B=$O(^NAME("A",B)) Q:(B="")!(NAM'=$E(B,1,LENGTH))
..... D DISPLAY1
```

12.   The sequence of operations in Frame 11 looks a little "awkward". Why not perform our $DATA operation first, then initialize the variables used for our $QRDER operation?

In subsequent frames, we will use this first line of code to initialize another variable - which is required in our DISPLAY1 module.

13.   To use this code with CH10EX1, we also need to perform the following functions:

- count the number of partial plus complete matches found

- if no partial or complete matches found, display the message "no matches found"

- display the accession number (unique identifier from primary file) for each partial or complete match identified.

14.   Now write a "complete" DISPLAY module for CH10EX1 to display and select exact plus partial matches, as described in Frames 11 - 13.

Here's how we did it:

```
CH10EX3 ; FIRST REVISION OF DISPLAY MODULE FROM CH10EX1
DISPLAY S COUNT=0,B=NAM,LENGTH=$L(NAM)
        I $D(^NAME("A",NAM)) D DISPLAY1
        F J2=0:0 S B=$O(^NAME("A",B)) Q:(B="")!(NAM'=$E(B,1,LENGTH))
...... DO DISPLAY1
        I COUNT=0 W !!,"NOT FOUND" Q
        D DISPLAY3
        Q
        ;
DISPLAY1 S C=""
        F J3=0:0 S C=$O(^NAME("A",B,C)) Q:C=""  D DISPLAY2
        Q
        ;
DISPLAY2 S COUNT=COUNT+1
        W !,"Accession number: ",C,?25,"Name: ",B
        W !?12,"Data = ",^NAME(C)
        Q
        ;
```

```
DISPLAY3 R !!,"Enter accession number to change: ",NUM I NUM="" Q
         I '$D(^NAME(NUM)) W !!,"NON-EXISTENT ACCESSION NUMBER!"
......   G DISPLAY3
         S NAME=$P(^NAME(NUM),"^")
         I $E(NAME,1,LENGTH)'=NAM W !!,"INCORRECT ACCESSION NUMBER!"
......   G DISPLAY3
         S FLAG=1,NAM=NAME
         Q
```

Notice the first line of our DISPLAY module. Since DISPLAY1 calls DISPLAY2 - and DISPLAY2 uses COUNT - we must initialize count before DOing DISPLAY1.

As pointed out in Frame 10, we need both $DATA and $ORDER: if the user enters an exact match, and we use this as the starting point for our $ORDER operation, $ORDER will "miss" this original entry!

Notice the $EXTRACT operation in DISPLAY3. When the user enters an accession number, our validity check must ensure that:

(1)   the number entered exists as a valid accession number in our pri-
       mary file (the $DATA check in line DISPLAY3 + 1)

(2)   the accession number entered corresponds to a node which matches
       the name entered.

The $EXTRACT operation provides a "check" in case the user enters a valid accession number - but one which does NOT appear on the list presented by our DISPLAY2 module.

We suggest you save this revised code as CH10EX3. You can then DO CH10EX3 from the first FOR loop in CH10EX1.

15.   Briefly describe the functions performed by each module from CH10EX3

DISPLAY   sets COUNT equal to zero (will be used to count the number of
                     matches found); sets B ($ORDER variable) equal to NAM; sets
                     LENGTH equal to $LENGTH of NAM.

                     DOes DISPLAY1 if an exact match is found via the $DATA func-
                     tion.

                     Searches second level of our "A" cross reference file, and QUITS
                     if:

```
```

- a null entry is found

- $EXTRACT(B,1,LENGTH) is no longer equal to NAM.

DOes DISPLAY1 until we QUIT the FOR loop.

If COUNT has not been incremented (no complete or partial match found in the DISPLAY 1-2 modules), outputs the message "not found" and QUITS the module. DOes DISPLAY3.

DISPLAY1	picks up unique identifiers from third level of "A" cross reference file and DOes DISPLAY2.
DISPLAY2	increments COUNT for each iteration of DISPLAY2 module
	Displays accession number and name from cross reference file, plus data from primary file.
DISPLAY3	prompts user to enter accession number, and QUITS on null entry.
	If node in primary file does not exist for accession number entered, displays error message and QUITS.
	Obtains full name from primary file.
	Performs $EXTRACT operation on full name from primary file, and compares this with NAM: if there is failure to match, displays an error message.
	Sets FLAG to '1', if the checks proceed without problems.

We can also depict this as a structure diagram (Figure 10-1) DISPLAY DOes DISPLAY1; DISPLAY1 DOes DISPLAY2; DISPLAY2 returns a value for COUNT. IF COUNT does not equal zero, we DO DISPLAY3.

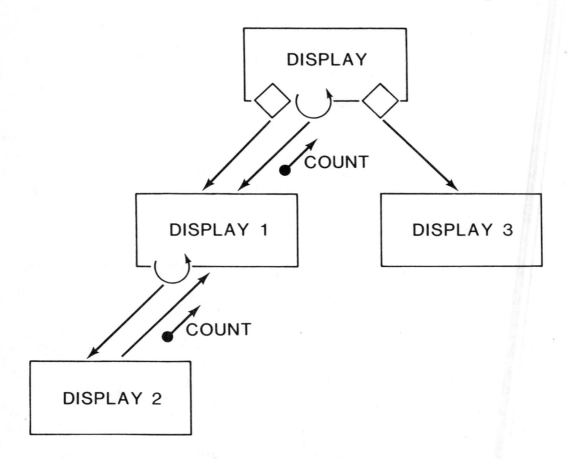

FIGURE 10-1. STRUCTURE CHART OF CH10EX3

16.   Rather than forcing the user to choose by accession number, it would be nice if we could number our matches sequentially as 1, 2, 3, 4... and so on. Also, it would be nice if in those cases where only one match was found, the program would automatically select this match.

To accomplish these objectives, we need to make the following changes in CH10EX3:

(1)   Store the name and accession number for each match in a local array with numeric subscripts.

(2)   Check if only one match was found - and in this case: (1) set NAM equal to the name from primary file; (2) set NUM equal to the unique accession number from primary file.

Study CH10EX3 in Frame 14, review how this code functions, and identify what modules will require changes:

_____

Our DISPLAY module goes through the second level of our cross reference file and DOes DISPLAY1.

DISPLAY1 goes through the third level of our cross reference file and DOes DISPLAY2.

DISPLAY2 increments COUNT, and prompts the user to enter an accession number. This looks like a good place to create a local array that stores the name and accession number for each match from our cross reference file. Each time we DO DISPLAY2, we can create a new node NM(COUNT) = B (second level subscript from our cross reference file) concatenated with C (third level subscript from our cross reference file).

DISPLAY3 prompts the user to enter an accession number. Here, we can prompt the user to enter a numeric subscript from our local array. We no longer need the two checks performed by our old DISPLAY3 module; instead we can perform a check on the numeric subscript from our local array.

At the end of DISPLAY3, we need to SET NUM equal to the second "piece" of our local array. Also, we need to KILL our local array - in preparation for the next iteration of our DISPLAY3 module.

Finally, we need a new line in our DISPLAY module to check if COUNT = 1. In this case, only a single match was found, and there is no need to display a "choice" via the DISPLAY3 module: we can set NAM equal to the first piece from our local array, set NUM equal to the second piece from our local array, and QUIT without DOing DISPLAY3.

17.   Try to modify CH10EX3 to accomplish these functions.

Here's how we did it:

```
CH10EX4 ; SECOND REVISION OF DISPLAY MODULE FROM CH10EX1
DISPLAY S COUNT=0,B=NAM,LENGTH=$L(NAM)
        I $D(^NAME("A",NAM)) D DISPLAY1
        F J2=0:0 S B=$O(^NAME("A",B)) Q:(B="")!(NAM'=$E(B,1,LENGTH))
...... D DISPLAY1
        I COUNT=0 W !!,"NOT FOUND" Q
        ;
        ;THE NEXT LINE DIFFERS FROM PREVIOUS EXAMPLE OF DISPLAY MODULE
        ;HERE WE WILL CHECK IF COUNT=1, IF SO, WE WILL SET THE VARIABLES
        ;NAM, NUM AND FLAG, AND THEN EXIT THE MODULE
        ;THE NM ARRAY HAS BEEN USED TO STORE NAME FROM THE SECOND LEVEL
        ;OF THE CROSS REFERENCE FILE AND THE UNIQUE IDENTIFIER FROM THE
        ;THIRD LEVEL OF THE CROSS REFERENCE FILE AS THE FIRST AND SECOND
        ;PIECES RESPECTIVELY
        ;
```

```
        I  COUNT=1  S  NAM=$P(NM(1),"^"),NUM=$P(NM(1),"^",2),FLAG=1  Q
        D  DISPLAY3
        Q
        ;
DISPLAY1 S C=""
        F  J3=0:0  S  C=$O(^NAME("A",B,C))  Q:C=""   D  DISPLAY2
        Q
        ;
DISPLAY2 ;THIS MODULE DIFFERS FROM THE PREVIOUS DISPLAY2 MODULE
        ;HERE, WE CREATE A LOCAL NM ARRAY WHICH CONTAINS THE SECOND AND
        ;THIRD LEVEL SUBSCRIPTS FROM OUR "A" CROSS REFERENCE FILE
        ;
        S  COUNT=COUNT+1,NM(COUNT)=B_"^"_C
        W  !,COUNT,?10,^NAME(C)
        Q
        ;
DISPLAY3 ;THERE IS A MINOR CHANGE IN THE PROMPT FOR OUR NEW DISPLAY3
        ;MODULE
        ;
        W  !!,"Choose a number between 1 and ",COUNT,": "  R NUM  I NUM=""  Q
        ;
        ;HERE, WE PERFORM A CHECK ON THE NUMBER ENTERED
        ;THIS REPLACES THE TWO CHECKS USED IN OUR PREVIOUS DISPLAY3 MODULE
        ;
        I  '$D(NM(NUM))  W  !,"ENTER A WHOLE NUMBER BETWEEN 1 AND ",COUNT
......  G  DISPLAY3
        ;
        ;HERE WE 'COLLECT' OUR NAM AND NUM VARIABLES FOR USE IN THE MAIN
        ;PROGRAM
        ;IN THE PREVIOUS PROGRAM, ACCESSION NUMBER WAS ENTERED 'DIRECTLY'-
        ;SO NO SET COMMAND WAS REQUIRED
        ;FINALLY, WE KILL THE NM ARRAY - IN CASE THIS MODULE IS CALLED A
        ;SECOND TIME BY THE MAIN PROGRAM
        ;
        S  FLAG=1,NAM=$P(NM(NUM),"^"),NUM=$P(NM(NUM),"^",2)
        K  NM
        Q
```

Notice there are relatively few changes in our code from CH10EX3.

18.   Some additional improvements are still possible.

First, we could add pattern matches and length checks in to our CHANGE module to ensure valid corrections - these were omitted for clarity.

Second, displaying an entire global node - as in our DISPLAY2 module - may lead to wrap-around. Wrap-around will make our display of matches hard to read. We can correct this problem with $EXTRACT:

```
        W  !,COUNT,?10,$E(^NAME(C),1,68)
```

This will ensure that each display line is only 80 characters long. We recommend that you use this in your own code.

Add this modification to CH10EX4. Now modify CH10EX1 to call CH10EX2 and CH10EX4 - rather than the original code used in Frame 1. Alternatively, you may prefer to modify CH10EX1 to incorporate the "new features" in CH10EX2 and CH10EX4.

Experiment with this program until you feel comfortable with it - and until you are sure it works properly!

PREVENTING PROBLEMS WITH "LONG ENTRIES" USED AS SUBSCRIPTS

19.   A potential problem with any cross reference file is that very long entries - such as name or town - may exceed the maximum allowable length for subscripts.

In some implementations of Standard MUMPS, the maximum allowable length for a single subscript is 31 characters. There may also be restrictions on the maximum allowable length for multiple subscripts of a single node.

In these implementations, the following code would produce an error message since it creates a subscript over 31 characters long:

```
S  NAM="ABCDEFGHIJKLMNOPQRSTUVWXYZ123456"
SET  ^NAME (NAM) =" "
```

20.   We can solve this problem by using $EXTRACT when we create our cross reference files. For example:

```
SET  NAM1=$EXTRACT (NAM, 1, 30)
```

Study the manual for your implementation to determine the maximum allowable length for:

- single subscripts

- multiple subscripts.

CHECKING NEW ENTRIES AGAINST A "DICTIONARY FILE"

21.   Assume we are creating a really large file, with several thousand names. We want to sort by town - to identify people who might join the same car pool. In planning our file, we want to avoid different spellings for the same town. For example:

MT JOY vs MOUNT JOY

MINNYAPOLIS vs MINEAPOLIS vs MINNEAPOLIS

NYC vs NEW YORK

NORTH BEND vs N. BEND

A "pattern match" which includes 100 or more different towns is not practical!

22.   One alternative is to create a "dictionary file" of possible town names. We can check each entry against this dictionary file - and reject the entry if no match is found.

23.   How would you use a dictionary file to check town names at the time of entry? One approach might be:

(1)   Create a dictionary file with string subscripts. The global might be called ^TOWN("nnn") where "nnn" represents a string subscript equal to town name. Contents of each global node would be equal to null, as with the cross reference files we created in Chapter Nine.

(2)   For each new entry, we would check $DATA. If $DATA(^TOWN("entry")) returned any number other than zero, the name entered would exist in our dictionary file.

(3)   If $DATA(^TOWN("entry")) returned zero, we could set a simple variable, LENGTH, equal to $L("entry"). We could then use $ORDER and $EXTRACT to identify any towns in our dictionary file whose first letters matched our entry. For example, an entry of "HA" would $ORDER through all towns whose first two letters were "HA".

24.   Here is a simple program to build our dictionary file:

```
CH10EX5 ;BUILD DICTIONARY FILE OF TOWN NAMES
        ;
        K
        F J=0:0 D ENTRY I TWN="" Q
        W !!,"Finished" Q
        ;
ENTRY   R !!,"Enter town name:  ",TWN I TWN="" Q
        I TWN'?1A.A W !,"ENTER ALPHA CHARACTERS ONLY!" S TWN=""
        I $L(TWN)>30 W !,"TOWN MAY NOT EXCEED 30 CHARACTERS!" S TWN=""
        I TWN="" G ENTRY
        S ^TOWN(TWN)=""
        Q
```

This simple program builds a ^TOWN(TWN) array with string subscripts, and null contents at each node.

25. Now write a routine to perform the following functions:

(1)   Allow user to enter name, address, town, state, zip code, and phone.

(2)   At each "town" entry, check $DATA in our ^TOWN file.

(3)   If the entry is not on file, then allow user to check entry against all towns in our dictionary file which begin with the same letters as our entry.

Here's how we did it:

```
CH10EX6   ;CREATE NAME FILE USING ^TOWN DICTIONARY FILE
          ;
          K  I '$D(^NAME) S ^NAME=1
          F J1=^NAME:1 D ENTRY I NAM="" Q
          W !!,"Finished" S ^NAME=J1 Q
          ;
ENTRY     R !!,"Enter name: ",NAM I NAM="" Q
          I NAM'?1A.AP W !!,"ENTER ALPHA CHARACTERS ONLY!",! S NAM=""
          I $L(NAM)>30 W !!,"NAME MAY NOT EXCEED 30 CHARACTERS!",! S NAM=""
          I NAM="" G ENTRY
ENTRY1    R !,"Enter address: ",ADR
          I $L(ADR)>80 W !!,"ADDRESS MAY NOT EXCEED 80 CHARACTERS!",!
.....     G ENTRY1
ENTRY2    R !,"Enter town: ",TWN
          D TWNFIND
          I TWN="" W !!,"NO MATCHES FOUND",! G ENTRY2
ENTRY3    R !,"Enter state: ",ST
          I ST'?2A W !!,"ENTER TWO LETTERS FOR STATE!",! G ENTRY3
ENTRY4    R !,"Enter zip code: ",ZIP
          I ZIP'?5N W !!,"ENTER FIVE NUMBERS FOR ZIP CODE!",! G ENTRY4
ENTRY5    R !,"Enter phone: ",TEL
          I (TEL'?3N1"-"3N1"-"4N)&(TEL'="U") D ERR G ENTRY5
          S ^NAME(J1)=NAM_"^"_ADR_"^"_TWN_"^"_ST_"^"_ZIP_"^"_TEL
          S ^NAME("A",NAM,J1)=""
          Q
          ;
TWNFIND   I TWN="" Q
          I $L(TWN)>30 W !!,"TOWN MAY NOT EXCEED 30 CHARACTERS!",!
......    S TWN="" Q
          I $D(^TOWN(TWN)) Q
          S LENGTH=$L(TWN),A=TWN
TWNFIND1  S A=$O(^TOWN(A))
          I (A="")!($E(A,1,LENGTH)'=TWN) S TWN="" Q
          W !!,A
          R !?5,"Is this correct? ",ANS
          I ANS?1"N".E G TWNFIND1
```

```
        S  TWN=A
        Q
        ;
ERR     W  !!,"ENTER PHONE NUMBER IN THE FORMAT 'nnn-nnn-nnnn'."
        W  !,"IF UNKNOWN, ENTER 'U'.",!
        Q
```

26.   Compared with programs from previous chapters, the only thing "new" about CH10EX6 is our TWNFIND module. This module performs functions similar to a pattern match.

Briefly describe how this module operates.

We DO TWNFIND from ENTRY2 + 1, after the prompt "Enter town:".

TWNFIND + 1 checks $LENGTH for our TWN entry; if this exceeds 30 characters, we display an error message, set TWN to a null value and QUIT the module.

TWNFIND + 2 checks if our entry already exists in the dictionary file.

TWNFIND + 3 creates the variables LENGTH and A for use with $ORDER through our dictionary file.

TWNFIND1 performs an $ORDER operation.

TWNFIND1 + 1 sets TWN equal to a null string and exits if $ORDER returns a null value or if $EXTRACT(A,1,LENGTH) does not equal TWN.

TWNFIND1 + 2 displays a value from our cross reference file

TWNFIND1 + 3 asks the user: "Is this correct?" On a "no" answer, we return to TWNFIND1; otherwise, we SET TWN equal to the subscript from our dictionary file.

27.   Can you think of a way to improve CH10EX6?

One way to improve this program would be to modify our TWNFIND module: rather than display names from our dictionary file "one at a time", we could display all names which match the latest entry, and allow a choice from this "menu". Let's change our TWNFIND module to:

(1)   Repeatedly perform our $ORDER operation to create a local array
        with numeric subscripts.

```
```

(2)   Display our local array, with a sequential number for each array element.

(3)   If there is only one element in our local array, SET TWN equal to this value and exit.

(4)   Prompt the user to select a town name from this local array. On a null entry, set TWN equal to " " and exit.

28.   Now write CH10EX6 with a revised TWNFIND module to perform these functions. Call this new program CH10EX7.

Here's how we did it:

```
CH10EX7 ;CREATE NAME FILE USING ^TOWN DICTIONARY FILE
        ;
        K  I '$D(^NAME) S ^NAME=1
        F J1=^NAME:1 D ENTRY I NAM="" Q
        W !!,"Finished" S ^NAME=J1 Q
        ;
ENTRY   R !!,"Enter name: ",NAM I NAM="" Q
        I NAM'?1A.AP W !!,"ENTER ALPHA CHARACTERS ONLY!",! S NAM=""
        I $L(NAM)>30 W !!,"NAME MAY NOT EXCEED 30 CHARACTERS!",!
......  S NAM=""
        I NAM="" G ENTRY
ENTRY1  R !,"Enter address: ",ADR
        I $L(ADR)>80 W !!,"ADDRESS MAY NOT EXCEED 80 CHARACTERS!",!
......  G ENTRY1
ENTRY2  R !,"Enter town: ",TWN
        D TWNFIND
        I TWN="" W !!,"NO MATCHES FOUND",! G ENTRY2
ENTRY3  R !,"Enter state: ",ST
        I ST'?2A W !!,"ENTER TWO LETTERS FOR STATE!",! G ENTRY3
ENTRY4  R !,"Enter zip code: ",ZIP
        I ZIP'?5N W !!,"ENTER FIVE NUMBERS FOR ZIP CODE!",! G ENTRY4
ENTRY5  R !,"Enter phone: ",TEL
        I (TEL'?3N1"-"3N1"-"4N)&(TEL'="U") D ERR G ENTRY5
        S ^NAME(J1)=NAM_"^"_ADR_"^"_TWN_"^"_ST_"^"_ZIP_"^"_TEL
        S ^NAME("A",NAM,J1)=""
        Q
        ;
TWNFIND I TWN="" Q
        I $L(TWN)>30 W !!,"TOWN NAME MAY NOT EXCEED 30 CHARACTERS!",!
......  S TWN="" Q
        I $D(^TOWN(TWN)) Q
        S LENGTH=$L(TWN),A=TWN
        F J2=1:1 S A=$O(^TOWN(A)) D TWNFIND1 I A="" S J2=J2-1 Q
```

```
            I  J2=0  S  TWN=""  Q
            I  J2=1  S  TWN=T(1)  Q
CHOICE   W  !,"Choose 1-",J2,":  "  R  ANS
            I  ANS=""  S  TWN=""  Q
            I  '$D(T(ANS))  W  !!,"ENTER A WHOLE NUMBER FROM 1 TO ",J2,!
......   G  CHOICE
            S  TWN=T(ANS)  K  T
            Q
            ;
TWNFIND1 I  (A="")!($E(A,1,LENGTH)'=TWN)  S  A=""  Q
            W  !?5,J2,?15,A
            S  T(J2)=A
            Q
            ;
ERR      W  !!,"ENTER PHONE NUMBER IN THE FORMAT 'nnn-nnn-nnnn'."
            W  !,"IF UNKNOWN, ENTER 'U'.",!
            Q
```

29.   Describe the operation of this revised version of our TWNFIND module.

The first four lines are identical to the first four lines of our TWNFIND module from CH10EX6.

Line TWNFIND+4 uses a FOR loop to:

(1)   repeatedly perform our $ORDER operation

(2)   create a local array with numeric subscripts via TWNFIND1

(3)   display our local array elements, together with their numeric subscripts, via TWNFIND1.

Line TWNFIND+5 exits if no matches are found.

Line TWNFIND+6 checks if only one match is found - and in this case, SETS TWN equal to our first array element.

Line CHOICE prompts the user to enter a number from the TWNFIND1 display.

If the entry at this point does not match any of the "choice numbers" for our local array, we display an error message. Otherwise, we SET TWN equal to one of our local array elements, and KILL our local array. Except for the changes in our TWNFIND module, this program is identical to CH10EX6.

30.   Although CH10EX7 is better than CH10EX6, there is room for further improvement: we might want to add a new town name to the dictionary file without the need to exit our program and DO CH10EX5. To do this we could modify CH10EX7 as follows:

> in line TWNFIND + 5, if J2 = 0 (from line TWNFIND + 4 after we DO our TWNFIND module), we can DO an ADD module which allows the user to enter a new town name in our ⌐TOWN dictionary file.

31.   Revise CH10EX7 to perform these functions. Call your new program CH10EX8. The only changes needed will be in line TWNFIND + 5, plus the addition of an ADD module.

Here's how we did it:

```
CH10EX8  ;CREATE NAME FILE USING ^TOWN DICTIONARY FILE
         ;NEW TOWNS MAY BE ADDED TO ^TOWN DICTIONARY FILE
         ;
         K  I '$D(^NAME) S ^NAME=1
         F J1=^NAME:1 D ENTRY I NAM="" Q
         W !!,"Finished" S ^NAME=J1 Q
         ;
ENTRY    R !!,"Enter name: ",NAM I NAM="" Q
         I NAM'?1A.AP W !!,"ENTER ALPHA CHARACTERS ONLY!",! S NAM=""
         I $L(NAM)>30 W !!,"NAME MAY NOT EXCEED 30 CHARACTERS!",!
......   S NAM=""
         I NAM="" G ENTRY
ENTRY1   R !,"Enter address: ",ADR
         I $L(ADR)>80 W !!,"ADDRESS MAY NOT EXCEED 80 CHARACTERS!",!
......   G ENTRY1
ENTRY2   R !,"Enter town: ",TWN
         D TWNFIND
         I TWN="" W !!,"NO MATCHES FOUND",! G ENTRY2
ENTRY3   R !,"Enter state: ",ST
         I ST'?2A W !!,"ENTER TWO LETTERS FOR STATE!",! G ENTRY3
ENTRY4   R !,"Enter zip code: ",ZIP
         I ZIP'?5N W !!,"ENTER FIVE NUMBERS FOR ZIP CODE!",! G ENTRY4
ENTRY5   R !,"Enter phone: ",TEL
         I (TEL'?3N1"-"3N1"-"4N)&(TEL'="U") D ERR G ENTRY5
         S ^NAME(J1)=NAM_"^"_ADR_"^"_TWN_"^"_ST_"^"_ZIP_"^"_TEL
         S ^NAME("A",NAM,J1)=""
         Q
         ;
TWNFIND  I TWN="" Q
         I $L(TWN)>30 W !!,"TOWN MAY NOT EXCEED 30 CHARACTERS!",!
......   S TWN="" Q
         I $D(^TOWN(TWN)) Q
         S LENGTH=$L(TWN),A=TWN
         F J2=1:1 S A=$O(^TOWN(A)) D TWNFIND1 I A="" S J2=J2-1 Q
```

```
            I J2=0 D ADD Q
            I J2=1 S TWN=T(1) Q
CHOICE   W !,"Choose 1-",J2,": " R ANS
            I ANS="" S TWN="" Q
            I '$D(T(ANS)) W !!,"ENTER A WHOLE NUMBER FROM 1 TO ",J2,!
......   G CHOICE
            S TWN=T(ANS) K T
            Q
            ;
TWNFIND1 I (A="")!($E(A,1,LENGTH)'=TWN) S A="" Q
            W !?5,J2,?15,A
            S T(J2)=A
            Q
            ;
ADD      R !?5,"Is this a new town? ",ANS
            I ANS'?1"Y".E S TWN="" Q
            I TWN'?1A.A W !!,"TOWN MUST BE ALPHA CHARACTERS ONLY!",!
......   S TWN="" Q
            I $L(TWN)>30 W !!,"TOWN MAY NOT EXCEED 30 CHARACTERS!"
......   S TWN="" Q
            S ^TOWN(TWN)=""
            Q
            ;
ERR      W !!,"ENTER PHONE NUMBER IN THE FORMAT 'nnn-nnn-nnnn'."
            W !,"IF UNKNOWN, ENTER 'U'.",!
            Q
```

32.   We could, of course, include our dictionary file within our ^NAME global. Here is one possible approach:

```
            <^NAME(1)=concatenated data
            <    .
            <^NAME(n)
            <^NAME("A",name,n)=""
            <    .
^NAME-<^NAME("A",name,nn)
            <^NAME("B",town,name,n)=""
            <    .
            <^NAME("B",town,name,nn)
            <^NAME("TOWN",town name)=""
            <    .
            <^NAME("TOWN",town name)
```

If you prefer to have all related global nodes in a single display, you may want to use this approach, rather than the separate dictionary file used in these examples.

SORTING ARRAYS WITH MIXED NUMERIC SUBSCRIPTS (CANONIC PLUS NON-CANONIC NUMBERS)

33.   In Chapter Eight we discussed the difference between "canonic numbers" and "non-canonic numbers". A canonic number has:

- no leading zeros

- no trailing zeros after a decimal.

From a numeric viewpoint, 001 has the same numeric value as 1, and 1.200 has the same numeric value as 1.2. In MUMPS, non-canonic numbers are treated as strings. And string values follow numeric values in the sorting sequence. Thus 001 would follow 9 - or 900! And 1.200 would follow 1.9!

34.   Let's assume we have a combined global file where the cross reference file has names sorted by date of birth. Here is one possible file structure:

```
                    <^NAME (1) =DATA
                    <      .
                    <^NAME (n)              <^NAME ("A", DOB, n)
        ^NAME   -   <^NAME ("A", DOB)   -   <^NAM
                    <      .                <^NAME ("A", DOB, nnn)
                    <      .
                    <^NAME ("A", DOB)
```

Assume we represent a DOB of January 3, 1983 as 830103; and July 4, 1904 as 040704.

With $ORDER, non-canonic numbers such as 040704 would appear AFTER canonic numbers such as 830103!

The solution is quite simple:

(1)   Append a prefix - such as "A" - to the mixture of canonic and non-canonic numbers used as subscripts in our cross reference file. Now, $ORDER will provide sorts in string sequence.

(2)   When we display subscripts from our cross reference file, use $EXTRACT to remove the first character.

For our date of birth cross reference file, we could append "A" in front of each date, using the format from frame 34. When we display dates, we could use $EXTRACT(DOB,2,7) to eliminate this alpha character from our display.

35.   A cross reference file using zip codes as subscripts provides a second example of "mixed" canonic and non-canonic numbers. We could append an alpha character in front of each zip code to ensure sorting in string order - then use $EXTRACT(ZIP,2,6) to eliminate this alpha character from our display.

36.   Time in military format is a third example of subscripts with mixed canonic and non-canonic numbers. Time values within a cross reference file might include:

```
0001  =  12:01 AM
0102  =   1:02 AM
0304  =   3:04 AM
0901  =   9:01 AM
1406  =   2:06 PM
```

Again, we could maintain times in proper sequence by concatenating an alpha character in front of each four digit number representing time in military format. When we print times, we could use $EXTRACT(TIME,2,5) to eliminate this alpha character from our display.

POINTER FILES

37.   You should consider this last section as "optional". We will not use "pointer files" in later chapters of this book. However, you may hear programmers talking about "pointer files". And you may see such files in the routines written by other programmers.

Most people who are new to MUMPS programming should skip this last section and go on to Chapter Eleven. People who are experienced programmers may want to review these examples of "pointer files" in MUMPS routines.

Rather than storing the same town name in our dictionary file and our primary file, it is possible to:

(1)   store the town name in a "pointer file", together with a number which serves as a unique identifier for this name

(2)   store only the numeric unique identifier in our primary file.

38.   Here is the program to build such a "pointer file" for town name:

```
CH10EX9  ;BUILD POINTER FILE OF TOWN NAMES
         ;
         K   I  '$D(^TOWN) S ^TOWN=1
         F  J=^TOWN:1 D ENTRY I TWN="" Q
         W !!,"Finished" S ^TOWN=J Q
         ;
ENTRY    R !!,"Enter town name: ",TWN I TWN="" Q
         I TWN'?1A.A W !,"ENTER ALPHA CHARACTERS ONLY!" G ENTRY
         I $L(TWN)>30 W !!,"TOWN MAY NOT EXCEED 30 CHARACTERS!" G ENTRY
         S ^TOWN(J)=TWN
         S ^TOWN("A",TWN,J)=""
         Q
```

The last value for our unique identifier is saved as the value of ^TOWN.

39.   We can now create a ^NAME file, in which we store the unique identifier from our

212

pointer file, rather than the "town name" itself. Here is the program to build such a ⸱NAME file:

```
CH10EX10  ;CREATE NAME FILE USING ^TOWN POINTER FILE
          ;
          K  I '$D(^NAME) S ^NAME=1
          F J1=^NAME:1 D ENTRY I NAM="" Q
          W !!,"Finished" S ^NAME=J1 Q
          ;
ENTRY    R !!,"Enter name: ",NAM I NAM="" Q
         I NAM'?1A.AP W !,"ENTER ALPHA CHARACTERS ONLY!" G ENTRY
ENTRY1   R !,"Enter address: ",ADR
         I $L(ADR)>80 W !!,"ADDRESS MAY NOT EXCEED 80 CHARACTERS!",!
......   G ENTRY1
ENTRY2   R !,"Enter town:  ",TWN
         D TWNFIND
         I TWN="" W !!,"NO MATCHES FOUND",! G ENTRY2
         S C="",C=$O(^TOWN("A",TWN,C)),TWN=C
ENTRY3   R !,"Enter state: ",ST
         I ST'?2A W !!,"ENTER TWO LETTERS FOR STATE!",! G ENTRY3
ENTRY4   R !,"Enter zip code: ",ZIP
         I ZIP'?5N W !!,"ENTER FIVE NUMBERS FOR ZIP CODE!",! G ENTRY4
ENTRY5   R !,"Enter phone: ",TEL
         I TEL'?3N1"-"3N1"-"4N D ERR G ENTRY5
         S ^NAME(J1)=NAM_"^"_ADR_"^"_TWN_"^"_ST_"^"_ZIP_"^"_TEL
         S ^NAME("A",NAM,J1)=""
         Q
         ;
TWNFIND  I TWN="" Q
         I $D(^TOWN("A",TWN)) Q
         S L=$L(TWN),B=TWN
TWNFIND1 S B=$O(^TOWN("A",B))
         I (B="")!($E(B,1,L)'=TWN) S TWN="" Q
         W !!,B
         R !?5,"Is this correct?  ",ANS
         I ANS?1"N".E G TWNFIND1
         S TWN=B
         Q
         ;
ERR      W !!,"ENTER PHONE NUMBER IN THE FORMAT 'nnn-nnn-nnnn'."
         Q
```

40.   In CH10EX10, the code is almost identical to CH10EX6 through line ENTRY2 + 2.

Line ENTRY2 + 3 is quite different - and represents a "new line" inserted into our old program, CH10EX6.

What is the function of this new line? Here, we want to find the first subscript at the third level within our pointer file. To do this, we perform a third level $ORDER operation, using the values of "A" and TWN at levels one and two. For any given town, there will be only one subscript at the third level. We then set TWN equal to this third level subscript from our pointer file, and store this entry in our primary file.

41.   Here is a "revised version" of CH10EX10, analogous to the CH10EX7 revision of CH10EX6:

```
CH10EX11  ;CREATE NAME FILE USING ^TOWN POINTER FILE
          ;
          K  I '$D(^NAME) S ^NAME=1
          F J1=^NAME:1 D ENTRY I NAM="" Q
          W !!,"Finished" S ^NAME=J1 Q
          ;
ENTRY     R !!,"Enter name: ",NAM I NAM="" Q
          I NAM'?1A.AP W !,"ENTER ALPHA CHARACTERS ONLY!" G ENTRY
ENTRY1    R !,"Enter address: ",ADR
          I $L(ADR)>80 W !!,"ADDRESS MAY NOT EXCEED 80 CHARACTERS!",!
......    G ENTRY1
ENTRY2    R !,"Enter town: ",TWN
          D TWNFIND
          I TWN="" W !!,"NO MATCHES FOUND",! G ENTRY2
          S C="",C=$O(^TOWN("A",TWN,C)),TWN=C
ENTRY3    R !,"Enter state: ",ST
          I ST'?2A W !!,"ENTER TWO LETTERS FOR STATE!",! G ENTRY3
ENTRY4    R !,"Enter zip code: ",ZIP
          I ZIP'?5N W !!,"ENTER FIVE NUMBERS FOR ZIP CODE!",! G ENTRY4
ENTRY5    R !,"Enter phone: ",TEL
          I TEL'?3N1"-"3N1"-"4N D ERR G ENTRY5
          S ^NAME(J1)=NAM_"^"_ADR_"^"_TWN_"^"_ST_"^"_ZIP_"^"_TEL
          S ^NAME("A",NAM,J1)=""
          Q
          ;
TWNFIND   I TWN="" Q
          I $D(^TOWN("A",TWN)) Q
          S L=$L(TWN),B=TWN
          F J2=1:1 S B=$O(^TOWN("A",B)) D TWNFIND2 I B="" S J2=J2-1 Q
          I J2=0 S TWN="" Q
          I J2=1 S TWN=T(1) Q
TWNFIND1  W !,"Choose 1-",J2,": " R ANS
          I ANS="" S TWN="" Q
          I '$D(T(ANS)) W !!,"ENTER A WHOLE NUMBER FROM 1 TO ",J2,!
......    G TWNFIND1
          S TWN=T(ANS) K T
          Q
          ;
TWNFIND2  I (B="")!($E(B,1,L)'=TWN) S B="" Q
          W !?5,J2,?15,B
          S T(J2)=B
          Q
          ;
ERR       W !!,"ENTER PHONE NUMBER IN THE FORMAT 'nnn-nnn-nnnn'."
          Q
```

42.   Notice the similarities to CH10EX7. Again, the code is almost identical through ENTRY2+2.

Line ENTRY2+3 represents a "new line" inserted into our old program. Again, we want to find the first subscript at the third level within our pointer file. And again, we store this numeric entry, rather than the town name, in our primary file.

43.   Here is a "revised version" of CH10EX11, analogous to the CH10EX8 revision of CH10EX7:

```
CH10EX12  ;CREATE NAME FILE USING ^TOWN POINTER FILE
          ;NEW TOWNS MAY BE ADDED TO ^TOWN POINTER FILE
          ;
          K  I '$D(^NAME) S ^NAME=1
          F J1=^NAME:1 D ENTRY I NAM="" Q
          W !!,"Finished" S ^NAME=J1 Q
          ;
ENTRY     R !!,"Enter name: ",NAM I NAM="" Q
          I NAM'?1A.AP W !,"ENTER ALPHA CHARACTERS ONLY!" G ENTRY
ENTRY1    R !,"Enter address: ",ADR
          I $L(ADR)>80 W !!,"ADDRESS MAY NOT EXCEED 80 CHARACTERS!",!
......    G ENTRY1
ENTRY2    R !,"Enter town: ",TWN
          D TWNFIND
          I TWN="" W !!,"NO MATCHES FOUND",! G ENTRY2
          S C="",C=$O(^TOWN("A",TWN,C)),TWN=C
ENTRY3    R !,"Enter state: ",ST
          I ST'?2A W !!,"ENTER TWO LETTERS FOR STATE!",! G ENTRY3
ENTRY4    R !,"Enter zip code: ",ZIP
          I ZIP'?5N W !!,"ENTER FIVE NUMBERS FOR ZIP CODE!",! G ENTRY4
ENTRY5    R !,"Enter phone: ",TEL
          I TEL'?3N1"-"3N1"-"4N D ERR G ENTRY5
          S ^NAME(J1)=NAM_"^"_ADR_"^"_TWN_"^"_ST_"^"_ZIP_"^"_TEL
          S ^NAME("A",NAM,J1)=""
          Q
          ;
TWNFIND   I TWN="" Q
          I $D(^TOWN("A",TWN)) Q
          S L=$L(TWN),B=TWN
          F J2=1:1 S B=$O(^TOWN("A",B)) D TWNFIND1 I B="" S J2=J2-1 Q
          I J2=0 D ADD Q
          I J2=1 S TWN=T(1) Q
CHOICE    W !,"Choose 1-",J2,": " R ANS
          I ANS="" S TWN="" Q
          I '$D(T(ANS)) W !!,"ENTER A WHOLE NUMBER FROM 1 TO ",J2,!
......    G CHOICE
          S TWN=T(ANS) K T
          Q
          ;
TWNFIND1  I (B="")!($E(B,1,L)'=TWN) S B="" Q
```

215

```
        W  !?5,J2,?15,B
        S  T(J2)=B
        Q
        ;
ADD     R  !?5,"Is this a new town?  ",ANS
        I  ANS'?1"Y".E S TWN="" Q
        I  TWN'?1A.A W !!,"TOWN NAME MUST BE ALPHA CHARACTERS ONLY!",!
......  S  TWN="" Q
        S  NEXT=^TOWN, ^TOWN(NEXT)=TWN
        S  ^TOWN("A",TWN,X)=""
        S  ^TOWN=X+1
        Q
        ;
ERR     W  !!,"ENTER PHONE NUMBER IN THE FORMAT 'nnn-nnn-nnnn'."
        Q
```

44.   Notice the similarities to CH10EX8 ENTRY2 + 2. Again, line ENTRY2 + 3 represents a new line inserted into our old program.

The ADD module is a little different. Here, ⌃TOWN has the next numeric subscript for our ⌃TOWN file. We set NEXT equal to ⌃TOWN, ⌃TOWN(NEXT) equal to the value of TWN, and then create a new entry in the "cross reference file" portion of our ⌃TOWN global.

45.   Does this "pointer file" offer significant advantages over our "dictionary file"?

Potentially, we can store more data within a single node of our primary file - which now contains numbers from the pointer file, rather than actual data.

However, this advantage is offset by:

(1)   Somewhat more complex code required to build our file

(2)   Somewhat more complex code required to "display" the contents of
       our primary file.

You will see "pointer files" used in routines written by other people. However, for most beginners, a "dictionary file" is adequate, and serves the same function.

SUMMARY OF NEW CONCEPTS - CHAPTER 10

Making changes in primary file plus cross reference files:

- read data from primary file into local array

- for each local array element display prompt plus old data

- read user response into local variable such as NAM

- for user response of RETURN, set local variable equal to existing local array element

- if old data does not match new entry, KILL old node of cross reference file and create a new node.

Using $EXTRACT function to select file entries for change:

- place length of user response (e.g. NAM) equal to a local variable such as LENGTH

- use $ORDER to display entries from cross reference file, with user response (e.g. NAM) as the "starting point"

- exit $ORDER operation if:
    (1) $ORDER returns null

    (2) NAM is no longer equal to $EXTRACT(NAM,1,LENGTH)

- check for an "exact match", since $ORDER will return the next subscript from our cross reference file.

  Example of code:

```
R !!,"Enter name: ",NAM
S B=NAM,LENGTH=$L(NAM)
F J=0:0 S B=$O(^NAME("A",B)) Q:(B="")!(NAM'=$E(B,1,LENGTH))
```

Using $EXTRACT function to prevent problems with "long entries" used as subscripts:

  Example:

```
SET NAM1=$EXTRACT(NAM,1,30)
SET ^NAME("A",NAM1,NAM)=""
```

Checking new entries against dictionary file:

- create dictionary file with string subscripts

- use $D to check whether new entry already exists in dictionary file

- use $ORDER to go through dictionary file, create local array, and exit if:

    (1) $ORDER returns a null

    (2) entry is no longer equal to $E(A,1,LENGTH)

- display local array, and allow user to make a selection

- check for an "extract match" - since $ORDER will return the next subscript from our dictionary file

- use of $EXTRACT permits display of "partial matches" from dictionary file, as well as from cross reference files.

Sorts with mixed numeric subscripts (canonic plus non-canonic numbers):

- concatenate alpha character in front of each subscript

- perform sort with $ORDER

- use $EXTRACT(variable,2,n) to eliminate leading alpha character from display or printout.

CHAPTER ELEVEN

CREATING, EDITING AND SEARCHING SUBFILES WITHIN A PRIMARY FILE

In this chapter, you will learn how to create, edit and search "subfiles" within a primary file. We will use the ^NAME file, from previous chapters, as an example for these subfiles. Topics include:

- creating "multi-node" subfiles for a primary file

- editing "multi-node" subfiles with the $FIND function

- searching subfiles with the contains operator

- programs for "file maintenance".

By the end of this chapter, you will be able to:

- create "multi-node" subfiles of "unlimited" length for a primary file

- edit data at the time of entry, using the $FIND function

- search subfiles for specific strings via the contains operator

- delete, add or change data within primary files and associated cross reference files.

INTRODUCTION

1.   The primary file for our ^NAME global, up to this point, has had only one level of subscripting:

```
                  <^NAME(1)=concatenated data
      ^NAME--<          .
                  <^NAME(n)
```

At this first level of subscripting, concatenated data has been stored as six pieces separated by the delimiter "^":

                    #1 = name
                    #2 = street
                    #3 = town
                    #4 = state
                    #5 = zip code
                    #6 = phone

2.   Within the primary file for our ^NAME global:

- each node represents the "record" for one person

- each piece represents one "data element", corresponding to a specific attribute for one person.

3.   Our implementation of Standard MUMPS allows up to 255 characters as the contents for one node. Some implementations of Standard MUMPS allow more. Study your user manual to determine the maximum for your system.

In the following frames, we assume up to 255 characters can be stored in a node.

4.   What if the data you want to store in your primary file exceeds 255 characters per node?

One answer is to use a second level of subscripting. Here is a possible file structure:

```
                          <^NAME(1,"COMMENT")
              <^NAME(1)--<^NAME(1,"ADDRESS")
      ^NAME--<        .     <^NAME(1,"PHONE")
              <^NAME(n)
```

This structure provides multiple "subfiles", with each subfile identified by a string subscript at the second level. At the third level, we can store data for each subfile:

```
                                                         <^NAME(1,"COMMENTS",1)
                                                         <        .
                              <^NAME(1,"COMMENTS")--<        .
                              <        .             <        .
            <^NAME(1)--<        .                    <^NAME(1,"COMMENTS",n)
  ^NAME--<        .             <        .
            <^NAME(n)     <^NAME(1,"PHONE")
```

This allows an unlimited number of "subfiles" within each record. Each subfile is identified by a second level string subscript, which specifies the type of data. Within each subfile, we have an "unlimited" number of nodes available for data storage.

5.   In the next section, we will demonstrate how to create this type of subfile.

CREATING "MULTI-NODE" SUBFILES FOR A PRIMARY FILE

6.   Outline the file structure, and write the code to build a ^NAME global with:

*   seven "pieces" in the first level of our primary file:

> #1 = name
> #2 = address
> #3 = town
> #4 = state
> #5 = zip code
> #6 = office phone (up to three office phones
> separated by sub-delimiters)
> #7 = home phone

*   an "A" cross reference file by name

*   a "B" cross reference file by name within town

*   a "comment" subfile which allows an unlimited number of comments, with each comment up to 60 characters in length

*   a "dictionary file" for town name (similar to the TWNFIND module used in Chapter Ten)

*   limits of 50 characters for names, 80 for address, and 50 for town.

Before you write this program, KILL ^NAME from Chapter Ten. Or, if you prefer, use a new global name, such as ^NAME1.

File structure:

```
                              <^NAME(1,"COMMENT",1)=data
                 <^NAME(1)--<          .
                 <      .          <^NAME(1,"COMMENT",n)=data
      ^NAME--<^NAME(n)
                 <^NAME("A",name,n)=""
                 <^NAME("B",town,name,n)=""
```

Code:

```
CH11EX1 ;CREATE NAME FILE WITH MULTI-NODE COMMENT 'SUBFILE'
        ;
        K  I '$D(^NAME) S ^NAME=1
        F NUM=^NAME:1 D ENTRY I NAM="" Q
        W !!,"Finished" S ^NAME=NUM Q
        ;
ENTRY   R !!,"Enter name: ",NAM I NAM="" Q
        I NAM'?1A.AP W !!,"ENTER ALPHA CHARACTERS ONLY!",! S NAM=""
        I $L(NAM)>50 W !!,"NAME MAY NOT EXCEED 50 CHARACTERS!",!
......  S NAM=""
        I NAM="" G ENTRY
ENTRY1  R !,"Enter address: ",ADR
        I $L(ADR)>80 W !!,"ADDRESS MAY NOT EXCEED 80 CHARACTERS!",!
......  G ENTRY1
ENTRY2  R !,"Enter town: ",TWN
        D TWNFIND
        I TWN="" W !!,"NO MATCHES FOUND",! G ENTRY2
ENTRY3  R !,"Enter state: ",ST
        I ST'?2A W !!,"ENTER TWO LETTERS FOR STATE!",! G ENTRY3
ENTRY4  R !,"Enter zip code: ",ZIP
        I ZIP'?5N W !!,"ENTER FIVE NUMBERS FOR ZIP CODE!",! G ENTRY4
        S (OTEL(1),OTEL(2),OTEL(3))=""
        F J2=1:1:3 R !,"Enter office phone: ",OTEL(J2) Q:OTEL(J2)=""
......  D PHONE
ENTRY5  R !,"Enter home phone: ",HTEL
        I HTEL'?3N1"-"3N1"-"4N&(HTEL'="U") D ERRHTEL G ENTRY5
        S OTEL=OTEL(1)_"\"_OTEL(2)_"\"_OTEL(3)
        S ^NAME(NUM)=NAM_"^"_ADR_"^"_TWN_"^"_ST_"^"_ZIP_"^"_OTEL_"^"_HTEL
        S ^NAME("A",NAM,NUM)=""
        S ^NAME("B",TWN,NAM,NUM)=""
        F J3=1:1 R !,"Enter comment: ",COM Q:COM=""  D COMMENT
        S ^NAME(NUM,"COMMENT")=J3-1
        Q
        ;
TWNFIND I TWN="" Q
        I $L(TWN)>50 W !!,"TOWN NAME MAY NOT EXCEED 50 CHARACTERS.",
......  ! S TWN="" Q
        I $D(^TOWN(TWN)) Q
        S LENGTH=$L(TWN),A=TWN
```

```
              F J1=1:1 S A=$O(^TOWN(A)) D TWNFIND1 I A="" S J1=J1-1 Q
              I J1=0 S TWN="" Q
              I J1=1 S TWN=T(1) Q
CHOICE        W !,"CHOOSE 1-",J1,":  " R ANS
              I ANS="" S TWN="" Q
              I '$D(T(ANS)) W !!,"ENTER A WHOLE NUMBER FROM 1 TO ",J1,!
......        G CHOICE
              S TWN=T(ANS) K T
              Q
              ;
  TWNFIND1    I (A="")!($E(A,1,LENGTH)'=TWN) S A="" Q
              W !?5,J1,?15,A
              S T(J1)=A
              Q
              ;
  PHONE       I OTEL(J2)?3N1"-"3N1"-"4N Q
              S J2=J2-1
              W !!,"ENTER PHONE NUMBER IN THE FORMAT 'nnn-nnn-nnnn'."
              W !,"YOU MAY ENTER UP TO THREE OFFICE PHONE NUMBERS"
              W !,"IF OFFICE PHONE UNKNOWN, ENTER 'RETURN'",!
              Q
              ;
  ERRHTEL     W !!,"ENTER PHONE NUMBER IN THE FORMAT 'nnn-nnn-nnnn'."
              W !,"IF UNKNOWN, ENTER 'U'.",!
              Q
              ;
  COMMENT     I $L(COM)<61 S ^NAME(NUM,"COMMENT",J3)=COM Q
              S J3=J3-1
              W !!,"COMMENT MAY NOT EXCEED 60 CHARACTERS!",!
              Q
```

7. Briefly discuss the functions performed by each module of CH11EX1.

Everything through ENTRY3 is identical to previous programs for building our ^NAME file.

The last two lines in ENTRY4 are new. First, we initialize the local variables OTEL(1), OTEL(2), OTEL(3); these will be used to store up to three office phone numbers for each name in our file. Second, we build our local OTEL array via a FOR loop.

Our PHONE module, DOne out of ENTRY4, performs two functions:

(1) QUITS if pattern match is ok

(2) if pattern match is not ok, decrements J2, displays an error message, and QUITS.

ENTRY5 is similar to previous programs. In ENTRY5+6, an open ended FOR loop incremented by one prompts for comments, and DOes the COMMENT module. Line ENTRY5+7 stores the third level subscript of our last comment as the value of ˄NAME(NUM,"COMMENT").

The COMMENT module checks length of the comment entry, and stores COM at the third level of our primary file. If length exceeds 60 characters, we decrement J3 and display an error message.

Our CH11EX1 program is quite similar to the routines presented in Chapter Ten. Only a few minor changes are needed to allow:

(1) multiple office phone numbers stored at the first level of our primary file

(2) multiple comments stored at the third level of our primary file.

The comments stored at the third level of subscripting represents a "subfile". We could easily create additional "subfiles", as depicted in Frame 4.

8. Now plan and write a program to display all data within our ˄NAME array, in alpha order by name.

To do this, we need to:

(1) use the third level of our "A" cross reference file to find subscripts in our primary file

(2) set the contents of each node equal to a local variable

(3) use a FOR loop to display the first five pieces of each node

(4) use a second FOR loop to display all subpieces within the sixth piece which do not equal a null entry

(5) use a third FOR loop with $ORDER to display the "COMMENT" subfile.

Here's how we did it:

```
CH11EX2 ;DISPLAY ^NAME GLOBAL IN ALPHA ORDER
        ;THIS PROGRAM SORTS NAME FILE IN ALPHA ORDER AND PRINTS CONTENTS OF
        ;THIS FILE, WHICH INCLUDES A MULTI-NODE 'COMMENT' SUBFILE
```

```
        ;
        K
        S  B=""
        F  J1=0:0  S  B=$O(^NAME("A",B))  Q:B=""   D  THIRD
        W  !!,"Finished"  Q
        ;
THIRD   ;FIND  SUBSCRIPT  FOR  PRIMARY  FILE  FROM  3RD  LEVEL  OF  CROSS
......  REFERENCE  FILE
        S  C=""
        F  J2=0:0  S  C=$O(^NAME("A",B,C))  Q:C=""   D  DISPLAY
        Q
        ;
DISPLAY ;DISPLAY  INFORMATION
        W  !!
        S  DATA=^NAME(C)
        F  J3=1:1:5  W  !,$P(DATA,"^",J3)
        S  PH=$P(DATA,"^",6)
        F  J4=1:1:3  S  TEL=$P(PH,"\",J4)  Q:TEL=""   W  !,TEL
        S  PH=$P(DATA,"^",7)
        I  PH="U"  S  PH="UNKNOWN"
        W  !,PH
        S  COM=""
        F  J5=0:0  S  COM=$O(^NAME(C,"COMMENT",COM))  Q:COM=""   W  !?5,
......  ^NAME(C,"COMMENT",COM)
        Q
```

EDITING A "MULTI-NODE" SUBFILE WITH THE $FIND FUNCTION

9.   The $FIND function returns information on the position of a specified substring within a string. The two argument form of $FIND returns a number specifying the position of the first character AFTER the specified substring. The syntax is:

$FIND(string,substring)

For example:

```
SET DATE="January 23, 1984"
SET POSITION=$FIND(DATE,",")
WRITE POSITION
```

would return 12.

The $FIND function returns the position of the first character after the ",". In this case, the position of the first character after "," is 12. If $FIND does not find a "," within our DATE variable, it will return a zero.

The three argument form of $FIND allows you to begin your search at some position other than the first character of the specified string. The syntax is:

$FIND(string,substring,position within string to begin search)

For example:

```
SET DATA="PART NO 7,324:January 7, 1984"
SET POSITION=$FIND(DATA,",",14)
WRITE POSITION
```

would return 25.

Here, the $FIND function begins its search at position #14, and returns a value of 25. By using the three argument syntax, we ignore the first comma within our data.

10.   The three argument form can be used to find every occurance of a substring within a string. To find every "," in the example above:

```
SET DATA="PART NO 7,324:January 7, 1984",POSITION=1
FOR J=1:1 SET POSITION=$FIND(DATA,",",POSITION) IF POSITION=0
......  W !,J-1 QUIT
```

The first time through the FOR loop, POSITION is SET to 11. The second time, POSITION is SET to 25; and the third time, POSITION is SET to zero - which is the QUIT condition for the FOR loop.

11.   The two argument form of $FIND can be used to "find" a specified substring within a portion of free text. Here is a simple example:

```
CH11EX3  ;ROUTINE TO EDIT PORTION OF TEXT ENTRY WITHOUT NEED TO
         ;RE-ENTER ENTIRE ENTRY
         ;
         R !,"Enter text: ",TEXT
         R !,"Replace: ",OLD,"  With: ",NEW D MOD
         W !!,"Finished" Q
         ;
MOD      I OLD=""
         S POSTN=$FIND(TEXT,OLD)
         S OLDLNGTH=$L(OLD)+1
         S FRSTTEXT=$E(TEXT,1,POSTN-OLDLNGTH)
         S LSTTEXT=$E(TEXT,POSTN,999)
         S TEXT=FRSTTEXT_NEW_LSTTEXT
         Q
```

12.   Describe what functions are performed by this code.

_____

Line CH11EX3+4:   (1) creates variables OLD for the old substring and NEW for the new substring;   (2) DOes MOD.

Line MOD+1 sets POSTN equal to the first position after the end of the old substring.

Line MOD+2 sets OLDLNGTH equal to $LENGTH of the old substring plus one.

Line MOD+3 sets FRSTTEXT equal to $EXTRACT of TEXT up to the position where our old substring begins.

Line MOD+4 sets LSTTEXT equal to $EXTRACT of TEXT, starting from the first position after the end of our old substring, to position 999.

Line MOD+5 concatenates FRSTEXT, NEW, and LSTEXT in appropriate order.

13.   We can use this program to "correct" free text - such as our "COMMENTS" in CH11EX1 - either at the time of entry or later. After each entry, we can ask "are you sure?" If the user replies "No", we can allow him to alter any portion of the entry.

14.   CH11EX4 represents a routine to edit comment entries, to be called by CH11EX1.

```
CH11EX4  ;EDIT THE COMMENTS IN ^NAME USING $FIND AND $EXTRACT
         ;THIS ROUTINE IS CALLED BY CH11EX1
         ;IF NO COMMENTS ENTERED,CH11EX1 LINE ENTRY5+7 SETS
......   ;^NAME(NUM,"COMMENT")=0
         ;
         I ^NAME(NUM,"COMMENT")=0 Q
         D DISPLAY
         R !!,"Do you want to edit any comments? YES=> ",ANS I ANS=""
.....    S ANS="Y"
         I ANS?1"Y".E D EDIT
         Q
         ;
DISPLAY  ;CREATE HEADINGS FOR THE COMMENT DISPLAY
         ;
         W !!!!!?3,"#",?10,"COMMENT",!?2,"---",?9,"---------"
         S C=""
         F J1=1:1 S C=$O(^NAME(NUM,"COMMENT",C)) Q:C=""  D DISPLAY1
         Q
         ;
DISPLAY1 ;SET COMMENT INTO LOCAL ARRAY 'COM'
         ;
         S COM(J1)=^NAME(NUM,"COMMENT",C)
         I COM(J1)="" K COM(J1) S J1=J1-1 Q
         W !?3,J1,?10,COM(J1)
         Q
         ;
EDIT     F J2=0:0 D DISPLAY,EDIT1 Q:NO=""  I NO="BAD" D ERROR
         Q
         ;
EDIT1    R !,"Edit which comment #: ",NO
         I NO="" Q
         I '$D(COM(NO)) S NO="BAD" Q
         ;
         ;REDISPLAY EDITED COMMENT AFTER EACH CHANGE
```

```
          ; STOP EDITING IF USER ENTERS 'RETURN' IN RESPONSE TO 'REPLACE'
          ; PROMPT
          ;
          F J3=0:0 W !!,COM(NO),!?5,"Replace " R OLD D EDIT2 I OLD="" Q
          ;
          ; TRUNCATE TO 60 CHARACTERS ANY COMMENT THAT EXCEEDS 60 CHARACTERS
          ; AFTER EDITING.
          ;
          S COM(NO)=$E(COM(NO),1,60)
          ;
          ; IF COMMENT IS NULL, DELETE IT
          ;
          I COM(NO)="" K COM(NO)
          ;
          ; KILL OLD COMMENTS AND SAVE EDITED COMMENTS
          ; COMMENT NODES ARE 'RENUMBERED' IF ANY COMMENTS ARE DELETED
          ;
          K ^NAME(NUM,"COMMENT")
          S A=""
          F J3=1:1 S A=$O(COM(A)) Q:A=""  S ^NAME(NUM,"COMMENT",J3)=COM(A)
          S ^NAME(NUM,"COMMENT")=J3-1
          K COM
          Q
          ;
EDIT2     ; POS2 = POSITION IN COMMENT AFTER THE 'OLD' STRING
          ; POS1 = POSITION IN COMMENT BEFORE THE 'OLD' STRING
          ;
          I OLD="" Q
          S POS2=$F(COM(NO),OLD)
          I POS2=0 W "      ???" Q
          S LENGTH=$L(OLD)
          S POS1=POS2-(LENGTH+1)
          R !?5,"With ",NEW
          S COM(NO)=$E(COM(NO),1,POS1)_NEW_$E(COM(NO),POS2,255)
          I $L(COM(NO))>60 D WARNING
          ;
          ; IF COMMENT IS NULL, DELETE IT AND SET OLD = NULL TO QUIT
          ; EDITING
          ;
          I COM(NO)="" S OLD="" W "     ...COMMENT DELETED"
          Q
          ;
ERROR     W !!,"THERE IS NO SUCH COMMENT NUMBER!",!
          Q
          ;
WARNING   W !!!?10,"* * * *  WARNING  * * * *"
          W !!,"THIS COMMENT EXCEEDS 60 CHARACTERS IN LENGTH!"
          W !,"CHARACTERS PAST POSITION #60 WILL BE TRUNCATED!",!!
          Q
```

What functions are performed by each module of this program?

The first two lines check whether any comments were entered, and if so, DO DISPLAY.

Our DISPLAY and DISPLAY1 modules: create two underlined headings; use $ORDER to create a local array from the contents of our COMMENT subfile; display each entry plus an entry number.

Line CH11EX4+6 displays the prompt "Do you want to edit any comments?" On a YES answer, we DO EDIT.

The EDIT module is a simple FOR loop, which: (1) does the DISPLAY module;   (2) DOes the EDIT1 module.

EDIT1 prompts the user to enter a comment number for editing. We QUIT on: (1) a null entry;   (2) an entry which represents an undefined node within our local COM array. In the latter case, we set NO equal to "BAD", and DO our ERROR module.

Line EDIT1+7:   (1) uses a FOR loop to display the comment selected for editing;   (2) prompts for an "OLD" string to be replaced;   (3) QUITS on a null entry;   (4) DOes EDIT2.

Line EDIT2+4 sets POS2 equal to the first position after the end of the old string. Line EDIT2+6 sets LENGTH equal to $LENGTH for the old string. Line EDIT2+7 sets POS1 equal to POS2 minus (LENGTH+1). Line EDIT2+8 prompts for a "NEW" string. Line EDIT2+9 sets COM(NO) equal to $EXTRACT of COM(NO) up to POS1 concatenated with NEW concatenated with $EXTRACT of COM(NO) from position 2 to the end of the string. If the new entry exceeds 60 characters in length, we do our WARNING module, to notify the user that characters past position #60 will be truncated. Finally, if the foregoing operations within our EDIT1 module delete COM(NO), we set OLD = " " and display a message "comment deleted".

Each time we do the EDIT module, we first DO DISPLAY, so the user can see "what's on file" before re-editing a specific comment.

CH11EX4 is unable to "stand alone". The variable NUM needs to be defined AND equal to a valid subscript in the primary file before CH11EX4 is called. CH11EX4 is, in effect, a large module saved as a routine to be called by CH11EX1.

15.   Now modify CH11EX1 to call CH11EX4. Name your new program CH11EX5.

Here's how we did it. The only changes needed were:

(1)   Omit a few comment lines

(2)   Add line ENTRY5+8 to DO^CH11EX4

```
CH11EX5  ;CREATE NAME FILE WITH UNLIMITED NUMBER OF COMMENTS FOR
         ;EACH NAME
         ;COMMENTS MAY BE EDITED AFTER INITIAL ENTRY
         ;
         K   I '$D(^NAME) S ^NAME=1
         F NUM=^NAME:1 D ENTRY I NAM="" Q
         W !!,"Finished" S ^NAME=NUM Q
         ;
ENTRY    R !!,"Enter name: ",NAM I NAM="" Q
         I NAM'?1A.AP W !!,"ENTER ALPHA CHARACTERS ONLY!",! S NAM=""
         I $L(NAM)>50 W !!,"NAME MAY NOT EXCEED 50 CHARACTERS!",!
......   S NAM=""
         I NAM="" G ENTRY
ENTRY1   R !,"Enter address: ",ADR
         I $L(ADR)>80 W !!,"ADDRESS MAY NOT EXCEED 80 CHARACTERS!",!
......   G ENTRY1
ENTRY2   R !,"Enter town: ",TWN
         D TWNFIND
         I TWN="" W !!,"NO MATCHES FOUND",! G ENTRY2
ENTRY3   R !,"Enter state: ",ST
         I ST'?2A W !!,"ENTER TWO LETTERS FOR STATE!",! G ENTRY3
ENTRY4   R !,"Enter zip code: ",ZIP
         I ZIP'?5N W !!,"ENTER FIVE NUMBERS FOR ZIP CODE!",! G ENTRY4
         S (OTEL(1),OTEL(2),OTEL(3))=""
         F J2=1:1:3 R !,"Enter office phone: ",OTEL(J2) Q:OTEL(J2)=""
......   D PHONE
ENTRY5   R !,"Enter home phone: ",HTEL
         I HTEL'?3N1"-"3N1"-"4N&(HTEL'="U") D ERRHTEL G ENTRY5
         S OTEL=OTEL(1)_"\"_OTEL(2)_"\"_OTEL(3)
         S ^NAME(NUM)=NAM_"^"_ADR_"^"_TWN_"^"_ST_"^"_ZIP_"^"_OTEL_
......   "^"_HTEL
         S ^NAME("A",NAM,NUM)=""
         S ^NAME("B",TWN,NAM,NUM)=""
         F J3=1:1 R !,"Enter comment:",COM Q:COM=""  D COMMENT
         S ^NAME(NUM,"COMMENT")=J3-1
         D ^CH11EX4
         Q
         ;
TWNFIND  I TWN="" Q
         I $L(TWN)>50 W !!,"TOWN NAME MAY NOT EXCEED 50 CHARACTERS.",!
......   S TWN="" Q
         I $D(^TOWN(TWN)) Q
         S LENGTH=$L(TWN),A=TWN
         F J1=1:1 S A=$O(^TOWN(A)) D TWNFIND1 I A="" S J1=J1-1 Q
         I J1=0 S TWN="" Q
         I J1=1 S TWN=T(1) Q
```

```
CHOICE   W  !,"CHOOSE 1-",J1,":  " R ANS
         I  ANS="" S TWN="" Q
         I  '$D(T(ANS))  W !!,"ENTER A WHOLE NUMBER FROM 1 TO ",J1,!
......   G  CHOICE
         S  TWN=T(ANS) K T
         Q
         ;
TWNFIND1 I  (A="")!($E(A,1,LENGTH)'=TWN)  S A="" Q
         W  !?5,J1,?15,A
         S  T(J1)=A
         Q
         ;
PHONE    I  OTEL(J2)?3N1"-"3N1"-"4N Q
         S  J2=J2-1
         W  !!,"ENTER PHONE NUMBER IN THE FORMAT 'nnn-nnn-nnnn'."
         W  !,"YOU MAY ENTER UP TO THREE OFFICE PHONE NUMBERS"
         W  !,"IF OFFICE PHONE UNKNOWN, ENTER 'RETURN'",!
         Q
         ;
ERRHTEL  W  !!,"ENTER PHONE NUMBER IN THE FORMAT 'nnn-nnn-nnnn'."
         W  !,"IF UNKNOWN, ENTER 'U'.",!
         Q
         ;
COMMENT  I  $L(COM)<61 S ^NAME(NUM,"COMMENT",J3)=COM Q
         S  J3=J3-1
         W  !!,"COMMENT MAY NOT EXCEED 60 CHARACTERS!",!
         Q
```

16.   As we make our comment entry at a terminal, it may be difficult to determine when we reach our 60 character limit. If we exceed this limit, we must re-enter the comment. We can change line ENTRY5+6 to provide a "marker" which clearly shows the user where the "limit" for a comment entry is located:

```
ENTRY5 R !,"Enter home phone: ",HTEL
        I  HTEL'?3N1"-"3N1"-"4N&(HTEL'="U")  D ERRHTEL G ENTRY5
        S  OTEL=OTEL(1)_"\"_OTEL(2)_"\"_OTEL(3)
        S  ^NAME(NUM)=NAM_"^"_ADR_"^"_TWN_"^"_ST_"^"_ZIP_"^"_OTEL_
......  "^"_HTEL
        S  ^NAME("A",NAM,NUM)=""
        S  ^NAME("B",TWN,NAM,NUM)=""
        F  J3=1:1 R !,"Enter comment:",?59,"v",!,COM Q:COM=""   D COMMENT
        S  ^NAME(NUM,"COMMENT")=J3-1
        D  ^CH11EX4
        Q
```

SEARCHING A "MULTI-NODE" SUBFILE WITH THE CONTAINS OPERATOR

17.   How might we design a program to: search our multi-node comment subfile in alphabetic order by name for a specified string; display all data for each name on which the comment subfile includes this string?

First, prompt the user to enter a string.

Second, use $ORDER to go through our "A" cross reference file in alphabetic order, and return third level subscripts (these subscripts represent unique identifiers in our primary file).

Third, use $ORDER to go through our multi-node "COMMENTS" file and:

(1)   Check each COMMENT node with the contains operator

(2)   Set a flag if the desired string is detected

(3)   If the flag is set, then DO our DISPLAY module from CH11EX2

18.   Now write the code to perform these functions. Call your new program CH11EX6.

Here's how we did it:

```
CH11EX6  ;SEARCH COMMENTS FOR SPECIFIED STRING
         ;THIS PROGRAM OPERATES WITH NAME FILE BUILT FROM CH11EX1
         ;THIS PROGRAM ALLOWS USER TO ENTER ANY STRING, THEN SEARCH
         ; THE COMMENT SUBFILE.
         ;
         K
         W !!!,"COMMENT SEARCH"
         F J1=0:0 R !!,"SEARCH FOR: ",SRCH Q:SRCH=""  D FIND
         W !!!,"Finished" Q
         ;
FIND     ;GET EACH NAME IN ALPHA ORDER
         W !!!!,"SEARCHING FOR ",SRCH,!!!!
         S B=""
         F J2=0:0 S B=$O(^NAME("A",B)) Q:B=""  D FIND1
         Q
         ;
FIND1    ;FIND SUBSCRIPT FOR PRIMARY FILE FROM 3RD LEVEL OF CROSS
......   ;REFERENCE FILE
         S C=""
```

```
          F  J3=0:0  S  C=$O(^NAME("A",B,C))  Q:C=""   D  FIND2
          Q
          ;
FIND2     ;GO  THROUGH  EACH  COMMENT  NODE  IN  PRIMARY  FILE
          S  C1="",FLAG="NOT  FOUND"
          F  J4=0:0  S  C1=$O(^NAME(C,"COMMENT",C1))  Q:(C1="")!
......    (FLAG="FOUND")    D  FIND3
          I  FLAG="FOUND"  D  DISPLAY^CH11EX2
          Q
          ;
FIND3     I  ^NAME(C,"COMMENT",C1)  [SRCH  S  FLAG="FOUND"
          Q
```

19.   Notice how line FIND2 + 3 uses the DISPLAY module from CH11EX2. You save a lot of time by "re-using" modules which perform similar or identical functions. This also makes your code easier to read: you can "skip over" those modules which are identical to other modules, and write only those portions which contain "new and different" code.

However, be careful when re-using a module. Make sure the re-used module does not alter variables from the calling routine in a manner which will affect the calling routine. For example, your module may KILL variables used by the calling routine.

PROGRAMS FOR "FILE MAINTENANCE"

20.   In the first four sections of this chapter, we presented some simple methods to create and edit multi-node subfiles.

After we have created a file, we will need to "maintain" this file. In this section, we will present examples of "file maintenance":

- delete entries from primary file and associated cross reference files

- add or change entries in the COMMENT subfile

- change data in the ˌNAME primary file, and associated cross reference files.

DELETE ENTRY FROM PRIMARY FILE AND ASSOCIATED CROSS REFERENCE FILES

21.   Let's consider the problem of deleting a particular name from our primary file, plus our "A" and "B" cross reference files. What functions need to be performed?

---

1.   Allow user to enter name for deletion.

2.   If $DATA exists for the name entered, then $ORDER through the third level of our cross

reference file to obtain unique identifiers from the primary file (there may be several "John Smiths" in our primary file).

      2.1   Create a temporary array of all people with this name, plus "identifiers" (such as address), so the user can elect "which John Smith should be deleted".

      2.2   Display names plus "identifiers" - ask user to choose a name for deletion.

      2.3   Ask user to verify the name to be deleted. If user verifies, delete entry from primary file and cross reference files.

   3.   If $DATA does not exist for the name entered, then look for a "partial match". To do this, $ORDER through the second level of our cross reference file. If $EXTRACT (for the number of characters entered) from the cross reference file provides a match, then perform functions 2.1-2.3.

   22.   Now write the code to perform these functions. We suggest you plan this program in modules.

Here's how we did it:

```
CH11EX7  ;DELETE AN ENTRY FROM THE NAME FILE
         ;THIS PROGRAM WILL OPERATE WITH MULTI-NODE COMMENT SUBFILE
         ;CREATED BY CH11EX1.   PRIMARY FILE AND BOTH CROSS REFERENCE
         ;FILES ARE DELETED
         ;
         K
         W !!!,"DELETE FILE ENTRIES",!
         ;
         ;SEARCH FOR NAME TO DELETE, DO DELETE MODULE IF NAME IS FOUND
         ;
         F K1=0:0 R !!,"Delete entry: ",NAME Q:NAME=""  D SELECT,
......   DELETE:NAME'=""
         W !!!,"Finished" Q
         ;
SELECT   ;SELECT FILE ENTRY
         ;THIS MODULE SETS THE FOLLOWING VARIABLES:
         ;     NAME = COMPLETE NAME OF ENTRY SELECTED  (NULL IF NO
         ; ENTRY FOUND)
         ;     NUM = UNIQUE IDENTIFIER OF ENTRY SELECTED
         ;     CNT = COUNTS # OF NAMES THAT MATCH SELECTED NAME
         ;     FL = FLAG
         ;     B = $ORDER VARIABLE
         ;NAM ARRAY IS KILLED TO 'ERASE' THE ARRAY - WHICH IS
```

```
              ;CREATED ON EACH CALL OF THE SELECT MODULE IN THIS ROUTINE
              ;THE NAM ARRAY IS CREATED IN SELECT3 TO DISPLAY TO USER ALL
              ;NAMES (PLUS UNIQUE IDENTIFIERS) WHICH MATCH THE NAME
              ; ENTERED FOR DELETION
              ;
              S (CNT,FL)=0,B=NAME,LEN=$L(NAME) K NAM
              ;
              ;CHECK IF SEARCH NAME ENTERED EXACTLY MATCHES A NAME IN FILE
              ;
              I $D(^NAME("A",NAME)) S FL=1
              ;
              ;FL IS USED TO DO SELECT2 WHEN AN EXACT MATCH
              ;IS FOUND. IF COMPLETE SEARCH NAME IS ENTERED, WE DO SELECT2
              ;
              I FL D SELECT2
              ;
              ; IF NO COMPLETE SEARCH NAME IS ENTERED, THEN WE LOOK FOR
              ;PARTIAL MATCHES.WE USE $ORDER AND $EXTRACT WITH OUR ALPHA
              ;CROSS REFERENCE FILE
              ;IF A PARTIAL MATCH IS FOUND, WE DO SELECT2 AND COUNT THE
              ;NUMBER OF PARTIAL MATCHES FOUND VIA SELECT3
              ;
              I 'FL F K2=0:0 S B=$O(^NAME("A",B)) Q:B=""!($E(B,1,LEN)'=NAME)
......  D SELECT2
              ;
              ;SET NAME = NULL IF NO MATCHES IN FILE ARE FOUND, THEN QUIT
              ;
              I CNT=0 S NAME="" Q
              ;
              ; IF ONE MATCH FOUND, SET NAME = FIRST PIECE FROM OUR TEMPORARY
              ;ARRAY.ALSO SET NUM = SECOND PIECE FROM OUR TEMPORARY ARRAY.
              ;
              I CNT=1 S NAME=$P(NAM(1),"^",1),NUM=$P(NAM(1),"^",2) Q
SELECT1 ;THIS PORTION OF CODE IS REACHED FROM SELECT WHEN
              ;MULTIPLE MATCHES ARE FOUND IN SELECT2 AND SELECT3
              ;
              W !,"CHOOSE 1-",CNT,": " R ANS
              ;
              ; IF NO MATCH IS CHOSEN, SET NAME = NULL AND QUIT
              ;
              I ANS="" S NAME="" Q
              I '$D(NAM(ANS)) W !!,"ENTER WHOLE NUMBER FROM 1 TO ",CNT,!
......  G SELECT1
              S NAME=$P(NAM(ANS),"^",1),NUM=$P(NAM(ANS),"^",2)
              ;THIS IS THE SAME CODE AS THE LAST LINE OF SELECT
              Q
              ;
SELECT2 ;WE ACCESS THIS MODULE FROM EITHER OF TWO POINTS IN SELECT -
              ;DEPENDING ON WHETHER A COMPLETE OR PARTIAL MATCH IS FOUND
              ;THIS MODULE FINDS UNIQUE IDENTIFIER, THEN DOES SELECT3
              ;REMEMBER - WE MIGHT HAVE MORE THAN ONE PERSON WITH EXACTLY
              ; THE SAME NAME
```

```
        ;
        S  C=""
        F  K3=0:0  S  C=$O(^NAME("A",B,C))  Q:C=""   D  SELECT3
        Q
        ;
SELECT3 ;CREATE  NAM  ARRAY  FOR  ALL  NAME  MATCHES  FOUND  IN  SELECT2
        ;LIST  ALL  NAME  MATCHES  FOUND  IN  SELECT1
        ;
        S  CNT=CNT+1
        ;
        ;PRINT  ASSIGNED  NUMBER  AND  NAME,  ADDRESS  &  TOWN  TO  IDENTIFY
        ;FILE  ENTRY
        ;
        W  !?5,CNT,?10,$P(^NAME(C),"^",1,3)
        ;
        ;SAVE  COMPLETE  NAME  ('B')  AND  UNIQUE  IDENTIFIER  ('C')  IN  NAM
        ;ARRAY
        ;
        S  NAM(CNT)=B_"^"_C
        Q
        ;
DELETE  ;DELETE  FILE  ENTRY,  FIRST  CONFIRM  DELETION
        ;THIS  CODE  IS  REACHED  FROM  CH11EX7
        W  !!!,"***** VERIFY  DELETION *****",!
        S  DATA=^NAME(NUM)
        ;
        ;PRINT  IDENTIFYING  INFORMATION
        ;SAVE  TOWN  NAME  TO  DELETE  TOWN  CROSS  REFERENCE
        ;IN  THE  LAST  PART  OF  FOR  LOOP,  WE  SET  TWN  EQUAL  TO  THIRD
        ;PIECE  OF  DATA  FROM  NODE  OF  PRIMARY  FILE
        ;
        F  K4=1:1:5  W  ?$X+5,$P(DATA,"^",K4)  I  K4=3  S  TWN=$P(DATA,"^",3)
        W  !,"Are  you  sure  you  want  to  delete  this  entry?  NO=> "  R  ANS
        I  ANS'="Y"  W  !!!,"*** ENTRY  NOT  DELETED!! ***",!  Q
        ;
        ;DELETE  ENTRY  AND  BOTH  CROSS  REFERENCES  FOR  ENTRY
        ;
        K  ^NAME(NUM),^NAME("A",NAME,NUM),^NAME("B",TWN,NAME,NUM)
        W  !!!,"***   DELETED!!   ***",!
        Q
```

23.   This program does NOT relate to our COMMENT subfiles - but only to the primary file and cross reference files.

ADD OR CHANGE ENTRIES IN COMMENT SUBFILE

24.   Now let's consider the problem of adding - or changing - entries in our multi-node COMMENT subfile. What functions need to be performed?

(1)   Allow user to enter a name.

(2)   Use our subroutine SELECT.CH11EX7 to go through the "A" cross reference file and look for complete - or partial - matches against the entry from #1 above. This subroutine also allows the user to select a specific name from those names which "match" the original entry.

(3)   Use our subroutine DISPLAY.CH11EX4 to display all comments from the primary file on the name selected.

(4)   Allow the user a choice of adding new comments or editing existing comments.

(5)   If the user wishes to edit existing comments, provide this function via our subroutine EDIT.CH11EX4.

(6)   If the user wishes to add comments, obtain the last third level "comment subscript" - value of .NAME(nnn,"COMMENT") - and increment this by one, to obtain the next third level "comment subscript".

(7)   Allow the user to enter comment: then check length (under 61 characters), and create new node in COMMENT subfile.

25. Now write the code to perform these functions. Call your new program CH11EX8.

Here's how we did it:

```
CH11EX8 ;ADD OR CHANGE DATA IN COMMENT SUBFILE
        ;THIS PROGRAM WORKS WITH MULTI-NODE COMMENT SUBFILE CREATED
        ;BY CH11EX1
        ;
        K
        W !!!,"ADD OR EDIT COMMENTS",!
        F K1=0:0 R !!,"Select entry: ",NAME Q:NAME=""  D MODIFY
        W !!!,"Finished" Q
        ;
MODIFY ;SELECT ENTRY THEN ADD OR EDIT COMMENTS
        D SELECT^CH11EX7
        ;
        ;KILL ALL NON-ESSENTIAL VARIABLES
        ;
        K (NAME,NUM,K1)
```

```
             ;
             ;QUIT IF SEARCH NAME NOT FOUND IN FILE (NAME IS NULL)
             ;
             I NAME="" Q
MODIFY1  ;LOOP
             ;DISPLAY ALL COMMENTS
             ;
             D DISPLAY^CH11EX4
             R !,"Add comments (A), Edit comments (E), or quit (RETURN)? ",ANS
             I ANS="" Q
             I ANS="A" D ADD
             I ANS="E" D EDIT^CH11EX4
             ;
             ;KILL ALL NON-ESSENTIAL VARIABLES
             ;
             K (NAME,NUM,K1)
             G MODIFY1
             ;
ADD       ;ADD COMMENTS TO ENTRY
             S NEXT=^NAME(NUM,"COMMENT")+1
             F K2=NEXT:1 R !,"Enter comment: ",?59,"v",!,COM Q:COM=""  D ADD1
             S ^NAME(NUM,"COMMENT")=K2-1
             Q
             ;
ADD1      ;CHECK COMMENT
             I $L(COM)<61 S ^NAME(NUM,"COMMENT",K2)=COM Q
             S K2=K2-1
             W !!,"COMMENT MAY NOT EXCEED 60 CHARACTERS!",!
             Q
```

In this code, most of the "work" is done by subroutines from other programs! There are less than 30 lines of "working code" - everything else is "comment lines".

CHANGE DATA IN ^NAME PRIMARY FILE AND ASSOCIATED CROSS REFERENCE FILES

26.   Let's consider the problem of allowing users to change data in our ^NAME file: including our primary file, cross reference file(s), and multi-node COMMENT file.

What functions need to be performed?

---

(1)   Allow user to enter the name for an entry in our primary file.

(2)   Use our subroutine SELECT^CH11EX7 to go through the "A" cross reference file and look for complete - or partial - matches against the

238

entry from #1 above. This subroutine also allows the user to select a specific name from those names which "match" the original entry.

(3) Read the data from the seven pieces of our primary file into a local array.

(4) Allow user to: leave name (the first piece) unchanged; modify name; or delete by entering "@".

(5) Allow user to: leave address (the second piece) unchanged; modify address; or delete by entering "@".

(6) Allow user to: leave town (the third piece) unchanged; modify town name; or delete by entering "@". Use TWNFIND^CH11EX5A subroutine to ensure that a "legitimate" town name is used as new entry. Before you run this new program, we suggest that you run ^CH11EX5 and add "none" to your town dictionary file for entries without a town.

(7) Allow user to: leave state (the fourth piece) unchanged; modify state; or delete by entering "@".

(8) Allow user to: leave ZIP code (the fifth piece) unchanged; modify zip code; or delete by entering "@".

(9) Allow user to: leave office phone(s) unchanged (sixth piece); modify office phone(s); delete one or more office phones by entering "@".

NOTE: if we delete the "first" office phone entry, this will present problems for our display program - which will not progress beyond the null string in our first "subpiece". To solve this problem, we will need to check our three office phone entries - and make sure that the "real entries" precede our "null strings".

(10) Allow user to: leave home phone (seventh piece) unchanged; modify home phone; delete by entering "@".

(11) Reset the node in our primary file with new concatenated data.

(12) Update cross reference file(s). Allow user to add or edit comments via ^CH11EX8.

27. Now write the code to perform these functions.

Here's how we did it:

```
CH11EX9  ;MODIFY ALL DATA IN ^NAME FILE
         ;THIS PROGRAM WORKS WITH THE MULTI-NODE COMMENT SUBFILE
         ;
         K
         W !!!,"MODIFY ALL FILE DATA",!!
         F J1=0:0 R !,"Modify what entry: ",NAME Q:NAME=""  D MODIFY
         W !!!,"Finished" Q
         ;
MODIFY   ;SELECT ENTRY THEN MODIFY ALL DATA
         D SELECT^CH11EX7
         ;
         ;KILL ALL NON-ESSENTIAL VARIABLES
         ;
         K (NAME,NUM,K1)
         ;
         ;QUIT IF SEARCH NAME NOT FOUND IN FILE (NAME IS NULL)
         ;
         I NAME="" Q
         ;
         ;SET FILE INFORMATION INTO DATA ARRAY
         ;
         F J2=1:1:7 S DATA(J2)=$P(^NAME(NUM),"^",J2)
EDIT     ;EDIT THE DATA
         W !!,"Name: ",DATA(1),"// " R NEWNAM
         ;
         ;IF NAME NOT CHANGED (NEWNAM="") SET NEWNAM = OLD NAME
         ;(DATA(1))
         ;
         I NEWNAM="" S NEWNAM=DATA(1)
         ;
         ;IF NEWNAM = @ DO DELETE MODULE OF CH11EX7
         ;IF ENTRY DELETED (ANS = 'Y') QUIT, ELSE RE-EDIT NAME
         ;
         I NEWNAM="@" D DELETE^CH11EX7 Q:ANS="Y"  S NEWNAM=""
         I NEWNAM'?1A.AP W !!,"ENTER ALPHA CHARACTER ONLY!",!
......   S NEWNAM=""
         I $L(NEWNAM)>50 W !!,"NAME MAY NOT EXCEED 50 CHARACTERS!",
......   ! S NEWNAM=""
         ;
         ;NEWNAM INVALID IF NULL AT THIS POINT
         ;
         I NEWNAM="" G EDIT
EDIT1    W !,"Address: ",DATA(2),"// " R NEW
         I NEW="" S NEW=DATA(2)
         ;
         ;IF ADDRESS IS DELETED, SET ADDRESS = 'NONE'
         ;
         I NEW="@" S (NEW,DATA(2))="NONE" W "    ...DELETED"
         I $L(NEW)>80 W !!,"ADDRESS MAY NOT EXCEED 80 CHARACTERS!",
......   ! G EDIT1
```

```
        S DATA(2)=NEW
EDIT2   W !,"Town: ",DATA(3),"// " R NEWTWN
        I NEWTWN="" S NEWTWN=DATA(3)
        I NEWTWN="@" S NEWTWN="NONE" W "    ...DELETED"
        ;
        ;TWN MUST BE DEFINED TO DO TWNFIND MODULE OF ^CH11EX5A
        ;
        S TWN=NEWTWN
        D TWNFIND^CH11EX5A
        I TWN="" W !!,"NO MATCHES FOUND",! G EDIT2
        S NEWTWN=TWN
EDIT3   W !,"State: ",DATA(4),"// " R NEW
        I NEW="" S NEW=DATA(4)
        I NEW="@" S (NEW,DATA(4))="NONE" W "    ...DELETED"
        I NEW'?2A&(NEW'="NONE") W !!,"ENTER TWO LETTERS FOR STATE!",
......  ! G EDIT3
        S DATA(4)=NEW
EDIT4   W !,"Zip code: ",DATA(5),"// " R NEW
        I NEW="" S NEW=DATA(5)
        I NEW="@" S (NEW,DATA(5))="NONE" W "    ...DELETED"
        I NEW'?5N&(NEW'="NONE") W !!,"ENTER FIVE NUMBERS FOR ZIP
......  CODE!",! G EDIT4
        S DATA(5)=NEW
        ;
        ;SET UP OTEL ARRAY FOR OFFICE PHONE
        ;
        F J3=1:1:3 S OTEL(J3)=$P(DATA(6),"\",J3)
EDIT5   ;EDIT OFFICE TELEPHONE NUMBERS
        F J4=1:1:3 W !,"Office telephone #",J4,": ",OTEL(J4),"// "
......  R NEW D ENTRTEL
        ;
        ;SET UP SORT ARRAY
        ;CNT WILL COUNT # OF NON-NULL OFFICE PHONE #'S
        ;
        S (SORT(1),SORT(2),SORT(3))="",CNT=1
        ;
        ;FOR LOOP MOVES NON-NULL PHONE NUMBERS INTO LOWER NUMBERED PIECES
        ;OF DATA(6)
        ;
        F J5=1:1:3 I OTEL(J5)'="" S SORT(CNT)=OTEL(J5),CNT=CNT+1
        ;
        ;RESET OTEL IN SORTED ORDER
        ;
        S OTEL(1)=SORT(1),OTEL(2)=SORT(2),OTEL(3)=SORT(3)
        S DATA(6)=OTEL(1)_"\"_OTEL(2)_"\ _OTEL(3)
EDIT6   W !,"Home phone: ",DATA(7),"// " R NEW
        I NEW="" S NEW=DATA(7)
        ;
        ;IF HOME PHONE IS DELETED, SET IT TO 'U' (UNKNOWN)
        ;
        I NEW="@" S (NEW,DATA(7))="U" W "    ...DELETED"
        I NEW'?3N1"-"3N1"-"4N&(NEW'="U") D ERRHTEL G EDIT6
```

```
        S  DATA(7)=NEW
        ;
        ;SET MODIFIED DATA INTO GLOBAL
        ;
        ;  S^NAME(NUM)=NEWNAM_"^"_DATA(2)_"^"_NEWTWN_"^"_DATA(4)_"^"_
......  DATA(5)_"^"_DATA(6)_"^"_DATA(7)
        ;
        ;UPDATE CROSS REFERENCE FILES IF NECESSARY
        ;
        I  NEWNAM'=DATA(1)  K  ^NAME("A",DATA(1),NUM)
......  S  ^NAME("A",NEWNAM,NUM)=""
        I  NEWNAM'=DATA(1)!(NEWTWN'=DATA(3))
......  K  ^NAME("B",DATA(3),DATA(1),NUM)
        ;
        ;ARGUMENTLESS IF TAKES SAME CONDITION AS ABOVE
        ;USED TO ELIMINATE WRAP-AROUND ON SET & KILL OF 'B' CROSS
        ;REFERENCE
        ;
        I   S  ^NAME("B",NEWTWN,NEWNAM,NUM)=""
EDIT7   ;ADD OR EDIT COMMENTS
        D  MODIFY1^CH11EX8
        Q
        ;
ENTRTEL I  NEW=""  Q
        I  NEW="@"  S  OTEL(J4)=""  W  "   ...DELETED"  Q
        I  NEW?3N1"-"3N1"-"4N  S  OTEL(J4)=NEW  Q
        W  !!,"ENTER PHONE NUMBER IN THE FORMAT 'nnn-nnn-nnnn'."
        ;
        ;RE-EDIT SAME PHONE NUMBER IF NEW PHONE IS INVALID
        ;
        S  J4=J4-1
        Q
        ;
ERRHTEL W  !!,"ENTER PHONE NUMBER IN THE FORMAT 'nnn-nnn-nnnn'."
        W  !,"IF UNKNOWN, ENTER 'U'.",!
        Q
```

28.   Notice how CH11EX9 "calls":

  (1)   subroutines from ^CH11EX7 and ^CH11EX5A

  (2)   ^CH11EX8.

Advantages of this approach include:

  (1)   less time required to write CH11EX9

  (2)   our program is shorter, and easier to understand.

242

If desired, we could further "break down" CH11EX9 to an even shorter "main program" - which would "call" a series of routines and subroutines to perform the "real work".

29.   Notice the three successive lines EDIT + 10 - EDIT + 13. If NEWNAM equals "@", we DO our subroutine DELETE^CH11EX7. If NEWNAM fails the pattern match, we set NEW-NAM equal to a null string. If NEWNAM is over 50 characters, we set NEWNAM equal to a null string.

30.   In the EDIT2 portion of our EDIT module, notice that we DO TWNFIND ^CH11EX5A even if town was not changed. Some programmers would prefer to DO this subroutine only if a change had been made.

31.   The EDIT5 portion of our EDIT module has some new code, which looks different from other programs up to this point.

Our problem here is that if we have three office phones, and then delete the first, our DISPLAY program will stop on a null entry (the first number, which was deleted) - and will not display our remaining two phone numbers. Let's assume we've deleted the first of three office phone numbers - and see how EDIT5 solves this problem.

First, we set up our OTEL array in line EDIT4 + 8.

Second, we display our OTEL array, accept a NEW entry, and DO the ENTRTEL module. If NEW is a "@", we set our OTEL array element equal to a null entry. If the pattern match is ok, we set our OTEL array element equal to our NEW entry.

Third, we set up our SORT array - with each array element equal to a null entry. We also set the simple variable CNT equal to one.

Fourth, we go through our OTEL array: if our array element is NOT equal to a null entry, then we set SORT(CNT) equal to the OTEL array element and increment CNT. Note that CNT counts the non-null telephone numbers.

Fifth, we re-create our OTEL array based on contents of our SORT array.

Sixth, we create DATA(6) as a concatenation of our OTEL array elements.

SUMMARY OF NEW CONCEPTS - CHAPTER 11

Multi-node subfile for a primary file:

- object is to store more than 255 characters for one record in primary file

- one possible file structure:

```
                                    <^NAME(1,"COMMENT")=data
                   <^NAME(1)--<
^NAME--<                            <^NAME(n,"COMMENT")=data
          <
```

  - can store value of next available subscript at third level as value for NAME(n,"COMMENT")

  - can build subfile at third level via FOR loop incremented by one

- display comment subfile via $ORDER operation on third level of primary file.

Two argument form of $FIND:

- returns a number specifying position of the first character after a specified substring

- syntax:

  $FIND(string,substring)

- example:

```
SET DATE="January 23, 1984"
WRITE $FIND(DATE,",")
```

  returns 12.

Three argument form of $FIND:

- allows you to begin search at some position other than first character of specified string

- syntax:

  $FIND(string,substring,position within string to begin search)

- example:

```
SET DATA="Part No 7,324:January 7, 1984"
WRITE $FIND(DATA,",",14)
```

   returns 25.

Editing strings with $FIND and $EXTRACT

- prompt user to enter OLD substring

- prompt user to enter NEW substring

- SET POSITION equal to $FIND(STRING,OLD)

- SET OLDLENGTH = $LENGTH(OLD)+1

- SET FRSTTEXT = $EXTRACT(STRING,1,(POSITION-OLDLENGTH))

- SET LASTTEXT = $EXTRACT(STRING,POSITION,999)

- SET NEWSTRNG = FRSTTEXT_NEW_LASTTEXT

CHAPTER TWELVE

DISPLAYING MENUS

You have now learned how to: build files; display files in a specific order (such as name within town); search files for data on a particular entry (such as specific name entered by the user); display all entries with specific data in common (such as the same name); delete entries in a primary file plus corresponding cross reference files; change data in a primary file plus corresponding cross reference files; use a "dictionary" (such as allowable names for towns or states) to check new entries against the "dictionary".

In this chapter, you will learn how to display a "menu" of programs relating to our ᐱNAME file, and make "selections" from this menu.

Topics presented include:

Displaying menus

- multiple WRITE commands

- the PRINT command

- the $TEXT function

Making selections from menus

- post conditionals vs multiple IF commands

- the $SELECT function (with and without indirection)

- the $TEXT function (with and without indirection)

- the $EXTRACT function

The $TEST special variable

- $TEST and the IF command

- $TEST and the ELSE command

- $TEST and the timed READ command

The HALT command

Special commands and functions related to menu display and selection:

- asterisk WRITE (implementation specific)

- the $CHAR function

- the $ASCII function

- asterisk READ

By the end of this chapter, you will be able to:

- display menus with any desired length and format

- make selections from menus

- use the $TEST variable with the argumentless IF command, the ELSE command, and the timed READ command to display "special instructions" if the user does not respond within a specified time period

- use asterisk syntax of the WRITE command (or the $CHAR function) to perform specific terminal functions - such as blanking a video screen and returning the cursor to upper left hand corner

- use asterisk syntax of the READ command to make menu selections via a single keystroke.

DISPLAYING MENUS

1. Let's assume we have nine related routines:

    NABLD - enter names and data into "name" file

    NATWNLST - list dictionary of "town" names

    NATWNBLD - build dictionary of "town" names

    NACOMSRC - search for a specified comment

    NAMOD - modify data in primary and cross reference files

    NADEL - delete a name and/or data from primary and cross
    reference files

    NADATA - display all data for a given name

    NAALPHA - report all names and data in alpha order by name

    NATWN - print all names and data in alpha order by town.

It would be helpful to display these options as a "menu" - so the user could see brief descriptions of all nine routines - and choose the desired program.

2. Check the user manual for your implementation of Standard MUMPS. Most systems will include utility programs for the following functions:

    *   global display - display the contents for a specified global (our system uses %G)

    *   global directory - display the names for all globals in alpha order (our system uses %GD)

    *   routine directory - display the names for all routines in alpha order (our system uses %RD)

When you use "routine directory" (or the equivalent for your system), it's convenient if related routines are listed together, in alphabetic order. For this reason, when you develop a group of related routines, we suggest that these routine names begin with the same first two letters.

MULTIPLE WRITE COMMANDS

3. Here is a simple way to display menus:

```
CH12EX1 ;DISPLAY MENU WITH MULTIPLE WRITE COMMANDS
        ;SELECTION VIA MULTIPLE IF COMMANDS
        ;
        F INDEX=0:0 D DISPLAY I ANS="" Q
        W !!,"Finished" K  Q
        ;
DISPLAY W !!,"Enter the number of desired option"
        W !,"Enter RETURN to exit program"
        W !!,"1.    Enter names and data"
        W !,"2.    List dictionary of town names"
        W !,"3.    Build dictionary of town names"
        W !,"4.    Search for a specified comment"
        W !,"5.    Modify data on file"
        W !,"6.    Delete data"
        W !,"7.    Display all data for a specified name"
        W !,"8.    Report all names and data in alpha order by name"
        W !,"9.    Print all names and data in alpha order by town"
        R !!,"Option: ",ANS
        I ANS="" Q
        I (ANS'?1N)!(ANS<1)!(ANS>9) W !!,"Choose 1 to 9, or enter
......  RETURN to quit" G DISPLAY
        I ANS=1 D ^NABLD Q
        I ANS=2 D ^NATWNLST Q
        I ANS=3 D ^NATWNBLD Q
        I ANS=4 D ^NACOMSRC Q
        I ANS=5 D ^NAMOD Q
        I ANS=6 D ^NADEL Q
        I ANS=7 D ^NADATA Q
        I ANS=8 D ^NAALPHA Q
        D ^NATWN Q
```

Notice that we do NOT need an IF for the last line of code - since this represents a "default" condition.

THE PRINT COMMAND

4.   A second way to display menus is via the PRINT command.

You have already used the PRINT command with direct execution in the "direct mode" - by entering PRINT directly after a system prompt (our implementation uses a right caret - some other implementations use an asterisk). Operation of the PRINT command with direct execution is implementation specific - with our system, this displays the program in our partition of main memory.

You can also use the PRINT command as part of a program, i.e. after a line start character (our implementation uses the tab as a line start character; some other implementations use a single space). Like PRINT with direct execution, this also is implementation specific. Here is an example:

```
        PRINT OPTIONS+1:OPTIONS+9 Q
        ;
OPTIONS ;
        1.    Enter names and data
        2.    List dictionary of town names
        3.    Build dictionary of town names
        4.    Search for specified comment
        5.    Modify data on file
        6.    Delete data
        7.    Display all data for a specified name
        8.    Report all names and data in alpha order by name
        9.    Print all names and data in alpha order by town
```

5.   The **PRINT** command allows us to display any desired lines within a program. These lines do **NOT** need to be executable MUMPS code. In this program, the QUIT is needed to prevent program execution from reaching line **OPTIONS + 1**.

6.   Rewrite CH12EX1 to use this PRINT module CH12EX2.

Here's how we did it:

```
CH12EX2 ;DISPLAY MENU WITH PRINT COMMAND
        ;SELECTION VIA MULTIPLE IF COMMANDS
        ;
        F INDEX=0:0 D DISPLAY I ANS="" Q
        W !!,"Finished" K  Q
        ;
DISPLAY W !!,"Enter the number of desired option"
        W !,"Enter RETURN to quit program",!!
        P OPTIONS+1:OPTIONS+9
        R !!,"Option: ",ANS
        I ANS="" Q
        I (ANS'?1N)!(ANS<1)!(ANS>9) W !!,"Choose 1 to 9, or
...... enter RETURN to quit"
G DISPLAY
        I ANS=1 D ^NABLD Q
        I ANS=2 D ^NATWNLST Q
        I ANS=3 D ^NATWNBLD Q
        I ANS=4 D ^NACOMSRC Q
        I ANS=5 D ^NAMOD Q
        I ANS=6 D ^NADEL Q
        I ANS=7 D ^NADATA Q
        I ANS=8 D ^NAALPHA Q
        D ^NATWN Q
        ;
OPTIONS ;
        1.    Enter names and data
```

```
          2.    List dictionary of town names
          3.    Build dictionary of town names
          4.    Search for specified comment
          5.    Modify data on file
          6.    Delete data
          7.    Display all data for a specified name
          8.    Report all names and data in alpha order by name
          9.    Print all names and data in alpha order by town
```

7.   With the PRINT command, when we read our program, we clearly see exactly what will be displayed on the screen. For this reason, some people find CH12EX2 easier to read than CH12EX1.

THE $TEXT FUNCTION

8.   A third way to display menus is via the $TEXT function. The $TEXT function, like the PRINT command, returns specified lines "exactly as written". Here is an example:

```
CH12EX3  ;DEMONSTRATION OF $TEXT FUNCTION
       ;
       F  INDEX=1:1:9  W  !,$TEXT(OPTIONS+INDEX)
       Q
       ;
OPTIONS ;
          1.    Enter names and data
          2.    List dictionary of town names
          3.    Build dictionary of town names
          4.    Search for specified comment
          5.    Modify data on file
          6.    Delete data
          7.    Display all data for a specified name
          8.    Report all names and data in alpha order by name
          9.    Print all names and data in alpha order by town
```

9.   In contrast to the PRINT command, we use a FOR loop, rather than a colon, to "step through" the nine lines of text. And in contrast to the PRINT command, $TEXT is NOT implementation specific.

The QUIT command prevents execution from "running over" into our OPTIONS module: if this happened, we would get an error message, such as <CMMD>, meaning "invalid command".

MAKING SELECTIONS FROM MENUS

POST CONDITIONALS VS MULTIPLE IF COMMANDS

10.   Up to this point, we have used a rather simple method to make selections from a menu:

- READ our used entry into a local variable such as ANS

- evaluate this local variable via a series of IF commands.

We could, of course, use multiple post conditionals, to shorten our code. For example:

D ^NABLD: ANS=1, ^NATWN: ANS=2, . . . etc.

This shortens our code. However, with post conditionals, every argument must be examined. With multiple IF commands, we QUIT as soon as we find a true condition.

NAME INDIRECTION

11.   "Name indirection" allows the current value of a variable to be interpreted as MUMPS code. The syntax for name indirection is expressed as: @(variable). The "at sign" means: "whatever is at (current value of variable)".

Here is a simple example of name indirection:

```
CH12EX4 ;EXAMPLE OF NAME INDIRECTION TO INTERPRET
        ;LITERAL STRING AS LINE LABEL
        ;
        F INDEX=0:0 D MOD Q:ANS=""  D @ANS
        W !!,"Finished" K  Q
        ;
MOD     W !,"Enter 'A' to add a new name and/or data."
        W !,"Enter 'C' to change name(s) and/or data ."
        W !,"Enter 'D' to delete name(s) and/or data."
        R !,"OPTION: ",ANS
        I (ANS'?1"A")&(ANS'?1"C")&(ANS'?1"D")&(ANS'="")  S ANS="ERR"
        Q
        ;
A       W !,"THIS MODULE ADDS NEW NAME(S) AND/OR DATA" Q
C       W !,"THIS MODULE ALLOWS USER TO CHANGE NAME(S) AND/OR DATA" Q
D       W !,"THIS MODULE ALLOWS USER TO DELETE NAME(S) AND/OR DATA" Q
ERR     W !!,"ENTER 'A', 'C' OR 'D' ONLY!" Q
```

12.   We can also use name indirection to access programs from disk. For example, instead of module A, we could access PGMA; instead of module C, we could access PGMC; instead of module D we could access PGMD. To do this, we would insert the following code before the DO command at the end of our FOR loop:

S ANS="^PGM"_ANS D @ANS

13.   Modify CH12EX2 from Frame 6 to use name indirection in place of the multiple IF commands. Call you new program CH12EX2A.

Here's how we did it:

```
CH12EX2A ;DISPLAY MENU WITH PRINT COMMAND
         ;SELECTION VIA NAME INDIRECTION IN PLACE OF MULTIPLE IF COMMANDS
         ;
         F INDEX=0:0 D DISPLAY Q:ANS=""   S ANS="^NA"_ANS D @ANS
         W !!,"Finished" K  Q
         ;
DISPLAY W !!,"Enter code for desired option"
         W !,"Enter RETURN to exit program",!!
         P OPTIONS+1:OPTIONS+9
         R !!,"Option: ",ANS
         I ANS="" Q
         I ANS="BLD"!(ANS="TWNLST")!(ANS="TWNBLD")!(ANS="COMSRC")!
......   (ANS="MOD")!(ANS="DEL")!(ANS="DATA")!(ANS="ALPHA")!(ANS="TWN") Q
         W !!,"Please enter correct code for function desired"
         G DISPLAY
         ;
OPTIONS ;
         BLD    - Enter names and data
         TWNLST - List dictionary of town names
         TWNBLD - Build dictionary of town names
         COMSRC - Search for specified comment
         MOD    - Modify data on file
         DEL    - Delete data
         DATA   - Display all data for specified name
         ALPHA  - Report all names and data in alpha order by name
         TWN    - Print all names and data in alpha order by town
```

THE $SELECT FUNCTION

14.   A third technique for making selections from menus involves the $SELECT function. Rather than multiple post conditionals on "one line" to replace a long sequence of IF commands, we can use the $SELECT function to execute a long sequence of IF commands. The syntax for $SELECT is:

    SELECT(logic expression#1:string#1,...,logic expression#n:string#n)

If logic expression#1 is true, string#1 is returned, and we exit the $SELECT function. Otherwise, $SELECT proceeds to evaluate the next expression in this sequence.

If $SELECT finds no "true" expression within the parentheses, program execution stops with an error message. For our implementation, the error message returned is <$SERR>.

15.   We can solve this problem of "no true expression" within the parentheses by entering a "1" for our last logic expression.

If no other expression is true, then the numeric value of "1" will be considered as true - and whatever string value we associate with the "1" will be returned.

16.   Here is an example, using $SELECT with indirection:

```
        F INDEX=0:0 D DISPLAY Q:ANS="" D @PGM
        W !!,"Finished" K  Q
        ;
DISPLAY PRINT OPTIONS+1:OPTIONS+7
        R !!,"Select option: ",ANS I ANS="" Q
        S PGM=$SELECT(ANS=1:"^NABLD",ANS=2:"^NATWNLST",
......  ANS=3:"^NATWNBLD",ANS=4:"^NACOMSRC",ANS=5:"^NAMOD",ANS=6:"^NADEL",
......  ANS=7:"^NADATA",ANS=8:"^NAALPHA",ANS=9:"^NATWN",1:"")
        I PGM="" W !,"ENTER AN OPTION NUMBER BETWEEN 1 AND 9",!!GDISPLAY
        Q
        ;
OPTIONS ;
        1.    Enter names and data
        2.    List dictionary of town names
        3.    Build dictionary of town names
        4.    Search for specified comment
        5.    Modify data on file
        6.    Delete data
        7.    Display all data for a specified name
        8.    Print all names and data in alpha order by name
        9.    Print all names and data in alpha order by town
```

In this example, if no entry is equal to a number between 1 and 9, $SELECT returns a null value.

However - look at that wrap around! Although $SELECT provides fewer lines than multiple IF commands - our code is NOT easier to read!

17.   Here is a solution to our wrap around problem:

```
S PGM=$S(ANS=1:"BLD",ANS=2:"TWNLST",ANS=3:"TWNBLD",1:"NEXT"
I PGM="NEXT" S PGM=$S(ANS=4:"COMSRC",ANS=5:"MOD",ANS=6:"DEL",1:"NEXT"
I PGM="NEXT" S PGM=$S(ANS=7:"DATA",ANS=8:"ALPHA",ANS=9:"TWN",1:""
S PGM="^NA"_PGM
I PGM="^NA" W !,"ENTER AN OPTION NUMBER BETWEEN 1 AND 9" G DISPLAY
Q
```

The next frames will demonstrate a more "advanced" method for menu selection, using the $TEXT function.

THE $TEXT FUNCTION

18.   We have already used the $TEXT function to display menus. We can also use $TEXT for menu selection. Here is a revised version of CH12EX3:

```
CH12EX5  ;DISPLAY MENU WITH $TEXT
         ;SELECT PROGRAM FROM MENU VIA $TEXT
         ;
         F INDEX=0:0 D DISPLAY I ANS="" Q
         W !!,"Finished" K  Q
         ;
DISPLAY  W !!,"Enter the number of desired option"
         W !,"Enter RETURN to exit program",!
         F J1=1:1:9 S DISPLY=$TEXT(OPTIONS+J1) W !,$P(DISPLY,"^")
         R !!,"Select option: ",ANS
         I ANS="" Q
         I (ANS?1N)&(ANS>0)&(ANS<10) D SELECT Q
         W !,"Choose 1 to 9, or enter RETURN to exit" G DISPLAY
         ;
OPTIONS  ;
         1.    Build file^^NABLD
         2.    List town names^^NATWNLST
         3.    Build town name dictionary^^NATWNBLD
         4.    Search for specified comment^^NACOMSRC
         5.    Modify data on file^^NAMOD
         6.    Delete data^^NADEL
         7.    Display data for specified name^^NADATA
         8.    Print data in alpha order by name^^NAALPHA
         9.    Print data in alpha order by name within town^^NATWN
         ;
SELECT   ;
         S CHOICE=$TEXT(OPTIONS+ANS)
         S PROGRAM=$PIECE(CHOICE,"^",2,3)
         D @PROGRAM
         Q
```

In our SELECT module, we set CHOICE equal to the line selected, set PROGRAM equal to the program name, and DO @PROGRAM.

We use the four argument form of $PIECE to return ^NATWN if the user selects option #9. Syntax for the four argument form of $PIECE is:

$PIECE(string,delimiter,starting field,ending field)

The four argument form of $PIECE - $PIECE(CHOICE,"^",2,3) - returns the second and

256

third "pieces" - based on the "^" delimiter - including all intermediate occurrences of this delimiter.

In this situation, the three argument form of $PIECE would not meet our needs: $PIECE(CHOICE,"^",2) returns a null string since the "second piece" is null; while $PIECE(CHOICE, "^", 3) returns "NATWN".

19.   The technique shown in CH12EX5 is commonly used by professional MUMPS programmers. We will use this method for subsequent examples.

THE $EXTRACT FUNCTION

20.   Can we allow users to enter the first few letters of an option name - rather than a numeric code as in CH12EX5? Yes! We can do this by combining $EXTRACT with $TEXT and name indirection. The following operations are required:

- allow user to enter a string of any length

- obtain the first piece from first item in our OPTIONS module

- if $EXTRACT of this piece to the length of user entry is not equal to user entry, examine the next item in our OPTIONS module.

A "nice touch" is to have the program: (1) "fill in" the first option name which matches those characters entered by the user; (2) ask if this option is the one intended; (3) DO the program selected.

21.   Now write a menu display and selection program, using $EXTRACT to provide these functions. Use CH12EX5 as a model. Call your new program CH12EX6.

Here's how we did it:

```
CH12EX6  ;DISPLAY MENU VIA $TEXT
         ;SELECTION VIA $TEXT WITH $EXTRACT
         ;
         F  INDEX=0:0 D DISPLAY I ANS="" Q
         W !!,"Finished" K  Q
         ;
DISPLAY  W !!,"Enter the first few characters of desired option, or
......   RETURN",!
         F J1=1:1:9 S DISPLAY=$T(OPTIONS+J1) W !,$P(DISPLAY,"^")
         R !!,"Select option: ",ANS
         I ANS="" Q
         ;
```

257

```
       ;NOW LOOP THRU OPTIONS MODULE TO FIND MATCH ON $EXTRACT
       ;
       S LENGTH=$L(ANS)
       F J2=1:1:9 S ITEM=$T(OPTIONS+J2) D MATCH I ANS=EXTRACT Q
       E  W !!,"THIS IS NOT AN OPTION!" Q
       R !,"Is this the correct option? YES=> ",RESPONSE
       I RESPONSE?1"N".E G DISPLAY
       S PROGRAM=$P(ITEM,"^",2,3)
       D @PROGRAM
       Q
       ;
MATCH  S EXTRACT=$E($P(ITEM,"^"),2,LENGTH+1)
       I ANS=EXTRACT W $E($P(ITEM,"^"),LENGTH+2,255)
       Q
       ;
OPTIONS ;
       Enter names and data^^NABLD
       List dictionary of town names^^NATWNLST
       Build dictionary of town names^^NATWNBLD
       Search for specified comment^^NACOMSRC
       Modify data on file^^NAMOD
       Delete data^^NADEL
       Display data for specified name^^NADATA
       Report data in alpha order by name^^NAALPHA
       Print data in alpha order by name within town^^NATWN
```

22.   In no case does the user have to enter more than two letters to choose a unique option from the list displayed by CH12EX6.

In line MATCH, we extract characters '2' to 'LENGTH + 1' for comparison with the user's response in order to skip the line start character returned along with the first piece of ITEM.

THE $TEST SPECIAL VARIABLE

23.   The $TEST special variable is reset by the:

- IF command

- "timed READ" command

- "timed OPEN" command

- "timed LOCK" command

- "timed JOB" command.

The timed READ command will be discussed later in this chapter. The timed OPEN command, LOCK command and JOB command will be presented in Chapter Fifteen.

Neither post conditionals nor $SELECT have any effect on the $TEST special variable.

$TEST AND THE IF COMMAND

24. When Standard MUMPS evaluates the argument on an IF command, it sets $TEST equal to the "truth value" of this argument. When the argument is true, $TEST is set to one, and all statements on the same line are executed. When the argument is false, $TEST is set to zero, and control passes to the next line.

25. For IF with a comparative argument:

        IF FLAG="OK" DO ENTRY

- if the variable FLAG equals the literal string "OK", the truth value of this argument is one, $TEST is set to one, and remaining statements on this line are executed

- if the variable FLAG does not equal the literal string "OK", the truth value of this argument is zero, $TEST is set to zero, and control passes to the next line of code.

26. For IF with a non-comparative argument:

        IF FLAG DO ENTRY

- if the value of FLAG is any value other than zero or null (for example, "OK", 1, or 10), the truth value of this argument is one, $TEST is set to one, and the remaining statements on this line are executed

- if the value of FLAG is zero or null, the truth value of this argument is zero, $TEST is set to zero, and control passes to the next line of code.

27. For IF with a non-comparative argument using the NOT operator:

        IF 'FLAG DO ENTRY

- if the value of FLAG is zero or null, the truth value of this argument is one, $TEST is set to one, and the remaining statements on this line are executed

- if the value of flag is any value other than zero or null (for example, "OK", 1, or 10), the truth value of this argument is zero, $TEST is set to zero, and control passes to the next line of code.

28.   An argumentless IF command evaluates the "current status" of $TEST:

    IF   DO ENTRY1 , ENTRY2 , ENTRY3

- if $TEST is one, the remaining statements on that line of code are executed

- if $TEST is zero, control passes to the next line of code.

The code following this IF command is executed ONLY if $TEST has been set to one. The value of $TEST is reset by: IF (with an argument), timed READ, timed OPEN, timed LOCK and timed JOB.

29.   We can consider IF with no argument as equivalent to the following code:

    IF $TEST

Remember - argumentless commands - such as KILL, QUIT and IF - must be followed by at least two spaces.

$TEST AND THE ELSE COMMAND

30.   The ELSE command can be considered as the "reverse" of an argumentless IF. The ELSE command never takes an argument.

The argumentless ELSE command evaluates the current status of $TEST:

- if $TEST is one, control passes to the next line of code

- if $TEST is zero, remaining statements on the same line of code are executed.

31.   For example:

    IF FLAG="OK" DO ENTRY
    ELSE   DO MODULE

The ELSE command will be executed ONLY if $TEST is zero. In this particular example, $TEST is set to zero if the variable FLAG does not equal "OK". But what might happen if ENTRY contained an IF command?

An IF command in our ENTRY module could reset $TEST - and thus affect execution of our ELSE command.

32.   Before you use the ELSE command (or an argumentless IF), make sure you will NOT have a problem with $TEST being reset by another portion of your program! Here is one way to solve our problem with the code from frame 31:

```
IF FLAG="OK" DO ENTRY QUIT
ELSE   DO MODULE QUIT
```

Now, we have no problem with $TEST being reset by ENTRY. If we DO ENTRY, we QUIT before executing the ELSE command.

In this case, we can omit the ELSE command with no effect on program execution:

```
IF FLAG="OK" DO ENTRY QUIT
DO MODULE QUIT
```

Here, we use a "default" condition, rather than the ELSE command. In our own code, we seldom use the ELSE command, except in combination with the timed READ command.

$TEST AND THE TIMED READ COMMAND

33.   For a menu display, what would happen if the user "walked away" without making an entry?

The program would wait indefinitely for a response!

34.   MUMPS provides a "timed READ" command, which enables us to check whether the user has responded within a specified time period. The syntax is:

```
READ ANS: (number of seconds)
```

For example:

```
READ ANS: 20
```

If the user does not respond within 20 seconds, $TEST is set to zero, and ANS is assigned the value of "".

35.   What if the user enters a partial response before timeout occurs - i.e. several characters, without a carriage return? In this case, Standard MUMPS accepts whatever characters were entered as the value of ANS, and sets $TEST to zero.

36.   We can use the ELSE command to check results of a timed READ example:

```
READ ANS:20 ELSE  W !,"TIMEOUT OCCURRED"
```

This combination of timed READ and ELSE is commonly used with either:

   (1)   the HALT command, which automatically terminates program execution, or

   (2)   asterisk syntax of the WRITE command, which allows us to perform functions such as "ringing the bell or buzzer" on a computer terminal.

THE HALT COMMAND

37.   The HALT command automatically terminates program execution, and "logs off" your terminal. For example:

```
READ ANS:20 ELSE   HALT
```

will wait 20 seconds for a user response, then terminate program execution and log off if the user does not strike RETURN.

This "log off" action is somewhat drastic - in many cases you may prefer to "wake the user up" by "ringing the bell" on his terminal. This can be performed by the asterisk syntax of the WRITE command.

SPECIAL COMMANDS AND FUNCTIONS RELATED TO MENU DISPLAY AND SELECTION

ASTERISK WRITE

38.   In most implementations, the asterisk WRITE command outputs a single ASCII character. Syntax is:

```
WRITE *number
```

The number specified represents a code in the ASCII character set. There are 128 ASCII characters, each associated with a numeric code (Table I).

From Table I, we see that the ASCII code for "A" is 65. Thus, to output an "A" we could use:

```
WRITE *65
```

262

TABLE I

CODE	CHARACTER	CODE	CHARACTER	CODE	CHARACTER	CODE	CHARACTER
0	NUL	32	SP	64	@	96	`
1	SOH	33	!	65	A	97	a
2	STX	34	"	66	B	98	b
3	ETX	35	#	67	C	99	c
4	EOT	36	$	68	D	100	d
5	ENQ	37	%	69	E	101	e
6	ACK	38	&	70	F	102	f
7	BEL	39	'	71	G	103	g
8	BS	40	(	72	H	104	h
9	HT	41	)	73	I	105	i
10	LF	42	*	74	J	106	j
11	VT	43	+	75	K	107	k
12	FF	44	,	76	L	108	l
13	CR	45	-	77	M	109	m
14	SO	46	.	78	N	110	n
15	SI	47	/	79	O	111	o
16	DLE	48	0	80	P	112	p
17	DC1	49	1	81	Q	113	q
18	DC2	50	2	82	R	114	r
19	DC3	51	3	83	S	115	s
20	DC4	52	4	84	T	116	t
21	NAK	53	5	85	U	117	u
22	SYN	54	6	86	V	118	v
23	ETB	55	7	87	W	119	w
24	CAN	56	8	88	X	120	x
25	EM	57	9	89	Y	121	y
26	SUB	58	:	90	Z	122	z
27	ESC	59	;	91	[	123	{
28	FS	60	<	92	\	124		
29	GS	61	=	93	]	125	}
30	RS	62	>	94	^	126	~
31	US	63	?	95	_	127	DEL

39.   Examine Table I closely. The first 32 characters are "non-printable characters" or "control characters", corresponding to the "ASCII control codes" 0 thru 31.

These ASCII control codes perform a variety of special functions. The ASCII code 7 corresponds to BEL - which means "ring the bell". The ASCII code 10 corresponds to LF - which means "line feed". The ASCII code 13 corresponds to CR - which means "carriage return". ASCII code 32 corresponds to SP - which means "space".

40.   Function of the asterisk WRITE command is implementation specific. For your system, try the following: enter WRITE *7 for direct execution at the next system prompt. Your terminal will probably "beep" or "buzz". If your terminal does NOT respond with an audible sound, then:

- your terminal may not have this capability, or

- your implementation of Standard MUMPS may handle asterisk WRITE in another manner.

41. Within a program, WRITE *7 can be used to "get the users attention" Here are some examples:

```
       I  $L (NAM) >50  W  !!,*7,"NAME  MAY  NOT  EXCEED  50
. . . . . .  CHARACTERS! "  G  ENTRY

       W  !,*7,"Are  you  sure  you  want  to  delete  this  entry? "  R  ANS

       R  ANS:20
       E   W  *7,*7,!,"Which  option  do  you  want  to  choose? "  R  ANS:60
. . . . . .  E   HALT
```

42. The ASCII code 8 corresponds to BS - which means "backspace". On a CRT, this control code moves the curser one position to the left. For your CRT terminal, enter at any right caret:

```
       >W  "AB",*8,*8,"C"
```

The output should be:

```
       CB
```

As soon as "AB" was output, the cursor moved two positions to the left, and C was output at the position where A initially was displayed.

43. Remember in Chapter Eleven how we used a "v" on the line above a comment entry to show the maximum length allowed? The backspace allows us to place this "marker" on the same line of our CRT display. For example:

```
       W  !,"Comment:  ",?$X+60,"<"  F  J1=1:1:61  W  *8
       R  COMMENT
```

Here, we display a prompt, place a marker in the correct position, then backspace so the cursor is re-positioned immediately after our prompt.

44. The ASCII code 27 corresponds to ESC, which means "escape".The ESCAPE control code allows you to perform terminal-specific functions such as:

```
       "clear the screen"
```

"erase from cursor to end of screen"

"erase from cursor to end of line"

To perform these terminal-specific functions, ESCAPE must be accompanied by other characters. The combination of ESCAPE plus one or more other characters is sometimes known as an "escape sequence". The escape sequence required to perform a given function is terminal-specific.

To clear the screen on our DEC (Digital Equipment Corp) VT52, two escape sequences are used:

ESCAPE H

ESCAPE J

To do this in a MUMPS program, we use:

W *27, *72, *27, *74

Notice from Table I that 72 and 74 are the ASCII codes for "H" and "J" respectively.

45.   The asterisk WRITE may also be used with variables. For example:

```
>S  BEL=7
>W  *BEL
```

will "ring the bell".

46.   Asterisk WRITE takes on different meanings when used with other devices such as mag tape drives. Thus, asterisk WRITE is both implementation specific and device specific. For information on this topic, consult the documentation provided by your system vendor.

THE $CHAR FUNCTION

47. $CHAR provides a function similar to asterisk WRITE. The syntax is:

CHAR (number #1, . . . number #n)

$CHAR returns the characters corresponding to the ASCII code in its arguments.

For example:

```
WRITE $C(65) returns:
A
```

This accomplishes the same thing as WRITE   *65. In contrast to asterisk WRITE, the results of $CHAR are not "implementation specific".

48.   The results of $CHAR may be SET into variables. For example:

>SET VAR=$CHAR (65, 7, 7, 7)

We can now use the expression W VAR to output "A" plus three "beeps".

THE $ASCII FUNCTION

49. $ASCII returns the ASCII code corresponding to a character in its argument. The one argument form:

ASCII (string)

returns the ASCII code of the first character in the string specified. For example:

>SET STRING="ABCD"
>WRITE $A (STRING)

returns 65.

The two argument form:

ASCII (string, n)

returns the ASCII code of the nth character in the string. For example:

WRITE $A (STRING, 4)

returns 68.

If the character position specified exceeds the length of the string, the $ASCII returns -1. For example:

WRITE $A (STRING, 5)

returns -1.

ASTERISK READ

50.   The asterisk READ command accepts a single character as input. Program execution continues after the first character is received, and does not wait for an entry of RETURN.

Syntax is:

```
READ  *ANS
```

The variable used with asterisk READ takes on a numeric value which is implementation specific. For some implementations, this numeric value corresponds to the ASCII code for the first character received.

At this point, you may want to experiment to determine the value assigned by asterisk READ in your system. Or you may want to look up asterisk READ in the user manual for your system.

The variable used with asterisk READ takes on a numeric value which is implementation specific. For some implementations, this numeric value corresponds to the ASCII code for the first character received.

At this point, you may want to experiment to determine the value assigned by asterisk READ in your system. Or you may want to look up asterisk READ in the user manual for your system.

51. The following code:

- provides a prompt

- accepts one character via asterisk READ

- checks whether this character was a carriage return (ASCII code #13)
  QUITS on an entry of carriage return

- otherwise:

  writes ASCII code for the character entered

  displays the character entered (if this is a non-printable character there may be no display).

```
F J1=0:0 R !,"Character:  ",*CH Q:CH=13   W !,CH,?10,$C(CH)
```

52. You can manually enter non-printable characters from the ASCII character set by holding down the control key and striking A, B, C and so on. Our routine in frame 51 will return the ASCII code, but in some cases, there will be no other output.

Table II provides a little more detail on the first 20 ASCII characters.

TABLE II

CODE	CHARACTER		CODE	CHARACTER	
0	NUL		14	CTRL N	
1	CTRL A		15	CTRL O	(suspends program output, but execution continues)
2	CTRL B		16	CTRL P	
3	CTRL C		17	CTRL Q	(resumes program execution after CTRL S)
4	CTRL D		18	CTRL R	
5	CTRL E		19	CTRL S	(suspends program execution)
6	CTRL F		20	CTRL T	
7	CTRL G	(bell)	21	CTRL U	
8	CTRL H	(backspace)	22	CTRL V	
9	CTRL I	(tab)	23	CTRL W	
10	CTRL J	(line feed)	24	CTRL X	
11	CTRL K		25	CTRL Y	
12	CTRL L	(form feed)	26	CTRL Z	
13	CTRL M	(carriage return)			

53.   Asterisk READ is useful to accept menu selections via a single keystroke with no RETURN. However, with asterisk READ, it is impossible to correct a "mistake" via the delete key.

Let's modify CH12EX5 to provide:

- asterisk READ for menu selection from numeric display of options

- timed READ for menu display (HALT if no selection made after ten minutes)

- $CHAR to convert code returned by asterisk READ into the appropriate character (with asterisk READ, an entry of "1" becomes "49")

- asterisk WRITE to "ring the bell" if the user makes an incorrect selection

- redisplay option selected, for confirmation by user.

54.   Here's how we did it:

```
CH12EX5A ;DISPLAY MENU WITH $TEXT
        ;SELECT PROGRAM FROM MENU VIA $TEXT
        ;
        F INDEX=0:0 D DISPLAY I ANS="" Q
        W !!,"Finished" K  Q
        ;
```

```
DISPLAY W !!,"Enter the number of desired option"
        W !,"Enter RETURN to exit program",!
        F J1=1:1:9 S DISPLY=$TEXT(OPTIONS+J1) W !,$P(DISPLY,"^")
        R !!,"Select option: ",*ANS:600 E  W !!,"Finished" H
        I ANS=13 S ANS="" Q
        S ANS=$C(ANS)
        I (ANS?1N)&(ANS'=0) D SELECT Q
        W !,*7,*7,"Choose 1 to 9, or enter RETURN to exit" G DISPLAY
        ;
OPTIONS ;
        1.    Build file^^NABLD
        2.    List town names^^NATWNLST
        3.    Build town name dictionary^^NATWNBLD
        4.    Search for specified comment^^NACOMSRC
        5.    Modify data on file^^NAMOD
        6.    Delete data^^NADEL
        7.    Display data for specified name^^NADATA
        8.    Print data in alpha order by name^^NAALPHA
        9.    Print data in alpha order by name within town^^NATWN
        ;
SELECT  ;
        S CHOICE=$TEXT(OPTIONS+ANS)
        S PROGRAM=$PIECE(CHOICE,"^",2,3),OPTION=$P($P(CHOICE,"^"),
......  "    ",2)
        W !!!,OPTION," Okay? Yes=> "
        R YN:60
        I YN?1"N".E Q
        D @PROGRAM
        Q
```

269

SUMMARY OF NEW CONCEPTS - CHAPTER 12

PRINT Command to display menu:

- implementation specific

- syntax: PRINT (initial line):(ending line)

- "program lines" appear exactly as displayed on video screen - and

- are NOT executed as MUMPS code.

$TEXT Function to display menu:

- syntax:

$$\text{F INDEX=1:1:n W !,\$TEXT(initial line+INDEX)}$$

- "program lines" appear exactly as displayed on video screen - and are NOT executed as MUMPS code.

Name Indirection:

- allows current value of a variable to be interpreted as MUMPS code

- example:

```
          D MOD Q:ANS=""   D @ANS
          ;
   MOD    W !,"Enter 'A' to add new name"
          W !,"Enter 'B' to delete name"
          R !,"Select option: ",ANS
          I ANS="" Q
          S ANS="^NA"_ANS
          Q
```

$SELECT Function:

- syntax:

```
$SELECT(logical expression1:string1,...,1:"")
```

- if none of the expressions are true, $SELECT sees the final value as "true", and returns a value of null.

$TEXT to make selection from menu using four argument form of $PIECE:

```
         F INDEX=1:1:END S DISPLAY=$TEXT(OPTIONS+INDEX)
. . . . . W !,$P(DISPLAY,"^")
         R ANS
         S CHOICE=$TEXT(OPTIONS+ANS)
         S PROGRAM=$P(CHOICE,"^",2,3)
         D @PROGRAM
```

$EXTRACT to make menu selection from alpha characters entered by user:

- check if $EXTRACT from entry in OPTION module (with $LENGTH of ANS) is equal to ANS. If so, redisplay for confirmation and DO program.

- example:

```
LABL    R !,"Select option: ",ANS
        S LENGTH=$L(ANS)
        F J=1:1:END S CHOICE=$T(OPTIONS+J) D MATCH
        R !,"Is this the correct option? ",RESPONSE
        I RESPONSE?1"N".E G LABL
        S PROGRAM=$P(CHOICE,"^",2,3)
        D @PROGRAM
        Q
        ;
MATCH   S EXTRACT=$E($P(CHOICE,"^"),2,LENGTH+1)
        I ANS=EXTRACT W $E($P(CHOICE,"^"),LENGTH+2,255
        Q
```

$TEST Special Variable set to one or zero depending on truth value of:

- IF command

- timed READ command

- timed OPEN command

- timed LOCK command

- timed JOB command.

IF with no argument:

- evaluates truth value of $TEST system variable

- remaining code on same line executed if $TEST equals one.

ELSE Command:

- never takes an argument

- evaluates truth value of $TEST system variable

- remaining code on same line executed if $TEST equals zero.

Timed READ:

- syntax: READ ANS:(number of seconds)

- if user does not respond with entry plus carriage return inside specified number of seconds, $TEST is set to zero, and variable is assigned a null value

  NOTE: for partial response (characters entered with no carriage return), some implementations assign variable the value of whatever characters were entered, while others assign a null value.

- often followed by ELSE command to check $TEST, for example;

                    READ ANS: 20 ELSE   HALT

HALT Command:

- automatically terminates program execution.

Asterisk syntax of WRITE command (implementation specific). Most implementations output a single ASCII character. For example:

                    W *65   outputs "A"

- can be used to output ASCII control codes. For example:

                    F INDEX=1: 1: 10 W *7

- some terminal functions may require "escape sequence" (strike ESCAPE key or W *27), followed by numeric entry

- specific terminal commands can be expressed in MUMPS code using asterisk syntax of WRITE command, for example:

                    ESCAPE, H, ESCAPE, J
                    W *27, *72, *27, *74

272

$CHAR:

- syntax:

    $CHAR (number#1, . . . number#n)

- returns character(s) corresponding to ASCII code(s) of argument(s). For example:

    WRITE $C (65) returns "A"

- can SET results of $CHAR into variables. For example:

    SET VAR=$CHAR (7, 7, 7, 7)

- sets VAR equal to four "bells".

$ASCII:

- one argument form: $ASCII(string) returns ASCII code of first character in string

- two argument form: $ASCII(string,n) returns ASCII code of nth character in string (returns -1 if n exceeds the length of the string).

Asterisk syntax of READ command:

- accepts single character as input for READ command. For example:

    READ *A

- For some implementations, the variable A takes on a numeric value corresponding to the ASCII code for the first character received.

- can be used to accept menu selections via a single keystroke.

- However, user cannot correct mistakes via the delete key.

CHAPTER THIRTEEN

ERROR TRAPPING
VARIABLE SCOPING
REPORT FORMATTING
DATE AND TIME FUNCTIONS

In the first twelve chapters, we introduced some fundamental commands, operators, and functions. These included:

Commands

DO	KILL
ELSE	PRINT
FOR	QUIT
GOTO	READ
HALT	SET
IF	WRITE

Operators

Arithmetic operators

+
–
*
/
>
<

Boolean operators

&
!
'

String operators

_ (concatenate)
=
[
]
? (pattern verification)

Functions

$DATA	$NEXT
$EXTRACT	$ORDER
$FIND	$PIECE
$LENGTH	$TEXT

We also introduced:

Special variable

$TEST

Indirection

name indirection

Postconditional syntax

on arguments of DO and GOTO
on all commands except ELSE, FOR, IF, and PRINT

Timed argument

on READ

And we introduced techniques to:

build a primary file plus cross reference files

change entries in a primary file plus cross reference files

delete items from a primary file plus cross reference files

display data from a primary file

Topics in this chapter include:

- Error trapping

  The BREAK command
  The "Error Trap"

- Controlling the "scope" of variables

  The KILL command
  The NEW command

- Report formatting

  The $JUSTIFY function
  The $Y special variable and "pagination"

- Date and time functions

  Timing speed of program execution with the $HOROLOG special variable
  Displaying date and time for printed output

- Integer divide and modulo

- Writing programs with the $HOROLOG special variable. When you have finished this chapter, you will be able to:

- Write programs which allow users to exit via striking the BREAK key; while avoiding problems from striking the BREAK key while a global is being SET

- Use the NEW command to control the "scope" of variables used in your programs

- Format columns of numbers via the $JUSTIFY function

- Use the $Y system variable to perform "pagination" for video displays as well as printed reports

- Time speed of program execution via the $HOROLOG special variable

- Display time and date on printed outputs.

ERROR TRAPPING AND THE BREAK COMMAND

THE BREAK COMMAND

1.   For our implementation, striking the BREAK key - or CONTROL/C - with programmer access interrupts our program, and outputs an implementation specific error message (<INTRPT>) with the line label, program name, and contents of command line where execution stopped.

However, striking the BREAK key with user access has no effect.

Study the manual for your system to determine how the BREAK key operates for YOUR implementation. You may want to "experiment" with the BREAK key to see how it works for your system.

Some implementations routinely:

- enable the BREAK key with programmer access

- disable the BREAK key with user access.

2.   For our implementation, the BREAK command can be used to:

- disable the BREAK key with programmer access

- enable the BREAK key with user access.

3.   In Chapter Five we used the argumentless BREAK command to stop program execution so we could examine local variables. The BREAK command with an argument is implementation specific. For our system:

    BREAK 0 disables BREAK key

    BREAK 1 enables BREAK key.

4.   Why bother disabling the BREAK key?

Suppose you are executing a program to create a large primary file with several cross reference files. During execution of the SET commands that create your globals, you inadvertently strike the BREAK key. Possibilities at this point include:

- You may have created a new entry in your primary file - with no corresponding entry in your cross reference files - if the SET command creating your primary file precedes the SET command creating your cross reference file.

- You may have created a new entry in your cross reference file - with no corresponding entry in your primary file - if the SET command creating your cross reference file precedes the SET command creating your primary file.

Since it is easier to "reconstruct" cross reference files from your primary file than vice versa - we recommend that you always SET your primary file globals BEFORE creating your cross reference files.

You can avoid such problems by disabling the BREAK key before executing the SET commands that create your globals.

5.   Why bother enabling the BREAK key?

Suppose a user is executing a program with many options. One of these options is "display all data in primary file". By mistake, the user chooses this option instead of "delete name from data base". If you have 50,000 names on file, and the user is unable to stop your program, this mistake will waste a lot of time and paper!

Or suppose, the user is printing all data from your primary file - but the printer has a paper jam. Again, there is a need to BREAK program execution in the user mode.

You can avoid these problems by:

(1)   enabling the BREAK key at the beginning of your program (BREAK 1)

(2)   disabling the BREAK key before executing those SET commands which create your globals (BREAK 0)

(3)   enabling the BREAK key after executing these SET commands (BREAK 1).

This will solve the problems described - both for user access and programmer access.

THE "ERROR TRAP"

6.   Remember how programs stop and display error messages - such as <SYNTX> for "syntax error" and <UNDEF> for "undefined variable"?

These error messages are implementation specific. Some error messages for our implementation include:

<CMMD>   "Command" - user tried to enter an undefined command, or used a command incorrectly. For example, entering EX1 at a right caret instead of DO EX1 results in a <CMMD> error.

<DIVER>   "Divide error" - an error in division occurred. Usually, this means an attempted division by zero. Dividing by an alpha string (alpha strings are considered zero) will cause this error.

<INRPT>   "Interrupt" - user interrupted a program by striking CONTROL/ C or the BREAK key.

<LINER>   "Line error" - a non-existent line was specified. An example would be DO LABL when the program being executed has no line with this label.

<MXSTR>   "Max string" - a variable was assigned the value of a string longer than 255 characters.

<NOPGM>   "No program" - attempt to reference a non-existent program. If you ZLOAD, or DO a program that does not exist on disk, this error message appears.

<SBSCR>   "Subscript" - illegal subscript such as a null string.

<SYNTX>   "Syntax" - the wrong format was used when entering code. Common examples include: no space between a command and first argument; an "extra" space in an argument list; failure to provide two spaces after a command with no argument, such as QUIT or KILL.

<UNDEF>   "Undefined" - attempt to reference a variable (local or global) with no assigned value. This error is usually caused by simple oversight, such as using a flag but forgetting to initialize it.

7.   "Error trapping" is implementation specific

Check your user manual to determine how your implementation provides for "error trapping".

Our implementation provides:

   (1)   a Z special variable, $ZERROR

   (2)   two utility programs, %ET ("error trap") and %ER ("error report").

For our system, "error trapping" can:

(1)   allow programs to continue running after one or more defined types of errors occur

(2)   output "additional messages" after one or more defined types of errors occur

(3)   prepare a "permanent record" of these errors.

8.   Remember - all Z commands, Z special variables, and utility programs are vendor specific. They may: (1) exist in your implementation with the same name and the same form; (2) exist in your implementation with the same name but a different form; (3) exist in your implementation with a different name but a similar form; (4) exist in your implementation with a different name and a different form; (5) be absent in your implementation.

Information on Z commands, Z special variables and utility programs is available in the reference manual provided by your system vendor.

9.   For our implementation, when there is an error message of ANY type:

(1)   if there is a line referenced by $ZERROR, program control passes to this line;

(2)   the system SETS $ZERROR equal to the error code and line reference which would have been printed out.

For example:

```
EXMPL  ;EXAMPLE OF ERROR TRAP
       S $ZE="ERROR"
       W !,"THIS VARIABLE IS UNDEFINED ",A,"SO WE WILL GET AN ERROR"
       W !,"FINISHED" Q
       ;
ERROR  W !!,"THE FOLLOWING ERROR OCCURRED: ",$ZE
       Q
```

Here is the output from this program:

```
>D EXMPL
THIS VARIABLE IS UNDEFINED

THE FOLLOWING ERROR OCCURRED:   <UNDEF>EXMPL+2

>
```

Notice: (1) program control passes to the line referenced by $ZE; (2) the error code is displayed; (3) control does NOT return to the "calling program": thus the error trap is similar to a GOTO command rather than a DO command.

To prevent our program from stopping on an error, we could change line ERROR + 1 to read:

    GOTO EXMPL

10. We can use error trapping via $ZE to ensure that:

(1)   After an <INRPT> message caused by striking the BREAK key, our
       program returns to a specific point, such as the main menu.

(2)   Error messages other than <INRPT> are saved by the %ET "error
       trap" utility program.

Here is a simple example:

```
CH13EX1  ;BUILD GLOBAL FILE WITH CROSS REFERENCE FILE
         ;THIS PROGRAM ILLUSTRATES USE OF BREAK COMMAND AND ERROR TRAP
         S  $ZE="ERROR^CH13EX1"  B  1
         K   I  '$D(^NAME1)  S  ^NAME1=1
         S  START=^NAME1
         F  J1=START:1  R  !,"Name:  ",NAM  Q:NAM=""    D  ENTRY
         S  ^NAME1=J1
         W  !!,"Finished"  Q
         ;
ENTRY    R  !,"Address:  ",ADR
         R  !,"Town:  ",TWN
         R  !,"State:  ",STATE
         R  !,"Ok to file?  ",ANS
         I  ANS'?1"Y".A  W  !,"*** NOT FILED ***"  S  J1=J1-1  Q
         B  0
         S  ^NAME1(J1)=NAM_"^"_ADR_"^"_TWN_"^"_STATE
         B  1  Q
         ;
ERROR    B  0
         I  $ZE["INRPT"  W  !!,"INTERRUPT:  HIT RETURN TO CONTINUE"
......   R  ANS  G  CH13EX1
         D  ^%ET  Q
```

11. In this example, for any error message other than INRPT:

● we DO our utility program ^%ET to "trap" the error message for later study and
   evaluation

● we exit the program via a QUIT command.

For an <INRPT> error message, we return to the first line of code.

Notice that we enabled the BREAK key in line CH13EX1 + 2, disabled the BREAK key in line

ENTRY + 5, and re-enabled the BREAK key in line ENTRY + 7.

12.   You can, of course, select your error messages, depending on the contents of $ZE. For example:

```
ERROR   I  ($ZE["DBDGD"]!($ZE["PLDER"])!($ZE["DKHER"])!($ZE["SYSER"])
......  W !!,*7,*7
        I  W !,"*** SERIOUS SYSTEM ERROR! ***"
        I  W !!,"NOTIFY THE SYSTEM MANAGER IMMEDIATELY!!"
        I  W !!,"DO NOT ATTEMPT TO RESTART PROGRAM!" D ^%ET Q
        .
        .
        .
```

Check the reference manual for your implementation, and determine which error messages represent serious problems for your system.

13.   You can, of course, SET $ZE equal to a program, such as:

```
     S  $ZE="^ERRPGM"
```

Here, after an error occurs, control passes to the program referenced in $ZE. The system also SETS $ZE equal to the "standard" error code plus line reference where the error occurred.

14.   Our implementation of ANS MUMPS provides two utilities: "error trap" (%ET) and "error report" (%ER). The "error trap" utility, %ET, saves information about "what happened" when the error occurred. In CH13EX1, we DO ,%ET to "trap" any error message other than "INTRPT". The error report utility, %ER, examines errors that have been recorded by %ET. Again, check the reference manual for your implementation, and determine how these functions are performed on your system.

CONTROLLING THE "SCOPE" OF VARIABLES

THE KILL COMMAND

15.   There are three forms of the KILL command:

KILL - (no argument)
            no effect on global variables
            deletes all local variables from your partition

KILL (NAM,ADR,PHONE) - (exclusive KILL)
            no effect on global variables
            deletes all local variables except those specified within parentheses

KILL ⌃NAME(4),NAM - (inclusive KILL)

        deletes the global and/or local variable specified, together with all
        descendants.

16.   The "scope" of a variable refers to its "range of action". Global variables are intended to be used by many programs - and have "unlimited scope". Local variables usually are intended to be used within a single program.

We might have the FOR loop:

        FOR I=START: 1 : END. . .

calling a module that uses 'I' as the interest on a loan. When we return to our FOR loop, we will have an incorrect value of I!

To prevent this problem, it is common practice to reserve the letters I, J, K and so on as FOR loop variables. We prefer to use these letters with a number, such as J1, J2, J3 and so on.

When one program DOes a subroutine from another program, we may have problems, if both programs use the same variable name for different purposes.

Assume we have a FOR loop:

        FOR INDEX=START: 1 : END. . .

calling a subroutine from a second program, which also assigns values to END. When we return to our first program, END will have an incorrect value!

One way to solve this problem is to identify:

    (1)   the variable names used in each program

    (2)   which programs are called by other program.

We can then compare variable names within the "called" and "calling" program - and look for potential problems.

A second approach is an exclusive KILL - to remove all "unwanted" variables which might "come over" from the called program. However, this is NOT satisfactory if: (1) VAR is assigned a value before our called program is DOne; (2) the called program assigns a new value to VAR; (3) we use VAR later on in our calling program.

THE NEW COMMAND

17.   The NEW command provides a solution to our problem with "called programs" which

assign new values to variables from the "calling program". The NEW command implies that all local variables - or specified local variables - are "new". The "old values" are "stacked" - or "saved" - until an implicit or explicit QUIT command terminating a DO is executed. At this time, the "stacked" or "saved" variables are restored to their original values.

Because the NEW command was recently approved by the MUMPS Development Committee, it is not yet provided by all implementations of Standard MUMPS. Check the manual for your system to determine whether the NEW command is provided. If the NEW command is not provided for your system, we suggest you move to frame 22.

18.   There are three forms of the NEW command, corresponding to the three forms of KILL:

NEW - no argument

      stacks all local variables from your partition until an implicit or explicit QUIT is executed

NEW (NAM,ADR,PHONE) - exclusive NEW

      stacks all local variables, except those within parentheses, until an implicit or explicit QUIT is executed

NEW NAM,ADR,PHONE - inclusive NEW

      stacks only the local variables specified, together with their descendants, until an implicit or explicit QUIT is executed.

19.   Here is an example of the NEW command with no argument:

```
EXMPL1  ;NEW COMMAND WITH NO ARGUMENT
        R !,"Enter name: ",NAM
        R !,"Enter address: ",ADR
        R !,"Enter phone: ",PHONE
        D MOD1
        W !!,"First name: ",NAM,!,"First address: ",ADR,!,
......  "First phone: ",PHONE
        Q
        ;
MOD1    NEW
        R !,"Enter name: ",NAM
        R !,"Enter address: ",ADR
        R !,"Enter phone: ",PHONE
        W !!,"Name: ",NAM,!,"Address: ",ADR,!,"Phone: ",PHONE
        Q
```

What will be displayed by line EXMPL1 + 5 if we make a "first set" of entries at the first prompts, and a "second set" of entries at the prompts in MOD1?

What will be displayed by line MOD1 + 4?

Line EXMPL + 5 will display the "first set" of entries: these were "stacked" by the NEW command on line MOD1, then "unstacked" by the explicit QUIT in line MOD1 + 5.

Line MOD1 + 4 will display the "second set" of values for NAM, ADR and PHONE.

20.   Here is an example of the exclusive NEW command:

```
EXMPL2  ; 'EXCLUSIVE' NEW COMMAND
        R !,"Enter name:  ",NAM
        R !,"Enter address:  ",ADR
        R !,"Enter phone:  ",PHONE
        D MOD1
        W !!,"First name:  ",NAM,!,"First address:  ",ADR,!,
......  "First phone:  ",PHONE
        Q
        ;
MOD1    NEW (NAM)
        R !,"Enter name:  ",NAM
        R !,"Enter address:  ",ADR
        R !,"Enter phone:  ",PHONE
        W !!,"Name:  ",NAM,!,"Address:  ",ADR,!,"Phone:  ",PHONE
        Q
```

What will be displayed by line EXMPL2 + 5 if we make a "first set" of entries at the first prompts, and a "second set" of entries at the prompts in MOD1?

Line EXMPL2 + 5 will display the "first set" of entries for address and phone: these were "stacked" by the NEW command on line MOD2, then "unstacked" by the explicit QUIT in line MOD1 + 5. However, the first entry for NAM was NOT "stacked": therefore line EXMPL2 + 5 will display the second value of NAM.

21.   Here is an example of the inclusive NEW command:

```
EXMPL3  ; 'INCLUSIVE' NEW COMMAND
        R !,"Enter name:  ",NAM
        R !,"Enter address:  ",ADR
        R !,"Enter phone:  ",PHONE
```

```
        D MOD1
        W !!,"First name: ",NAM,!,"First address: ",ADR,!,
...... "First phone: ",PHONE
        Q
        ;
MOD1    NEW NAM
        R !,"Enter name: ",NAM
        R !,"Enter address: ",ADR
        R !,"Enter phone: ",PHONE
        W !!,"Name: ",NAM,!,"Address: ",ADR,!,"Phone: ",PHONE
        Q
```

What will be displayed by line EXMPL3+5 if we make a "first set" of entries at this first prompt, and a "second set" of entries at the prompts in MOD1?

Line EXMPL3+5 will display the "first entry" for name: this was "stacked" by the NEW command on line MOD1, then "unstacked" by the explicit QUIT in line MOD1+5. However, the first entries for ADR and PHONE were NOT stacked: therefore line EXMPL2+5 will display the "second values" for ADR and PHONE.

REPORT FORMATTING

THE $JUSTIFY FUNCTION

22.   We can use the format control character "?" to align a series of outputs so they begin at the same left hand position on different lines. Alignment of outputs at the left hand end of each string is called "left justification". For example:

```
        SMITH, RODGER
        JONES, CYNTHIA
        EINSTEIN, ALBERT
```

23.   In some cases, we want to align a series of outputs so they end at the same right hand position on different lines. Alignment of outputs at the right hand end of each string is called "right justification". For example:

```
         0.37
         3.70
        33.37
```

The $JUSTIFY function provides right justification - but operates in a different manner than the "?" used for left justification.

24.   Syntax for the two argument form of $JUSTIFY is:

        JUSTIFY(`string`,`field width`)

One way to understand the concept of "field width" is to consider that $JUSTIFY takes the specified string, and transforms it to the specified "field width" by "padding" the left hand portion of the string with blank spaces. For example:

```
S  STRING(1)="1.003"
S  STRING(2)="1000"
S  STRING(3)=".1"
F  J1=1:1:3  W  !,"VALUE IS",$JUSTIFY(STRING(J1),10)
```

will return:

```
VALUE  IS    1.003
VALUE  IS    1000
VALUE  IS       .1
```

Here, each string was "padded" with blank spaces and output in a field width of ten characters. A string of eleven characters would have "overflowed" the field width, extending to the right of the other strings. Thus, $JUSTIFY does NOT truncate strings which exceed the specified field width.

Here is a second example:

```
SET  DATA(1)=10,DATA(2)=1,DATA(3)=100
FOR  J=1:1:3  W  !,$JUSTIFY(DATA(J),20)
```

will return:

```
 10
  1
100
```

If we begin each output from $JUSTIFY after other output on the same line, our "field width" is "added on" to the current position of our print head.

Here is another example:

```
S  DATA(1)=10,DATA(2)=1,DATA(3)=100,DATA(4)=1/4,DATA(5)=1/5,
......  DATA(6)=1/6
F  J=1:2:6  W  !,$JUSTIFY(DATA(J),20),$JUSTIFY(DATA(J+1),20)
```

will return:

```
              10                   1
             100                0.25
             0.2         0.166666666
```

Each time through the FOR loop, our second $JUSTIFY operation "begins the field width" of 20 characters at column 20. Thus the concept of "field width" can also be understood as "right hand distance from current position of the print head (or cursor)".

25.   The three argument form of $JUSTIFY allows us to specify any desired number of decimal places, as well as string name and field width.

Syntax for the three argument form of $JUSTIFY is:

```
$JUSTIFY(string,field width,number of decimal places)
```

For example:

```
S DATA(4)=1/4,DATA(5)=1/5,DATA(6)=1/6
F J=4:1:6 W !,$J(DATA(J),20,2)
```

will return:

```
                0.25
                0.20
                0.17
```

Notice that:

- $JUSTIFY returns a leading zero for non-integers between -1 and 1

- $JUSTIFY adds "non significant" zeros as needed

- $JUSTIFY performs a rounding operation, rather than simple truncation.

THE $Y SPECIAL VARIABLE AND "PAGINATION"

26.   What if you output 30 lines onto a screen which only displays 24 lines? On most screens, the display will "scroll" - and you lose your first six lines. If you move quickly, you may be able to "stop" the display. CONTROL/S suspends program execution and stops the display - CONTROL/Q continues program execution and completes the display.

27.   Remember how the $X special variable counts horizontal columns? The $Y special variable counts vertical lines.

$Y is incremented by one for each line feed executed by your program. You can use $Y to "keep track" of your vertical position when displaying "pages" on a CRT, or a hard copy terminal.

28.   The READ and WRITE commands update the value of $Y based on the two format control characters: "!" (line feed) and "#" (form feed):

```
                READ # or
                WRITE #
```

set $Y to zero;

```
                READ ! or
                WRITE !
```

increment $Y by one.

For our implementation, $Y is automatically reset to zero when $Y exceeds 255.

29.   For our system, the form feed character, "#", also causes a "top-of-form" operation on hard copy devices: the printer moves to the top of next page. Check the manual for your system to determine whether # causes a "top-of-form" operation, as well as setting $Y to zero.

30.   How could we solve our problem with a CRT display which exceeds 24 lines?

One way is to check $Y after each line feed specified in our MUMPS code. When $Y is equal to or greater than 22, we stop the output and display a prompt: "Enter carriage return to continue display". On a carriage return, we reset $Y to zero, and continue our display. Write the code to perform these functions.

```
    I $Y'<22 W !,"Enter carriage return to continue display" R ANS W #
```

31.   In "real life", we might "blank the screen" after W #, before starting the next display. For CRTs, this is usually done via asterisk syntax of the WRITE command, as demonstrated in Chapter Twelve.

32.   How can we ensure that hard copy output will begin on separate pages, rather than "running together"?

Most printers print six lines per vertical inch. Thus a 8-1/2"X 11" page has a total of 66 lines. Usually, one inch margins at the bottom and top limit us to 66 minus 12, or 54 useful lines of information per printed page.

We can check $Y after each line feed specified in our MUMPS code. When $Y is equal to or greater than 60, we can perform a form feed and reset $Y to zero.

Write the code to perform these functions:

```
        I $Y'<60 W #!!!!!!
```

In this code, we check if $Y is greater than or equal to 60. This allows six lines (one inch) at the bottom of a page. After we form feed, we perform six line feeds to allow a one inch margin at the top of the new page.

33.   For hardcopy output, we may want to print page numbers.

Here is some code to print page numbers at the bottom of each page:

```
PAGEMOD ;  THIS MODULE HANDLES PAGINATION AS PART OF A PROGRAM
         ;WHICH PRINTS HARDCOPY REPORTS.
         ;
         ;  STARTING VALUE OF 'PAGE' MUST BE INITIALIZED BY THE
         ;  CALLING PROGRAM.
         ;  RECOMMEND THAT CALLING PROGRAM PERFORM A FORM FEED
         ;  TO BEGIN REPORT ON A NEW PAGE.
         ;
         I $Y<60 Q
         W !!!,?35,PAGE,#!!!!!! S PAGE=PAGE+1 Q
         ;
         ;  THIS MODULE SHOULD BE CALLED AFTER EACH LINE FEED
         ;  OPERATION.
```

TIME AND DATE FUNCTIONS

TIMING SPEED OF PROGRAM EXECUTION WITH THE $HOROLOG SPECIAL VARIABLE

34.   The $HOROLOG special variable returns two numbers separated by a comma. The format of this string is "D,S" where:

> D = number of days since December 31, 1840, i.e. D = 1 for January 1, 1841.

> S = number of seconds since midnight for the current day.

35.   We can use $H special variable to time speed of program execution. Here is a simple program to evaluate execution speed:

```
CH13EX2 ;TIME SPEED OF EXECUTION WITH $HOROLOG
        ;
        S TIME1=$P($H,",",2),^TEST(1,1,1,0)=0
        F INDEX=1:1:5000 S ^TEST(1,1,1,INDEX)=INDEX
        S TIME2=$P($H,",",2)
        W !!,"TEST PROGRAM REQUIRED ",(TIME2-TIME1)," SECONDS
......  FOR EXECUTION."
        Q
```

Execution speed is affected by several factors including:

(1)   number and type of programs running on the system at time of test

(2)   efficiency of the MUMPS implementation

(3)   efficiency of the operating system

(4)   type of hardware.

A variety of "test programs" are available from system vendors, as well as from the MUMPS Users' Group. However, relative execution speeds of "real life programs" on different systems do not always show perfect correlation with relative execution speeds of "test programs".

DISPLAYING DATE AND TIME FOR PRINTED OUTPUT

36. $HOROLOG can be used to calculate the current date and time. Two programs to do this are outlined at the end of this chapter, beginning with Frame 42.

However, most implementations of Standard MUMPS provide utility programs to display the current date and time. These utility programs are implementation specific. Check your system documentation to determine whether such utility programs are included with your system, and if so, how they operate.

The rest of this frame briefly describes the %D and %T utility programs provided for our implementation of Standard MUMPS. The "date" and "time" utility programs for your system may be different.

The %D utility program for our implementation outputs date as MMM DD YY. The %T utility program for our implementation outputs time as HH:MM AM/PM.

To use these utility programs, simply tab to where you want the date and time, then DO ˄%D and ˄%T. Here is an example:

```
EXMPL ;UTILITY PROGRAMS FOR DATE AND TIME
      ;THESE UTILITY PROGRAMS ARE IMPLEMENTATION SPECIFIC
      W !!,"PRINTED AT " D ^%T W " " D ^%D
      W !!!,"FINISHED" Q
```

For our implementation, if you enter this example into local memory (but do NOT save it onto disk), and DO it, you will get an error message - <NOPGM>.

When you DO a program on disk from within another program, the calling program is automatically reloaded from disk when the called program QUITs - provided the calling program was saved to disk before the called program was DOne.

Thus, EXMPL will work properly ONLY if it is saved onto disk before you DO .%T. Study the date and time utility programs for YOUR system - and write some simple programs which call these utilities.

If your implementation does NOT provide date and time utility programs, you may want to use the program presented in the last section of this chapter. A similar program is presented in the MUMPS Primer (Walters RF, Bowie J, and Wilcox JC, 1983, published by MUMPS Users' Group).

INTEGER DIVIDE AND MODULO

37.   Integer divide is like regular division, except the answer is truncated at the decimal point. The integer divide operator is expressed as a backslash ("\"). For example:

$$3 \backslash 2 = 1$$
$$1 \backslash 3 = 0$$
$$9 \backslash 4 = 2$$

38.   Integer divide is commonly used to:

- obtain the number of weeks in a specified number of days (integer divide by 7)

- obtain the number of minutes in a specified number of seconds (integer divide by 60)

- eliminate the decimal portion of a real number (integer divide by 1).

The last section of this chapter demonstrates use of integer divide to obtain time and date from $HOROLOG.

39.   Modulo can be thought of as the remainder of a positive number after integer division. The modulo operator is expressed as a pound sign (#). For example:

$$3 \# 5 = 3$$
(integer divide of 3 by 5 gives zero, with a remainder of 3)

$$14 \# 5 = 4$$
(integer divide of 14 by 5 gives two, with a remainder of 4)

40.   The formal definition of modulo is:

```
A#B = A-(A\B*B)+(absolute value of B if A<0)
```

Thus:

$$3\#5 = 3 - (3 \setminus 5 * 5)$$
$$= 3 - (0 * 5)$$
$$= 3 - 0$$
$$= 3$$

And:

$$-3\#5 = -3 - (-3 \setminus 5 * 5) + 5$$
$$= -3 - (0 * 5) + 5$$
$$= -3 - 0 + 5$$
$$= -3 + 5$$
$$= 2$$

Notice that modulo gives different results for positive and negative numbers.

However, since most uses of modulo involve only positive numbers, we can think of modulo as the remainder of a positive number after integer division.

41.   Modulo can be used with $HOROLOG to obtain the current "second" within the current minute: if $P($H,",",2)#60 returns 10, we are 10 seconds into the current minute.

The last section of this chapter demonstrates use of modulo to obtain time and date from $HOROLOG.

WRITING PROGRAMS WITH THE $HOROLOG SPECIAL VARIABLE

42.   If your system provides utility programs to display the current date and time, we suggest you read only thru Frame 46 - and then go on to Chapter Fourteen.

43.   We can extract the "seconds" portion of $HOROLOG by using $PIECE:

```
S  TM=$P ($H, " , "2)
```

returns the number of seconds after midnight.

We can obtain seconds after the minute by:

```
S  SEC=TM#60
```

We can obtain the minutes after midnight by:

```
S  MINPAST=TM\60
```

We can obtain hours after midnight by:

```
S  HR=MINPAST\60
```

We can obtain minutes after the hour by:

```
S MIN=MINPAST#60
```

We can obtain the suffix for AM or PM by:

```
S SUFFIX="AM"
I TM'<43200 S SUFFIX="PM",TM=TM-43200
```

If the time is Noon (TM = 43200) or later, we subtract 43200 from TM to correctly obtain time in the 12 hour format.

44.   Now write the code to output time in the format HR:MIN:SECONDS (AM/PM)

```
CH13EX3 ;TIME IN HRS. MIN. AND SEC. USING $H
        S TM=$P($H,",",2),SUFF="AM",SEC=TM#60
        I TM'<43200 S SUFF="PM",TM=TM-43200
        S MINPAST=TM\60,HR=MIN\60,MIN=MINPAST#60
        I 'HR S HR=12
        W !!,"THE TIME IS ",HR,":",MIN,":",SEC,SUFF Q
```

45.   Describe the functions performed by each line of code in CH13EX3:

In line 1, the $PIECE operation returns seconds after midnight. The suffix for time is set to AM (later, we will reset this to PM if minutes past midnight is equal to or greater than 43200). Finally, modulo 60 of seconds after midnight gives us seconds after the minute.

Line 2 is executed only if the time is 12 noon or later: i.e. if TM is greater than or equal to 43200. Line 2 changes the suffix to PM, and subtracts 43200 from TM, so subsequent operations will obtain answers based on a 12 hour clock rather than a 24 hour clock.

In line 3, the first calculation returns minutes past midnight or noon (since we subtract 43200 from times past noon). The second calculation returns hours past midnight or noon. The third calculation returns minutes past the hour. With these operations, the hours "12 midnight" and "12 noon" will be set to zero.

Line 4 checks if HR equals zero, and if so, resets HR to equal 12.

Line 5 simply outputs the variable HR, MIN, SEC and SUFF.

46.   As written, CH13EX3 outputs 1:09:06PM as 1:9:6PM

We can modify line 5 to output 1:09:06 PM rather than 1:9:6 PM:

```
W !!,"THE TIME IS ",HR,": ",MIN\10,MIN#10,": ",SEC\10,SEC#10," ",
```

. . . . . .   SUFF Q

How does this work?

```
9\10  equals  0              12\10  equals  1
9#10  equals  9              12#10  equals  2
```

This code provides a convenient way to insert leading zeros for those numbers less than ten.

47.   If your system provides utility programs to display the current date and time, we suggest you pass over this section - and go on to Chapter Fourteen. We can extract the "date" portion of $HOROLOG by using $PIECE:

```
S  DT=$P($H,",")
```

returns the number of days since December 31, 1840.

However, there was one extra day in the year 1900. So we should add one day before we begin calculating the date:

```
S  DT=$P($H,",")+1
```

48.   We can correct for leap years if we know that the number of days within any four years (this will include a leap year) will be 1461. Thus the number of leap years that have occurred since 1840 will be:

```
DT\1461
```

The year of the last leap year will be:

```
S  YEAR=(DT\1461)*4+1841
```

The number of days since the last leap year will be:

```
S  DAYS=DT#1461
```

49.   To obtain the current year and the number of days into this current year, we can use a FOR loop:

```
F J1=1:1:3 Q:DAYS'>365   S YEAR=YEAR+1,DAYS=DAYS-365
```

After completing this FOR loop, DAYS is equal to days into the current year, and YEAR is equal to the current year.

50.   Now we must check if DAYS is equal to zero. Why is this necessary?

Jan 1 of 1981 is the first day of a leap year cycle, so DT#1461 equals 1. Dec 31 of 1980 is the last day of a leap year cycle - so DT#1461 equals zero. At this point in our program, the DAYS variable is the number of days into the current year - for Dec 31 of 1980 (or any other leap year) DAYS should be 366 rather than zero. Therefore, we must check if DAYS is equal to zero. We can do this via:

```
I DAYS=0  S DAYS=366,YEAR=YEAR-1
```

51.   Here is the code to obtain month:

```
       S MO=1,DAYMO=DAYS
       F J2=31,(YEAR#4=0)+28,31,30,31,30,31,31,30,31,30,31
. . . . . .   Q:DAYYR'>J2   S MO=MO+1,DAYMO=DAYMO-J2
```

With this type of FOR loop, we list specific values to be assigned to J2. The FOR loop is executed for each of these values, until DAYYR is equal to or less than the accumulated total.

Notice the expression $(YEAR\#4 = 0) + 28$.

The expression in parenthesis will yield a truth value of either zero or one, which is added to 28. If YEAR#4 is zero, then the truth value is one, so one day is added to 28 for leap years.

This FOR loop gives us: (1) the number of the month; (2) the day of the month.

52.   We now have year, month and day.

We can attach a leading zero to month and day:

```
       S M=MO\10_MO#10
       S D=DAYMO\10_DAYMO#10
```

53.   Now write a program to output date in numeric format using $H.

```
```

```
CH13EX4  ;DATE USING $H
        S DT=$P($H,",")+1
        S YEAR=(DT\1461)*4+1841,DAYS=DT#1461
        F J1=1:1:3 Q:DAYS'>365  S YEAR=YEAR+1,DAYS=DAYS-365
        I DAYS=0 S DAYS=366,YEAR=YEAR-1
        S MO=1,DAYMO=DAYS
        F J2=31,(YEAR#4=0)+28,31,30,31,30,31,31,30,31,30,31
......  Q:DAYMO'>J2  S MO=MO+1,DAYMO=DAYMO-J2
        W !,"THE DATE IS ",MO\10,MO#10,"/",DAYMO\10,DAYMO#10,
......  "/",YEAR Q
```

Line 5 initializes the value of MO as one, and the value of DAYMO (day of month) as DAYS (day of year), in preparation for the FOR loop in line 6.

Line 6 uses a FOR loop to determine month of year and day of month. Each time through this FOR loop, the FOR loop variable, J2, takes on the value of the number of days in the "next" month of the year. Each time through the FOR loop we: (1) SET MO equal to MO + 1; (2) subtract the value of J2 from DAYMO (initialized as equal to DAYS in line 5). We QUIT this FOR loop when DAYMO finally becomes equal to or less than J2.

Line 7 uses the same technique described in Frame 46 to insert leading zeros for numbers less than 10.

If MO is 3, MO\10 equals zero and MO#10 equals 3. If DAYMO is 25, DAYMO\10 equals 2, and DAYMO#10 equals 5. Notice that the expression MO\10, MO#10 and DAYMO\10, DAYMO#10 are similar to the code used in frame 41. If MO is 3, MO\10 equals zero and MO#10 equals 3. If DAYMO is 25, DAYMO\10 equals 2, and DAYMO#10 equals 5. This "trick" ensures that leading zeros are inserted when needed and omitted when NOT needed!

SUMMARY OF NEW CONCEPTS - CHAPTER 13

BREAK:

- effect of BREAK key and operation of BREAK command are implementation specific

- may disable BREAK key before executing SET commands to create globals

- may enable BREAK key so user can stop programs.

ERROR TRAP:

- error trapping is implementation specific

- some implementations provide $ZERROR special variable which can direct program control to specified line when error condition occurs (i.e. when an error message would be produced).

KILL COMMAND:

- KILL (no argument)
  no effect on global variables
  deletes all local variables from partition

- KILL (VAR1,VAR2)
  exclusive KILL has no effect on global variables
  deletes all local variables except for those specified

- KILL VAR1,VAR2
  inclusive KILL deletes local and/or global variables specified together with their descendants.

NEW COMMAND:

- NEW (no argument)
  stacks all local variables until implicit or explicit QUIT is executed

- NEW (VAR1,VAR2)
  exclusive NEW stacks all local variables except for those specified

- NEW VAR1,VAR2
  inclusive NEW stacks local variables specified.

$JUSTIFY FUNCTION:

- two argument form: $JUSTIFY(string,field width) returns specified string right justified within specified field width

- three argument form: $JUSTIFY(string,field width,number of decimal places) returns specified string right justified within specified field width rounded to specified number of decimal places.

$Y SPECIAL VARIABLE:

- returns vertical position of cursor or print head

- reset to zero by WRITE# or when $Y exceeds 255.

$HOROLOG SPECIAL VARIABLE:

- returns "D,S" where:
  D = number of days since December 31, 1840
  S = number of seconds past midnight for current date

- most implementations provide utility programs to return current time and date (see user manual for your system).

INTEGER DIVIDE ARITHMETIC OPERATOR:

- expressed as "\"

- performs division with answer truncated at decimal point (returns "integer number" rather than "real number").

MODULO ARITHMETIC OPERATOR:

- expressed as "#"

- can be considered as the remainder of a positive number after integer divide.

INSERTING LEADING ZEROS WITH INTEGER DIVIDE AND MODULE:

- the following code inserts leading zeros if the value of VAR is less than 10:

```
W !,VAR\10,VAR#10
```

- the following code inserts leading zeros if the value of VAR is less than 100:

```
W !,VAR\100,VAR#100
```

CHAPTER FOURTEEN

WRITING GENERALIZED PROGRAMS WITH INDIRECTION

We briefly introduced name indirection in Chapter Twelve. This chapter will provide a more detailed discussion of indirection, and a more detailed discussion of the $DATA function.

The term "indirection" means that a data value is "indirectly" interpreted as MUMPS code. This data value is, in effect, temporarily inserted into the program at time of execution (Walters RF, Bowie J, Wilcox JC: MUMPS Primer, 1983). The MUMPS language provides five types of indirection:

- name indirection - a variable, line label or routine name is inserted at time of execution

- pattern indirection - a pattern match is inserted at time of execution

- argument indirection - a command argument is inserted at time of execution

- subscript indirection - a subscript is inserted at time of execution

- command indirection - a command line is inserted at time of execution.

Topics presented include:

- the $DATA function

- name indirection

- pattern indirection

- argument indirection

- command indirection - the XECUTE command.

We will not present subscript indirection in this chapter. Subscript indirection is discussed briefly in Chapter Seventeen.

The last section of this chapter will present a form of MUMPS syntax called "naked reference". This should be regarded as "optional reading". We do not use naked reference in our own code: however, you may see it in routines written by other programmers.

By the end of this chapter, you will be able to use:

- name indirection - so the same code can operate with any desired global

- pattern indirection - so you can use a "library" of pattern matches with many different programs

- argument indirection - so you can insert new command arguments at the time of program execution (this technique is a little difficult to follow, and we do not recommend it for beginners)

- command indirection - using the string value of a variable as a line of MUMPS code.

THE $DATA FUNCTION

1. Up to now, we have used $DATA to check whether a global exists. For example:

```
I  $D(^NAME)=0  S  ^NAME=1
```

or:

```
I  '$D(^NAME)  S  ^NAME=1
```

If ^NAME has an assigned value, $DATA returns 1; if ^NAME does not have an assigned value, $DATA returns zero.

2. The $DATA function, applied to a local or a global variable, returns one of four values:

0	means	NO DATA and NO DESCENDANTS
1	means	HAS DATA and NO DESCENDANTS
10	means	NO DATA and HAS DESCENDANTS
11	means	HAS DATA and HAS DESCENDANTS

3. What is a descendant? A descendant variable has the same name as another variable, plus one or more additional levels of subscripting.

For example:

```
                                  <NAME(1,1,1)
                    <NAME(1,1)--<     .
                    <       .     <NAME(1,1,3)
        <NAME(1)---<    .
        <     .     <NAME(1,4)
```

302

```
NAME-<
      <
      <
      <
```

NAME(1) is a descendant of NAME

NAME(1,1) and NAME(1,4) are descendants of NAME(1,1) as well as descendants of NAME

NAME(1,1,1) and NAME(1,1,3) are descendants of NAME(1,1), but NOT of NAME(1,4)

4.   An ancestor variable has the same name as another variable, but one or more fewer levels of subscripting. Thus NAME(1,1) is an ancestor of NAME(1,1,1) and NAME(1,1,3). And NAME is the ancestor of NAME(1), NAME(1,1), and NAME(1,4).

5.   Assume the following nodes of a ^NAME array have been created:

```
^NAME
^NAME (3) ="HAMILTON,  ALEXANDER"
^NAME (3, 1) ="SECRETARY  OF  THE  TREASURY"
^NAME (4)
^NAME (4, 1) ="SECRETARY  OF  STATE"
^NAME (6) ="SMITH,  JOHN"
```

Also, assume that: the ^NAME node was created "automatically" via creation of ^NAME(3); the ^NAME(4) node was created "automatically" via creation of ^NAME(4,1).

What values would you expect to be returned by $DATA for each of the above nodes?

10

11

1

10

1

1

6.   We would expect that when we create ^NAME via SET ^NAME(3) = "HAMILTON, ALEXANDER", $DATA for ^NAME returns 10.

And we would expect that when we create ^NAME(4) via SET ^NAME(4,1) = "SECRETARY

OF STATE",$DATA for ^NAME(4) returns 10.

However, for some implementations, $DATA(^NAME) will return 11 while $DATA(^NAME(4) returns 10. These implementations are non-standard in their treatment of the $DATA function since the "head node" for a global, when created "automatically", is assigned a value of null.

7. Evaluate your own system in terms of:

```
SET  NAM(1,1)="CAT"
SET  ^NAM(1,1)="DOG"
WRITE  $DATA(NAM)
WRITE  $DATA(^NAM)
```

According to the Standard, $DATA should return 10 in both instances. However, our implementation returns 10 for $DATA(NAM) and 11 for $DATA(^NAM).

NAME INDIRECTION

NAME INDIRECTION - LOCAL ARRAYS

8. Name indirection allows you to insert any desired:

- variable

- line label, or

- routine name

into your code at the time of program execution.

The syntax for name indirection is expressed as:

@(variable or literal string).

The "at sign" means: "whatever is at (variable or literal string)".

9. Assume we have created a NAME(nnn) array by the following code:

```
F J1=1:1:10 R !,"Enter name:  ",NAM S NAME(J1)=NAM
```

We can display this local array via:

```
F J2=1:1:10 W !,NAME(J2)
```

Or we can display this local array via name indirection:

```
S  ARRAYNAM="NAME(J2)"
F  J2=1:1:10  W  !,@ARRAYNAM
```

This last FOR loop writes out "whatever is at ARRAYNAM".

What if we had a PROJECT(nnn) local array with ten array elements? We could use our same FOR loop to display this array via indirection:

```
S  ARRAYNAM="PROJECT(J2)"
F  J2=1:1:10  W  !,@ARRAYNAM
```

Indirection enables us to use the same code - regardless of our array name.

NAME INDIRECTION - GLOBAL ARRAYS

10.   With local arrays, there is little need for indirection. However, name indirection can be useful when we want to examine a large number of global arrays, using a single program.

Imagine that we have 100 global arrays on disk. Using indirection, we can write a program which:

(1)   allows the user to enter a global name

(2)   displays a message if this global does not exist

(3)   searches through this global to any desired level of subscripting.

The only limitation is that our global array must have a "structure" compatible with the logic of our search program.

11.   Remember how we used a FOR loop, incremented by zero, with $ORDER, to list a single-level global array with numeric or string subscripts? For example:

```
S  A=""
F  INDEX=0:0  S  A=$O(^NAME(A))  Q:A=""   W  !,A,?30,^NAME(A)
W  !!,"FINISHED"  Q
```

Name indirection allows us to write this code in a form that can be used to search the first level of any global, regardless of global name.

12.   Here is a program to examine any global array at the first level, regardless of global name.

```
CH14EX1  ;EXAMINE ANY GLOBAL ARRAY AT FIRST LEVEL USING
         ; INDIRECTION
         ;
         F J1=0:0 R !!,"Global name: ",GLOBAL Q:GLOBAL=""  D MOD
         W !!,"Finished" K  Q
         ;
MOD      S GL="^"_GLOBAL
         I '$D(@GL) W !,*7,"THIS GLOBAL DOES NOT EXIST!" Q
         S GL=GL_"(A)",A=""
         F J2=0:0 S A=$O(@GL) Q:A=""   I ($D(@GL)=1)!($D(@GL)=11)
......   W !,A,"=",@GL
         Q
```

Notice the use of $DATA in line MOD+3. In our previous programs, we knew in advance which nodes had data, and which had descendants. However, with this generalized program, we might encounter a node with descendants, but no data. If we try to WRITE a node with no data, our program would halt and display an error message. Thus, for a node where $DATA returns 10, we would have a problem! Our previous code:

    I 'DATA(global name)

is inadequate for those situations where we do not know in advance whether a particular node contains data. For this reason, we use the code:

    I ($DATA(global name)=1)!($DATA(global name)=11)

We could also express this as:

    I $DATA(GLOBAL NAME)#10

since $DATA will return a 1 as the remainder from modulo operation on either 1 or 11.

13.   For CH14EX1, outline what happens to the values of GLOBAL and GL if we enter NAME in response to the prompt "Global name":

The first FOR loop sets GLOBAL = NAME

Line MOD sets GL = ^NAME

Line MOD+1 checks whether ^NAME exists.

Line MOD+2 sets GL equal to ^NAME(A)

The FOR loop in MOD can be considered as equivalent to:

```
        F  J2=1:1  S  A=$O(^NAME(A))...
```

Our $DATA function ensures that no WRITE commands will be attempted on nodes where $DATA returns zero or ten.

14.   By entering a familiar global name such as NAME, we can see this code is similar to the code we previously wrote to examine our ˌNAME array. However, with indirection, we can enter any array name we wish.

15.   Here is the same program, extended to include four levels of any global array.

```
CH14EX2  ;EXAMINE ANY GLOBAL ARRAY AT UP TO FOUR LEVELS
        ;
        F  INDEX=0:0  R !!,"Global name: ",GLOBAL Q:GLOBAL=""
......  D  LEVEL1
        W  !!,"Finished" K  Q
        ;
LEVEL1  S  GL="^"_GLOBAL
        I  '$D(@GL) W !,*7,GL," DOES NOT EXIST!" Q
        W  !,"GLOBAL NAME=",GLOBAL
        I  $D(@GL)#10 W !,GL,"=",@GL
        S  GL1=GL_"(A)",A=""
        F  J1=0:0  S A=$O(@GL1)  Q:A=""   W !?2,A,"=" W:$D(@GL1)#10
......  @GL1 D  LEVEL2
        Q
        ;
LEVEL2  S  GL2=GL_"(A,B)",B=""
        F  J2=0:0  S B=$O(@GL2)  Q:B=""   W !?4,B,"=" W:$D(@GL2)#10
......  @GL2 D  LEVEL3
        Q
        ;
LEVEL3  S  GL3=GL_"(A,B,C)",C=""
        F  J3=0:0  S C=$O(@GL3)  Q:C=""   W !?6,C,"=" W:$D(@GL3)#10
......  @GL3 D  LEVEL4
        Q
        ;
LEVEL4  S  GL4=GL_"(A,B,C,D)",D=""
        F  J4=0:0  S D=$O(@GL4)  Q:D=""   W !?8,D,"=" W:$D(@GL4)#10
......  @GL4
        Q
```

16.   What are the advantages of using this "general purpose program", rather than writing a "specific program"?

First, this "general purpose program" saves time. You simply enter any global name, and the program either:

        displays a message that this global does not exist, or

        displays the subscripts and global contents at each level.

Second, you can use this routine as a "module" in other programs. Not only does this save the time of writing a new module - but you eliminate the need for "proof reading" to pick up syntax errors caused by missing commas, unclosed parentheses, and so on.

Indirection does have some disadvantages. First, your code becomes more difficult to read. Second, programs with indirection will execute more slowly than programs which specify the global names.

NAME INDIRECTION - LINE LABELS

17. We have seen how name indirection allows us to replace a global name with any desired global name. Name indirection also allows us to replace a line label with any desired line label. This was demonstrated in Chapter Twelve.

NAME INDIRECTION - PROGRAMS FROM DISK

18. Name indirection can be used to access programs from disk. For example, instead of calling a module 'A', we could call ·PGMA, and so on.

PATTERN INDIRECTION

19. For name indirection, the indirection operator (expressed by the @ symbol) replaces a variable, a line label, or a program name.

Pattern indirection can be considered as a special form of name indirection, where the indirection operator replaces a pattern match.

For pattern indirection, the indirection operator (expressed by the @ symbol) follows the pattern match operator ('?'). Here is an example:

```
        S  PHONE="3N1""-""3N1""-""4N"
        F  J1=0:0  R !,"Phone: ",PH Q:PH=""   I PH'?@PHONE D ERR
        Q
        ;
ERR     W !!,"ENTER PHONE NUMBER IN THE FORMAT 'nnn-nnn-nnnn'"
        Q
```

If you plan to use many complex pattern matches in a group of related programs, pattern indirection can:

- ensure consistent formats for the pattern matches in different programs

- simplify changes in the pattern match for a particular entry such as phone.

ARGUMENT INDIRECTION

20.   For argument indirection, the indirection operator (expressed by the @ symbol) replaces a command argument. Here is an example:

```
S  NAM="^NAME(20)"
S  ^NAME(20)="JONES,ROBERT"
S  ^PROJECT(37)="CLEAN GARAGE THIS SATURDAY"
S  @NAM=^PROJECT(37)
```

With this code, at run time, we SET ^NAME(20) equal to "CLEAN GARAGE THIS SAT-URDAY".

Here is another example.

```
S  NAM="^NAME(20)"
S  ^NAME(20)="JONES,ROBERT"
S  ^PROJECT(37)="CLEAN THE GARAGE THIS SATURDAY"
S  ^PROJECT(37)=@NAM
```

With this code, at run time, we set ^PROJECT(37) equal to "JONES,ROBERT".

Code which uses argument indirection can be difficult to read. We will not use argument indirection for further examples in this chapter.

COMMAND INDIRECTION - THE XECUTE COMMAND

USING THE STRING VALUE OF A VARIABLE AS A LINE OF MUMPS CODE

21.   The XECUTE command allows us to interpret a literal string as a line of MUMPS code. Consider this line of code:

```
S  Y="F INDEX=1:1:4 W !,""HELLO"""
```

The command WRITE !,Y will output:

```
F  INDEX=1:1:4  W !,"HELLO"
```

The command XECUTE Y will output:

```
HELLO
HELLO
HELLO
HELLO
```

The XECUTE command interprets our value of Y - the literal string - as a line of MUMPS code, and executes this code.

Of course, we must use the XECUTE command with a literal string which represents a valid line of MUMPS code.

22.   We can use the XECUTE command with global nodes, as well as with local variables. For example:

```
S ^Y="F INDEX=1:1:4 W !,""HELLO"""
```

The command W !,^Y will output:

```
F INDEX=1:1:4 W !,"HELLO"
```

The command XECUTE ^Y will output:

```
HELLO
HELLO
HELLO
HELLO
```

23.   We can use the XECUTE command to perform a specific function for several different programs. For example:

```
S ^PHONE="W !,""ENTER PHONE NUMBER IN FORMAT
......  'nnn-nnn-nnnn'."",!,""IF TELEPHONE NUMBER IS UNKNOWN,
......  ENTER 'U'."",!,"" IF THIS INDIVIDUAL IS KNOWN NOT TO HAVE
......  A PHONE, ENTER 'N'."""
```

Then, at the beginning of each program, we can use the code:

```
S PHONE=^PHONE
```

and use the command:

```
X PHONE
```

to display the desired message. We prefer to XECUTE PHONE as a local variable since this provides faster execution than XECUTEing ^PHONE as a global variable.

XECUTEING AN ARRAY IN SEQUENTIAL ORDER

24.   What if we need more than 255 characters for the code to be "called" by our XECUTE command?

A simple solution is to put our code into several variables, and XECUTE these in sequence. For example:

```
        S ^DATACHK(1)="R !,""File this data? Yes=> "",ANS
......  I ANS="""" S ANS=""Y"""
        S ^DATACHK(2)="I ANS?1""N"".E W !!,""NOT FILED"""
        S ^DATACHK(3)="I (ANS'?1""Y"".E)&(ANS'?1""N"".E)
......  W !!,*7,""PLEASE ENTER 'Y' OR 'N'"" S FLAG=""ERR"""
```

At the beginning of each program, we can read this DATACHK array into a local array:

```
        F J1=1:1:3 S DATACHK(J1)=^DATACHK(J1)
```

We can then use the following code later in our program:

```
        F J2=1:1:3 X DATACHK(J2)
```

25.   Thus the XECUTE command allows us to store MUMPS code as a series of variables set to literal strings. When we encounter an implicit or explicit QUIT, program control returns to that point immediately after the XECUTE command.

26.   If a given routine will be used by many programs, you may either:

   (1)   re-write this routine for each program

   (2)   use the DO command to call this routine from disk:
          eg. DO ^DATACHK

   (3)   enter this code into a global array, and use XECUTE as shown in
          Frame 24.

XECUTEING AN ARRAY IN NON-SEQUENTIAL ORDER

27.   In Frame 24, we used a FOR loop to XECUTE an array in sequential order The following form of FOR loop allows us to XECUTE an array in any order we desire:

```
        F J1=1,3,6,4 XECUTE ELEMENTS(J1)
```

Here, our FOR loop XECUTES array elements 1, 3, 6 and 4 - then stops.

28.   Instead of using a FOR loop, we can use one variable to XECUTE another. Here is an example:

```
        S RENAM1="F J1=0:0 R !!,""Program name: "",PGM Q:PGM="""""
......  X RENAM2,RENAM3"
        S RENAM2="F J2=0:0 R !,""New name: "",NEW Q:NEW?1A.AN
......  W ?$X+5,""ALPHA CHARACTERS ONLY"""
        S RENAM3="ZL @PGM ZS @NEW"
```

29.   RENAM1 prompts for program name, and QUITS on a null entry. Otherwise, we XECUTE RENAM2 and RENAM3.

RENAM2 prompts for entry of a new program name and QUITS on a correct pattern match.

RENAM3 uses indirection to load the original program, and then saves contents of local memory under the new name.

30.   When we use one variable to XECUTE a second, we have "nested XECUTE commands" - similar to nested DO commands.

When we first presented the DO command, we described how:

        DO MOD places line label MOD on the stack

and:

        DO ^PGM1 places program name ^PGM1 on the stack.

These line label names and program names are removed from the stack when an implicit or explicit QUIT command is encountered.

31.   With the code in Frame 28:

```
    X RENAM1            places RENAM1 on the stack
    X RENAM2            adds RENAM2 to the stack
```

When we QUIT RENAM2 on a valid entry for "New name:", RENAM2 is removed from the stack. We then return to RENAM1 and X RENAM3 places RENAM3 on the stack. When we QUIT RENAM3 (an implicit QUIT), this removes RENAM3 from the stack. When we QUIT RENAM1 (an implicit QUIT), this removes RENAM1 from the stack.

WRITING UTILITY PROGRAMS WITH THE XECUTE COMMAND

32.   A utility program is a "general purpose" program which performs "general functions" rather than the "specialized functions" of an application program. Your MUMPS system vendor probably provides a number of utility programs - described in the user manual for your system. The names and functions of utility programs are implementation specific. Your program editor is one example of a utility program.

For our system, we call the editor via X ^%. For your system, you probably call the editor via XECUTE, rather than a DO command.

When you call a program with the DO command, the existing program in your partition is automatically replaced by the "called" program. Thus, if you called the editor via a DO

312

command, the existing program - which you wished to edit - would disappear from your partition!

33.   Most implementations of Standard MUMPS solve this problem via the XECUTE command. When we XECUTE our editor, the calling program does NOT disappear from our partition. The command X ˏ% XECUTES the code stored on disk as the contents of our global ˏ%.

34.   To write "programs to operate on other programs", use the XECUTE command so the program operated on won't disappear from your partition! Here is a complete utility program, based on our code from Frame 28:

```
%RENAME1 ;This routine allows programs to be renamed.
        ;Optional deletion of old program name.
        ;
        W !!,"This routine allows you to rename programs"
        R !!,"Would you like to see the Routine Directory? Yes=> ",ANS
        I ANS'?1"N".E D ^%RD
        W !!,"After a program has been saved under the new name,"
        R !,"do you want the 'old' program name deleted? No=> ",DEL
        I DEL?1"Y".E D WARNING
        S RNAM1="F J1=0:0 R !!,""Program name: "",PGM Q:PGM="""" "
...... X RNAM2,RNAM3"
        S RNAM2="F J2=0:0 R !,""New Name: "",NEW Q:NEW?1A.AN
...... W ?$X+5,""Bad Name"""
        S RNAM3="ZL @PGM ZS @NEW X RNAM4"
        S RNAM4="I DEL?1""Y"".E ZR  ZS @PGM"
        X RNAM1
        Q
        ;
WARNING W !!!,"* * *  WARNING  * * *"
        W !!,"All programs that refer to the renamed programs
...... will have to"
        W !,"be updated to reflect the new program name."
        R !,"Are you sure you want old program name deleted? ",DEL
        Q
```

Notice that our program name begins with a "%" character: this is common practice for "utility programs". However, for some implementations, program names which begin with "%" can be saved to disk only by the System Manager. Check your user manual for additional information on this topic.

35.   This particular utility program would be called via DO ˏ%RENAME1. Let's examine the functions performed by each line of code:

> %RENAME1 + 5:   if ANS does not pattern match one "N" followed
> by any number of other characters, we DO the utility program %RD
> (routine directory). Your implementation may have a different

name for the utility program which displays your routine directory.

%RENAME1 + 7:   prompts for an answer to the query "do you want the old program name deleted?", and reads this answer into the local variable DEL.

%RENAME1 + 8:   displays warning message on a "Y" response to the prompt in previous line. The user is allowed to modify this response via the WARNING module.

Lines %RENAME1 + 9:   through %RENAME1 + 12 set up a small program within the local variables RENAM1 thru RENAM4. This small program will be used to rename the program specified by the code in the variable RENAM1.

%RENAME1 + 9:   SETS RNAM1 equal to a literal string of executable MUMPS code. This code prompts for "Program name:", QUITS on a null entry, then XECUTES RNAM2 and RNAM3.

%RENAME1 + 10:   SETS RNAM2 equal to a literal string of executable MUMPS code. This code prompts for "New name", QUITS on any entry which pattern matches one alpha character followed by any number of alpha characters or numbers; if the QUIT command is not executed, an error message is displayed.

%RENAME1 + 11:   SETS RNAM3 equal to a literal string of executable MUMPS code. This code loads whatever is "at" PGM; saves this routine under whatever name is "at" NEW; and XECUTES RNAM4. Remember - the ZLOAD and ZSAVE commands are implementation specific!

%RENAME1 + 12:   SETS RNAM4 equal to a literal string of executable MUMPS code. This code checks whether DEL pattern matches 1 "Y" followed by any number of other characters - if so, a ZREMOVE command followed by ZSAVE saves an empty partition onto disk using whatever name is "at" PGM.

%RENAME1 + 13:   XECUTEs RNAM1

36.   Which lines in this program MUST be executed via the XECUTE command?

Lines %RENAME1 + 11-12 MUST be executed via the XECUTE command - since they operate on another program.

Lines %RENAME1 + 9-10 do NOT require execution via the XECUTE command - since they do NOT operate on another program.

37.   What would happen if at RNAM1 the user enters a program name which does not exist in the routine directory?

%RENAME1 will stop with an implementation specific error message such as "<NOPGM>" at RNAM3.

38.   How could you "trap" such an error?

You could use the implementation-specific "error trap" provided with your system. For our implementation, this is the Z-special variable $ZERROR.

39.   Now rewrite %RENAME1 to:

(1)   Use the XECUTE command only where it is essential

(2)   Use the "error trap" to prevent this routine from stopping when a non-existant program name is entered by the user

(3)   Display a message to user after old program is deleted.

Here's how we did it:

```
%RENAME2 ;This routine allows programs to be renamed.
         ;Optional deletion of old program name.
         ;
         S $ZE="ERR^%RENAME2"
         W !!,"This routine allows you to rename programs"
         R !!,"Would you like to see the Routine Directory? Yes=>
......    ",ANS
```

315

```
         I  ANS'?1"N".E D ^%RD
         W  !!,"After a program has been saved under the new name,"
         R  !,"do you want the 'old' program name deleted? No=> ",DEL
         I  DEL?1"Y".E D WARNING
         S  RNAM1="ZL @PGM ZS @NEW X RNAM2"
         S  RNAM2="I DEL?1""Y"".E ZR  ZS @PGM W ?$X+5,""...""",PGM,"
......   " deleted..."""
OLD      F J1=0:0 R !!,"Program name: ",PGM Q:PGM=""  D NEW X RNAM1
         Q
         ;
NEW      F J2=0:0 R !,"New Name: ",NEW Q:NEW?1A.AN  W ?$X+5,"Bad Name"
         Q
         ;
WARNING  W !!!,*7,"* * *  WARNING  * * *"
         W !!,"All programs that refer to the renamed programs will
......   have to"
         W !,"be updated to reflect the new program name."
         R !,"Are you sure you want old program name deleted?  ",DEL
         Q
         ;
ERR      I $ZE'["<NOPGM>" W !!,*7,"Error...",$ZE Q
         W !!,*7,PGM," does not exist!" S $ZE="ERR^%RENAME2"
         G OLD^%RENAME2
```

40. Notice in our revised program:

- we XECUTE only two lines of code

- at the start of our program we set $ZERROR equal to "ERR ‿%RENAME2". The ERR module QUITS our routine if $ERROR does NOT contain the implementation-specific error message "<NOPGM>". Otherwise, we display a message that the named program does not exist, reset $ZERROR, and return to OLD‿%RENAME2.

- we use the asterisk syntax of WRITE to "ring the bell" if user enters "YES" to the prompt: "do you want the original program name deleted?".

- in line %RENAME2 + 11, we display a message that the program was deleted to "let the user know what's going on".

NAKED REFERENCE

41. We suggest you consider this section as "optional reading". We do NOT use naked reference for the programs presented in this manual. However, you may see naked reference in the code written by other programmers.

42. Naked reference refers to a partial subscript, whose complete definition depends on

the last subscript used for global access. The term "global access" means a global accessed from disk, e.g. via a WRITE command, or the SET command. The following code:

```
W !,A,^NAME("A",A)
S B=""
F I=0:0 S B=$O(^NAME("A",A,B) Q:B=""  W !!,B,?30,^NAME
...... ("A",A,B)
```

can be rewritten with naked reference as:

```
W !,A,^NAME("A",A)
S B=""
F I=0:0 S B=$O(^NAME("A",A,B)) Q:B=""  W !!,B,?30,^(B)
```

Our partial subscript ^(B) is defined by the last subscript used for global access: ^NAME("A",A,B).

43.   With naked reference, MUMPS looks at the previous global access, then uses this complete global name, with all associated subscripts.

For some implementations, naked reference provides faster execution since it eliminates the need for a "second look up" on your global name.

Here is a simple program you can use to evaluate how naked reference affects the speed of program execution for your implementation of ANS MUMPS:

```
CH14EX3  ; IMPACT OF NAKED REFERENCE ON SPEED OF SET COMMAND
         ; IN FOR LOOP
         ;
A        S ^XXX(1,1,1,0)=0,T1=$P($H,",",2)
         F J1=1:1:5000 S ^XXX(1,1,1,J1)=J1
         S T2=$P($H,",",2)
         W !,T2-T1," SECONDS REQUIRED FOR 5000 ITERATIONS OF SET
......   COMMAND" W !!
B        K  S ^XXX(1,1,1,0)=0,T1=$P($H,",",2)
         F J2=1:1:5000 S ^(J2)=J2
         S T2=$P($H,",",2)
         W !,T2-T1," SECONDS REQUIRED FOR 5000 ITERATIONS OF SET
......   COMMAND"
         W !,"USING NAKED REFERENCE"
         W !!,"Finished" Q
```

45.   You may find that for your implementation, naked reference does not provide a significant decrease in the time required for execution.

Other factors which influence execution speed include:

- number of users on the system

- other programs running at the same time as your "test program".

46. Even if naked reference does decrease the time required for executing your programs, you may prefer to avoid using naked reference.

Naked reference can be confusing to read, since the most recent global access is sometimes unclear. For example:

```
W ! , ^NAME (1 , 5)
S ^PROJECT (2 , 5) =^(5)
```

Here "^(5)" in our set command refers to ^NAME(1,5), rather than to ^PROJECT(2,5).

Naked reference refers to the last global accessed from disk - NOT to the last global name in your code!

We recommend that you avoid using naked reference - at least until you are an experienced MUMPS programmer.

SUMMARY OF NEW CONCEPTS - CHAPTER 14

$DATA FUNCTION:

0	means no data, no descendants
1	means data, no descendants
10	means no data, descendants
11	means data, descendants

NAME INDIRECTION:

- allows insertion of any desired variable name, line label or routine name into a routine at the time of execution.
  For example:

```
R !,"Program name:  ",ANS
S PGMNAM="^"_ANS
D @PGMNAM
```

PATTERN INDIRECTION:

- allows insertion of any desired pattern match into a routine at the time of execution.
  For example:

```
S SSN="3N1""-""2N1""-""4N"
I ANS'?@SSN D ERR
```

ARGUMENT INDIRECTION:

- allows insertion of any desired argument into a routine at the time of execution.

COMMAND INDIRECTION:

- implemented via the XECUTE command

- interprets literal string as a line of MUMPS code
  Example:

```
S RNAM1="ZL @PGM ZS @NEW X RNAM2"
S RNAM2="I DEL?1""Y"".E ZR  ZS @PGM"
X RNAM1
```

CHAPTER FIFTEEN

USING MULTIPLE DEVICES FROM A SINGLE TERMINAL
ACCESSING FILES IN A MULTI-USER ENVIRONMENT

Up to this point, we have assumed you are performing all your input and output at a single terminal. In this chapter, we will present techniques for displaying reports - or program listings - on a device other than your own terminal. We will also demonstrate two methods to run "background jobs".

Up to this point, we have also assumed that global files will be accessed by only one person at a time. In this chapter, we will demonstrate how to avoid problems when several users access the same global files.

Topics include:

- Using multiple devices from a single terminal - the OPEN, USE and CLOSE commands

- Running "background jobs" via the $IO special variable or the JOB command

- Accessing files in a multi-user environment - the LOCK command.

By the end of this chapter you will be able to:

- output reports - or program listings - on devices other than your own terminal

- run "background jobs"

- use the LOCK command to avoid problems which otherwise would arise when several users simultaneously attempt to change the same global node.

USING MULTIPLE DEVICES FROM A SINGLE TERMINAL - THE OPEN, USE AND CLOSE COMMANDS

1.   For most implementations of Standard MUMPS, each device has a unique identification number. These device numbers may be "standard" for the implementation - and independent of hardware configuration. For example, with our implementation:

Device #1	=	console terminal
Device #3	=	line printer
Device #47-50	=	mag tape drives
Device #64-143	=	terminals

The device numbers for your system may differ from those above. Study the user manual for your implementation, to determine how device numbers are specified for your system.

2.   For our implementation, when you log onto the system, the terminal at which you log on is considered your "Principal Device". This principal device can be identified by two numbers: the number assigned to it by the system and device number zero. For example, if you log on at a terminal which is device number 64, your principal device can be identified as device number 64 or device number 0. All input/output operations are directed to this Principal Device - unless otherwise specified by the OPEN and USE commands.

Study the user manual for your implementation, to determine how numbering for the Principal Device is handled for your system.

3.   When you log onto the system, you establish "ownership" of your Principal Device. You may "claim ownership" of additional devices via the OPEN command.

After executing an OPEN command, the calling program owns the device and no other program can use it. For example:

```
OPEN  3, 64, 65
```

claims ownership of devices 3, 64 and 65.

For our system, device 3 is the line printer, and devices 64 and 65 user terminals. Your system manager can provide the device numbers for your system.

4.   If a device is already "owned" by someone else and you attempt to claim it via an OPEN command, your program waits until this device is released by the other program. It is common practice to attach a timeout on the OPEN command:

```
OPEN  3: : 60
```

Within the double colon, you may use an implementation specific device parameter. If you do not specify this parameter, a default value is supplied by your system. On our system, we can specify the column width for a specific display. For example:

```
OPEN 3:110:60 means:
```

"Attempt to OPEN device 3 for a display width of 110 columns; if OPEN command cannot be executed within 60 seconds, set the $TEST special variable equal to zero."

5.   Remember how the $TEST special variable is affected by timeouts? If the OPEN is successful, $T is set to one. Otherwise, $T is set to zero. Here is the code to OPEN device #3, check $T after a 20 second timeout, and display a message if device #3 is not available:

```
OPEN 3::60 E  W !,"Line printer not available"
```

The message would be displayed if someone else had "gotten there first" and established ownership of device #3 via his own OPEN command.

6.   Execution of an OPEN command establishes ownership - but neither directs output to the "owned" device, nor accepts input from the "owned" device.

The USE command enables you to perform input/output on an OPENed device. You may OPEN several devices at once, but can USE only one device at a time. The syntax for USE allows a "parameter" as for OPEN. However, no timeout is permitted, and only one colon is applied. Here are two examples:

```
USE 3
USE 3:110
```

The first command does not specify display width: the default value is used. The second command specifies 110 column display width.

Again, the "parameter" is implementation specific. Study the user manual for your implementation to determine how this operates for your system.

7.   When a USEd device is no longer needed, you should release it via the CLOSE command. For example:

```
SELECT OPEN 3::60 I  USE 3:110 D REPORT CLOSE 3 Q
       W !,"Line printer not available" Q
       ;
REPORT ;MODULE TO PRODUCE DESIRED REPORT
```

Your CLOSE command allows another program to OPEN the specified device. Unlike OPEN and USE, CLOSE does not accept timeouts or parameters.

8.   For our implementation, OPEN, USE and CLOSE also operate under direct execution.

Thus, to output a program on our printer, we could enter:

```
>O 3::30  W $T
```

if $T were equal to one we would continue with:

```
>U 3 P
>C 3
```

Study your user manual to see how these three commands operate under direct execution for your system. In earlier chapters, we noted that the operation of MUMPS commands for direct execution is implementation specific.

9.   Once you have executed an OPEN and USE command, all input/output - i.e. all READ and WRITE operations - will be performed on the device specified, until the next USE command, or a CLOSE command.

You can use one device for input and another for output by executing a USE for each operation. Here is an example:

```
O 3,64 U 64 R !,"Name:  ",NAM
U 3 W !,"Name entry was ",NAM
U 64 R !,"Address:  ",ADR
U 3 W !,"Address entry was ",ADR
.
.
.
C 3,64
```

In this case, all input is on device 64, and all output on device 3.

Modify the above code, so input is on your principal device, and output on device 64.

```
O 64::10
E  W !,"Device #64 not available" Q
U 0 R !,"Name:  ",NAM
U 64 W !,"Name entry was ",NAM
U 0 R !,"Address:  ",ADR
U 64 W !,"Address entry was ",ADR
.
.
.
C 64
```

Device zero does not have to be opened. The command USE 0 shifts control from device 3 to device zero.

10.   In Frame 9, we retained ownership of device #64 until the end of our program. In "real life", we probably would "save" our data as a local or global array, then output a single report "all at once".

11.   OPEN, USE and CLOSE can have post conditionals on the command, but not on the argument. Here is some code to OPEN device #3 if ANS?1"Y".E, with a timeout of 5 seconds:

```
R !,"Output report on line printer? (Y or N): ",ANS
O:ANS?1"Y".E 3::5
```

We could then have an ELSE command followed by USE:

```
E  W !,"LINE PRINTER UNAVAILABLE" D CHOICE Q
U 3:110 D REPORT C 3 Q
```

12.   A common use of OPEN, USE, and CLOSE is to direct output to a line printer. Let's write a routine to do this. This routine should:

(1)   allow the user to direct output to either the line printer (device 3) or the terminal currently in use (device 0)

(2)   if the terminal is selected and is available, print report

(3)   if the line printer is selected and is available, print report

(4)   if the line printer is selected, but is not available, user should have option to either:

(a)   wait for line printer
(b)   use the terminal, or
(c)   stop without a printout.

13.   Here's how we did it:

```
LPSELECT ;THIS ROUTINE ALLOWS THE USER TO DIRECT OUTPUT TO EITHER
         ;A LINE PRINTER (DEVICE #3) OR THE TERMINAL IN USE (DEVICE #0)
         ;THE DEVICE NUMBERS ZERO AND 3 ARE IMPLEMENTATION SPECIFIC
         ;CHANGES MAY BE NEEDED WITH YOUR IMPLEMENTATION.
         ;
         R !,"Output report on line printer (L) or your terminal
......  (T)? ",ANS
         I (ANS'?1"L".E)&(ANS'?1"T".E) W ?$X+5,*7,"PLEASE ENTER
......  T OR L" G LPSELECT
         I ANS?1"T".E D REPORT Q
         O 3::10 I  U 3:110 D REPORT C 3 Q
         D LPBUSY
         I FLAG="NOTDONE" W !,"REPORT NOT DONE BECAUSE LINE PRINTER
......  WAS BUSY"
```

```
          Q
          ;
LPBUSY  S  FLAG="OK"
        W  !,"Line printer not available"
        W  !,"Would you like to wait for line printer (W),"
        W  !,"display report on terminal(T)"
        R  !,"or exit program(E)? ",ANS
        I  ANS?1"T".E  D REPORT Q
        I  ANS?1"E".E  S FLAG="NOTDONE" Q
        I  ANS'?1"W".E  W !,*7,"PLEASE ENTER 'W', 'T' OR 'E'" G LPBUSY
        W  !!,"NOW WE WILL TRY TO OUTPUT REPORT ON LINE PRINTER"
        O  3::30 I  U 3:110 D REPORT C 3 Q
        W  !,"LINE PRINTER STILL UNAVAILABLE"
        G  LPBUSY
```

RUNNING "BACKGROUND JOBS"

THE $IO SPECIAL VARIABLE

14.   The $IO special variable contains the number of the device presently in use. For example:

```
>W $IO
```

returns the number of your principal device. Another example:

```
>O 3 U 3 W $IO
```

prints 3 on device 3.

15.   For our implementation, we can use $IO to run a program "in background" via:

```
U 0 C $IO
```

This code "closes" our principal device - so subsequent code will "run in background". In this context, "running in background" means "running on its own" without user interaction. The U 0 before closing $IO makes sure we are closing our principal device and not another device.

16.   Here is a revised version of LPBUSY which "runs in background" if the line printer is unavailable:

```
LPBUSY  W  !,"Line printer not available"
        W  !!,"Would you like to: "
        W  !," 1.   Display report on your terminal"
        W  !," 2.   Have program wait for line printer, and free
.....  up this terminal"
        W  !," 3.   Exit program at this point"
```

```
R !,"Select option: ",ANS
I (ANS<1)!(ANS>3) W *7,*7 G LPBUSY
I ANS=1 D REPORT Q
I ANS=3 Q
W !!!,"*** THIS TERMINAL IS NOW FREE ***",!!,"EXIT" U O C $IO
O 3 U 3 D REPORT H
```

Since there is no timeout on our OPEN command, this last line of code will "run in background" until the line printer becomes available.

Notice the "exit message" in line LPBUSY + 9: this tells the user that the terminal will be available for other programs (after executing C $IO). Since device 0 is already in use, we could omit USE 0 before CLOSEing $IO.

Notice that this code HALTs itself automatically when it is finished to "free up" the partition used for "running in background".

We do NOT need to CLOSE Device 3 - since all OPENed devices are automatically closed by the HALT command.

17.   Running a routine "in background" can be useful for programs which do not require interaction with the user. Examples include:

 • printing long reports

 • searching large globals

 • creating a new cross reference file for a large file.

THE JOB COMMAND

18.   Another way to run background jobs is via the JOB command.Unlike CLOSING $IO, the JOB command is not implementation specific.

The JOB command is based on the content of a "job number". In a multi-user environment, your computer's operating system allows a limited number of MUMPS programs to execute at the same time. Each program running on your system is called a "job". Every time you log on to your system, you are assigned a "job number" that identifies your job to the operating system. Your job number remains the same until you log off: if you log on again, yo 1 probably will be assigned a different job number.

19.   MUMPS stores your job number in the special variable $JOB. At a right caret enter:

>W $JOB

This returns the job number you were assigned when you logged on.

20. The JOB command allows you to start a job (i.e. a program)to run in background in another partition. Syntax is:

    JOB ^ROUTINE: job parameters: timeout

Both job parameters and timeout are optional.

The job parameters are implementation specific: see your system manual for information.

21. Here is an example of the JOB command with our LPBUSY module from Frame 16:

```
LPBUSY W !,"Line printer not available"
       W !!,"Would you like to: "
       W !," 1.    Display report on your terminal"
       W !," 2.    Have program wait for line printer, and free up
...... this terminal"
       W !," 3.    Exit program at this point"
       R !,"Select option: ",ANS
       I (ANS<1)!(ANS>3) W *7,*7 G LPBUSY
       I ANS=1 D REPORT Q
       I ANS=3 Q
       JOB REPORT^PROGRAM: : 60
       E  W !!,"NO PARTITION AVAILABLE FOR BACKGROUND JOB AT
...... THIS TIME" G LPBUSY
       W !!,"REPORT WILL BE PRINTED WHEN LINE PRINTER BECOMES
...... AVAILABLE" Q
```

22. In this program, the JOB command attempts to start REPORT.PROGRAM in another partition. If this attempt is unsuccessful, after 60 seconds, a message is displayed and we GOTO LPBUSY. If this attempt is successful, the message in our last line of code is displayed, and we QUIT the module.

We recommend that you use a timeout with your JOB command. When the new job is started, your program will continue - independent of the new job.

23. The devices that a new job owns can be determined in two ways. First, the program executed by the new job can specify devices via the OPEN command. Second, the job parameters of the JOB command may allow you to specify devices. Check your user manual to see if the job parameters provide this function for your system.

24. When you start a background job via CLOSE $IO, your background job has access to your original local variables. However, when you start a background job with JOB, your background job does not have access to your original variables. When using the JOB command, we suggest that you first store any local variables needed by the background job in a global file. The background job can then examine this global as needed.

25. After starting a background job via CLOSE $IO, you must log on again to continue the

program you were running. The JOB command allows you to continue your program after the background job is started.

Why might JOB be unable to start a new job? Your MUMPS system allows a limited number of jobs to be processed at one time - and, there may be no "job slots" available. In this case, a JOB command without a timeout will wait until somebody logs off. Out of courtesy to others, you should only have one background job running at a time. Otherwise, your background jobs could "hog" the system and prevent others from logging on. Every background job you start means one less person can log on to the system. If you need to run several background jobs at the same time, ask your system manager first!

ACCESSING FILES IN A MULTI-USER ENVIRONMENT - THE LOCK COMMAND

26.   In a single user environment, you will not need the LOCK command. In a multi-user environment, where multiple terminals access and modify the same globals, the LOCK command becomes necessary.

Consider a global array ^NAME, where ^NAME has the value of the last "unique identifier" for our primary file. Suppose that two users are updating this file from different terminals. If both programs simultaneously access the value for ^NAME, both users could end up with the same value for the next available subscript. Then, when our second user executes the SET command:

    S ^NAME (J1)=DATA(1)_DATA(2) , ^NAME ("A", DATA(1) , J1)=" "

new data will over write the previous data at ^NAME(J1).

This problem can be avoided by ensuring that only one user can access and update certain critical globals at a given time.

27.   LOCK claims ownership of either a global, or part of a global. In contrast to OPEN, this ownership is NOT exclusive. LOCK does NOT prevent other programs from access to a LOCKed node. But LOCK does prevent other programs from LOCKing a LOCKed node.

28.   The syntax for LOCK allows a timed argument to take two forms:

    LOCK ^NAME (A)

    LOCK ^NAME (A) : 10

If you try to LOCK ^NAME(A) and this node is already LOCKed by another program, your program simply stops until the node becomes available.

With a timeout on LOCK, $T is set to zero if ^NAME(A) is not LOCKed within the specified number of seconds.

We suggest that you always use timeout with LOCK, and test $T to determine whether the attempted LOCK has been successful.

29.   The LOCK command, by itself, does not provide any protection for your data. In Frame 28, following execution of the LOCK command, other programs can modify our ^NAME(A) global. However, following execution of the LOCK command, other programs can not LOCK the ancestors or descendants of our locked node.

If you LOCK a node, both the descendants and the "ancestors" of that node are locked. We can consider all nodes in a direct line from a given node to the top of the tree as "ancestors".

In this example:

```
                                      <^A (1, 1, 1)
                      <^A (1, 1)  -  <^A (1, 1, 2)
        <^A (1)  -  <^A (1, 2)       <^A (1, 1, 3)
^A  -  <^A (2)       <^A (1, 3)
        <^A (3)
```

(1)   if we LOCK ^A(1,1), what other nodes are locked?

(2)   what other nodes are NOT locked?

---

        descendents A(1,1,1), A(1,1,2), and A(1,1,3) are locked

        ancestors A(1) and A are locked

        "siblings" A(1,2) and A(1,3) are NOT locked

30.   LOCK is effective only if other programs also use LOCK. LOCK is not effective if other programs which access your globals fail to use LOCK.

For example:

    PGM1   LOCK ^NAME (A) : 10

    PGM2   S ^NAME (A) =NAM

The LOCK command in PGM1 is executed. Since LOCK does NOT exclude access to a LOCKed node, the SET command in PGM2 is also executed.

A second example:

    PGM1   LOCK ^NAME (A) : 10

```
PGM2    LOCK ^NAME(A)
        S  ^NAME(A)=NAM
```

Now, PGM2 will wait until ^NAME is unlocked by PGM1.

31.   We could rewrite this second example with $T:

```
PGM1    F J1=1:1:3 L ^NAME(A):10 Q:$T W "."
        E W !,*7,"THIS ENTRY IS BEING EDITED, SELECT ANOTHER ONE" Q
        D UPDATE

PGM2    F J1=1:1:3 L ^NAME(A):10 Q:$T  W "."
        E W !,*7,"SOMEONE ELSE IS USING THIS ENTRY, PLEASE
......  RE-SELECT" Q
        S ^NAME(A)=NAM
```

In PGM1, the first FOR loop, repeatedly tries to LOCK ^NAME(A). If the LOCK is successful, we QUIT the FOR loop. If the LOCK is not successful, we output a "." to let the user know "something is going on".

If the LOCK is not accomplished after three attempts, we output a message that the entry is being edited.

32.   The LOCK command accepts post conditionals. For example:

```
LOCK:ANS?1"Y". E  ^NAME(A)
```

33.   The LOCK command can specify one node, several nodes, or an entire global.

Using the global in Frame 29, we can LOCK ^A(1,1,1) and ^A(1,1,2) by the command:

```
LOCK (^A(1,1,1),^A(1,1,2))
```

Notice that both arguments are enclosed in parentheses. Without the parentheses:

```
LOCK ^A(1,1,1),^A(1,1,2)
```

will LOCK ^A(1,1,1), then unLOCK ^A(1,1,1) when the second LOCK command is executed.

34.   Timeouts may be used on LOCK for multiple global nodes. For example:

```
LOCK (^A(1,1,1),^A(1,1,2)):10
E W !,"GLOBALS ^A(1,1,1) AND ^A(1,1,2) ARE LOCKED BY
...... ANOTHER PROGRAM"
```

35.   What about unLOCKing nodes?

Executing a new LOCK command will unlock all previously locked nodes. For example:

```
PGM1    LOCK ^A(1,1,1) D UPDATE LOCK ^A(1,1,2)
```

Our first LOCK command locks ^A(1,1,1); our second LOCK command unlocks ^A(1,1,1) and locks ^A(1,1,2). However, we do NOT recommend this approach!

First, neither LOCK command has a timeout: if either node is LOCKed by another user, your program will hang until the desired node becomes available.

Second, another user might have the following code in a program:

```
PGM2   LOCK ^A(1,1,2) D UPDATE LOCK ^A(1,1,1)
```

If PGM1 and PGM2 are run at the same time, it is possible that neither program can execute its second LOCK command. In this case, both programs could hang indefinitely!

36. To unlock previously locked nodes, we recommend that you use LOCK with no argument.

LOCK with no argument releases all globals currently "owned" by that user. For example:

```
PGM1    LOCK ^A(1,1,1):10
        E  W !,"^A(1,1,1) IN USE BY ANOTHER PROGRAM" G PGM1
        D UPDATE LOCK
        LOCK ^A(1,1,2):10
        E  W !,"^A(1,1,2) IN USE BY ANOTHER PROGRAM" G PGM1+3
        D UPDATE LOCK

PGM2    LOCK ^A(1,1,2):10
        E  W !,"^A(1,1,2) IN USE BY ANOTHER PROGRAM" G PGM2
        D UPDATE LOCK
        LOCK ^A(1,1,1):10
        E  W !,"^A(1,1,1) IN USE BY ANOTHER PROGRAM" G PGM2+3
        D UPDATE LOCK
```

Here, using LOCK with no argument to unlock our global nodes avoids the "conflict" between PGM1 and PGM2.

SUMMARY OF NEW CONCEPTS - CHAPTER 15

Device number:

- implementation specific

- Principal Device (device zero):

  - may be defined as your log on terminal
  - automatically "OPENED" at log on.

OPEN command:

- claims ownership of the specified device

- if device is already OPENed by other user, program hangs until device is released by implicit or explicit CLOSE command (HALT is considered an implicit CLOSE command)

- syntax:

```
OPEN  3
OPEN  3: : 60
OPEN  3: 110: 60
```

> timeout = 60 seconds
> parameter = 110 columns
> NOTE: default parameter assigned by system if no parameter specified.
> Parameter syntax is implementation specific.

- may be post conditionalized:

```
OPEN: FLAG="LP"  3: 110: 60
```

USE:

- directs input/output to specified device after execution of OPEN command

- accepts parameter but no timeout

- syntax:

```
USE  3
USE  3: 110
```

> NOTE: default parameter assigned by system if no parameter specified.
> Parameter syntax is implementation specific.

- may be post conditionalized:

        USE: FLAG="LP" 3 : 110

CLOSE:

- releases owned device from OPEN command

- syntax:

        CLOSE 3

- may be post conditionalized:

        CLOSE: FLAG="DONE" 3

SPECIAL VARIABLES:

        $TEST - set to zero when:
            - timeout occurs for READ, OPEN, JOB or LOCK commands
            - argument to IF command has truth value of zero (false)

        $IO special variable - contains device number for current device in
        use

        $JOB special variable - returns job number assigned when you log
        on

Background job:

- refers to program that runs without user interaction

- may be started by use of:
        CLOSE command with $IO special variable (implementation
        specific)
        JOB command
        - example with CLOSE command

                W !,"THIS TERMINAL IS NOW FREE"
                U 0 C $IO
                O 3 U 3 D REPORT

        The last two commands will "run in background" until ex-
        ecuted. As soon as the CLOSE $IO command is executed, ter-
        minal is free for other users

- example with JOB command

```
JOB  REPORT^PROGRAM: : 60
   E  W ! , "NO PARTITION AVAILABLE"  G LPBUSY
```

The JOB command is commonly used with a timeout; otherwise your program will "hang" until JOB is executed.

LOCK:

- claims ownership of specified global (or part of global)

- does NOT prevent other programs from access to LOCKed node

- DOES prevent other programs from LOCKing specified node, together with descendants and ancestors of this node

- applies only to multi-user environment

- can specify several nodes to be LOCKed at one time:

```
LOCK  ^ (A(1,1,1), ^A(1,1,2))
```

- LOCK with no argument releases all globals LOCKed by your program

- accepts timeout.

CHAPTER SIXTEEN
PUTTING IT ALL TOGETHER

This chapter demonstrates how the routines from the previous chapters can"work together" as a single program that allows you to:

(1)   Create new records in a "name and address file". Each record provides fields for name, address, town, state, zip code, home phone, office phone, keywords (referenced against a keyword dictionary file) and comments.

(2)   Automatically check entries for town and keyword against dictionary files.

(3)   Edit information within this file.

(4)   Display data

(5)   Search for records that include a specified keyword.

(6)   Search for records that include a specified character string in the comment field.

This program was originally written by Mr. Gustavo San Roman, a third year student at the Pennsylvania State University School of Medicine, as a class project for our course "An Introduction to Computer Programming". Subsequently, the code was rewritten by Mr. Bressler. If you wish to use this program, but need to "save partition space", you could:

(1)   Maintain two versions of the program - a "documented version" with comments, and a "working version" with the comments removed.

(2)   Some MUMPS installations provide "stripper" software that allows you to remove comments before the program is run.

(3)   Some program editors allow you to keep comments in a special global file - separate from your program.

(4)   "Break up" the routines into several smaller routines.

Our objective in including this program is to provide an example of how the routines in this book can "work together" in a single program. The authors would welcome suggestions for improved clarity or functionality.

337

```
NAMEFILE ;
         ;         This routine starts the Name File program.  It just DOes
         ;         ^NAMENU.  The sole purpose of this routine is to make
         ;         remembering the start routine for this Name File program
         ;         easier to remember - DO ^NAMEFILE is easier to remember
         ;         than DO ^NAMENU.  We could rename ^NAMENU, but then the
         ;         routine's name would not reflect the routine's function.
         ;
         D ^NAMENU Q



NAMENU ; Main Menu Display and Selection
         ;         This routine is a modification of CH12EX6.
         ;         This routine displays the main menu via $TEXT.
         ;         Modifications include:
         ;             Menu selection by numeric or alpha entry
         ;             Timed read for menu selection
         ;             HELP function to aid user
         ;             CLEAR,NEWPAGE, and HOLD are XECUTEd throughout the program
         ;             to prevent "scrolling" when using a CRT
         ;
         ;         Other routines in this program:
         ;             NADD               NAEDIT
         ;             NADELETE           NADDKEY
         ;             NALSTKEY           NADISPLY
         ;             NASEARCH           NAHELP1
         ;             NAHELP2
         ;
         ;         Global variables:
         ;           ^NAME - holds data for the Name file.  This includes
         ;                   the COMMENT and KEY subfiles.  The Name file
         ;                   is cross referenced by name and name within
         ;                   town.
         ;             Structure:
         ;               ^NAME=next available subscript
         ;                 ^NAME(n)=name^address^town^state^zip^office tel.
         ;                       ^home tel.
         ;                       office tel. = phone1\phone2\phone3
         ;                 ^NAME(n,"COMMENT")=next comment number
         ;                   ^NAME(n,"COMMENT",x)=comment
         ;                 ^NAME(n,"KEY",keyword)=""
         ;                 ^NAME("A",name,n)=""
         ;                 ^NAME("B",town,name,n)=""
         ;           ^KEYWORDS - holds the keyword dictionary file.
         ;             Structure:
         ;               ^KEYWORDS(keyword)=""
         ;           ^TOWN - holds the town dictionary file.
         ;             Structure:
         ;               ^TOWN(town)=""
         ;
```

```
;            Common local variables:
;               ANS is used to accept a user response, usually to a
;                  'yes/no' type question.  When the value of ANS must
;                  be preserved throughout a routine, ANS1 is used for
;                  additional user responses.
;               CLEAR XECUTEs throughout the routines.  It simply
;                  clears the screen for CRT terminals.
;               HOLD is commonly XECUTEd in conjunction with CLEAR.
;                  It prevents scrolling by prompting the user to 'Hit
;                  RETURN to Continue'. Therefore, program output will
;                  continue when the user is ready. HOLD freezes output
;                  for CRTs only.
;               J1, J2...are FOR loop variables.  J1 is used whenever
;                  possible, except when FOR loops are nested.  The
;                  number associated with the 'J' indicates the level
;                  of nesting.
;               K1, K2...are FOR loop variables.  These FOR loop
;                  variables are only used in modules called by more
;                  than one routine.  This avoids conflict with the
;                  'J' FOR loop variables.
;               NEWPAGE XECUTEs throughout the routines.  It DOes
;                  PAGE^NADISPLY to prevent scrolling on CRT terminals.
;               NUM is always used to denote the unique identifier for
;                  the Name file.
;
;
;
;            %IS is a vendor-specific utility program that assists in
;            device selection.  DOing CURRENT^%IS returns variables
;            that describe the device currently in use.  The variables
;            contain information about the device such as page (screen)
;            width & length, device type, and the ASCII codes required
;            to perform backspacing and form feeds (clear screen).  For
;            this program, we will only use the variables FF, SL and
;            SUB.  These variables are described below:
;               FF = this variable contains a string which is the
;                     argument of a WRITE command.  When used with
;                     indirection, i.e., WRITE @FF, MUMPS performs a
;                     form feed (clear screen).  For example, FF is
;                     '#,*27,*72,*27,*74' for a VT-52 terminal. You may
;                     recognize this 'Escape H, Escape J' sequence from
;                     Chapter 12.  In this string, the '#' only resets
;                     $X and $Y to zero - this reflects the cursor's
;                     new position at the top of the page (screen).
;                     For an LA120 printer terminal, FF is simply '#'.
;               SL = this variable is equal to the Screen Length.  We
;                     use this variable in the module PAGE^NADISPLY to
;                     determine if the output is close enough to the
;                     bottom of the screen to hold the display and wait
;                     for a user response before clearing the screen.
;               SUB = this variable contains a string which includes the
;                     device's classification and type.  The device
;                     classification can be one of three types - 'C', 'P'
```

```
;         or'PK', which stand for 'CRT', 'Printer' and
;         'Printer with Keyboard' respectively.  For a VT-52,
;         SUB is 'C-VT-52', while SUB is 'PK-DEC' for an
;         LA120.  For this program, we are only concerned
;         with the device classification.  This variable is
;         checked via a pattern match in the variables CLEAR,
;         NEWPAGE, and HOLD.  This allows the program to hold
;         the display and clear the screen only on CRTs.
;         This is not done on printer devices because the
;         hardcopy output makes holding the display
;         unneccessary, and disregarding the form feed saves
;         paper.
;
;         Your implementation should have a similar utility program.
;
D CURRENT^%IS
S CLEAR="I SUB'?1""P"".E W @FF",NEWPAGE="I SUB'?1""P"".E D
.....PAGE^NADISPLY"
S HOLD="I SUB'?1""P"".E R !!!,""ENTER 'RETURN' TO CONTINUE"",
......CONTINUE"
;
;         Display title screen with HELP instructions
;
X CLEAR
W !!!!!!!!!
F J1=1:1:55 W "*"
W !,"*****         WELCOME TO THE NAME FILE!               *****"
W !,"*****         INSTRUCTIONS ARE PROVIDED AT EACH       *****"
W !,"*****         PROMPT, BUT IF YOU RUN INTO TROUBLE      *****"
W !,"*****         JUST ENTER 'HELP' TO PRINT A             *****"
W !,"*****         COMPLETE SET OF INSTRUCTIONS.            *****",!
F J1=1:1:55 W "*"
X HOLD
F INDEX=0:0 D DISPMENU I OPTION="" Q
W !!,"NAME FILE FINISHED" K  Q
;
DISPMENU ;
;         Print the menu, read the entry and then do the selected
;         option.  The screen is cleared each time the menu is
;         printed.
;
X CLEAR
W !!,"TO CHOOSE OPTION:  ENTER OPTION NUMBER OR FIRST LETTER(S)
......OF DESCRIPTION"
W !!,"ENTER 'RETURN' TO EXIT FROM PROGRAM",!!!!,"OPTIONS:",!
F J1=1:1:7 S DISPLAY=$TEXT(OPTIONS+J1) W !,$P(DISPLAY,"^")
;
;         A timed read is used inorder to terminate the program if
;         more than 10 minutes elapse before choosing an option.
;
R !!,"SELECT OPTION: ",OPTION:600 E  W !!,"*** TIMEOUT HAS
......OCCURED ***" H
```

```
         I  OPTION=""  Q
         I  OPTION="HELP"  D ^NAHELP1  G DISPMENU
         ;
         ;        Check to see if entry was a number, if so find option via
         ;        NUMBER module, otherwise find option with ALPHA module.
         ;
         I  (OPTION?1N)&(OPTION>0)&(OPTION<8)  D NUMBER D SETUP G DISPMENU
         S  LENGTH=$L(OPTION)
         ;
         ;        ITEM = the 'program' line from the OPTIONS module that
         ;               corresponds to the option selected.
         ;
         F  J1=1:1:7  S ITEM=$T(OPTIONS+J1)  D ALPHA  I OPTION=EXTRACT  Q
         E  W !!!,"THIS IS NOT AN OPTION!!",!!  X HOLD  G DISPMENU
         D  SETUP  G DISPMENU
         ;
SETUP    ;
         ;        Verify option selected and run the corresponding routine
         ;        using indirection.
         ;
         R  !,"IS THIS THE CORRECT OPTION? YES=>",ANS
         I  ANS?1"N".E  Q
         I  ANS="HELP"  D YESNO^NAHELP2  X HOLD  Q
         S  PROGRAM=$P(ITEM,"^",2,3)
         D  @PROGRAM  X HOLD
         Q
         ;
NUMBER   ;
         ;        Determine the option selected for numeric entries.
         ;
         S  ITEM=$T(OPTIONS+OPTION)
         W  $E($P(ITEM,"^"),3,255)
         Q
         ;
ALPHA    ;
         ;        Determine the option selected for alpha entries.
         ;
         S  EXTRACT=$E($P(ITEM,"^"),6,LENGTH+5)
         I  OPTION=EXTRACT  W $E($P(ITEM,"^"),LENGTH+6,255)
         Q
         ;
OPTIONS  ;***** This is the menu and program for each option *****
         1.    ADD A NEW ENTRY^^NADD
         2.    EDIT(CHANGE) DATA INCLUDING THE COMMENTS^^NAEDIT
         3.    REMOVE AN ENTRY^^NADELETE
         4.    MODIFY OR ADD KEYWORDS^^NADDKEY
         5.    LIST THE KEYWORDS^^NALSTKEY
         6.    DISPLAY NAMES PLUS DATA IN ALPHA ORDER^^NADISPLY
         7.    SEARCH BY KEYWORD OR COMMENTS^^NASEARCH
```

```
NADD    ;  Add a New Entry to Name File
        ;       This routine is a modification of CH11EX1.
        ;       Modifications include:
        ;           If an exact match is not found in the town dictionary,
        ;           a list of towns with the same first letter may be
        ;           displayed.  The user can choose from this list or
        ;           enter a new town into the dictionary.
        ;
        ;       To maintain consistency, address, town, state, zip code
        ;       and home phone will appear as 'UNKNOWN' if there is no
        ;       entry for those data items.
        ;
        ;       KILL all non-essential variables.
        ;       Initialize ^NAME global if it does not yet exist.
        ;
        K (FF,SL,SUB,CLEAR,NEWPAGE,HOLD) I '$D(^NAME) S ^NAME=1
        F NUM=^NAME:1 X CLEAR D ENTRY I NAM="" Q
        W !!,"ADDING NEW ENTRY FINISHED" S ^NAME=NUM Q
        ;
ENTRY   ;
        ;
        R !!,"ENTER NAME:  ",NAM I NAM="" Q
        I NAM'[","  W !!,$C(7),"ENTER NAME IN FORMAT ""LAST NAME,
......FIRST NAME""." ,!
G ENTRY
        I NAM'?1A.AP W !!,$C(7),"ENTER ALPHA CHARACTERS ONLY!",! S
......NAM=""
        I $L(NAM)>30 W !!,$C(7),"NAME MAY NOT EXCEED 30 CHARACTERS!",
......! S NAM=""
        I NAM="" G ENTRY
ENTRY1  R !,"ENTER STREET ADDRESS:  ",ADR
        I ($L(ADR)>80)!(ADR="HELP")  W !!,$C(7),"ADDRESS MAY NOT EXCEED
......80 CHARACTERS!",! G ENTRY1
        I ADR="" S ADR="UNKNOWN" W ?$X+5,ADR
ENTRY2  R !,"ENTER TOWN:  ",TWN
        I TWN="HELP" D TOWN1^NAHELP2 G ENTRY2
        D TWNFIND
        I TWN="" G ENTRY2
ENTRY3  R !,"ENTER STATE:  ",ST
        I (ST'?2A)&(ST'="UNKNOWN")  W !!,$C(7),"ENTER TWO LETTER
......ABREVIATION OR 'UNKNOWN' FOR STATE!",! G ENTRY3
ENTRY4  R !,"ENTER ZIP CODE:  ",ZIP
        I (ZIP'?5N)&(ZIP'="UNKNOWN")  W !!,$C(7),"ENTER FIVE NUMBERS
......OR 'UNKNOWN' FOR ZIP CODE!",! G ENTRY4
        S (OTEL(1),OTEL(2),OTEL(3))=""
        F J1=1:1:3 R !,"ENTER OFFICE PHONE:  ",OTEL(J1) Q:OTEL(J1)=""
......D PHONE
        S OTEL=OTEL(1)_"\"_OTEL(2)_"\"_OTEL(3)
ENTRY5  R !,"ENTER HOME PHONE:  ",HTEL
        I HTEL'?3N1"-"3N1"-"4N&(HTEL'="UNKNOWN")  D ERRHTEL G ENTRY5
        BREAK 0
        S ^NAME(NUM)=NAM_"^"_ADR_"^"_TWN_"^"_ST_"^"_ZIP_"^"_OTEL_"^"_HTEL
```

```
          S  ^NAME("A",NAM,NUM)=""
          S  ^NAME("B",TWN,NAM,NUM)=""
          BREAK 1
          D  KEYCOM
          F  COMNUM=1:1 D ENTCOM I COM="" Q
          BREAK 0
          S  ^NAME(NUM,"COMMENT")=COMNUM-1
          BREAK 1
          Q
          ;
TWNFIND   ;
          ;        Initialize ^TOWN global if it does not exist.
          ;
          I  '$D(^TOWN) S ^TOWN("UNKNOWN")=""
          ;
          ;        Reject town entry if it is null.
          ;
          I  TWN="" W !!,"IF TOWN IS NOT KNOWN, ENTER 'UNKNOWN'." Q
          I  $L(TWN)>30 W !!,$C(7),"TOWN NAME MAY NOT EXCEED 30
......CHARACTERS!",! S TWN="" Q
          ;
          ;        If entry matches a town exactly, QUIT.
          ;        Otherwise, check for partial matches.
          ;
          I  $D(^TOWN(TWN)) Q
          S  LENGTH=$L(TWN),A=TWN
          F  J1=1:1 S A=$O(^TOWN(A)) D TWNFIND1 I A="" S J1=J1-1 Q
          ;
          ;        If there are no partial matches, DO TWNMENU
          ;
          I  J1=0 D TWNMENU Q
TWNONE    ;
          ;        There is one partial match, DO TWNOK to confirm town.
          ;
          I  J1=1 D TWNOK Q
TWNSELEC  ;
          ;        Multiple partial matches have been found, select correct
          ;        town from the matches - or hit return if town is not in
          ;        the list.
          ;
          W  !!,"AN EXACT MATCH WAS NOT FOUND!!"
          W  !,"ENTER 'RETURN' OR CHOOSE FROM THOSE LISTED"
          W  !!,"CHOOSE 1-",J1,": " R ANS
          I  ANS="HELP" S SENDER="TOWN" D MENU^NAHELP2 G TWNSELEC
          I  ANS="" D TWNCHK Q
          I  '$D(T(ANS)) W !!,$C(7),"ENTER A WHOLE NUMBER FROM 1 TO ",J1,!
......G TWNSELEC
          ;
          ;        SET TWN equal to town selected from list.
          ;
          S  TWN=T(ANS) K T
          Q
```

```
        ;
TWNFIND1 ;
        I  (A="")!($E(A,1,LENGTH)'=TWN)  S  A=""  Q
        ;
TWNFIND2 ;
        ;           Display  partial  matches  found.
        ;
        W  !?10,J1,?15,A
        S  T(J1)=A
        Q
        ;
TWNOK  ;
        ;           Verify  town  selected.
        ;           If  town  is  not  verified,  DO  TWNMENU
        ;
        R  !!,"IS  THIS  THE  TOWN  THAT  YOU  WANT?    YES=>  ",ANS
        I  ANS'?1"N".E  S  TWN=T(1)  Q
        D  TWNMENU
        Q
        ;
TWNMENU  ;
        W  !!,$C(7),"*** WARNING ***",!,"'",TWN,"'  IS  NOT  IN  THE  TOWN
......FILE!!!"
        W  !,"PLEASE  SELECT  AN  ACTION  FROM  THE  OPTIONS  LISTED  BELOW
...... (ENTER  NUMBER)"
TWNOPT  W  !!?10,"1   REENTER  TOWN  NAME"
        W  !?10,"2   LIST  ALL  TOWNS  WITH  SAME  1ST  LETTER"
        R  !?10,"3   ADD  THIS  TOWN  AS  A  NEW  TOWN",!,"#",ANS
        I  ANS=1  S  TWN=""  Q
        I  ANS="HELP"  D  TOWN2^NAHELP2  G  TWNOPT
        I  ANS=3  D  TWNADD  Q
        I  ANS'=2  W  !,$C(7),"PLEASE  ENTER  A  NUMBER  FROM  1  TO  3"  G  TWNOPT
        S  A=$E(TWN)
        K  T
        F  J1=1:1  S  A=$O(^TOWN(A))  Q:$E(A)'=$E(TWN)    D  TWNFIND2
        S  J1=J1-1
        I  J1=0  W  !!,"THERE  ARE  NO  TOWNS  WITH  THE  SAME  FIRST  LETTER!!"
......G  TWNOPT
        I  J1=1  D  TWNOK  Q
        D  TWNSELEC
        Q
        ;
TWNCHK  ;
        ;           If  a  town  is  not  selected  from  the  list,  do  you  want  to
        ;           add  your  entry  to  the  town  dictionary  file?
        ;
        W  !!,$C(7),"DO  YOU  WISH  TO  ENTER  '",TWN,"'  AS  A  NEW  TOWN?
......YES=>  "
        R  ANS
        I  ANS="HELP"  D  YESNO^NAHELP2  G  TWNCHK
        I  ANS?1"N".E  S  TWN=""  Q
        D  TWNADD
```

```
            Q
            ;
TWNADD      ;
            ;            Verify intention to add the town to the town dictionary
            ;            file.
            ;
            W  $C(7),!!,"*** WARNING ***"
            W  !,"ARE YOU SURE '",TWN,"' IS A NEW TOWN? NO=> "
            R  ANS
            I  ANS="HELP" D YESNO^NAHELP2 G TWNADD
            I  ANS'?1"Y".E S TWN="" Q
            I  TWN'?1A.AP W !!,$C(7),"TOWN MUST BE ALPHA CHARACTERS ONLY!",
......! S TWN=""Q
            I  $L(TWN)>30 W !!,$C(7),"TOWN MAY NOT EXCEED 30 CHARACTERS!"
......S TWN="" Q
            S  ^TOWN(TWN)=""
            Q
            ;
KEYCOM      ;
            ;            Enter keywords into the 'KEY' subfile.
            ;
            X  CLEAR R "DO YOU WISH TO LIST THE KEYWORDS?  NO=> ",ANS
            I  ANS?1"Y".E D ^NALSTKEY
            S  KEY=""
            W  !!,"ENTER KEYWORDS ONE AT A TIME."
            F  J1=0:0 D KEYCOM1 I KEY="" Q
            Q
            ;
KEYCOM1     ;
            ;
            R  !!,"ENTER KEYWORD: ",KEY
            I  KEY="" Q
            I  '$D(^KEYWORDS(KEY)) W !,$C(7),"KEYWORD DOES NOT EXIST" Q
            I  $D(^NAME(NUM,"KEY",KEY)) W !,$C(7),"THIS KEYWORD IS ALREADY
......ON FILE!" Q
            BREAK 0
            S  ^NAME(NUM,"KEY",KEY)=""
            BREAK 1
            Q
            ;
ENTCOM      ;
            ;            Marks the 61st character position to show maximum size
            ;            of a comment.
            ;
            W  !,"ENTER COMMENT: ",?$X+60,"<" F K2=1:1:61 W $C(8)
            R  COM I COM'="" D COMMENT
            Q
            ;
COMMENT I $L(COM)<63 BREAK 0 S ^NAME(NUM,"COMMENT",COMNUM)=COM
......BREAK 1 Q
            S  COMNUM=COMNUM-1 D LWARNING^NAHELP2 Q
            ;
```

```
PHONE  I  OTEL(J1)?3N1"-"3N1"-"4N Q
       S  J1=J1-1
       W  !!,$C(7),"ENTER PHONE NUMBER IN THE FORMAT '000-000-0000'."
       W  !,"YOU MAY ENTER UP TO THREE OFFICE PHONE NUMBERS."
       W  !,"IF OFFICE PHONE IS UNKNOWN, ENTER 'RETURN'.",!
       Q
       ;
ERRHTEL W  !!,$C(7),"ENTER PHONE NUMBER IN THE FORMAT '000-000-0000'."
       W  !,"IF HOME PHONE IS UNKNOWN, ENTER 'UNKNOWN'.",!
       Q
       ;


NAEDIT ;  Edit All the Data in Name File
       ;        This routine is a modification of CH11EX9.
       ;        This program works with the multi-node COMMENT and
.......KEYWORD subfiles
       ;
       K  (FF,SL,SUB,CLEAR,NEWPAGE,HOLD)
       X  CLEAR
       W  !!!,"TO EDIT THE FOLLOWING DATA:"
       W  !!?5,"1)   ENTER 'RETURN' TO LEAVE THE DATA UNCHANGED"
       W  !?5,"2)   ENTER A NEW VALUE TO CHANGE THE DATA"
       W  !?5,"3)   ENTER '@' TO DELETE THE DISPLAYED ITEM."
       R  !!?5,"DO YOU NEED MORE INSTRUCTIONS?   NO=> ",ANS
       I  ANS?1"Y".E D EDIT^NAHELP2
       F  J1=0:0 X CLEAR R !!,"MODIFY WHAT ENTRY:  ",NAME Q:NAME=""
......D MODIFY
       W  !!!,"EDIT IS FINISHED",!!!!
       Q
       ;
MODIFY ;
       ;        Select the entry to be modified via SELECT^DELETE and
       ;        then edit all data.
       ;
       I  NAME="HELP" S SENDER="MODIFY" D SELECNAM^NAHELP2 Q
       D  SELECT^NADELETE I NAME="" Q
       S  DATA=^NAME(NUM)
       F  J2=1:1:7 S DATA(J2)=$P(DATA,"^",J2)
EDIT   X  CLEAR
       W  !!,"NAME:  ",DATA(1),"// " R NEWNAM
       I  NEWNAM="" S NEWNAM=DATA(1)
       I  NEWNAM="@" D DELETE^NADELETE Q:ANS="Y"  G EDIT
       I  NEWNAM'[","  W !!,"ENTER NAME IN FORMAT 'LAST NAME,FIRST
......NAME'." S NEWNAM=""
       I  NEWNAM'?1A.AP W !!,"ENTER ALPHA CHARACTERS ONLY!",!
......S NEWNAM=""
       I  $L(NEWNAM)>30 W !!,"NAME NAY NOT EXCEED 30 CHARACTERS!",!
......S NEWNAM=""
       I. NEWNAM="" X HOLD G EDIT
```

```
EDIT1 ;
        W !,"ADDRESS: ",DATA(2),"// " R NEW
        I NEW="" S NEW=DATA(2)
        I NEW="@" S (NEW,DATA(2))="UNKNOWN" W "    ...DELETED"
        I $L(NEW)>80 W !!,"ADDRESS MAY NOT EXCEED 80 CHARACTERS!",!
......G EDIT1
        S DATA(2)=NEW
EDIT2 ;
        W !,"TOWN:  ",DATA(3),"// " R NEWTWN
        I NEWTWN="" S NEWTWN=DATA(3)
        I NEWTWN="@" S NEWTWN="UNKNOWN" W "    ...DELETED"
        S TWN=NEWTWN
        D TWNFIND^NADD
        I TWN="" G EDIT2
        S NEWTWN=TWN
EDIT3 ;
        W !,"STATE:  ",DATA(4),"// " R NEW
        I NEW="" S NEW=DATA(4)
        I NEW="@" S (NEW,DATA(4))="UNKNOWN" W "    ...DELETED"
        I NEW'?2A&(NEW'="UNKNOWN") W !!,"ENTER TWO LETTERS OR 'UNKNOWN'
...... FOR STATE!",! G EDIT3
        S DATA(4)=NEW
EDIT4 ;
        W !,"ZIP CODE:  ",DATA(5),"// " R NEW
        I NEW="" S NEW=DATA(5)
        I NEW="@" S (NEW,DATA(5))="UNKNOWN" W "    ...DELETED"
        I NEW'?5N&(NEW'="UNKNOWN") W !!,"ENTER FIVE NUMBERS OR 'UNKNOWN'
......FOR ZIPCODE!",! G EDIT4
        S DATA(5)=NEW
        F J2=1:1:3 S OTEL(J2)=$P(DATA(6),"\",J2)
EDIT5 ;
        F J2=1:1:3 W !,"OFFICE TELEPHONE #",J2,": ",OTEL(J2),"// "
......R NEW D ENTRTEL
        S (SORT(1),SORT(2),SORT(3))="",CNT=1
        F J2=1:1:3 I OTEL(J2)'="" S SORT(CNT)=OTEL(J2),CNT=CNT+1
        S OTEL(1)=SORT(1),OTEL(2)=SORT(2),OTEL(3)=SORT(3)
        S DATA(6)=OTEL(1)_"\"_OTEL(2)_"\"_OTEL(3)
EDIT6 ;
        W !,"HOME PHONE: ",DATA(7),"// " R NEW
        I NEW="" S NEW=DATA(7)
        I NEW="@" S (NEW,DATA(7))="UNKNOWN" W "    ...DELETED"
        I NEW'?3N1"-"3N1"-"4N&(NEW'="UNKNOWN") D ERRHTEL G EDIT6
        S DATA(7)=NEW
        BREAK 0
        S ^NAME(NUM)=NEWNAM_"^"_DATA(2)_"^"_NEWTWN_"^"_DATA(4)_"^"_
......DATA(5)_"^"_DATA(6)_"^"_DATA(7)
        I NEWNAM'=DATA(1) K ^NAME("A",DATA(1),NUM) S ^NAME("A",NEWNAM,
......NUM)=""
        I NEWNAM'=DATA(1)!(NEWTWN'=DATA(3)) K ^NAME("B",DATA(3),DATA(1)
......,NUM)
        I  S ^NAME("B",NEWTWN,NEWNAM,NUM)=""
        BREAK 1
```

```
EDIT7 ;
        ;           Edit the keywords.
        ;
        D EDITKEY
        ;
EDIT8 ;
        ;           Display the COMMENT subfile and then ask whether to
        ;           add, edit or quit.
        ;           This module is a modification of MODIFY^CH11EX8.
        ;
        D DISPCOM1
        R !!,"ADD COMMENTS (A),EDIT COMMENTS (E), OR QUIT (RETURN)? ",
......ANS
        I ANS="" Q
        I ANS="A" D COMADD
        I ANS="E" D COMED1
        I ANS="HELP" D EDITCOM^NAHELP2 X HOLD
        G EDIT8
        ;
COMADD ;
        ;           Add comments to the COMMENT subfile.
        ;           This module is a modification of ADD^CH11EX8.
        ;
        I '$D(^NAME(NUM,"COMMENT")) S ^NAME(NUM,"COMMENT")=0
        S NEXT=^NAME(NUM,"COMMENT")+1
        F COMNUM=NEXT:1 D ENTCOM^NADD I COM="" Q
        S ^NAME(NUM,"COMMENT")=COMNUM-1
        Q
        ;
COMED1 ;
        ;           This module is modified from CH11EX4.
        ;
        F J2=0:0 D DISPCOM1,COMED2 Q:NO=""   I NO="BAD" D NUMERR^NAHELP2
        Q
        ;
COMED2 ;
        ;           This module is modified from CH11EX4.
        ;
        R !!,"EDIT WHICH LINE NUMBER: ",NO
        I NO="HELP" S SENDER="COMMENT" D MENU^NAHELP2 X HOLD Q
        I NO="" Q
        I '$D(COM(NO)) S NO="BAD" Q
        F J3=0:0 D COMED3 I OLD="" Q
        S COM(NO)=$E(COM(NO),1,61)
        I COM(NO)="" K COM(NO)
        BREAK 0
        K ^NAME(NUM,"COMMENT")
        S A=""
        F J3=1:1 S A=$O(COM(A)) Q:A=""   S ^NAME(NUM,"COMMENT",J3)=COM(A)
        S ^NAME(NUM,"COMMENT")=J3-1
        BREAK 1 K COM
        Q
```

```
        ;
COMED3  ;
        ;           Set up the display to edit the COMMENT subfile.
        ;
        W !!!,"EDIT COMMENT:  ",COM(NO)
        W !!,?5,"IN THE ABOVE LINE REPLACE:  "
        R OLD
        D COMED4
        Q
        ;
COMED4  ;
        ;           This module is modified from EDIT2^CH11EX4.
        ;
        I OLD="" Q
        I OLD="@" S (OLD,COM(NO))="" W "       ...COMMENT DELETED" X HOLD Q
        S POS2=$F(COM(NO),OLD)
        I POS2=0 W "       ???" Q
        S LENGTH=$L(OLD)
        S POS1=POS2-(LENGTH+1)
        R !?5,"WITH:  ",NEW
        S COM(NO)=$E(COM(NO),1,POS1)_NEW_$E(COM(NO),POS2,255)
        I $L(COM(NO))>62 D LWARNING^NAHELP2
        I COM(NO)="" S OLD="" W "       ...COMMENT DELETED" X HOLD
        Q
        ;
DISPCOM1 ;
        ;           Creates the headings for the display of the COMMENT
        ;           subfile. This module is modified from DISPLAY^CH11EX4
        ;
        K COM
        S C=""
        F COMNUM=1:1 S C=$O(^NAME(NUM,"COMMENT",C)) Q:C=""  D DISPCOM2
        D DISPCOM3
        Q
        ;
DISPCOM2 ;
        ;           SET the COMMENT subfile into the local array COM.
        ;           This module is modified from DISPLAY1^CH11EX4.
        ;
        S COM(COMNUM)=^NAME(NUM,"COMMENT",C)
        I COM(COMNUM)="" K COM(COMNUM) S COMNUM=COMNUM-1 Q
        Q
        ;
DISPCOM3 ;
        ;           Print the heading for the edit display of the COMMENT
        ;           subfile.
        ;
        X CLEAR
        W ?3,"#",?12,"COMMENT",!?2,"---",?11,"---------"
        F J3=1:1:COMNUM-1 W !?3,J3,?10,COM(J3) X NEWPAGE
        Q
        ;
```

349

```
ENTRTEL  ;
         ;          This module is ENTERTEL^CH11EX9
         ;
         I NEW="" Q
         I NEW="@" S OTEL(J2)="" W "    ...DELETED" Q
         I NEW?3N1"-"3N1"-"4N S OTEL(J2)=NEW Q
         W !!,"ENTER PHONE NUMBER IN FORMAT '000-000-0000'."
         W !,"UP TO THREE OFFICE PHONE NUMBERS MAY BE ENTERED."
         W !,"IF OFFICE PHONE IS UNKNOWN, ENTER 'RETURN'."
         S J2=J2-1
         Q
         ;
ERRHTEL  ;
         ;          This module is ERRHTEL^CH11EX9
         ;
         W !!,"ENTER PHONE NUMBER IN FORMAT '000-000-0000'."
         W !,"IF UNKNOWN ENTER 'UNKNOWN'.",!
         Q
         ;
EDITKEY  ;
         ;          Display the keywords and then the edit options.
         ;
         X CLEAR
         D KEYLIST^NADISPLY
         R !!,"ADD KEYWORDS (A), DELETE KEYWORDS (D), OR QUIT (RETURN):
......   ",ANS
         I ANS="" Q
         I ANS="HELP" D EDITKEY^NAHELP2 X HOLD G EDITKEY
         I ANS="A" D KEYCOM^NADD
         I ANS="D" D DELKEY
         G EDITKEY
         ;
DELKEY   ;
         ;          Delete keywords from the KEY subfile.
         ;
         X CLEAR
         W "DELETE KEYWORDS FROM RECORD"
         D KEYLIST^NADISPLY
         R !!,"DELETE WHICH KEYWORD: ",KEY
         I KEY="" Q
         I $D(^NAME(NUM,"KEY",KEY)) K ^NAME(NUM,"KEY",KEY) W "...DELETED"
......G DELKEY
         W !!,KEY," IS NOT A KEYWORD FOR THIS RECORD!"
         X HOLD
         G DELKEY




NADELETE ; Delete Records from Name File
         ;          This routine is a modification of CH11EX7.
         ;          Modifications include:
```

```
        ;           Asks for name verification if only one match is found.
        ;       The SELECT & DELETE modules are used by other routines.
        ;
        K  (FF,SL,SUB,CLEAR,NEWPAGE,HOLD)
ENTRY  ;
        X  CLEAR
        R  !!,"DELETE ENTRY:  ",NAME
        I  NAME="" W !!,"DELETE IS FINISHED" Q
        I  NAME="HELP" S SENDER="DELETE" D SELECNAM^NAHELP2 G ENTRY
        D  SELECT
        I  NAME'="" D DELETE
        G  ENTRY
        ;
SELECT  ;
        S  (CNT,FLAG)=0,B=NAME,LENGTH=$L(NAME) K NAM
        I  $D(^NAME("A",NAME))  S FLAG=1
        I  FLAG=1 D SELECT2
        I  'FLAG F K1=0:0 S B=$O(^NAME("A",B))  Q:B=""!($E(B,1,LENGTH)'=
......NAME) D SELECT2
        I  CNT=0 S NAME="" W !!,"***  NAME NOT FOUND  ***",!! Q
        I  CNT=1 D SELECTOK Q
SELECT1 ;
        W  !!,"PLEASE CHOOSE BY NUMBER, FROM 1-",CNT,":  " R ANS
        I  ANS="" S NAME="" Q
        I  ANS="HELP" S SENDER="NAME" D MENU^NAHELP2 G SELECT1
        I  '$D(NAM(ANS)) W !!,"ENTER WHOLE NUMBER FROM 1 TO ",CNT,!
......G SELECT1
        S  NAME=$P(NAM(ANS),"^",1),NUM=$P(NAM(ANS),"^",2)
        ;
        ;       The variables used in the SELECT module are KILLed to
        ;       free these variables for use in the routines that call
        ;       this module.  The variables NAME and NUM return the name
        ;       and the unique identifier of the record selected - and
        ;       therefore are not KILLed.
        ;
        K  B,C,CNT,FLAG,K1,K2,LENGTH,NAM,ANS,SENDER
        Q
        ;
SELECT2 ;
        S  C=""
        F  K2=0:0 S C=$O(^NAME("A",B,C))  Q:C=""   D SELECT3
        Q
        ;
SELECT3 ;
        S  CNT=CNT+1
        X  NEWPAGE
        W  !?5,CNT,?10,$P(^NAME(C),"^",1,3)
        S  NAM(CNT)=B_"^"_C
        Q
        ;
SELECTOK ;
        ;           Confirm the name selected.
```

```
        ;
        R !!,"IS THIS THE NAME YOU WANT?   YES=> ",ANS
        I ANS="HELP" D YESNO^NAHELP2 G SELECTOK
        I ANS'?1"N".E S NAME=$P(NAM(1),"^",1),NUM=$P(NAM(1),"^",2) Q
        S NAME=""
        Q
        ;
DELETE  ;
        ;
        X CLEAR
        W !!!,"***** VERIFY DELETION *****",$C(7,7,7,7),!
        S DATA=^NAME(NUM)
        F K1=1:1:5 W ?$X+5,$P(DATA,"^",K1) I K1=3 S TWN=$P(DATA,"^",3)
        R !!,"ARE YOU SURE YOU WANT TO DELETE THIS ENTRY? NO=> ",ANS
        I ANS="HELP" D YESNO^NAHELP2 X HOLD G DELETE
        I ANS'?1"Y".E W !!!,"*** ENTRY NOT DELETED!! ***",! X HOLD Q
        BREAK 0
        K ^NAME(NUM),^NAME("A",NAME,NUM),^NAME("B",TWN,NAME,NUM)
        BREAK 1
        W !!!,"*** DELETED!! ***",! X HOLD
        Q



NADDKEY ; Add or Modify Keyword Dictionary File
        ;
        X CLEAR
        W !!,"OPTIONS ARE AS FOLLOWS:   (ENTER NUMBER)"
        W !,?5,"1   ADD A NEW KEYWORD"
        W !,?5,"2   MODIFY AN EXISTING KEYWORD"
        W !,?5,"3   LIST THE EXISTING KEYWORDS"
        W !,?5,"4   QUIT"
        R !!,"#",ANS
        I ANS=4 W !,"KEYWORD MODIFICATION FINISHED! " Q
        I (ANS<1)!(ANS>3) W !!,$C(7),"PLEASE ENTER A NUMBER FROM 1 TO 4"
        I ANS=3 D ^NALSTKEY
        I ANS=2 D MOD
        I ANS=1 D NEW
        X HOLD
        G NADDKEY
        ;
NEW     ;
        ;       Add new keywords to the dictionary file.
        ;
        R !!,"ENTER NEW KEYWORD:   ",NEW
        I NEW="" Q
        S ^KEYWORDS(NEW)=""
        W "     ...HAS BEEN ENTERED AS A NEW KEYWORD."
        Q
        ;
MOD     ;
```

352

```
             ;        Select keyword for modification.
             ;
             R !!,"WHICH KEYWORD DO YOU WISH TO MODIFY?    ",KEY
             I KEY="" Q
             I $D(^KEYWORDS(KEY)) D CHANGE Q
             W !!,"THAT KEYWORD DOES NOT EXIST!!",!!
             Q
             ;
CHANGE  ;
             ;        Change or delete a keyword.
             ;
             W !!,"ENTER '@' TO DELETE THE KEYWORD"
             W !,"MODIFY:   ",KEY," // " R NEW
             I (NEW="")!(NEW=KEY) W ?$X+3,"...NO CHANGE" Q
             I NEW="@" D VERIFY I ANS1'?1"Y".E G CHANGE
             K ^KEYWORDS(KEY)
             I NEW'="@" S ^KEYWORDS(NEW)=""
             W !!,"UPDATING KEYWORD IN NAME FILE..."
             S NUM=""
             F J1=0:0 S NUM=$O(^NAME(NUM)) Q:NUM=""   D UPDATE
             Q
             ;
UPDATE  ;
             ;        This module updates the NAME file, i.e., if a keyword is
             ;        changed in the dictionary file, this module goes through
             ;        the NAME file and changes each occurrence of the modified
             ;        keyword.  A '.' is printed for each record which is so
             ;        modified.  The module QUITs immediately if the keyword is
             ;        not contained in the record being examined.
             ;
             I '$D(^NAME(NUM,"KEY",KEY)) Q
             W "."
             ;
             ;        KILL old keyword in record.
             ;
             K ^NAME(NUM,"KEY",KEY)
             ;
             ;        QUIT here if the keyword was deleted from the dictionary
             ;        file.
             ;
             I NEW="@" Q
             ;
             ;        SET new keyword into the record.
             ;
             S ^NAME(NUM,"KEY",NEW)=""
             Q
             ;
VERIFY  ;
             ;        Verify intention to delete a keyword.
             ;
             W !!,$C(7),"ARE YOU SURE YOU WANT TO DELETE '",KEY,"'?   NO=> "
             R ANS1
```

```
          I  ANS1="HELP"  D  YESNO^NAHELP2  G  VERIFY
          Q




NALSTKEY  ;  List Keywords in Dictionary File
          ;
          X  CLEAR
          W  !!,"THE FOLLOWING IS THE LIST OF KEYWORDS: ",!!?5
          S  KEY=""
          F  J1=0:0  S  KEY=$O(^KEYWORDS(KEY))  Q:KEY=""   D LIST
          Q
          ;
LIST      ;
          ;       Print keywords side by side on a line until the keyword
          ;       about to print would exceed column 74,  then start a new
          ;       line.
          ;
          I  ($X+$L(KEY))>74  W  !?5
          W  KEY,?$X+3
          Q
          ;




NADISPLY  ;  Display Name File
          ;         This routine is a modification of CH11EX2.
          ;         This routine prints selected data items in the NAME
          ;         file, including  the multi-node COMMENT and KEY subfiles,
          ;         in alpha order.
          ;         Modifications include:
          ;             print titles for the data
          ;             print the whole file vs one name
          ;             print all data items vs selected data items
          ;
          K  (FF,SL,SUB,CLEAR,NEWPAGE,HOLD)
ALL       X  CLEAR
          R  !,"DO YOU WISH TO DISPLAY ALL OF THE NAMES? NO=> ",ANS
          I  ANS="HELP"  D  DISPNAM^NAHELP2  G  ALL
          I  ANS'?1"Y".E  D  SELECTN
          I  ANS?1"Y".E  D  SECOND
          W  !!,"DISPLAY IS FINISHED"
          Q
          ;
SELECTN   ;
          ;         Allow the user to enter a name,  then using the
          ;         SELECT^NADELETE module,  return the unique identifier
          ;         for that name,  and finally,  print the data via
          ;         the DISPLAY module.
          ;
```

```
        X CLEAR
        R !!,"WHOSE DATA FILE WOULD YOU LIKE TO DISPLAY? ",NAME I
......NAME="" Q
        I NAME="HELP" S SENDER="DISPLAY" D SELECNAM^NAHELP2 G SELECTN
        D SELECT^NADELETE I NAME="" G SELECTN
        D DISPLAY
MORE    R !!,"DO YOU WISH TO DISPLAY ANOTHER NAME?   NO=> ",ANS1
        I (ANS1'?1"Y".E)&(ANS1'="HELP") Q
        I ANS1="HELP" D YESNO^NAHELP2 G MORE
        G SELECTN
        ;
SECOND ;
        ;      Find next name from 2nd level of cross reference file.
        ;
        S B=""
        F J1=0:0 S B=$O(^NAME("A",B)) Q:B=""   D THIRD
        Q
        ;
THIRD  ;
        ;      Find unique identifier from 3rd level of cross reference
        ;      file.
        ;
        S NUM=""
        F J2=0:0 S NUM=$O(^NAME("A",B,NUM)) Q:NUM=""   D DISPLAY
        Q
        ;
DISPLAY ;
        ;      Displayed information can be for all the names in the
        ;      file, one selected name or, via the search option, all
        ;      the names found by the search.
        ;
        ;      Display the data items indicated by the user.  If SELECT
        ;      does not exist, the user has not yet selected the data
        ;      items to be displayed.  DO the SELFIELD module.
        ;
        I '$D(SELECT) D SELFIELD S SELECT=1
        X NEWPAGE
        W !!
        S DATA=^NAME(NUM)
        F K3=1:1:5 I DISPFLD(K3)'?1"N".E D TITLE
        S PH=$P(DATA,"^",6)
        F K3=1:1:3 D OPHONE
        S PH=$P(DATA,"^",7)
        I DISPFLD(7)'?1"N".E X NEWPAGE W !,"HOME PHONE: ",?14,PH
        D KEYDSPLY,COMMENT1
        Q
        ;
SELFIELD ;
        ;      Prompt the user to select all or some data items for
        ;      display.
        ;
        R !!!,"DO YOU WISH TO DISPLAY ALL FIELDS FOR EACH NAME?
```

```
. . . . . . NO=> ",ANS1
        I ANS1="HELP" D DISP^NAHELP2 X HOLD,CLEAR G SELFIELD
        I ANS1'?1"Y".E D DISPFLD Q
        ;
        ;       If user wants all data items displayed, SET all elements
        ;       of the DISPFLD array to 'YES'.
        ;
        F K3=1:1:9 S DISPFLD(K3)="YES"
        Q
        ;
DISPFLD ;
        ;       Allow the user to select which data item(s) to display
        ;       for each record.
        ;
        W !!,"FOR EACH OF THE FOLLOWING FIELDS, ENTER 'RETURN' TO
. . . . . SELECT THAT"
        W !,"FIELD FOR DISPLAY.  ENTER 'N' TO PREVENT THE FIELD FROM
. . . . . APPEARING."
        R !!,"DO YOU NEED MORE HELP?  NO=> ",ANS1
        I ANS1?1"Y".E D DISPMORE^NAHELP2
        R !!,"DISPLAY NAME?   YES=> ",DISPFLD(1)
        R !,"DISPLAY ADDRESS?   YES=> ",DISPFLD(2)
        R !,"DISPLAY TOWN?   YES=> ",DISPFLD(3)
        R !,"DISPLAY STATE?   YES=> ",DISPFLD(4)
        R !,"DISPLAY ZIP?   YES=> ",DISPFLD(5)
        R !,"DISPLAY OFFICE PHONE?   YES=> ",DISPFLD(6)
        R !,"DISPLAY HOME PHONE?   YES=> ",DISPFLD(7)
        R !,"DISPLAY KEYWORDS?   YES=> ",DISPFLD(8)
        R !,"DISPLAY THE COMMENTS?   YES=> ",DISPFLD(9)
        X CLEAR
        Q
        ;
TITLE   ;
        ;       Determine the correct title for each data item and print
        ;       the title and data item.
        ;
        S TITLE=$S(K3=1:"NAME: ",K3=2:"ADDRESS: ",K3>2:"NEXT")
        I TITLE="NEXT" S TITLE=$S(K3=3:"TOWN: ",K3=4:"STATE: ",
. . . . . .K3=5:"ZIP CODE: ")
        X NEWPAGE W !,TITLE,?14,$P(DATA,"^",K3)
        Q
        ;
OPHONE  ;
        ;
        S TEL=$P(PH,"\",K3)
        I (TEL="")!(DISPFLD(6)?1"N".E) S K3=4 Q
        X NEWPAGE
        W !,"OFFICE PHONE: ",?14,TEL
        Q
        ;
KEYDSPLY ;
        ;       Display the keywords, if specified for output.  Use the
```

```
        ;        module LIST^NALSTKEY to print the keywords.
        ;
        I DISPFLD(8)?1"N".E Q
KEYLIST W !,"KEYWORDS: ",!?5
        S KEY=""
        F K3=0:0 S KEY=$O(^NAME(NUM,"KEY",KEY)) Q:KEY=""  D
......LIST^NALSTKEY
        Q
        ;
COMMENT1 ;
        ;        Display COMMENT subfile, if specified for output.
        ;
        ;
        I DISPFLD(9)?1"N".E Q
        S COM=""
        X NEWPAGE
        W !!,"COMMENTS: ",!
        F K3=0:0 D COMMENT2 I COM="" Q
        Q
        ;
COMMENT2 ;
        ;
        S COM=$O(^NAME(NUM,"COMMENT",COM))
        I COM="" Q
        X NEWPAGE
        W !,^NAME(NUM,"COMMENT",COM)
        Q
        ;
PAGE    ;
        ;        Called by the variable NEWPAGE.  Compare $Y to SL-2
        ;        (screen length minus 2) to determine if the output is
        ;        within two lines of the bottom of the screen.  If so,
        ;        hold the display until the user hits 'Return', then
        ;        clear the screen.
        ;
        I $Y<(SL-2) Q
        W !!,"** ENTER RETURN TO CONTINUE DISPLAY **"
        R WAIT:600 E  W !,"TIMEOUT OCCURED" H
        X CLEAR
        Q
        ;



NASEARCH ; Search Name File
        ;        This routine is a modification of CH11EX6.
        ;        This routine searches the COMMENT subfile for any
        ;        user specified string, or searches for a KEYWORD.
        ;        Modifications include:
        ;            Search for "keyword" or any user specified string.
        ;
```

357

```
        K  (FF, SL, SUB, CLEAR, NEWPAGE, HOLD)
        X  CLEAR
        W  !!!,?5, "YOU  ARE  IN  THE  SEARCH  MODULE"
        W  !, "THIS  MODULE  WILL  ALLOW  YOU  TO:   1)  SEARCH  THE"
        W  !, "COMMENTS  FOR  ANY  STRING  THAT  YOU  SO  DESIRE;"
        W  !, "2)  SEARCH  FOR  A  KEYWORD."
        X  HOLD
OPTS    ;
        X  CLEAR
        W  !!!,?5, "SEARCH  OPTIONS:  (ENTER  NUMBER)"
        W  !,?10, "1   SEARCH  COMMENTS  FOR  USER  SPECIFIED  STRING"
        W  !,?10, "2   SEARCH  FOR  KEYWORD"
        W  !,?10, "3   QUIT"
        R  !, "#",ANS
        I  ANS=3  W  !!, "SEARCH  IS  FINISHED"  Q
        ;
        ;       NOMATCH = 1  indicates  the  search  found  no  matches.
        ;       NOMATCH  controls  the  printing  of  the  'No  matches  found'
        ;       message.
        ;       SELECT  is  KILLed  so  it  is  undefined  when  the
        ;       DISPLAY^NADISPLY  module  is  called.   See  comments  on
        ;       this  module  for  more  details.
        ;       KEYSRCH  is  defined  only  when  searching  for  a  keyword.
        ;       This  determines  whether  to  search  for  keywords  (KEYFIND
        ;       module)  or  to  search  the  COMMENT  subfile  (COMFIND  &
        ;        COMFIND1  modules).
        ;
        S  NOMATCH=1  K  KEYSRCH,SELECT
        I  (ANS'=1)&(ANS'=2)  W  !,$C(7), "ENTER  A  NUMBER  FROM  1  TO  3"
......X  HOLD  G  OPTS
        I  ANS=2  S  KEYSRCH=1  D  KEYWSRCH
        I  ANS=1  D  STRING
        ;
        ;       Print  a  message  if  the  search  was  unsuccessful
        ;       (NOMATCH=1).
        ;
        I  NOMATCH  W  !!, "SORRY,  THE  SEARCH  FOUND  NO  MATCHES"


        X  HOLD  G  OPTS
        ;
STRING  ;
        ;       Accept  entry  of  the  COMMENT  search  string.
        ;
        R  !!!, "SEARCH  'COMMENTS'  FOR:  ",SRCH  I  SRCH=""  Q
        D  FIND
        Q
        ;
FIND    ;
        ;       Get  each  name  in  alpha  order  from  the  cross  reference
        ;       file.
        ;
```

```
        X CLEAR
        S B=""
        F J1=0:0 S B=$O(^NAME("A",B))  Q:B=""   D FIND1
        Q
        ;
FIND1 ;
        ;       Find the unique identifier for the ^NAME file from the
        ;       third level of the cross reference file.  DO KEYFIND
        ;       module if KEYSRCH variable is defined.
        ;
        S NUM=""
        F J2=0:0 S NUM=$O(^NAME("A",B,NUM))  Q:NUM=""   D COMFIND:'$D(KEYSRCH),
.....   KEYFIND:$D(KEYSRCH)
        Q
        ;
COMFIND ;
        ;       Check each COMMENT node in the record for the search
        ;       string. Stop searching COMMENT nodes when the search
        ;       string is found.
        ;
        S COMNUM="",FLAG="NOT FOUND"
        F J3=0:0 S COMNUM=$O(^NAME(NUM,"COMMENT",COMNUM))  Q:(COMNUM="")
......!(FLAG="FOUND")   D COMFIND1
        Q
        ;
COMFIND1 ;
        ;       If the search string is found in a COMMENT node, display
        ;       the record (DO DISPLAY^NADISPLY) and SET NOMATCH = 0
        ;       since at least one match has been found.
        ;
        I ^NAME(NUM,"COMMENT",COMNUM)[SRCH S FLAG="FOUND",NOMATCH=0
......D DISPLAY^NADISPLY
        Q
        ;
KEYWSRCH ;
        X CLEAR
        R !!!,"DO YOU WISH TO LIST THE KEYWORDS? YES=> ",ANS1
        I ANS1="HELP" D YESNO^NAHELP2 G KEYWSRCH
        I ANS1'?1"N".E D ^NALSTKEY
        D ENTKEYW
        I SRCH="" Q
        D FIND
        Q
        ;
ENTKEYW ;
        ;       Accept keyword for search and check if it is in the
        ;       KEYWORDS dictionary file.
        ;
        R !!!,"ENTER KEYWORD TO SEARCH FOR: ",SRCH
        I SRCH="" Q
        I '$D(^KEYWORDS(SRCH)) W !,$C(7),"THIS KEYWORD IS NOT ON
......FILE" G ENTKEYW
```

```
        Q
        ;
KEYFIND ;
        ;       Check for the search keyword in the KEY subfile of the
        ;       record in question.  If found, SET NOMATCH = 0 since at
        ;       least one match has been found.
        ;
        S FLAG="NOT FOUND"
        I '$D(^NAME(NUM,"KEY",SRCH)) Q
        S FLAG="FOUND",NOMATCH=0 D DISPLAY^NADISPLY
        Q




NAHELP1 ;
        ;       This routine provides instructions on how to choose
        ;       the desired option and what the capabilities of each
        ;       option are.
        ;
OPTION  ;
        ;
        X CLEAR
        W !!,"YOU ARE IN THE VERY BEGINNING OF THE PROGRAM.  CHOOSE THE"
        W !,"LISTED OPTIONS YOU WOULD LIKE TO USE."
        W !!,"DO THIS BY ENTERING THE NUMBER TO THE LEFT OF THE OPTION,"
        W !,"OR BY ENTERING THE FIRST LETTER(S) OF THE OPTION
......DESCRIPTION"
        R !,"DO YOU NEED MORE HELP?  NO=> ",ANS
        I ANS'?1"Y".E Q
        ;
OPTION1 ;
        ;
        R !!,"PLEASE ENTER THE OPTION # THAT YOU WANT DESCRIBED: ",ANS
        I ANS="HELP" G OPTION
        I ANS=1 D DISPLAY Q
        I ANS=2 D EDIT Q
        I ANS=3 D REMOVE Q
        I ANS=4 D ADD Q
        I ANS=5 D SEARCH Q
        I ANS=6 D LSTKEY Q
        I ANS=7 D ADDKEY Q
        W !,"** PLEASE ENTER A NUMBER FROM 1 TO 7 **"
        G OPTION1
        ;
ADD     ;
        ;
        X CLEAR
        W !!,"THE 'ADD' OPTION IS USED TO ENTER A NEW RECORD (NAME) "
        W !,"INTO THE CARD FILE."
        X HOLD
        Q
```

```
        ;
EDIT    ;
        ;
        X CLEAR
        W !!,"THE 'EDIT' OPTION IS USED TO CHANGE ANY INFORMATION "
        W !,"WITHIN THE CARD FILE."
        X HOLD
        Q
        ;
REMOVE  ;
        ;
        X CLEAR
        W !!,"THE 'REMOVE' OPTION IS USED ONLY TO DELETE AN ENTIRE
......RECORD"
        W !,"FROM THE FILE."
        X HOLD
        Q
        ;
ADDKEY  ;
        ;
        X CLEAR
        W !!,"THE 'MODIFY OR ADD KEYWORD' OPTION ALLOWS YOU TO ADD NEW"
        W !,"KEYWORDS AS WELL AS CHANGE OR DELETE EXISTING ONES."
        X HOLD
        Q
        ;
LSTKEY  ;
        ;
        X CLEAR
        W !!,"THE 'LIST' OPTION DISPLAYS A LIST OF KEYWORDS."
        W !!,"EACH RECORD CAN BE IDENTIFIED BY ONE OR SEVERAL KEYWORDS."
        W !,"FOR EXAMPLE, ONE PERSON MIGHT BE IDENTIFIED BY THE "
        W !,"KEYWORDS 'CONSULTANT', 'PROGRAMMER', AND 'ABC SOFTWARE
......COMPANY'."
        X HOLD
        Q
        ;
DISPLAY ;
        ;
        X CLEAR
        W !!,"THE 'DISPLAY' OPTION IS USED TO OBTAIN ANY INFORMATION "
        W !,"WITHIN THE CARD FILE.  WHILE IN THIS OPTION YOU CANNOT "
        W !,"CHANGE ANY INFORMATION."
        X HOLD
        Q
        ;
SEARCH  ;
        ;
        X CLEAR
        W !!,"THE 'SEARCH' OPTION ALLOWS YOU TO SEARCH THE COMMENT OR"
        W !,"KEYWORD SECTIONS OF ANY RECORD FOR A PARTICULAR STRING OR"
        W !,"A COMBINATION OF STRINGS.  THOSE RECORDS THAT CONTAIN ALL"
```

```
        W !,"THE DESIRED STRINGS WILL BE DISPLAYED."
        X HOLD
        Q
        ;




NAHELP2 ;
        ;       This routine provides various HELP messages.
        ;       The modules marked 'sender needed' are called by more than
        ;       one routine.  The variable SENDER in these modules
        ;       identifies the option calling the help module or the data
        ;       item for which help is required.  This allows us to use
        ;       the same help modules for different situations.
        ;
YESNO   ;
        ;       This will explain the default sign "=>"
        ;
        W !!,"ANSWER EITHER YES OR NO.  WHEN THERE IS THE SYMBOL '=>'"
        W !,"AT THE END OF A QUESTION, YOU CAN ENTER 'RETURN' AND"
        W !,"THE ANSWER DISPLAYED BEFORE '=>' WILL BE ACCEPTED AS YOUR"
        W !,"RESPONSE."
        Q
        ;
MENU    ;       ***** SENDER NEEDED *****
        ;
        W !!,"TO CHOOSE THE ",SENDER," THAT YOU WANT,  ENTER THE NUMBER"
        W !,"TO THE LEFT OF THAT ",SENDER,"."
        I SENDER="COMMENT" Q
        W !,"IF THE ",SENDER," IS NOT ON THIS LIST, OR IF YOU WISH"
        W !,"TO ENTER A DIFFERENT ",SENDER,",  ENTER 'RETURN'."
        Q
        ;
EDIT    ;
        ;
        W !!,"ONE DATA ITEM WILL BE DISPLAYED FOLLOWED BY '//'.  IF "
        W !,"YOU WISH TO LEAVE THAT DATA ITEM UNCHANGED, ENTER"
        W !,"'RETURN'. IF YOU WISH TO CHANGE THAT DATA ITEM, ENTER "
        W !,"THE NEW DATA.EVERYTHING ON THE LEFT OF THE '//' WILL "
        W !,"BE REMOVED AND REPLACED BY YOUR ENTRY.  IF YOU WISH TO "
        W !,"DELETE A DATA ITEM, ENTER '@' TO THE RIGHT OF THE '//'."
        R !!!,"ENTER 'RETURN' TO BEGIN EDITING",CONTINUE
        Q
        ;
EDITKEY ;
        ;
        W !!,"IF YOU WISH TO ADD KEYWORDS, JUST ENTER 'A'."
        W !,"IF YOU WISH TO DELETE KEYWORDS, JUST ENTER 'D'."
        W !,"IF YOU WISH TO LEAVE THE KEYWORDS UNCHANGED, ENTER
......'RETURN'."
        Q
```

```
        ;
EDITCOM ;
        ;
        W !!,"IF YOU WISH TO ADD A COMMENT JUST ENTER 'A'."
        W !,"IF YOU WISH TO CHANGE OR DELETE A COMMENT ENTER 'E'."
        W !,"IF YOU WISH TO LEAVE THE COMMENTS UNCHANGED ENTER
......'RETURN'."
        Q
        ;
TOWN1   ;
        ;
        W !!,"THE TOWN YOU ENTER MUST BE FOUND IN THE TOWN DICTIONARY"
        W !,"FILE.  IF NOT, YOU CAN ENTER A NEW TOWN.  HOWEVER, BE "
        W !,"SURE THAT IT IS INDEED A NEW TOWN AND NOT JUST A DIFFERENT"
        W !,"SPELLING OR ABREVIATION."
        W !!,"IF THE TOWN IS NOT KNOWN ENTER 'UNKNOWN'.",!!!
        Q
        ;
TOWN2   ;
        ;
        W !!,"IF YOU MADE A TYPING ERROR, ENTER CHOICE 1.  IF YOU ARE"
        W !,"NOT SURE WHETHER THE TOWN THAT YOU SELECTED IS A NEW TOWN, "
        W !,"ENTER CHOICE 2.  IF YOU ARE POSITIVE THAT THIS IS A NEW"
        W !,"TOWN, ENTER CHOICE 3.   (CHOICE 2 IS THE SAFEST!!!)"
        Q
        ;
NUMERR  ;
        ;
        R !!,"THERE IS NO SUCH NUMBER!!",!,WAIT:2
        Q
        ;
LWARNING ;
        ;
        W !!!!?10,"* * * *   WARNING   * * * *",$C(7,7,7)
        W !!,"THIS COMMENT EXCEEDS 60 CHARACTERS IN LENGTH!"
        W !,"CHARACTERS PAST POSITION #60 WILL BE TRUNCATED!",!!
        Q
        ;
DISPNAM ;
        ;
        W !!,"YOU MUST DECIDE WHETHER YOU WISH TO DISPLAY ALL THE NAMES"
        W !,"OR JUST ONE."
        Q
        ;
DISP    ;
        ;
        W !!,"THERE ARE SEVERAL DATA ITEMS FOR EACH NAME.  YOU MUST "
        W !,"DECIDE WHICH DATA ITEMS YOU WISH TO DISPLAY.  YOU CAN "
        W !,"DISPLAY THEM ALL OR IN ANY COMBINATION."
        Q
        ;
DISPMORE ;
```

```
        ;
        W !!,"THERE ARE NINE FIELDS OF DATA FOR EACH NAME ON FILE"
        W !,"THEY ARE AS FOLLOWS:"
        W !!?5,"NAME, ADDRESS, TOWN, STATE, ZIP CODE"
        W !?5,"OFFICE PHONE, HOME PHONE, KEYWORDS, COMMENTS"
        W !!,"YOU CAN SELECT ANY COMBINATION OF THESE NINE FIELDS"
        W !,"TO BE DISPLAYED."
        Q
        ;
SELECNAM ;      ***** SENDER NEEDED *****
        ;
        W !!,"ENTER THE NAME OF THE PERSON WHOSE DATA FILE YOU WISH TO"
        W !,"SENDER.  ENTER THE NAME IN THE FORMAT 'LAST NAME,FIRST "
        W !,"NAME'. IF YOU ENTER ONLY THE FIRST FEW LETTERS OF THE LAST "
        W !,"NAME, THEN ALL NAMES THAT BEGIN WITH THOSE LETTERS WILL BE"
        W !,"DISPLAYED. YOU CAN THEN CHOOSE A NAME FROM THIS LIST."
        Q
        ;
```

CHAPTER SEVENTEEN

THE MUMPS LANGUAGE: STRUCTURE AND SYNTAX

In the previous chapters, we have presented commands, functions, special variables, operators, and utilities in the context of specific programs.

In this chapter, we will **discuss** MUMPS from the perspective of "language elements" and the rules for putting these elements together.

Topics will include:

- Elements of the MUMPS language

- Commands

- Functions

- Operators

- Special variables.

For a more complete review of MUMPS language elements, we recommend the ANS MUMPS Programmer's Reference Manual, and the MUMPS Primer, both published by the MUMPS Users' Group, 4321 Hartwick Road, #510, College Park, MD 20740.

ROUTINES, LINES AND PROGRAMS

A routine is a group of lines that are saved on disk under a specific name such as CH1EX4, or NABUILD. The routine name is usually, but not necessarily, the same as the first line label. This routine name is used to:

- save the routine on disk .

- load the routine from disk.

A routine name can be up to eight characters long: any characters beyond the first eight are ignored. Routine names:

- must begin with an alpha character or the "%" character (for some implementations, only Utility Programs in the Manager's UCI may begin with %)

- may include numeric characters (however, no decimal numerics are allowed).

It is considered "good practice" for a single routine:

- to perform a single group of related functions (such as building or modifying a specific global)

- to contain "comment lines" which explain the functions performed by each module or "subroutine".

A line within a routine must begin with a line start character: typically a single space or a tab, depending on the implementation. Line labels are optional and placed before the line start character. Three types of lines are:

- Comment lines, which begin with a semi colon and contain comments which explain the logic of a routine or subroutine.

- Text lines, which contain text in the exact format used for output (typically accessed by a PRINT command or the $TEXT function).

- Command lines, which contain at least one command, with or without arguments.

The length of a routine line is limited to 255 characters, including the line label, line start character, code and comments.

A line label is optional and used to:

- name routines

- identify subroutines or "modules" which are "done" by the DO command

- provide "access points" within a routine for the GOTO command.

Line labels follow the same rules as routine names - except that a line label may start with a numeric character as well as an alphabetic character or "%". As with routine names, no punctuation is allowed, and length is limited to eight characters.

A module or subroutine is one or several lines of executable code within a routine which:

perform a specific function; are accessed by the DO command through a specific line label. One routine can access the subroutine of another routine via the DO command.

A program is a collection of routines, which perform a group of closely related functions. In some cases, one routine can be considered as a short "program". In other cases, a program may include a dozen or more routines, saved on disk under separate names.

A package is a collection of related programs. It is considered "good practice" to have all names for programs in a package start with the same first two letters.

COMMANDS AND COMMAND LINES

Like other routine lines, a command line is always preceded by a line start character - such as a tab or a space. A command line begins with a command, and includes one or more commands, with or without arguments. For example:

```
QUIT
DO ENTRY
IF '$D(^NAME)  SET ^NAME=1
```

The new MUMPS standard allows one or more spaces between the line start character and the beginning of a command line: check your user manual to see if your implementation allows such "extra" spaces.

A command specifies an action to be performed. Typical commands include: QUIT, SET, HALT, IF, DO, GOTO and FOR. Some commands - such as HALT - never take an argument. Some commands - such as IF - may or may not take arguments. Some commands - such as GOTO and FOR - require arguments.

A command is separated from its first argument by a single space. Multiple arguments on one command are separated by commas, without spaces between the arguments.

A command and its arguments are separated from the next command on that line by at least one space. Some implementations of MUMPS (based on the 1977 Standard) allow only one space to separate a command and its arguments from the next command on the same line.

An argumentless command must be separated from the next command on the same line by at least two spaces (the second space signifies a "null argument").

There are two types of commands in Standard MUMPS:

Regular Commands
Z Commands.

All Z commands are implementation specific. Of those commands not preceded by a "Z", two are implementation specific:

> PRINT
> WRITE with no argument.

Timeouts on Commands

Timeouts are allowed on arguments of the READ, OPEN, JOB and LOCK commands. For example:

> READ ANSWER:90 will wait for 90 seconds

> READ ANSWER:TIME will wait for a number of seconds equivalent to the value of TIME

> OPEN 3::90 will wait for 90 seconds

> OPEN 3::TIME will wait for a number of seconds equivalent to the value of TIME

> LOCK ˄NAME(A):90 will wait for 90 seconds

> LOCK ˄NAME(A):TIME will wait for a number of seconds equivalent to the value of TIME

> JOB ˄REPORT::90 will wait for 90 seconds

> JOB ˄REPORT::TIME will wait for a number of seconds equivalent to the value of TIME.

Post Conditionals on Commands and Arguments

Post conditionals are allowed on all commands except FOR, IF and ELSE. Interpretation of a post conditional on a command is as follows:

(1)   if the post conditional is true the command is executed

(2)   if the post conditional is false, the command is not executed.

For example:

> DO:ANS?1"Y".E ENTRY
> OPEN:ANS?1"Y".E 3::30

```
SET: ANS?1"Y".E ^NAME(J1)=DATA(1)_"^"_DATA(2)_"^"_DATA(3)
```

Unlike the IF command, post conditionals do not affect the value of $TEST.

Post conditionals are allowed on the arguments of DO, GOTO, and XECUTE. For example:

```
DO MOD1:ANS["Y",MOD2
```

In this example, the post conditional on our first argument affects only that argument, and not the second argument. Thus, we will always DO MOD2, regardless of the value for ANS.

If there are post conditionals on both a command and its argument, the latter is evaluated only if the post conditional on the command is true. For example:

```
DO:ANS["Y" ENTRY:FLAG="OK"
```

will evaluate the post conditional on ENTRY only if ANS contains Y.

FUNCTIONS

While a command specifies an action to be performed, a function: (1) performs an operation on a specified variable, string, number or program line; (2) returns a value based on the outcome of this operation. Each function is designated by the initial character "$", followed by a unique name which may be abbreviated to its initial letter. The function name is followed by one or more expressions in parentheses. For example:

```
SET NAME="SMITH, JOHN"
WRITE $EXTRACT(NAME)
WRITE $LENGTH("RODGERS, ROBERT")
WRITE $TEST(11)
WRITE $CHAR(65)
FOR I=1:1:3 WRITE $TEXT(OPTIONS+I)
```

There are two types of functions in Standard MUMPS:

> Regular functions
> Z functions

The regular functions are included in all implementations of Standard MUMPS. The Z functions are implementation specific.

VARIABLES

A variable is a name for an entity whose value may be changed. Standard MUMPS provides three types of variables:

- local variables (subscripted and simple)

- global variables (subscripted and simple)

- special variables.

Variable names can be up to eight characters long: any characters beyond the first eight are ignored. As with routine names, variable names:

- must begin with an alpha character or the "%" character

- may include numeric characters - however, no decimal numerics are allowed.

Local variables can be created by the READ or SET command, and deleted by the KILL command. They are NOT saved on disk, but disappear when you log off at your terminal.

Global variables can be created by the SET command, and are stored on disk until deleted by a KILL command.

Simple variables are designated solely by the variable name. For example: ^NAME.

Subscripted variables are designated by a variable name plus one or more subscripts. For example:

^NAME ("A" , B, C, 4)

Subscripts may be assigned either as:

- literal strings - such as "A" in the foregoing example

- variables - such as B and C in the foregoing example

- numbers - such as 4 in the foregoing example.

An array refers to a group of subscripted variables with the same variable name.

A "node" refers to an individual array element.

LITERAL STRINGS

A literal string, or "string literal", is any combination of characters with constant value. A string literal is defined by being enclosed in quotation marks. For example:

```
SET NAME(J1)="SMITH, JOHN"
SET NAME(J1)="" (null string)
```

If quotation marks are to be included within a string literal, two quotation marks together signify a single quotation mark within the string literal. For example:

```
SET RESULT(1)="ANSWER IS ""INCORRECT"""
```

NUMERIC LITERALS

In Standard MUMPS, a number is considered as a special type of string, rather than a separate data type. Standard MUMPS identifies two types of numbers:

- integers - whole numbers with no fractional component; may or may not be preceded by a positive or negative sign

- real numbers - a whole number with a decimal fraction.

Exponential notation is expressed by a number followed by E followed by a power of ten. The following are examples of numeric literals:

```
0.8
18
1.8E2 (represents 180)
12E-2 (represents 0.12)
```

Standard MUMPS provides a minimum of 9 digits of precision, both for integers and endless fractions such as 1/3. Thus a number such as 0.33333333333 might be retained as 0.333333333. Some implementations provide even greater accuracy. We suggest you check your user manual for information.

With regard to exponential notation, Standard MUMPS specifies that numbers between 1E-25 and 1E25 will be accepted. Again, some implementations offer even greater ranges.

EXPRESSIONS

The simplest expressions in Standard MUMPS are: variables, string literals, numeric literals, and functions. For example:

```
NAME
"SMITH, JOHN"
1.8E6
$EXTRACT(^NAME(12))
```

Such simple expressions are sometimes called "expression atoms". Complex expressions can be built by linking expression atoms with commands and operators. For example:

```
READ NAM
SET NAM="SMITH, JOHN"
SET ^NAME(J1)=DATA(1)_"^"_DATA(2)
SET RESULT=1/2*4+3
```

All MUMPS expressions are evaluated from left to right. Parentheses can be used to modify the order of evaluation. For example:

```
1/2*4+3=5
1/(2*4)+3=3.125
1/2*(4+3)=3.5
```

OPERATORS

Operators are symbols that specify arithmetic and logical operations to be performed. The MUMPS Operators can be classified into four general groups, based on the type of operation performed:

1. Arithmetic operators
   - arithmetic binary operators
   - arithmetic unary operators
   - arithmetic relational operators

2. String operators
   - string relational operators
   - string binary operator

3. Logical operators (Boolean operators)
   - logical binary operators
   - logical unary operator

4. Indirection
   - argument indirection
   - name indirection
   - pattern indirection
   - subscript indirection
   - command indirection (XECUTE command)

THE ARITHMETIC OPERATORS INCLUDE:

1.1 Arithmetic binary operators (operate on two expressions)

+   add

372

```
-          subtract
*          multiple
/          divide
\          integer divide
#          modulo
```

1.2   Arithmetic unary operators (operate on one expression)

```
+          plus
-          minus
```

1.3   Arithmetic relational operators (depict relationship between two expressions)

```
>          greater than
<          less than
```

THE STRING OPERATORS INCLUDE:

2.1   String relational operators (depict relationship between two expressions)

```
=          equals
[          contains
]          follows
?          pattern match
```

2.2   String binary operator (operates on two expressions)

```
_          concatenate
```

THE LOGICAL OPERATORS (sometimes called Boolean operators) include:

3.1   Logical binary operators (operate on two expressions)

```
&          and
!          or
```

3.2   Logical unary operator (operates on one expression)

```
not
```

INDIRECTION

Indirection allows the value of an expression to be inserted temporarily into a MUMPS program.

4.1   Indirection at the argument level uses the value of an expression as one or more arguments of a command. For example:

```
        S P=3,T=0
SELECT  R !,"Enter 3 for printer or 0 for terminal: ",ANS
        I (ANS'=3)!(ANS'=0) G SELECT
        OPEN @(ANS_"::30") E  W !,*7,"PRINTER NOT AVAILABLE" G SELECT
```

4.2   Indirection at the name level uses the value of an expression as the name of a variable, a line label, or a routine. For example:

```
        R !,"Enter program name:  ",NAME
        S PGM="^"_NAME
        D @PGM
```

4.3   Indirection at the pattern level uses the value of an expression in place of a pattern. For example:

```
        S TEL="3N1""-""3N1""-""4N"
        R !,"Enter phone:  ",PHONE
        I PHONE'?@TEL D ERROR
```

4.4   Indirection at the subscript level uses the value of an expression in place of a subscript. The following code could be used to create an array with date of birth entries as subscripts:

```
        R !,"Name:  ",NAM
        R !,"Date of birth:  ",DOB
        S FILE="^NAME(NAM)",@FILE@(DOB)=""
```

sets ^NAME(NAM,DOB) equal to null.

4.5   Indirection at the command level is accomplished via the XECUTE command. For example:

```
        SET CODE="WRITE!,""THIS IS AN EXAMPLE"""
```

XECUTE CODE will output:

```
        THIS IS AN EXAMPLE
```

The value of CODE is treated as a command line, and is executed as if it were inserted into the program.

SPECIAL VARIABLES

Special variables may be regarded as functions that return a value based on internal operation of the system.

Standard MUMPS provides two types of special variables:

- regular special variables

- Z special variables.

Examples of regular special variables include:

```
$TEST
$X
$Y
```

The Z special variables are implementation specific: consult your user manual for implementation on your system.

FORMAT CONTROL CHARACTERS

The following characters are used for format control:

?	specifies tab to the column specified - for example ?40 tabs to column 40; ?$X+5 tabs five positions to the right of current positions for cursor or print head
!	specifies a new line operation (carriage return and line feed on hard copy device)
#	specifies form feed and sets $Y to zero.

BREAK

BREAK without an argument suspends program executions - allowing you to display current values for variables or perform some other function. For our implementation, the ZGO command is used to resume program execution after a BREAK command.

Some implementations allow a single argument to the BREAK command. For our implementation, BREAK 0 disables the BREAK key, while BREAK 1 enables the BREAK key.

The BREAK command accepts a post conditional. For example:

```
BREAK: I>10000
```

The BREAK command may be inserted into a routine during debugging, so the programmer can examine values for variables during program execution.

CLOSE

CLOSE with one or more arguments is used to release designated device(s) from ownership, making it (them) available to other users.

The CLOSE command accepts post conditionals. For example:

```
CLOSE: $T=1  1,64,65
```

The CLOSE command may be used with indirection. For example:

```
CLOSE: $T=1  @DEVICE
```

DO

DO provides temporary transfer of control to a specified line; control returns to that point immediately after the DO command when an implicit or explicit QUIT is encountered. For example:

```
DO MOD1 W !,"FINISHED MOD1"
DO ^CH1EX4,^CH1EX5,^CH1EX6 W !,"FINISHED ^CH1EX4, ^CH1EX5,
...... ^CH1EX6"
DO MOD^CH1EX4
```

The first line of code transfers control to line MOD1, then returns to that point immediately after the DO command when an implicit or explicit QUIT is encountered.

The second line of code DOes three routines, then returns to the WRITE command.

The third line of code loads CH1EX4, begins execution at the line labelled MOD, then returns to the calling routine when an implicit or explicit QUIT is encountered. In this third example, the DO command is used to access a subroutine from a named program.

The DO command accepts post conditionals. Also, arguments of the DO command may have post conditionals. For example:

```
DO: FLAG=0  MOD1
DO  MOD1: FLAG=0
```

The DO command may be used with indirection. For example:

```
DO  @LINE
```

The DO command may be used in direct mode (i.e. entered at a system prompt to DO a specified program starting at any desired line.

ELSE

ELSE executes those statements following on the same line if the value of $T is zero. If the value of $T is one, remainder of line to right of ELSE command is not executed. ELSE is always followed by at least two spaces - since it never takes an argument.

The $TEST special variable may be set by:

> IF command with arguments
>
> timed READ
>
> timed LOCK
>
> timed OPEN
>
> timed JOB.

ELSE itself does not affect the value of $T. When ELSE is paired with an IF command, ELSE should be placed on the following line. For example:

```
IF  SEX="M"  DO ENTRY1 ELSE   DO ENTRY2
ELSE   D MOD2
```

In this example, the first ELSE command is never executed.

ELSE may be paired with a timeout on the same line. For example:

```
OPEN 3::60 ELSE  WRITE !,"LP BUSY" DO MOD
```

FOR

FOR specifies the repeated execution of those following statements on the same line. We can identify three forms of FOR loop, where FLV stands for "FOR loop variable":

```
FOR FLV=START:STEP
FOR FLV=START:STEP:END
FOR FLV=VALUE1,VALUE2...VALUEn
```

The first form is an open FOR loop: execution is ordinarily terminated by QUIT with a post conditional. Termination with GOTO is recommended only when:

(1)   a particular condition requires that you "GOTO" the end of the program, and

(2)   it is awkward to reach "end of the program" in some other manner.

The second form is a closed FOR loop where execution is terminated when FLV reaches or would pass the value of END. The value of STEP may be either positive or negative.

The third form provides specific values for the FOR loop variable. This may be used to access specific nodes of an array in non-sequential order: for example, an array with multiple nodes containing MUMPS code executed via the XECUTE command.

The FOR command does not accept post conditionals.

Name indirection can be used with the FOR parameters. For example:

```
FOR FLV=@A:@B:@C WRITE !,FLV
```

You can use more than one FOR statement on the same line: the "inner FOR loops" on the right are nested within the "outer FOR loops" to the left. For example:

```
FOR FLV=1:1:10 FOR J=1:1 QUIT:J>10
FOR FLV=1:1:10 FOR J=1:1 GOTO END:J>10
```

If the inner FOR loop is terminated by a QUIT, only the inner FOR loop is terminated. If the inner FOR loop is terminated by a GOTO, both the inner FOR loop and all outer FOR loops are terminated. Killing the FOR loop variable within the scope of the FOR loop will result in an error.

GOTO

GOTO transfers program execution to the specified line or routine. In contrast to the DO command, this transfer is "permanent": program control does NOT return to that point immediately after the GOTO command when an implicit or explicit QUIT is encountered.

As with the DO command, both the GOTO command and its arguments may have post conditionals. For example:

```
GOTO: ANS["N"  MOD
GOTO  MOD: ANS["N"
```

As with the DO command, indirection may be used. For example:

```
GOTO: ANS["N"  @MOD
```

We recommend that you avoid the GOTO command, except:

(1)   to return to the same line - when performing a pattern match

(2)   to return to the first line of a routine or module

(3)   to exit to the last line of a routine or module.

HALT

HALT unlocks any global nodes you may have locked, closes all owned devices, and terminates execution of your program. The HALT command accepts post conditionals. For example:

```
READ !, "DO YOU WISH TO LOG OFF?  ", ANS HALT: ANS["Y"
```

HANG

HANG suspends program execution for a specified number of seconds. For example:

```
HANG 30
```

suspends program execution for 30 seconds. The HANG command accepts post conditionals. For example:

```
HANG: ANS["N"  30
```

You can use indirection in combination with the HANG command. For example:

        HANG @ANS

The HANG command can be used to slow down output to a speed that can be followed by humans. However, we seldom use HANG for this purpose in our own code.

IF

IF provides conditional execution of statements on the same line. We can identify four forms of the IF command:

        IF (no argument - command followed by at least two spaces)

        IF A (non-comparative argument)

        IF A>B (comparative argument)

        IF A,A>B (multiple arguments).

IF with no argument is the inverse of ELSE: those statements following on the same line are executed if the value of $T is one. If the value of $T is zero, the code to the right of IF is not executed.

IF with a non comparative argument evaluates the truth value of this argument as one or zero. If this argument has any value other than zero or null, the remainder of line is executed. If this argument has a value of zero or null, remainder of line is not executed. For example:

```
READ !,"Enter results of 5x3 ",ANS:30
IF  WRITE !,"ANSWER RECEIVED WITHIN 30 SECONDS"
IF ANS'=15 WRITE !,"BUT INCORRECT RESULT" QUIT
ELSE  WRITE !,"AND RESULT IS CORRECT" QUIT
```

IF with a comparative argument is perhaps the most common form of this command.

IF with multiple arguments performs a logical AND operation: remainder of line is executed only if all arguments are true.

Neither the IF command nor its arguments accept post conditionals.

Argument indirection can be used with the IF command.

JOB

JOB starts another job independent of your current job. Program execution is suspended until the new job is started.

A timeout is commonly attached to the argument of the JOB command. If MUMPS cannot start the new job within the number of seconds specified, $TEST is set to zero and program execution continues.

Post conditionals can be attached to the JOB command.

The JOB command can be used with indirection.

Here are some examples:

```
JOB ^REPORT
JOB BEGIN^REPORT
JOB BEGIN^REPORT::10
JOB:ANS?1"Y".E ^REPORT
S PGM="^REPORT" JOB @PGM
```

The third example uses a timeout on the argument.

The fourth example uses a post conditional.

The fifth example uses indirection.

Job parameters may be attached to the argument of the JOB command. The job parameters are implementation specific: check your user manual to determine the nature of the job parameters for your system.

KILL

KILL deletes local or global variables. We can identify three forms of the KILL command:

KILL - KILL with no argument removes all local variables from your partition, but has no effect on global variables

KILL ^NAME(3),^NAME(4) - inclusive KILL removes the local or global variables specified, together with all descendent nodes

KILL (NAM,ADR,PHONE) - exclusive KILL removes all local variables except for those specified within parentheses - this form of KILL has NO EFFECT on global variables.

The KILL command accepts post conditionals. For example:

KILL: ANS ["Y" ^NAME

The KILL command can be used with indirection. For example:

K: ANS ["Y" @GLOBAL

LOCK

LOCK makes specified global nodes unavailable for locking by another user. When you lock a global, MUMPS prevents other users from executing a LOCK command for that global.

When you unlock a global, MUMPS again allows other users to execute a LOCK command for that global. Thus LOCK provides a "notice" to other users that you are modifying a global, or adding new nodes to the global. We can identify four forms of the LOCK command:

LOCK - with no argument, unlocks all previously locked globals.

LOCK ^B(1,2) - with one argument locks the global specified - if LOCK cannot be accomplished, program execution waits until the global specified is free for locking. When the LOCK command is executed, all descendants AND all ancestors of ^B (1,2) are also locked.

LOCK ^B(1,2):30 - timed LOCK waits for up to 30 seconds for the global specified to be free for locking. If a LOCK cannot be accomplished within 30 seconds, $TEST is set to zero, and program execution is resumed.

LOCK (^A,^B(1,2)) - with multiple arguments enclosed in parentheses, locks ^A, and locks ^B(1,2). In most cases, it is "better practice" to LOCK and unLOCK nodes separately, rather than use this form of the LOCK command. We suggest you avoid LOCK with multiple arguments NOT enclosed in parentheses - only the last argument is LOCKed when the command is executed.

The LOCK command accepts post conditionals, and can be used with indirection.

NEW

The NEW command is not yet included in the ANSI standard. Check your user manual to determine whether this is included with your system.

NEW specifies that the local variables named as arguments are "stacked" or "saved". Following execution of a NEW command, these variable names may acquire "new" values, without affecting those values "saved" by the NEW command.

When an implicit or explicit QUIT command terminating a DO or an XECUTE is encountered, the "saved" variables are restored. We can identify three forms of the NEW command:

NEW NAM,DATE - stack the local variable(s) listed
NEW (NAM,DATE) - stack all local variables except those in parentheses
NEW - stack all local variables

For example, the code:

```
MOD1      SET NAM="SMITH,JOHN"
          DO MOD2
          WRITE !,NAM
          QUIT
MOD2      NEW NAM
          SET NAM="DOE,JANE"
          QUIT
```

will output:

SMITH, JOHN

OPEN

OPEN claims exclusive ownership of a device such as CRT, printer, or magnetic tape drive. Before you can use any device except your principal device (assigned when you log on), you must first execute an OPEN command, and then execute a USE command. Two users cannot OPEN the same device. If you attempt to open a device owned by another user, MUMPS suspends program execution until the device is free.

When OPEN is followed by a timeout, if MUMPS cannot OPEN the device within specified number of seconds, $TEST is set to zero, and program execution is resumed.

Some devices, such as mag tape drives and line printers, may require a device parameter with the OPEN command: for information, see the user's manual for your implementation. For other devices, such as CRT's and printers, the "device parameter" is optional, and specifies number of columns to be displayed.

The OPEN command accepts post conditionals and can be used with indirection. For example:

```
SET DEVICE=DEVICE_"::60" OPEN @DEVICE
```

PRINT

The PRINT command is NOT specified as part of Standard MUMPS! However, we include it here because:

(1)   many implementations provide either PRINT or an equivalent command

(2)   we find PRINT a useful command in "real life" applications.

For our implementation, PRINT with no argument can be entered at a right caret to display the routine in your partition of memory (direct execution).

For our implementation, PRINT can also be used as part of a program. We can identify three forms of the PRINT command:

PRINT will print all routine lines in your partition

PRINT A will print line A

PRINT A:A + N will print line A through line A + N where N is any integer.

This last form of the PRINT command can be used to display a menu of options.

QUIT

QUIT terminates the execution of a FOR loop, a DO command, an XECUTE command, or a routine. In the context of a FOR loop, when a QUIT is executed, program control passes to the next line. In combination with a DO command, QUIT returns program control to that point immediately after the DO command "paired" with the QUIT. In combination with an XE-CUTE command, QUIT returns program control to that point immediately after the XECUTE command "paired" with the QUIT.

When a routine "runs out of code" this is considered an "implied QUIT", and program execution stops. Alternatively, an explicit QUIT command can be used at the end of each routine.

QUIT does not take an argument, and therefore is always followed by at least two spaces. QUIT may take a post conditional argument. For example:

```
FOR I=0:0 READ @PROMPT,ANS QUIT:ANS=""
```

READ

READ: (1) outputs a literal string and/or format control(s); (2) inputs the value for a variable. For example:

```
READ ! , "Name:  " , NAM
WRITE ! , "Name:  "
READ NAM
```

We can identify eight forms of the READ command:

READ ANS - input the value for a variable after prompt displayed by WRITE command

READ !, "Enter result: ", ANS - outputs a format control character as well as a literal string, and inputs the value for a variable

READ:SEX = "F" "Number of pregnancies: ", NUM - post conditional on READ command

READ @PROMPT1, ANS - command used with name indirection

READ !, "Enter name: ", NAM#30 - fixed length READ which accepts a maximum of 30 characters in the variable NAM

READ !, "Enter name: ", NAM:10 - timeout on argument of READ command; if no entry is made and a timeout occurs, NAM is given the value of " "

READ !, "Enter name: ", NAM#30:10 - fixed length READ with timeout

READ *ANS - "asterisk syntax" of READ command.

The asterisk syntax of READ indicates that a single character will be read, and that there is no need for the user to strike return after this single character entry. Thus, the input is only one character long. For our implementation, the assigned value of ANS will be the decimal ASCII equivalent of the first character entered. For your implementation, ANS might be assigned a different value (such as the hexadecimal ASCII equivalent of the first character entered). Table I of Chapter Twelve presents the ASCII character set, and the decimal ASCII equivalents for these characters.

The READ command accepts post conditionals, and can be used with indirection.

SET

SET assigns the value(s) to one (or several) variables.

We can identify six forms of the SET command:

        SET ˆNAME(J1)=NAM_ADR_PHONE

        SET (START,STEP)=1

        SET:'$DATA(ˆNAME) ˆNAME=1

        SET @ENTRY=START

        SET A=1,B=2,C=3

        SET $PIECE(ˆNAME(24),"ˆ",5)="203-444-7777"

The SET command can be used with $PIECE to change one piece of a node without rebuilding the entire node.

The SET command accepts post conditionals, and can be used with indirection.

USE

USE designates a specific device as the current device for input and output. Unless this device is your principal device, you must first establish ownership with an OPEN command.

The specified device is used until either:

(1)   you close the device with a CLOSE command - and return to your principal device

(2)   you execute another USE to select a new device

(3)   program execution stops, e.g. due to a HALT command or an error message.

The USE command allows you to specify a device parameter; however, no timeout is permitted. For example:

        USE 3

        USE 3:80

For our implementation, the 80 is a device parameter which specifies an 80 column width.

Device parameters are implementation specific.

The USE command accepts post conditionals. For example:

    USE: $T 64

Parameters may be specified in combination with a post conditional. For example:

    USE: $T 64: 80

The USE command may be used with indirection. For example:

    OPEN @ENTRY
    USE: $T @ENTRY

In our implementation, the USE command provides access to video terminals, hard copy terminals, line printers, and mag tape drives.

VIEW

VIEW provides a means for examining information specific to a given implementation of Standard MUMPS. The type of information which may be examined by the VIEW command includes:

- contents of a specific data block on disk

- contents of a specific location in main memory

- value of a local variable

- contents of routine directory

- contents of global directory.

The VIEW command may also allow you to alter contents of a specific data block on disk, or contents of a specific location in main memory.

Use of the VIEW command renders a program non-portable, since operation of this command will vary for different systems.

We do not use the VIEW command, and do not recommend it for beginners. Unless you are an experienced programmer, using VIEW in your code can cause serious problems.

Some implementations restrict use of the VIEW command to the system manager.

WRITE

WRITE: (1) outputs a literal string and/or format controls; (2) outputs the value for a variable. We can identify seven forms of the WRITE command:

WRITE	direct execution (WRITE entered at any right caret). This form of the WRITE command is implementation specific. For our system, direct execution of WRITE with no argument displays all variables in our partition of memory.
WRITE !!!	output format controls - commas between multiple format controls are optional, and can be omitted.
WRITE !!,A,B	output format controls and values for one or more variables.
WRITE !!,"Enter number ""N"""	output literal string (quotation marks within string must be represented by two adjacent quotes).
WRITE *27,*72,*27,*74	asterisk syntax of WRITE: can be used to perform functions such as "ringing the bell", cursor addressing or "blanking the screen". The codes for some of these functions are terminal specific.
WRITE:FLAG = 1 "OK"	post conditional on WRITE command.
WRITE @A,!!,@B	WRITE command with indirection.

The WRITE command accepts post conditionals and can be used with indirection.

XECUTE

Each argument of the XECUTE command is interpreted as if it were a line of MUMPS code. For example:

```
SET A="WRITE !,""THIS IS AN EXAMPLE"""
SET B="WRITE "" OF THE XECUTE COMMAND"""
XECUTE A,B
```

would produce as output:

```
THIS IS AN EXAMPLE OF THE XECUTE COMMAND
```

If an XECUTE statement contains a DO command, MUMPS will execute whatever code is specified in the DO arguments. For example:

```
SET A="DO ^B,^C,^D,^F"
XECUTE A
```

will DO the routines ^B, ^C, ^D, ^E and ^F

Each XECUTE argument functions like a subroutine called by a DO command and terminated with a QUIT.

Both the XECUTE command and its arguments accept post conditionals.

$ASCII

$ASCII returns the decimal ASCII code for a specified character in a specified string. The one argument form of $ASCII returns the decimal ASCII code for the first character. For example:

```
SET STRING="TEST"
SET B=$ASCII(STRING)
```

will set B equal to the decimal ASCII code for T.

The two argument form of $ASCII returns the decimal ASCII code for a specified character position. For example:

```
SET STRING="TEST"
SET A=$ASCII(STRING,3)
```

will set A equal to the decimal ASCII code for S.

If the string is empty, or if the integer value in the position argument is larger than the number of characters, $ASCII returns -1.

$CHAR

$CHAR acts as the inverse of $ASCII: it returns the character whose decimal ASCII code is specified. For example:

```
SET A=$CHAR(27)
```

will set A equal to the character whose decimal ASCII code is 27 (the escape character).

The $CHAR function will accept multiple arguments. For example:

```
WRITE $CHAR(65,77)
```

will return AM.

If you specify a number less than zero, no character is returned. If you specify a number greater than 127, the result is implementation specific.

$DATA

$DATA returns an integer that indicates whether the named variable has: neither data nor decendants, data but no decendants, decendants but no data, or both data and decendants. The values returned and their meanings are:

```
 0 - neither data nor descendants
 1 - data but no descendants
10 - descendants but no data
11 - data and descendants.
```

The MUMPS language standard specifies that a previously undefined root is given a $DATA of 10 when you create this root by defining a lower level node. For example:

```
KILL ^NAME SET ^NAME(1)="SMITH,ROBERT"
WRITE $DATA(^NAME)
```

will return a 10.

However, some implementations "automatically" assign a null value to ^NAME - so that:

```
WRITE $DATA(^NAME)
```

will return 11.

We suggest that you check how your implementation handles the above sequence. In some cases, results on global arrays may differ from the results on local arrays.

The MUMPS language standard specifies that when you KILL all decendants of a node, the value of $DATA reflects the "current status" of its argument.

```
KILL ^A SET ^A=1,^A(1)=1,^A(2)=2
KILL ^A(1),^A(2)
WRITE $DATA(^A)
```

will return 1, since all decendants of A have been killed.

We suggest that you check how your implementation handles the above sequence both for global arrays and local arrays: for earlier versions of MUMPS, the value of $DATA remained unchanged after decendants of a node were KILLed.

The $DATA function may be used with indirection. For example:

```
SET ^NAME=1,^NAME(1)="SMITH,JOHN",A="^NAME"
WRITE $DATA(@A)
```

returns 11.

$EXTRACT

$EXTRACT returns the specified character(s) from a specified string. We can identify three forms of $EXTRACT: one argument, two argument, and three argument.

The one argument form of $EXTRACT returns the first character of the specified string. For example:

```
SET NAME="SMITH, JOHN"
WRITE $EXTRACT(NAME)
```

will return "S".

The two-argument form of $EXTRACT returns one character at the position specified. For example:

```
WRITE $EXTRACT(NAME,4)
```

will return "T";

```
WRITE $EXTRACT(NAME,20)
```

will return a null string.

The three argument form of $EXTRACT returns all characters from the first position specified to the second position specified. For example:

```
WRITE $EXTRACT(NAME,1,3)
```

will return "SMI";

```
WRITE $EXTRACT(NAME,1,20)
```

will return "SMITH, JOHN";

```
WRITE $EXTRACT(NAME,20,30);
```

will return a null string;

```
WRITE $EXTRACT(NAME,-1,30)
```

will return "SMITH, JOHN".

$FIND

$FIND returns the position of a specified substring within a specified string.

The two argument form of $FIND returns the character position immediately following a specified substring within a specified string. For example:

```
SET NAME="SMITH, JOHN"
SET A=$FIND(NAME,",")
```

returns "7" - the character position immediately following "," within "SMITH, JOHN".

From here, we can then obtain first initial by the two argument form of $EXTRACT:

```
SET FI=$EXTRACT(NAME,A+1).
```

We can obtain last name by the three argument form of $EXTRACT:

```
SET LN=$EXTRACT(NAME,1,A-2).
```

The three argument form of $FIND includes as a third argument, the position at which $FIND will start its search for the specified substring. For example:

```
SET TEXT="THIS IS A LINE OF TEXT"
SET WORD=$FIND(TEXT," ",12)
```

returns "16" - the character position immediately following the first space after the twelfth character in the specified string.

$JUSTIFY

We can identify two forms of $JUSTIFY.

The two argument form of $JUSTIFY returns a specified string, right-justified within a field of specified length. For example:

```
SET A(1)=10,A(2)=5,A(3)=100
FOR I=1:1:3 WRITE !,$JUSTIFY(A(I),10)
```

returns:

```
        10
         5
       100
```

Notice that for each output, the right most character is at position 10. This form of $JUSTIFY can be used with alpha character strings, as well as numeric strings.

The three argument form of $JUSTIFY converts the string to a numeric value, and specifies the number of decimal places desired. For example:

```
SET A(1)=10.566,A(2)=5,A(3)=.006,A(4)="CAT",A(5)=1/3
FOR I=1:1:3 WRITE !,$JUSTIFY(A(I),10,2)
```

returns:

```
10.57
 5.00
 0.01
 0.00
 0.33
```

Notice that $JUSTIFY "rounds up" numbers rather than performing a simple truncation, adds leading or trailing zeros as needed, and evaluates a non-numeric literal string as zero. We could further round off these numbers via:

```
FOR I=1:1:3 WRITE !,$JUSTIFY(A(I),10,0)
```

to return:

```
 11
  5
100
  0
  0
  0
```

$LENGTH

The one argument form of $LENGTH returns the number of characters in a specified string. If the specified string is a null string, $LENGTH returns a zero. For example:

```
SET ^A="THIS IS A STRING"
WRITE $LENGTH(^A)
```

returns 16. And:

```
SET ^B=""
WRITE $LENGTH(^B)
```

returns 0.

You can use the one argument form of $L to test two or more strings before concatenation. For example:

```
        IF  $L(NAM)+$L(ADR)+$L(TEL)'>255 SET ^NAME(I)=NAM_ADR_TEL
        E   WRITE !,"NAME+ADDRESS+PHONE MUST NOT EXCEED 255 CHARACTERS"
. . . . . . GOTO MOD
```

Another way to accomplish the same thing:

```
        IF  $L(NAM_ADR_TEL)<256 SET ^NAME(I)=NAM_ADR_TEL
        E   WRITE !,"NAME+ADDRESS+PHONE MUST NOT EXCEED 255 CHARACTERS"
. . . . . . GOTO MOD
```

The two argument form of $LENGTH returns the number of times, plus one, that a specified delimiter occurs within a specified string or variable. This variation on $LENGTH returns the number of "pieces" within a string for a specified delimiter. For example:

```
        SET DELIM="^"
        SET ^NAME="SMITH,JOHN^422 LINDEN DRIVE^HERSHEY^PA"
        WRITE $LENGTH(^NAME,"^")
```

returns 4. And:

```
        WRITE $LENGTH(^NAME,DELIM)
```

also returns 4.

$NEXT

$NEXT works in the same manner as $ORDER, except the starting and ending values are "-1" rather than "" (a null string).

Although negative subscripts can be used with $NEXT, the results may be misleading. Since $ORDER has no problems with negative subscripts, we recommend you use $ORDER rather than the $NEXT function.

$ORDER

$ORDER returns the next subscript in a local or global array, based on the ASCII collating sequence. From a starting point of "" (a null string), $ORDER returns the first subscript at a specified level. After returning the last subscript, $ORDER then returns "" as a default. For example:

```
        SET A1=""
        FOR I=0:0 SET A2=$ORDER(^NAME(A1)),A1=A2 QUIT:A2=""  WRITE !,A2
```

returns all subscripts at the first level for the global ^NAME.

This code can be shortened to:

```
SET A=""
FOR I=0:0 SET A=$ORDER(^NAME(A)) QUIT:A=""  WRITE !,A
```

Returning subscripts in true numeric order presents a potential problem: 0001, 1, and 1.00 all have the same numeric value - but different values in the ASCII collating sequence (Table I of Chapter Twelve). To solve this problem, Standard MUMPS uses a convention whereby "canonic numbers" are returned first, followed by all other strings in the ASCII collating sequence.

A "canonic number" has no non-significant leading or trailing zeros:

Canonic numbers	Non-canonic numbers
.5	0.5
1.2	1.20
7	007
130	130.0

The $ORDER function returns subscripts in the order of canonic numbers in true numeric sequence, followed by all other subscripts in ASCII collating sequence.

If the following fifteen values were subscripts returned by $ORDER, they would appear in the following sequence:

```
.1
.5
1.2
1.65
120
012
0600
100.0
2.0
SMITH
SMITH, R
SMITH, R.
Smith, R.
smith, R.
```

The first five subscripts, as canonic numbers, appear in true numeric order.

The second four subscripts appear in "string order" based on the ASCII collating sequence. Notice that this sequence appears analogous to "alphabetic order".

The last five subscripts appear in "string order" based on the ASCII collating sequence. Notice that upper case alpha characters precede lower case alpha characters (Table I of Chapter Twelve).

$PIECE

$PIECE returns one or more pieces of a specified string, based on positions relative to a specified delimiter.

The two argument form of $PIECE returns the first "piece" of a specified string relative to a specified delimiter. For example:

```
SET NAM="JONES,ROBERT"
SET ADR="500 UNIVERSITY DRIVE"
SET PHONE="111-111-1111"
SET NAME=NAM_"^"_ADR_"^"_PHONE
WRITE $PIECE(NAME,"^")
```

returns:

```
JONES,ROBERT
```

If the delimiter does not exist, then the whole string is returned:

```
WRITE $PIECE(NAME,"#")
```

returns:

```
JONES,ROBERT^500 UNIVERSITY DRIVE^111-111-1111
```

The three argument form of $PIECE returns the piece specified by the third argument. For example:

```
WRITE $PIECE(NAME,"^",2)
```

returns:

```
500 UNIVERSITY DRIVE
```

as the "second piece" of NAME.

If the specified number is greater than the number of pieces, $PIECE returns a null. For example:

```
WRITE $PIECE(NAME,"^",6)
```

returns "",since the sixth "piece" does not exist.

If the specified delimiter does not exist, and the third argument is 1, $PIECE returns the entire string. For example:

```
WRITE $PIECE(NAME,"#",1)
```

returns:

```
JONES,ROBERT^500 UNIVERSITY DRIVE^111-111-1111
```

as the "first piece" to the left of the non existent specified delimiter.

If the specified delimiter does not exist, and the "third argument is greater than 1, $PIECE returns a null string. For example:

```
WRITE $PIECE(NAME,"#",2)
```

returns "",since the "second piece" relative to this non-existent delimiter does not exist.

The four argument form of $PIECE allows multiple pieces to be extracted. The syntax is:

```
$PIECE (string,delimiter,position of first piece,position of last piece).
```

For example:

```
SET ^DATA="A^B^C^D^E^F^G"
WRITE $PIECE(^DATA,"^",3,6)
```

returns:

```
C^D^E^F
```

as the third, fourth, fifth and sixth "pieces".

If the fourth argument is greater than the number of pieces for the entire string, $PIECE returns everything from the "first specified piece" to the end of the string. For example:

```
WRITE $PIECE(^DATA,"^",3,500)
```

returns:

```
C^D^E^F^G
```

If the specified number for the "first piece" is greater than the number of pieces for the entire string, $PIECE returns a null string. For example:

```
WRITE $PIECE(^DATA "^",200,500)
```

returns a null string.

The same thing happens if the specified number for the "first piece" exceeds the specified number for the "last piece".

If the specified delimiter does not exist, and the third argument is 1, $PIECE returns the entire string. If the third argument exceeds 1, $PIECE returns a null string.

Both forms of $PIECE can be nested. For example:

```
WRITE $PIECE($PIECE(NAME,"^",3),"-",1)
```

returns the telephone area code,111.

$PIECE allows us to "break apart" long strings constructed by concatenation. Using $PIECE, it is relatively easy to retrieve substrings from long data strings stored as the values of global nodes. This function, easily performed by $PIECE, would require complex code in most other computer languages.

The SET command can be used with $PIECE to change one part of a node without rebuilding the entire node. For example:

```
SET $PIECE(^DATA,"^",5)="EEE"
WRITE !,^DATA
```

returns:

```
A^B^C^D^EEE^F^G
```

$RANDOM

$RANDOM returns a random integer uniformly distributed in an interval from zero to one less than a specified number. For example:

```
SET X=$RANDOM(100)
```

will return a random number between 0 and 99;

```
SET X=$RANDOM(2)
```

will randomly return either 0 or 1;

```
SET X=$RANDOM(1)
```

will always return zero;

```
    FOR I=1:1:100 SET X(I)=$RANDOM(101)
```

generates an array of random numbers from zero to 100.

The $RANDOM function can be used to write programs which simulate unpredictable events such as the roll of dice, or outcomes following a decision. If you need to write a "simulation program" which does NOT operate in a strictly predictable manner, $RANDOM will be quite useful!

$SELECT

$SELECT returns, from a list of arguments, the right hand portion of the first argument whose truth value is true. If all values are false, an error message is returned, and the program halts. Therefore, $SELECT ordinarily is used with a final argument whose truth value is true; the right hand portion of this argument is then returned if all others are false.

Each $SELECT argument represents two expressions separated by a colon: the left hand expression is evaluated for its truth value, and the right hand expression is returned if this truth value is true.

$SELECT evaluates the arguments from left to right. When $SELECT discovers a truth-valued expression with the value of one (true), it returns the matching expression on the right of the colon. For example:

```
    SET MON="FEB"
    S MO=$S(MON="JAN":"01",MON="FEB":"02",MON="MAR":"03",
.....  MON="APR":"04",MON="MAY":"05",MON="JUN":"06",MON="JUL":"07",
.....  MON="AUG":"08",MON="SEP":"09",MON="OCT":"10",MON="NOV":"11",
.....  MON="DEC":"12",1:"ERROR"
```

returns "02".

$SELECT may be used with indirection to call a routine from disk, based on user response entered at a prompt. For example:

```
    READ !,"Option 1,2,3 OR 4? ",ANS
    DO @$SELECT(ANS=1:"^CH1EX4",ANS=2:"^CH2EX4",ANS=3:"^CH3EX6",
.....  ANS=4:"^CH3EX8",1:"^ERROR")
```

Here, the $SELECT function allows us to select from a number of different routines, using a single line of code. Since $SELECT exits as soon as a "true condition" is found, $SELECT will execute more rapidly than a long list of post conditionals.

$TEXT

$TEXT returns the text of a specified line from the current routine in memory. If the line specified does not exist, $TEXT returns a null string.

$TEXT provides a useful method to display menus. For example:

```
        FOR J1=1:1:6 WRITE !?5,$TEXT(OPTIONS+J1)
        QUIT
OPTIONS ;
        1.      BUILD FILE
        2.      PRINT FILE - ORDER ACCESSION NUMBER
        3.      PRINT FILE - ALPHA ORDER
        4.      ADD NEW ENTRY
        5.      DELETE OR MODIFY PREVIOUS ENTRY
        6.      DISPLAY DATA FOR SPECIFIED FILE ENTRY
```

Here, $TEXT returns the text of lines OPTIONS+1 through OPTIONS+6.

$TEXT is often used with $PIECE. For example:

```
        FOR J2=1:1:6 SET A=$TEXT(OPTIONS+J2) WRITE !?5,$PIECE(A,"^^",1)
        QUIT
OPTIONS ;
        1.      BUILD FILE^^FIBLD
        2.      PRINT FILE - ORDER ACCESSION NUMBER^^FIACC
        3.      PRINT FILE - ALPHA ORDER^^FIALP
        4.      ADD NEW ENTRY^^FIADD
        5.      DELETE OR MODIFY PREVIOUS ENTRY^^FIDEL
        6.      DISPLAY DATA FOR SPECIFIED FILE ENTRY^^FIDIS
```

This allows us to DO @$PIECE(A,"^",2,3).

$VIEW

$VIEW is an implementation specific function which returns the contents of a specified memory location. Thus, the $VIEW function is similar to the VIEW command.

Use of the $VIEW function renders a program non-portable, since operation of this function will vary for different systems. We do not use the $VIEW function, and do not recommend it for beginners. Specific information on the $VIEW function is provided in the users manual for your implementation.

BINARY ADD

Binary add produces the sum of two numeric expressions.

If an expression has no leading numeric characters, binary add gives it a value of zero. For example:

```
        WRITE  "8"+"CATS"          returns 8
```

If an expression has leading numeric characters followed by non-numeric characters, the non-numeric characters are dropped. For example:

```
        WRITE  8+"4 CATS"          returns 12
```

Leading zeros do not affect the result. For example:

```
        WRITE  "001"+10            returns 11
```

BINARY SUBTRACT

Binary subtract produces the difference between two numeric expressions.

If an expression has no leading numeric characters, binary subtract gives it a value of zero. For example:

```
        WRITE  "8"-"CATS"          returns 8
```

If an expression has leading numeric characters followed by non-numeric characters, the the non-numeric characters are dropped. For example:

```
        WRITE  8-"4 CATS"          returns 4
```

BINARY MULTIPLY

Binary multiply produces the product of two numeric expressions.

If an expression has no leading numeric characters, binary multiply gives it a value of zero. For example:

```
        WRITE  "8"*"CATS"          returns 0
```

If an expression has leading numeric characters followed by non-numeric characters, the non-numeric characters are dropped. For example:

```
WRITE 8*"4 CATS"          returns 32
```

BINARY DIVIDE

Binary divide produces the result of dividing two numeric expressions.

If an expression has no leading numeric characters, binary divide gives it a value of zero. For example:

```
WRITE "CATS"/8            returns zero
```

But:

```
WRITE 8/"CATS"
```

will produce a system error - due to attempted division by zero. For our system, you can use $ZERROR to resume program execution after an error occurs: check the user manual for your system to determine how "error recovery" is accomplished.

If an expression has leading numeric characters followed by non-numeric characters, the the non-numeric characters are dropped. For example:

```
WRITE 8/"2 CATS"          returns 4
```

A "special" application of binary divide is to produce close approximations for important constants. The following approximations are from Brodie L, Starting FORTH, Prentice Hall, Englewood Cliffs, NJ, 1981:

NUMBER	APPROXIMATION
3.141... (pi)	355/113
1.414... (square root of 2)	19601/13860

BINARY INTEGER DIVIDE

Binary integer divide produces the integer result of dividing two numeric expressions. An "integer result" means "a whole number with nothing after the decimal point". For example:

```
8/3 = 2.6666...

8\3 = 2
```

If an expression has no leading numeric characters, binary divide gives it a value of zero. For example:

```
        WRITE "CATS"\8              returns zero
```

As with binary divide, attempted division by zero will produce a system error.

If an expression has leading numeric characters followed by non-numeric characters, the non-numeric characters are dropped. For example:

```
        WRITE 8\"2 CATS"            returns 4
```

A common application of binary integer divide is to extract the integer part of a number. For example:

```
        SET A=1.74321
        SET B=A\1
        WRITE B                    returns 1
```

We can modify this code to perform a rounding operation:

```
        SET A=1.74321
        SET B=A+.5\1
        WRITE B                    returns 2
```

BINARY MODULO

Binary modulo is defined as:

```
        A#B=A-(B*floor(A/B))
```

where floor(A/B) is the largest integer which is less than or equal to A/B.

The following examples are adapted from Walters RF, Bowie J, Wilcox JC:MUMPS Primer, 1982, p 15, published by the MUMPS Users' Group. For example:

```
        SET A=13,B=5
        A#B=13-(5*floor(13/5))
           =13-(5*floor(2.6))
           =13-(5*2)
           =13-10
           =3

        SET A=20,B=5
        A#B=20-(5*floor(20/5))
           =20-(5*floor(4.0))
           =20-(5*4)
           =20-20
           =0
```

If both A and B are positive, we can think of modulo as "what's left over" after an integer divide.

If A and/or B is negative, the results are more difficult to predict. For example:

```
SET A=4,B=-3
A#B=4-(-3*floor(4/-3))
   =4-(-3*floor(-1.333...))
   =4-(-3*-2)
   =4-(6)
   =-2
```

UNARY PLUS

Unary plus gives its argument a numeric interpretation, without affecting the sign.

If the argument has no leading numeric characters, unary plus gives it a value of zero. For example:

```
SET A="CATS"
WRITE +A          returns 0
```

If the argument has leading numeric characters followed by non-numeric characters, the non-numeric characters are dropped. For example:

```
SET A="8 CATS"
WRITE +A          returns 8
```

Unary plus does NOT alter the sign of positive or negative numbers. For example:

```
SET A=-10,B=10
WRITE +A,+B       returns -10 and 10
```

Like the binary arithmetic operators, unary plus "strips off" leading zeros. For example:

```
SET A=007
WRITE +A          returns 7
```

Like other arithmetic operators, unary plus can be used with exponential notation. For example:

```
SET A="9E2ABC"
WRITE +A
```

will return 900 (the value of 9E2).

UNARY MINUS

Unary minus gives its argument a numeric interpretation, and reverses the sign.

If the argument has no leading numeric characters, unary minus gives it a value of zero. For example:

```
SET A="FOUR PLUS 4"
WRITE -A          returns 0
```

If the argument has leading numeric characters followed by non-numeric characters, the non-numeric characters are dropped. For example:

```
SET A="8 CATS"
WRITE -A        returns -8
```

A negative number will be changed to a positive number. For example:

```
SET A=-8
WRITE -A        returns 8
```

Like the unary plus, unary minus "strips off" leading zeros. For example:

```
SET A="007"
WRITE -A        returns -7
```

GREATER THAN

This arithmetic relational operator tests whether the first argument is numerically greater than the second. Like the six arithmetic binary operators, and the two arithmetic unary operators, this relational operator converts alpha strings into numeric values: it then performs a comparison based on numeric values of these arguments.

An argument with no leading numeric characters is given a value of zero. For example:

```
SET A="FOUR PLUS 20"
SET B=1
IF A>B WRITE !,"A GREATER THAN B"
ELSE  WRITE !,"A NOT GREATER THAN B"
```

will return "A NOT GREATER THAN B".

For an argument with leading numeric characters followed by non-numeric characters, the non-numeric characters are dropped. For example:

```
SET A="02 PLUS FOUR"
SET B=1
IF A>B WRITE !,"A GREATER THAN B"
ELSE  WRITE !,"A NOT GREATER THAN B"
```

will return "A GREATER THAN B"

As with the other arithmetic operators, exponential notation can be used. For example:

```
SET A=3E2
SET B=100
IF A>B WRITE !,"A GREATER THAN B"
ELSE  WRITE !,"A NOT GREATER THAN B"
```

will return "A GREATER THAN B".

This operator can be used with the unary not (see section on logical operators) as follows:

```
A'>B is interpreted as:
```

"A not greater than B" (A equal to or less than B).

LESS THAN

This arithmetic relational operator tests whether the first argument is numerically less than the second. Like the six arithmetic binary operators and the two arithmetic unary operators, this relational operator converts alpha strings into numeric values: it then performs the comparison based on numeric values of the arguments.

An argument with no leading numeric characters is given a value of zero. For example:

```
SET A="FOUR PLUS 20"
SET B=1
IF A<B WRITE ! , "A LESS THAN B"
ELSE   WRITE ! , "A NOT LESS THAN B"
```

will return "A LESS THAN B".

For an argument with leading numeric characters followed by non-numeric characters, the non-numeric characters are dropped. For example:

```
SET A="20 PLUS FOUR"
SET B=1
IF A<B WRITE ! , "A LESS THAN B"
ELSE   WRITE ! , "A NOT LESS THAN B"
```

will return "A NOT LESS THAN B".

As with the other arithmetic operators, exponential notation can be used. For example:

```
SET A=3E2
SET B=100
IF A<B WRITE ! , "A LESS THAN B"
ELSE   WRITE ! , "A NOT LESS THAN B"
```

will return "A NOT LESS THAN B".

This operator can be used with the unary not (see section on logical operators) as follows:

A'<B is interpreted as:

"A not less than B" (A equal to or greater than B).

CONCATENATE

This operator, expressed by the underline character, creates a new string composed of the right hand argument and the left hand argument. For most implementations, if the new string is longer than 255 characters, a system error results. Some implementations may allow longer strings. You may want to experiment, or check the user manual for your implementation, to determine the maximum length allowed in your system.

Here is a simple example:

```
SET NAM="SMITH, JOHN"
SET DOB="JULY 1, 1982"
SET ^NAME=NAM_" : "_DOB
WRITE ^NAME
```

will return

SMITH, JOHN : JULY 1, 1982

EQUALS

This string relational operator compares two strings for "string equality", rather than "numeric equality". Unlike the two arithmetic relational operators (greater than and less than), there is NO conversion to a "numeric equivalent". For example:

```
SET A=100
SET B=10E2
IF A=B WRITE ! ,"A EQUALS B BY STRING COMPARISON"
ELSE  WRITE ! ,"A NOT EQUAL TO B BY STRING COMPARISON"
```

will return "A NOT EQUAL TO B BY STRING COMPARISON"

To test numeric equality, use the unary plus to force a numeric interpretation. The following code performs numeric comparison of A and B:

```
IF +A=+B WRITE ! ,"A EQUALS B BY NUMERIC COMPARISON"
ELSE  WRITE ! ,"A NOT EQUAL TO B BY NUMERIC COMPARISON"
```

For the above values of A and B, this code returns "A EQUALS B BY NUMERIC COMPARISON".

The "equals" string relational operator may be used as an arithmetic relational operator by preceding both arguments with a unary plus.

CONTAINS

This string relational operator tests whether the sequence of characters in the right hand argument is contained within the sequence of characters in the left hand argument. For example:

```
SET A="COST ANALYSIS"
SET B="COST"
SET C="CST"
SET D="C"

IF A[B WRITE ! ,"A CONTAINS B"
IF B[A WRITE ! ,"B CONTAINS A"
IF A[C WRITE ! ,"A CONTAINS C"
IF A[D WRITE ! ,"A CONTAINS D"
```

will return:

```
"A CONTAINS B"
"A CONTAINS D"
```

FOLLOWS

This string relational operator tests whether the sequence of characters in the left hand argument follows the sequence of characters in the right hand argument. Comparison is based on the ASCII collating sequence (Table I of Chapter Twelve)

Earlier versions of Standard MUMPS used this operator to perform sorts in alphabetic order. Today, such sorts are done "automatically" via string subscripts. Occasionally, the follows operator may be useful to check the alpha order of two strings. For example:

```
IF A]B DO MOD1
IF B]A DO MOD2
ELSE DO MOD3
```

The follows operator can be used to display only those entries which follow a specific character. For example:

```
IF NAM]"MZZZZZ" DO DISPLAY
```

could display all names starting with N through Z.

PATTERN MATCH

This string relational operator tests whether the characters in the left hand argument match the pattern specified in the right hand argument. The characters used and their meanings are:

N	the ten numeric characters from 0 through 9
U	the 26 upper case alphabetic characters from A through Z
L	the 26 lower case alphabetic characters from a through z
P	the 33 punctuation characters specified in the ASCII collating sequence (Table I of Chapter Twelve)
A	the 26 upper case alphabetic characters from A through Z plus the 26 lower case alphabetic characters from a to z
C	the 33 control characters specified in the ASCII collating sequence (Table I of Chapter Twelve)
E	every character in the ASCII collating sequence.

You can also use in a pattern match:

(1)   string literals enclosed in quotation marks: such as ".", "_", "N", "YES".

(2)   composite pattern codes. For example:

        AP - alpha characters or punctuation marks

        "."","" - periods or commas

        A"." - alpha characters or periods.

(3)   a number to specify how many occurrences are required for a specified character or string literal. For example:

              IF PHONE? 3N"-"3N"-"4N

        specifies 3 numbers followed by one hyphen followed by 3 numbers followed by one hyphen followed by four numbers.

(4)   a period preceding the pattern match character or string literal to specify "any number including zero". For example:

        IF NAM?.A specifies "any number of alpha characters including zero".

(5)   a number, a period, and a second number to specify "any number from (first number) to (second number)" for the pattern match character or string literal. For example:

        IF NAM?1.30A specifies between 1 to 30 alpha characters

(6)   a number followed by a period to specify "at least (number)" for the pattern match character or string literal. For example:

        IF NAM?2.A will require "two or more alpha characters".

(7)   a number preceded by a period to specify "any number from zero to (number)" for the pattern match character or string literal. For example:

        IF NAM?.20A specifies between zero and 20 alpha characters.

BINARY AND

This operator - also known as the "Boolean And" and expressed as "&" - tests whether both of two arguments are true. It is possible to combine three or more arguments with multiple "Boolean And" operators. For example:

```
        FOR J1=1:1 READ !,"Enter number: ",NUM QUIT:NUM=""  DO ENTRYCHK
        ;
ENTRYCHK IF (NUM'?1N.N)&(NUM'?1N.N1".".N)&(NUM'?1"-"1N.N)&
......  (NUM'?1"-"1N.N1".".N) DO ERR QUIT
        SET DATA(J1)=NUM QUIT
ERR     WRITE !,"NUMERIC ENTRIES ONLY, PLEASE!"
        WRITE !,"FOR ENTRIES LESS THAN ONE, PLEASE ENTER A LEADING ZERO"
        WRITE !,"FOR NEGATIVE NUMBERS, PLEASE PRECEDE YOUR ENTRY BY
......  A MINUS SIGN DIRECTLY BEFORE THE NUMBER (NO SPACE NEEDED)"
        WRITE !,"FOR POSITIVE NUMBERS, PLEASE DO NOT ENTER A 'PLUS'
......  SIGN"
        QUIT
```

If our entry fails the first pattern match AND the second pattern match AND the third pattern match AND the fourth pattern match, we display an error message and QUIT ENTRYCHK. Otherwise, we create a new mode in our array, then QUIT ENTRYCHK.

When you combine multiple arguments with Boolean And, we suggest you use parentheses to ensure proper interpretation.

We can evaluate the truth value for the test performed by a Boolean And. For example:

```
        SET A=1,B=1,C=0
        WRITE A&B                       returns 1
        WRITE B&C                       returns 0
```

BINARY OR

This operator - also known as the "Boolean Or" and expressed as "!" - tests whether either of two arguments is true. It is possible to combine three or more arguments with multiple "Boolean Or" operators. For example:

```
        FOR J1=1:1 READ !,"Enter number: ",NUM  QUIT:NUM=""  DO ENTRYCHK
ENTRYCHK IF (NUM?1N.N)!(NUM?1N.N1".".N)!(NUM?1"-"1N.N)!
......  (NUM?1"-"1N.N1"."N) SET  DATA(J1)=NUM QUIT
        DO ERR QUIT
```

If our entry passes the first pattern match OR the second pattern match OR the third pattern match OR the fourth pattern match, we SET DATA(J1)=NUM and QUIT ENTRYCHK. Otherwise, we display an error message and QUIT ENTRYCHK.

When you combine comparative arguments with the Boolean Or, we suggest you use parentheses to ensure proper interpretation.

We can evaluate the truth value for the test performed by a Boolean Or. For example:

```
SET  A=1, B=0, C=0
WRITE  A!B                        returns 1
WRITE  B!C                        returns 0
```

UNARY NOT

This operator - also known as the "Boolean Not" and expressed as an apostrophe - reverses the truth value of any arithmetic or string relational operator. For example:

```
'>      A'>B        A is less than or equal to B
'<      A'<B        A is greater than or equal to B
'=      A'=B        A is unequal to B
'[      A'[B        A does not contain B
']      A']B        A does not follow B
'?      A'?"B"      A does not pattern match"B"
'&      A'&B        Either A or B or both are false - same as '(A&B)
'!      A'!B        Both A and B are false - same as '(A!B)
```

The Unary Not can be used on arguments, as well as on operators. For example:

```
SET  A=0, B=1
IF  'A WRITE  "A EQUALS ZERO"     returns "A EQUALS ZERO"
WRITE  'A&B                       returns 1
WRITE  'A&'B                      returns 0
WRITE  A!'B                       returns 0
WRITE  'A!'B                      returns 1
```

$HOROLOG

The $HOROLOG special variable returns a string of two numbers, separated by a comma. These two numbers represent the current time and date. The first number represents the number of days since December 31, 1840. The second number represents the number of seconds past midnight for the current day.

We find $HOROLOG useful for timing execution speed of routines of subroutines. For example:

```
        SET A=$PIECE($HOROLOG,",",2)
        FOR J1=1:1:10000 DO SUB
        SET B=$PIECE($HOROLOG,",",2)
        WRITE !,"EXECUTION TIME= ",B-A,"   SECONDS"
        QUIT
SUB     SET ^NAME=J1+J1
        QUIT
```

A program to obtain current time and date from $HOROLOG is presented at the end of Chapter Thirteen. However, most implementations of Standard MUMPS provide a utility program to accomplish this function.

$IO

The $IO special variable returns the number of the current I/O device.

Using CLOSE with the $IO special variable is implementation specific: check your user manual for information.

With our system, $IO can be used with the CLOSE command to perform "background jobs" (see Chapter Fifteen).

$JOB

The $JOB special variable returns the job number for the routine currently executing in your partition. Your job number remains constant throughout your terminal session. The MUMPS Primer published by the MUMPS Users' Group (MUG) suggests that $JOB can be used as the initial subscript for a "scratch file" on disk. For example:

```
        SET ^UTILITY($JOB,J1)=NAME(J1)
```

The global ^UTILITY is used as a scratch global by convention. Since no two users will have the same $JOB number, several programs can simultaneously use the same scratch global.

$STORAGE

The $STORAGE special variable returns the number of bytes of free space available in your partition. You may want to consider checking $STORAGE when working with:

(1)   very large local arrays

(2)   very long programs.

However, if you keep local arrays and programs relatively short, it is unlikely you will run out of space in your partition. A potential use of $STORAGE is to decide whether to file data from a local array. For example:

```
DO ^ROUTINE   IF $STORAGE<500 DO ^FILE
```

However, we have not used the $STORAGE special variable for this purpose in our own programs.

$TEST

The $TEST special variable reflects the truth value from:

(1)   the latest IF command with an argument, or

(2)   the latest OPEN, LOCK, JOB or READ command with a timeout.

The $TEST special variable enables us to use the argumentless IF command, and its converse, the ELSE command. Here are two simple examples:

```
READ !,"Enter phone number:  ",PHONE
IF PHONE?1"?" DO HELP1
ELSE  DO PATMATCH

READ !,"Enter phone number:  ",PHONE
IF PHONE?1"?" D HELP1
IF  SET TERM=$IO,TIME=$HOROLOG
IF  SET ^PROBLEM(TERM,TIME)="FORMAT FOR PHONE ENTRY"
```

We suggest that you use the $TEST special variable with the timed OPEN, LOCK, and JOB commands - otherwise program execution may "hang" for a prolonged period.

Post conditionals do NOT affect $TEST.

$X

The $X special variable returns a positive integer equal to current horizontal position of the cursor or print head. $X is reset to zero for each carriage return, line feed (!) or form feed (#). Also, $X is automatically reset to zero whenever it exceeds 255. Thus $X potentially can have any value between zero and 255.

A common application of $X is in the expression:

    ? $X+n

which moves the cursor or print head the specified number of characters.

Some implementations allow the SET command to revise the value of $X. For example:

    SET $X=1

This application of the SET command allows you to "correct" the value of $X after use of cursor control on a CRT. Otherwise, after the cursor control is used, your program has no way to identify the "current" cursor location.

$Y

The $Y special variable returns a positive integer equal to current vertical position of the cursor or print head. $Y is reset to zero for each form feed (#), and incremented by one for each line feed (!). Also, $Y is automatically reset to zero whenever it exceeds 255. Thus $Y potentially can have any value between zero and 255.

Common applications of $Y are to execute a form feed when a printed page is full, or "stop" a screen display when a specified number of lines (usually 24) have been output. For example:

    WRITE: $Y>60 #
    IF $Y>22 READ "Enter carriage return to continue display",ANS

Some implementations allow the SET command to revise the value of $Y. For example:

    SET $Y=1

This application of the SET command allows you to "correct" the value of $Y after use of cursor control on a CRT. Otherwise, after the cursor control is used, your program has no way to identify the "current" cursor location.

APPENDIX A

THE ASCII CHARACTER SET

TABLE I

CODE	CHARACTER	CODE	CHARACTER	CODE	CHARACTER	CODE	CHARACTER
0	NUL	32	SP	64	@	96	
1	SOH	33	!	65	A	97	a
2	STX	34	"	66	B	98	b
3	ETX	35	#	67	C	99	c
4	EOT	36	$	68	D	100	d
5	ENQ	37	%	69	E	101	e
6	ACK	38	&	70	F	102	f
7	BEL	39	'	71	G	103	g
8	BS	40	(	72	H	104	h
9	HT	41	)	73	I	105	i
10	LF	42	*	74	J	106	j
11	VT	43	+	75	K	107	k
12	FF	44	,	76	L	108	l
13	CR	45	−	77	M	109	m
14	SO	46	.	78	N	110	n
15	SI	47	/	79	O	111	o
16	DLE	48	0	80	P	112	p
17	DC1	49	1	81	Q	113	q
18	DC2	50	2	82	R	114	r
19	DC3	51	3	83	S	115	s
20	DC4	52	4	84	T	116	t
21	NAK	53	5	85	U	117	u
22	SYN	54	6	86	V	118	v
23	ETB	55	7	87	W	119	w
24	CAN	56	8	88	X	120	x
25	EM	57	9	89	Y	121	y
26	SUB	58	:	90	Z	122	z
27	ESC	59	;	91	[	123	{
28	FS	60	<	92	\	124	|
29	GS	61	=	93	]	125	}
30	RS	62	>	94	^	126	~
31	US	63	?	95	_	127	DEL

GLOSSARY

ACCESS TIME - the time required to obtain data or a named routine from main memory (typically about one microsecond) or from a storage device such as magnetic disk (typically about 30-300 millisecond).

ADDRESS - the location at which data or a named routine is stored within main memory or a storage device such as magnetic disk.

ALGORITHM - a sequence of logical steps to carry out a specified task.

ALPHANUMERIC - the letters, numbers and other printable characters contained in the ASCII character set (see ASCII).

ANCESTOR - a node within an array in a direct line between a specified node and the root of the array.

ANS - an acronym for American National Standard.

ANSI - an acronym for American National Standards Institute.

APPLICATION PROGRAM - a program which meets specific user needs, such as maintaining a file of names with addresses and phone numbers.

ARITHMETIC LOGIC UNIT - that part of the central processing unit which performs arithmetic and logical operations; also known as ALU.

ARITHMETIC OPERATOR - an operator which gives its associated operands(s) a numeric interpretation, and performs an arithmetic function such as add, subtract, multiply, divide, integer divide, or modulo.

ARGUMENT - an expression which is operated on by a command or a function.

ARRAY - a set of nodes, referenced by subscripts, which share the same variable name.

ASCII - American Standard Code for Information Interchange: a series of 128 characters which include upper and lower case alpha characters, numbers, punctuation, special symbols, and control characters. See Tables I and II in Chapter 12.

ASCII CONTROL CHARACTERS - those members of the ASCII character set which cause specific operations to be performed: for example BS for backspace, BEL for bell, CR for carriage return, ACK for acknowledge transmission, EOT for end of transmission, and FF for form feed. The ASCII characters 0-31 represent control characters, rather than printable characters. Control characters typically are produced by pressing the control key and a specific letter key at the same time. Some control characters, such as CTRL/C, have similar meanings in all implementations of Standard MUMPS. Other control characters are used in ways which are implementation specific.

ASCII PRINTABLE CHARACTERS - those members of ASCII character set which output characters on a hard copy terminal or CRT screen. The ASCII characters 32-127 represent printable characters.

ASYNCHRONOUS - a communications method in which data is sent one character at a time as it is produced, rather than at specific time intervals.

AUXILLIARY STORAGE - see Secondary Storage.

BACKUP - the process of creating duplicate data files and/or program copies as a "reserve" in case the original is lost or damaged.

BACKGROUND - refers to running a program that has no interaction with a user. Programs run in background may have lower priority than interactive programs that provide user interaction.

BASIC - an acronym for Beginners All-Purpose Symbolic Instruction Code, a widely used programming language developed at Dartmouth College during the late 1960's.

BAUD - a measure of data transmission speed, roughly equivalent to one bit per second (bps). Commonly used Baud rates include 300, 1200, 2400 and 9600.

BINARY - refers to a number system using the base 2. In this system, there are only two digits: 0 and 1. The instructions prepared in a programming language such as MUMPS must be translated into binary code for machine execution.

BIT - a term that represents the contraction of binary digit. The binary number 101, composed of three bits, is equivalent to decimal 5. All data within a computer is expressed as a combination of binary digits.

BLOCK - a designated space on disk which typically contains 1024 bytes.

BUG - an error in a program. Bugs may be caused by syntax errors, logic errors, or a combination of both.

BUS - a group of electrical connections that carry signals between components of a computer.

BYTE - a group of eight bits, handled by the computer as a single unit. One byte represents one ASCII character.

CANONIC NUMBER - a number with no leading zeros to the left, and no trailing zeros to the right of the decimal point. For example: 1.2 is a canonic number, but 1.20 and 01 are non-canonic numbers.

CARET - a symbol expressed as ⌃ (up caret), < (left caret) or > (right caret). In many MUMPS systems, a right caret is used as a system prompt. The right caret is also referred to as a "right angle bracket".

CATHODE RAY TUBE (CRT) - a vacuum tube which guides electrons onto a screen to display characters or graphics. Also called VDT (video display tube) or VDU (video display unit).

CENTRAL PROCESSING UNIT (CPU) - those parts of computer hardware that: carry out arithmetic and logic operations (arithmetic logic unit or ALU); control the sequence of operations performed (control unit); and contain the stored program of instructions (internal memory).

CHANNEL - a pathway for data into or out of a computer system.

CHANNEL CAPACITY - maximum data transmission rate for a given channel, usually expressed as "bits per second" or "baud rate".

CODE - instructions written in computer language. For example "a line of MUMPS code".

COLLATING SEQUENCE - the sequence in which group of items are arranged. True numeric order implies a sequence based on numeric values: for example 001, 002, 3.0, 3.1, and so on. String order implies an "alphabetic order" based on the 128 ASCII characters: for example 001, 0010, 0014, 002, 00463, 01, 01:, 01?, 01W, 01a, 02 and so on. See Table I of Chapter 12.

COLUMN - the position along the horizontal axis at which a character is displayed.

COMMAND - a combination of characters which instructs the computer to perform a specific operation. In MUMPS, commands may be entered directly at a system prompt (direct execution), or embedded within a program.

COMMENT - in a MUMPS program, a comment is free text used to describe program operation. Comments are preceded by semicolons to distinguish them from executable code.

COMPUTER SYSTEM - a computer system includes:

(1)   computer hardware - a CPU and various peripheral devices (terminals, printers and disk drives)

(2)   computer software - programs that specify operations to be performed by the hardware components.

CONCATENATE - to join together two expressions into a single string, by use of the concatenate operator. In MUMPS, the concatenate operator is depicted by the underline character.

CONDITIONAL TRANSFER - a transfer of program control that occurs only if a certain condition is met. For example: IF AGE>120 DO ERRORMOD; IF NAM'?1A.E GOTO ENTRY. Conditional transfers may be temporary (the DO command) or permanent (the GOTO command).

CONFIGURATION - the type and arrangement of hardware in a particular system. This includes the type of CPU, type and number of disk drives, type and number of terminals, amount of main storage, and so on.

CONSTANT - a numeric value which does not change during program execution; also referred to as a "numeric literal".

CONTROL CHARACTERS - see ASCII control characters.

CORE - a synonym for main memory; also referred to as primary storage. During the 1960's, this term referred to tiny circles of ferrite, in which bits of data were represented by the direction of magnetization. Today, the term "core memory" is used to indicate other types of storage, which do not use magnetized rings.

CPU - see central processing unit.

CRT - see cathode ray tube.

CURRENT DEVICE - the device used for I/O operations at any given time during program execution.

CURSOR - a movable spot of light - usually a blinking square or an underline character - that shows the next point where characters can be entered or deleted on a video screen.

DATA - characters which are stored in the computer system, as the values of local or global variables. Information can be considered as data which has meaning and value to humans.

DATA BASE - an organized collection of data related to a particular topic. For example: names, addresses and phone numbers for people working in a given department, arranged by date of employment.

DATA PROCESSING - logical and/or arithmetic operations performed on data: these may be performed manually (e.g. sorting through a card file by hand), mechanically (e.g. using a mechanical device to obtain cards from a file), or electronically (e.g. using a computer to perform these functions).

DATA TYPE - the range of values that a variable may assume. Typical data types for computer languages such as BASIC and Pascal include:

   integers (whole numbers)
   real (decimal numbers)
   character (characters strings of a specified length).

Standard MUMPS uses a single data type: the variable length character string, which may be assigned a numeric value based on the rules described in Chapter Three of this text.

DEBUG - to correct logic and/or syntax errors in a computer program.

DESCENDANT - any node in an array that shares the same name and subscript as the specified node, but has one or more additional levels ofsubscripting.

DEVICE - any hardware in a computer system, other than the CPU. A device may exist as a subdivision within a given piece of hardware: for example, the sequential disk processor of a hard disk. NOTE: Some implementations of Standard MUMPS allow a single disk to be divided into two areas: random access and sequential disk processor. See the user manual on your system for additional information.

DIGITAL COMPUTER - a computer in which data is handled as discrete bits, rather than a continuous variable such as voltage. Almost all computers used today are digital computers. Analog computers, used during the 1960's, represented data as a continuous variable such as voltage.

DIRECT EXECUTION - execution of a command entered "directly" at a system prompt (such as a right caret) with no intervening line start character. In Standard MUMPS, operation of commands via direct execution is implementation specific. For our implementation, direct execution of PRINT displays the program currently in your partition, while direct execution of WRITE displays the local variables in your partition.

DIRECT MODE - see direct execution.

DISK - a device for storing data as magnetized spots in concentric tracks commonly classified as hard disks and floppy disks. Hard disks have faster access times and larger capacities than floppy disks (also known as diskettes).

DISK DRIVE - a peripheral device that can be used to "read" and "write" on a hard disk or diskette.

DISKETTE - sometimes called "floppy disk" in contrast to "hard disk". A diskette is a piece of flexible plastic coated with metallic oxide. Common sizes include 5 1/4 inch and 8 inch diameter. Typical access times range from about 200 msec to 400 msec. Typical capacity is relatively small, ranging from 200 Kbytes to 1 Mbyte

DOCUMENTATION - User documentation refers to the instruction manuals which provide users with sufficient information to use a system. System documentation refers to the descriptions of hardware and operating system provided by a system vendor. Program documentation refers to the description of how a program is organized and how it operates. This is intended as an aid to those programmers who will be responsible for revising the original program.

DOWNTIME - the period of time when a computer system is not working. Often classified as:

> scheduled downtime - computer unavailable due to scheduled activities, such as preventive maintenance on disk drives

> unscheduled downtime - computer unavailable due to hardware or software failure.

EDITOR - a routine that can be used to edit, or modify, programs from internal storage.

ENTRY REFERENCE - the reference to a routine, or a routine line, used as the argument of a DO or GOTO command. Typical entry references may include:

- a line label

- a line label plus an offset

- a routine name

- a line label and a routine name

- a line label plus an offset and a routine name.

ERROR MESSAGE - text displayed by the computer when a system error occurs. The error messages used in Standard MUMPS are implementation specific.

EXECUTE - to perform an instruction specified in a computer program.

EXECUTION TIME - the time required for a computer system to perform a specified routine. This will vary according to the hardware, the operating system (some implementations are more efficient than others), the routine, and whether multiple jobs are being run at the same time.

EXPONENTIAL NOTATION - in Standard MUMPS a method for expressing exponents using the letter E. For example: 2,200,000 can be expressed as 2.2E6, and 0.0000022 can be expressed as 2.2E-6.

EXPRESSION - a character string which, when executed as part of a command argument, creates a value.

EXPRESSION ATOM - the smallest character string which, when executed as part of a command argument, creates a value. Typical expression atoms include:

ADR - a variable name

"SMITH, JOHN" - a literal string

$PIECE(^ NAM(1)," ^ ",3) - a function

111 - a constant

EXTERNAL STORAGE - storage of data and programs outside the computer: for example, on a magnetic disk or tape.

FIELD - a reserved area in a record used for storage of specific information. For example, in a global array, each node might have specific fields or "pieces" reserved for name, address and phone number.

FIELD LENGTH - the maximum number of characters allowed for a given field.

FILE - a collection of related records. Typical examples include files of names, projects, or accounts receivable.

FLOPPY DISK - an informal synonym for diskette.

FUNCTION - in Standard MUMPS, a function, abbreviated by a dollar sign followed by a capital letter, performs an operation on an argument, and returns a value. Typical functions include $DATA, $EXTRACT and $PIECE.

GLOBAL VARIABLE - a variable which is stored on disk, and potentially available to any user. Global variables usually exist as parts of global arrays. The term "global" may refer either to a global variable or a global array. For some systems, globals may be output to magnetic tape: for our implementation, this is done via a utility program, Global Output.

HARDCOPY - characters and/or graphic displays produced on paper, rather than in temporary form via CRT. Also see softcopy.

HARD DISK - a disk which is rigid rather than flexible, in contrast to a "floppy disk".

HARDWARE - the physical components of a computer system: e.g."the computer", plus peripheral devices such as disk drives, CRT terminals, printers, magnetic tape drives.

INCREMENT - a value used to increase a counter in a loop. For example, in the program line: FOR J1 = A:B DO MOD Q:FLAG = 0, B represents the increment. Negative increments are known as decrements.

INDIRECT EXECUTION - execution of a command as part of a computer program,rather than execution of a command entered directly at a system prompt. Code for indirect execution is preceded by an implementation specific line start character (such as a tab or a space following the system prompt).

INDIRECT MODE - see indirect execution.

INDIRECTION - a method for using the current value of an expression as executable MUMPS code. When MUMPS finds an example of indirection, it uses the current value of this expression as executable code. This allows execution of the same code using different values for an expression following the @ sign.

INFORMATION - data which has meaning and value for humans.

INITIALIZE -to create a variable with a specified value.In MUMPS, the $DATA function is commonly used to check whether a variable must be initialized.

INPUT - data or programs put into a computer.

INPUT DEVICE - a device which can be used to "read" data or programs into a computer. Typical examples include CRT units, magnetic tape drives, and those disk drives which accept removable disks or disk cartridges.

INTERACTIVE - a computer system which carries out a "dialog" with the user. Most MUMPS systems are interactive: they display prompts for data entry, display error messages immediately after an incorrect entry, and produce output within a few seconds after input has been completed. The "interactive" nature of a computer system is based on hardware, operating systems, and the application program.

INTERFACE - the hardware and software that links a computer to a peripheral device.

INTERNAL MEMORY- the storage area in a computer system where programs and data are placed immediately before execution. In some cases, internal memory includes a small cache memory unit, which operates at very high speed and contains the variables and/or routines most recently executed.

INTERNAL STORAGE - see internal memory.

INTERPRETER - a program which translates code one line at a time prior to execution. This is contrasted with a compiler, which typically translates an entire program at one time, prior to execution.

JOB - any system activity which requires the use of a partition: for example, running a program, or issuing commands for direct execution.

JUSTIFY - the process of moving alphanumeric data to the left, or to the right, to produce consistent margins. The $JUSTIFY function in MUMPS produces output which is right justified in a field of specified length.

K - the symbol for kilobyte, also abbreviated as Kb or Kbyte. One Kbyte actually means 1024 bytes, rather than an even thousand.

KILOBAUD - a data transmission speed of approximately 1,000 bits per second.

LIBRARY UTILITY - a utility routine which can be incorporated into routines written by end users. The names of library utilities are commonly preceded by %.

LINE - a string of characters entered as executable code and terminated by a carriage return. MUMPS allows up to 255 characters within a single line of code. Also see wrap around.

LINE LABEL - a name at the beginning of a routine line, which can be used as an identifier for that line. The first character of a line label must be either %, an uppercase alpha character, or a number. The remaining characters can be any combination of uppercase alpha characters or digits; however, no punctuation characters are allowed.

LINE REFERENCE - a reference to a program line, which may be either: (1) a line label, or (2) a line label and an offset.

LINE START CHARACTER - an implementation specific character such as a tab or a single space, placed after a system prompt to indicate that the subsequent code will be executed indirectly as part of a program, rather than directly (as soon as the user enters a carriage return).

LITERAL - a string of characters within a routine that does not change in value during execution of the routine. MUMPS recognizes two types of literals: (1) string literals, which must be enclosed in quotation marks; (2) numeric literals, for which quotation marks are omitted. A string literal might be: SET A = "12 + 33". A numeric literal might be: SET B = 12 + 33. In these cases, WRITE A returns 12 + 33, while WRITE B returns 45.

LOCAL VARIABLE - a variable which exists in your partition of main memory, and disappears when you log off.

LOG OFF - see LOGOFF.

LOG ON - see LOGON.

LOGICAL OPERATOR - an operator which produces a truth-valued result based on the truth value of its operand(s). The three logical operators in MUMPS are: the Boolean AND (binary operator), the Boolean OR (binary operator) and the NOT operator (unary operator).

LOGOFF - the process of exiting from access to a computer system. For our implementation, this is done by entering a HALT command.

LOGON - the process of gaining access to a computer system, in order to: (1) run existing programs (User Access); write new programs as well as run existing programs (Programmer Access). For our system, Programmer Access requries entry of a User Class Identifier (UCI), followed by a Programmer Access Code (PAC).

MACHINE LANGUAGE - instructions which can be executed by a computer without further translation. These instructions usually are in the form of binary numbers, and are specific to a given type of computer.

MAGNETIC DISK - a rotating disk on which data is recorded as magnetized spots. Also see hard disk, floppy disk, and Winchester disk.

MAGNETIC TAPE - also known as mag tape: plastic or mylar tape, coated on one side with iron oxide, commonly stored on reels or cassettes.

MAGNETIC TAPE DRIVE - a device that reads and writes data on magnetic tape. Commonly classified as:

(1)   reel tape or "industry compatible tape"

(2)   cassette tape.

MAIN STORAGE - see internal memory.

MAINTENANCE - program maintenance refers to two activities:

(1)   Correction of "bugs" which appear in the course of program operation. Some bugs become obvious only after a program has been in use for several months.

(2)   Modification of programs to provide new functions, which were not initially planned.

Hardware maintenance refers to preventive maintenance on hardware such as disk drives, mag tape drives, and printers.

MAP - an implementation-specific term referring to an amount of disk storage. For our system, one map consists of 400 data blocks (each block contains 1024 bytes).

MEAN TIME BETWEEN FAILURES - sometimes abbreviated as MTBF, refers to the mean period of time between consecutive failures for specific hardware, such as a disk drive or printer. A MTBF of 2000 hours for a disk drive is considered excellent performance.

MEDIUM - the physical material on which programs or data are stored. Magnetic media include tapes, cards, and removable disks.

MEMORY - a term used to indicate data storage. See internal storage and external storage.

MODULE - a logical subunit within a routine, accessed by a DO command and terminated by a QUIT command.

MODULO - a mathematical means of obtaining the remainder of a division operation. Thus 40 modulo 5 equals 0; 42 modulo 5 equals 2.

MUMPS - an acronym for Massachusetts General Hospital Utility Multi-Programming System.

NAKED REFERENCE - a shorthand method for referring to a node in a global array. You can refer to the sibling or descendant of the last referenced node by a circumflex ($\wedge$) plus the unique portion of the desired node. For example: if $\wedge$NAME ("A",1) were the last global reference, $\wedge$(3) would refer to $\wedge$NAME("A",3).

NESTING - refers to a relationship between two commands. When two commands are nested, the second command statement is contained within the range of the first statement. An example is: FOR J1 = 1:1:5 WRITE !J1 FOR J2 = 10:1:15 WRITE !,?5, J2. Here the second FOR loop (using the variable J2) is executed completely for each value of J1 in the first FOR loop. This second FOR loop is referred to as the "inner" FOR loop, since it operates "inside" the scope of the "outer" FOR loop. This second FOR loop is "nested" within the first FOR loop. In MUMPS, the FOR, DO and XECUTE commands can be nested.

NODE - an array element characterized by a name and a unique subscript. Thus the terms node, array element and subscripted variable are synonymous.

NULL STRING - a string which contains no data, i.e. " "

NUMBER EQUIVALENT - refers to the comparison of decimal numbers to numbers in other systems such as octal or binary. For example:

DECIMAL	OCTAL	BINARY
1	1	001
2	2	010
3	3	011
4	4	100
5	5	101
6	6	110
7	7	111
8	10	1000
9	11	1001
10	12	1010

NUMERIC EXPRESSION - an expression evaluated as a number. For example, any character string can be converted to a numeric expression via the unary plus.

NUMERIC LITERAL - a series of characters evaluated as a numeric expression. For example, + "10 CATS" is evaluated as a numeric expression via the unary plus. Other examples of numeric literals include 35, 035, 35.0, 0.35 and 10E2.

OBJECT CODE - the set of instructions in machine language which is produced by a compiler.

OCTAL SYSTEM - the number system with eight values as the base, rather than the ten values used in the decimal system. See number equivalent.

OFF-LINE - not in direct communication with a computer system. For example, a terminal is "off line" when it is either: (1) disconnected from the computer; (2) turned off; or (3) isolated from the computer via an "on line/off line" switch.

OFFSET - a positive whole number used with a line label to reference a specified line of code.

ON-LINE - in direct communication with a computer system. For example, a terminal is "on line" when it is: (1) turned on, (2) connected to the computer, and (3) placed "on line" via an "on line/off line" switch.

OPERAND - an expression which is operated on by a command or a function.

OPERATOR - a symbolic character which specifies an action to be performed. MUMPS provides ten arithmetic operators (six binary operators, two unary operators, and two relational operators); five string operators (four relational operators and one binary operator); and three logical operators (Boolean AND, Boolean OR and Boolean NOT).

OUTPUT - the results of a data processing operation.

OUTPUT DEVICE - a device on which output is displayed or stored. Printers and CRT units are commonly used as output devices. Less commonly, output may be produced on mag tape or diskettes, for transport to another computer system.

PARENT - for any node in an array, the parent is that ancestor at the "next higher level", moving toward the root of the array. Also see ancestor.

PARTITION - that portion of main memory dedicated to an individual user. This partition contains the current routine, and all local variables in use at a given time.

PASSWORD - a string of characters which must be entered to gain access to a computer system or a program. A password helps identify "authorized" users of a computer system or program.

PERIPHERAL DEVICE - any hardware device other than the computer itself (central processing unit plus internal memory). Typical examples include card readers (input devices), printers (output devices), CRT units (I/O devices), and disk drives (secondary storage).

POST CONDITIONAL EXPRESSION - a truth-valued expression appended to a command or argument, so that execution of the command or argument is conditional on the truth value of this expression. If the expression is true, the command or argument is executed; if the expression is false, the command or argument is not executed.

PRINCIPAL DEVICE - the device on which a computer system conducts all I/O operations, in the absence of specific OPEN and USE commands. In most cases, your principal device is the terminal you used to log onto the system.

PROGRAM - a list of instructions for computer operations, written in a programming language.

PROGRAMMER ACCESS - access to a computer system that allows you to write programs. For our system, Programmer Access is specified during logon via entry of a User Class Indentifier (UCI) followed by a Programmer Access Code (PAC). Programmer access allows processing of MUMPS code via direct execution as well as indirect execution. Your system may have a different name for Programmer Access (e.g. "programmer mode").

PROGRAMMER ACCESS CODE (PAC) - a form or password used to gain programming access to a MUMPS system.

PROMPT - a message displayed by the computer which requests some action from the user. For example: "NAME:" is a prompt to enter name, while "PHONE:" is a prompt to enter phone number.

RADIX - the base of a number system. For example 10 is the radix of the decimal system, 8 is the radix of the octal system, 2 is the radix of the binary system.

RANDOM ACCESS - refers to a device in which it is possible to retrieve any record with essentially the same speed, usually within 300 milliseconds or less. For example: a magnetic disk (or part of a magnetic disk) organized so that each record has a specific address - thus the read/write head can move to this address without sequentially reading all preceding records on the disk.

RANDOM NUMBER GENERATOR - a routine which will produce random numbers. In MUMPS, this is provided by the $RANDOM function.

READ/WRITE HEAD - a device can "read" data from magnetic tape or disk, and "write" data to magnetic tape or disk.

REAL TIME - taking place in a time frame relevant to "real life" events. For example, an on-line interactive display of "name, address, phone number and current bank balance" would be considered "real time" if results were displayed within one or two seconds when customers phoned to inquire about their current bank balance; a twenty second delay might not be relevant to the "real life" event of a phone query for information.

RECORD - a collection of data items which refer to a specific entity. For example, in a name-address-phone number file, each record would contain a collection of data relating to one person.

RELATIONAL OPERATOR - an operator which produces a truth-valued result based on the relationship of its operands. Thus relational operators in MUMPS are binary operators. The two arithmetic relational operators are "less than" (<) and "greater than" (>). The four string relational operators are "equals" (=), pattern match (?), contains ([) and follows (]). If the relation expressed by the operator and its operands is true, MUMPS returns a truth value of one; if this relation is false, MUMPS returns a truth value of zero. These truth values can be examined via the $TEST special variable.

ROOT - the unsubscripted name of a local or global array, sometimes referred to as the "top level" of the array.

ROUTINE - a group of program lines which are saved, loaded and called as a single unit, via a specific name.

SECONDARY MEMORY - devices other than internal memory used to store programs and data. Most MUMPS systems use disk units as secondary memory.

SEQUENTIAL ACCESS - in contrast to random access, refers to devices that do not retrieve every record with essentially the same speed. With sequential access, the retrieval time for a given record depends upon its position in a sequence of records. For example, most magnetic tapes are organized so that each record does NOT have a specific address: thus the read/write head must review all records in sequential order until the desired record is identified. Some implementations of Standard MUMPS allow certain portions of disk to be organized as sequential access (Sequential Disk Processor).

SERIAL TRANSMISSION - transmission of "one bit at a time", in contrast to parallel transmission of multiple bits at the same time. For most implementations of MUMPS on small computers, data transmission is characterized as "asynchronous serial ASCII". Also see Asynchronous and ASCII.

SIBLING - for any node in an array, all nodes which have the same immediate ancestor (parent). Siblings have the same number of subscripts, and differ only in their last subscripts.

SOFTCOPY - displays produced on a CRT screen, rather than on paper.

SOFTWARE - the programs which control computer operations. These are commonly classified as:

(1)   system software or operating system

(2)   applications software.

The operating system controls overall operations of the computer. For some implementations, the MUMPS interpreter is "embedded" within the operating system. For other implementations, MUMPS may run as a "separate entity", distinct from the operating system, either as: (1) an interpreted language; or (2) a compiled language.

SPECIAL VARIABLE - a variable whose value is defined by system operation. Examples include $HOROLOG, $IO, and $TEST.

STACK - the central location in the CPU where data (in the form of numbers) is temporarily stored immediately before arithmetic and logical operations are performed. Data is added "onto the stack", then taken "off the stack" as execution of a command is completed. If you have nested DO...QUIT modules, each "nested DO" is added to the stack, and then removed as execution of the DOne module is completed. If you have "deeply nested" DO modules, it is possible to get an implementation specific error message which indicates "stack overflow". A similar message may occur with "deeply nested" XECUTE or FOR commands.

STATEMENT - a simple logical unit consisting of a command (and in most cases its argument) which specifies an operation to be performed. For example:SET ⌃ NAME = NAM.

STRING - a sequential set of ASCII characters. For most MUMPS implementations, string length may range from one to a maximum of 255 characters.

STRING EXPRESSION - an expression to which MUMPS does not give a numeric interpretation.

STRING LITERAL - a string of characters enclosed in double quotation marks.

STRING ORDER - see collating sequence.

SUBROUTINE - another term for module.

SUBSCRIPT - a numeric or string value that: is enclosed in parentheses; is appended to the
name of a local or global variable; identifies a specific node within an array. A node
may have multiple subscripts, separated by commas.

SUBSCRIPTED VARIABLE - a node within a local or global array.

SUBSTRING - a sequence of characters within a specified string, that can be accessed by the
$EXTRACT or $PIECE function.

SYSTEM - a combination of hardware and software designed to perform specific functions.

SYSTEM PROMPT - an implementation specific character displayed as a prompt to the user
that a response is expected. Code may be entered at a system prompt for direct
execution (no line start character), or indirect execution (line start character follows
the system prompt and precedes the first character of code).

TAB - refers to horizontal spacing achieved by using the question mark as a horizontal format
control.

TAPE DRIVE - see magnetic tape drive

TAPE TRANSPORT - see magnetic tape drive

TIMEOUT - a whole number appended to the argument of a READ, OPEN, JOB or LOCK
command. This number specifies the number of seconds in which the operation should
be completed. If the operation is NOT completed within this time interval, $TEST is
set to zero.

TRACK - the portion of a moving storage medium, such as disk or tape, that is accessible to the
read/write head. Magnetic tape typically has seven or nine linear tracks, while a
magnetic disk typically has several hundred circular tracks. On a magnetic disk, the
outermost track is the longest, and the innermost the shortest: however, each track
may contain the same number of bits.

TREE STRUCTURE - a term sometimes used to describe the structure of a MUMPS array.
This has the same structure as a family tree, with the root at the top, and ancestor

nodes arranged below, according to their depth of subscripting. All nodes with one subscript are at the first level, all nodes with two subscripts at the second level, and so on.

TRUTH-VALUED EXPRESSION - an expression that is evaluated as either true or false. A true expression has the value of one, while a false expression has the value of zero. Typical examples include:

(1)   Arguments of the IF command.

(2)   Timeouts on READ, LOCK, JOB and OPEN.

        Value of most recently evaluated truth-valued expression is stored as value of the $TEST special variable.

USER ACCESS - access to a computer system that allows you to run a program, but not to write or modify programs. For our system, user access is specified during logon via entry of a User Class Identifier (UCI) followed by a program name. After execution of the specified program, the user is logged off by the system. Your system may have a different name for and User Access (e.g. "users mode").

USER CLASS IDENTIFIER (UCI) - the first of the two codes to identify users at time of log on.

UTILITY - a routine which provides "special services" such as listing global names or routine names for a particular UCI. Library utilities perform services for programmers: by convention, these routine names begin with a percent sign (%). System utilities perform services for the system manager.

VARIABLE - a name under which data may be stored. MUMPS recognizes three types of variables: local variables, global variables, and special variables such as $HOROLOG and $TEST.

WINCHESTER DISK - a hard disk with very light read/write head and a relatively low "flying height" (distance between read/write head and disk surface) which often is permanently sealed within a drive unit.

WORD - the greatest number of bits that a computer can handle in any one operation. Typical word lengths are 8, 16 and 32 bits. Each word is made up of one or more 8 bit bytes.

WRAPAROUND - the automatic shifting of characters from one line to the next line. Since "one line of MUMPS code" may contain up to 255 characters, this "wraparound" can extend "one line of code" to three or even four lines on an eighty column CRT.

INDEX

Organizations Provi ... **this Book:**

Clinical Data, Inc.
1172 Commonwealth Avenue
Boston, MA 02146
(617) 734-3700

...cords.

Digital Equipment Corporation
Two Iron Way
Marlboro, MA 01752
(617) 467-2351

T... n provides applications and systems to
th... velopment, sales, and support activities
fo... d an active role in the development of
N... ucts: DSM-11, a multi-user operating
s... amily of processors, VAX-11 DSM, a
N... nputer systems.

Eclectic Systems Corporation
4301 Poche Court West
New Orleans, LA 70129
(504) 254-3500

E... MUMPS) single and multi-user operat-
in... oprocessors. Hardware systems range
fr... systems with streaming tape. Imple-
m... and Commodore.

Inteck, Inc.
695 S. Colorado Blvd.
Suite 20
Denver, CO 80222
(303) 733-5900

Inte... urnkey applications software written in
MUM... ccess to a patient's record of prior visits,
compu... e of the patients file. The ADMINISTRA-
TOR is a... ng, electronic filing, electronic mail, meet-
ing sched... ges. Inteck also offers an ANSI Standard
MUMPS for... both single user and multi-user versions.

Interpretive Data Systems
1500 Shelburne Road
Box C-1070
Burlington, VT 05402
(802) 862-1022

IDS supplies M... lical industry. Sales and service offices
are nationwide. ... nt billing, outpatient billing, accounts
receivable, accou... management, physician billing and accounts receivable, ... omated medical records, and patient
registration.

InterSystems Corporation
210 Commercial, 3rd Floor
Boston, MA 02109
(617) 227-1555

InterSystems Corporation develops and markets ANSI Standard MUMPS products for the DEC computer family. The M products satisfy a wide range of needs, from single user systems running under a
general operating system (M/PRO for the PRO 350), to high performance compiled MUMPS in a dedicated PDP-11 environment (M/11+), to systems requiring a large number of terminals in a multi-
lingual environment (M/VX for the VAX). Additionally, InterSystems provides increased flexibility
with networking software that allows the creation and use of distributed MUMPS databases.

MedRx Systems, Inc.
747 Main Street, Suite 221
Concord, MA 01742
(617) 369-3010

MedRx Systems, Inc. is committed to practical COSTAR-based systems for the private practice physician. We provide all of the consulting, installation, and training necessary to insure a successful
COSTAR-based medical system. Our comprehensive cost-effective systems cover the entire range of
private practice needs from financial recordkeeping to clinical quality medical records, word processing and automatic recall.

MedRx developed the Talking Medical Record (tm) which can read all or selected parts of any
medical record over the telephone. Now no physician is ever more than a phone call away from
critical patient medical record information.

Micronetics Design Corporation
932 Hungerford Drive, #11
Rockville, MD 20850
(301) 424-4870

Micronetics Design Corporation offers multi-user MUMPS operating systems for microprocessors including Motorola 68000 and 6809, Intel 8086 and 80186, as well as several other microprocessor
types. Hardware configurations range from small floppy disk systems thru large Winchester disk
systems with tape drives. Implementations are available for Motorola Information Systems (Four-
Phase), NCR, Convergent Technologies, Perkin-Elmer, Apple, IBM PC, Radio Shack, and many more
including most UNIX* based systems. Available applications include word processing, financial and
general business packages, and medical applications including COSTAR.